*i*NFORMATION
LITERACY
SOURCEBOOKS

INFORMATION LITERACY INSTRUCTION

THEORY AND PRACTICE

Esther S. Grassian and Joan R. Kaplowitz

Neal-Schuman Publishers, Inc.

New York   **London**

Published by Neal-Schuman Publishers, Inc.
100 Varick Street
New York, NY 10013

Library of Congress Cataloging-in-Publication Data

Grassian, Esther S.
   Information literacy instruction : theory and practice / Esther S.
Grassian, Joan R. Kaplowitz.
      p. cm.
   ISBN 1-55570-406-9 (alk. paper)
   1. Information literacy—Study and teaching. 2. Information
retrieval—Study and teaching. I. Kaplowitz, Joan R.

ZA3075.G73 2001
025.5'24'071—dc21   00-067866

DEDICATION

My portions of this book are dedicated to the one I love, Howard Cowan, and to you, dear reader. As my late, beloved father, Rabbi E.D. Stampfer, used to say, "May you go from strength to strength."

ESTHER S. GRASSIAN

I would like to dedicate this book to all my redwood friends (you know who you are); to Hillary and Greg, who continue to be the best work I have ever done; to Barnabus, Josette, and Zen, who prove daily that only cats know how to live; and finally, to every student who ever asked me a question, challenged my ideas, or stimulated my thinking. Without your inspiration, this book could not have been written.

JOAN R. KAPLOWITZ

Table of Contents

PART II.   INFORMATION LITERACY INSTRUCTION
BUILDING BLOCKS

PART IV. DELIVERING INFORMATION LITERACY INSTRUCTION

Figure List

CD-ROM Contents List

Read Me

Mode Selector Form

Mode Selection Web Pages

Mode Selection Tables

Sample PowerPoint Show On Distance Learning

"Read More About It . . ." from each chapter (with live links)

"Synchronous In-Person Group Instruction: Preparation
and Teaching with Technology Checklist"

Foreword

In the 1940s, when I was readying myself for the joyous experience I have had in my library career, preparation in graduate school consisted of courses in reference skills, techniques, and sources, the rules and reason of cataloging, and policies and methods of acquiring materials. No mention was made of teaching potential librarians ways of helping library users make the best use of the resources of their libraries. It is in this area of information literacy instruction that Esther Grassian and Joan Kaplowitz shine, offering guidance, knowledge, and wisdom in assisting library users in their pursuit of information.

There were no courses for potential librarians in bibliographic instruction, or library instruction, or, for that matter, information literacy, when they started their careers. In truth, when it was suggested to ALA in the early 1970s that there was a crying need for librarians to meet at a national level under the ALA's auspices, in order to help each other develop means and modes of helping users fathom the breadth and depth of knowledge libraries contained for them, there was almost insurmountable objection to the concept. A small group of determined and brave people pounded on doors for a long, long time before their needs were recognized and rooms at the inn were made available. Now, of course, ACRL has an Instruction Section devoted to the subject, there is an ALA Library Instruction Round Table, an ACRL Institute for Information Literacy, a National Forum on Information Literacy, and an ALA Information Literacy Community Partnerships Initiative.

Librarians have learned from each other and from their own experiences, have established courses designed to help users make effective use of library resources, have developed many different types of instructional aids, and have published a large body of literature documenting and expanding upon these efforts. *Information Literacy Instruction* draws upon and synthesizes material from this body of literature, as well many others. For these reasons, and more, I think this book is of great importance to all our populace, and particularly to those who are studying the complexities of helping library users.

In my years of retirement and decreasing contact with information sources, with their increasing complexity, I have been fortunate to continue my education with these two women, who have endless patience and understanding of the special learning problems of those of us who came along a little too soon.

MIRIAM DUDLEY
Emeritus Reference/Instruction Librarian,
UCLA College Library

The ACRL Instruction Section established the Miriam Dudley Instruction Librarian Award in 1984, to honor her "pioneering efforts in the field of bibliographic instruction [which] led to the formation of the Instruction Section." (ACRL, IS, 2000 [online])

Preface

Imagine, if you will, the following scenarios . . .

Scenario 1: The phone rings off the hook, 15 voicemail messages wait for an answer, and e-mail never seems to end. Administrators press for experimental pilot projects using new, untested, or difficult-to-use products. They insist on complete statistics, fully trained staff, and frequent progress reports. Meanwhile, instructional staff worry about being overloaded, having too little time to prepare, and looking foolish trying to teach without full understanding of, or comfort with, a broad range of instructional modes—not to mention an endless parade of new equipment, hardware, and software. Instruction schedules need to be set up for ongoing programs, equipment checked and maintained, and handouts and Web pages/sites created or updated.

Scenario 2: Your phone is silent. Your e-mail messages are mostly from listservs, colleagues, and friends. You rarely get requests for information literacy instruction (ILI), and very few people attend library workshops, or visit your instructional Web pages. You wonder where all the learners have gone. You also wonder how they are evaluating the quality of materials they find, particularly on the Web, and if they even know about your library's licensed databases, much less how to use them effectively.

Four basic *questions*—what to do, how to do it, when to do it, and how to measure success—weigh most heavily on all librarians involved in ILI. If your situation falls under Scenario 1, Scenario 2, or somewhere in-between, *Information Literacy Instruction: Theory and Practice* is designed to help, whether you are a student, a new librarian, or a seasoned professional.

Why write *Information Literacy Instruction* and devote an entire book to this topic? It seems as though librarians have always taught people how to use libraries and research tools. Over the past 30 years instruction has grown in importance in libraries and other information settings, even, according to some, eclipsing traditional reference service. As computers entered library settings, training employees, staff, and our various publics became an expected part of the librarian's job in all realms, including both public and technical service. For much of this thirty-year period though, few library schools have supported this instructional role by offering full-length credit courses to help prepare library school students, or by offering continuing education for practicing instruction librarians.

In those few exemplary institutions that have offered such courses, both faculty and students have treasured a number of textbooks, but the last one in this field, *Library Instruction for Librarians* (Roberts and Blandy, 1989), has been out of print for some time. As wonderful as it is, much of it is sadly out of date, especially in relation to technology and technology-related issues. Furthermore, there are few opportunities for in-depth continuing education in information literacy instruction, and no useful texts for practicing librarians who wish to educate themselves by deepening their background knowledge and expanding their instructional skills. *Information Literacy Instruction: Theory and Practice* attempts to fill this dual need by serving as a textbook for library school ILI courses, as well as a support and self-education tool for the practicing instruction librarian.

We have been instruction librarians and instruction coordinators for many years. We proposed a "User Education/Bibliographic Instruction" course to the UCLA library school in 1989, and, when it was approved, we designed and taught it together the first time it was offered. Since 1990 we have alternated teaching this class each year at the UCLA Graduate School of Education and Information Studies, Department of Information Studies. We have based this book on our course, on our own practical instructional planning and delivery experience, on our educations, and on our intensive study of publications and other materials in information literacy and related fields, such as psychology, education, management, and technology.

To acquire a thorough understanding of the theory and practice of ILI, we recommend reading the entire book, sampling additional suggested readings (from the "Read More About It" sections at the end of each chapter or the complete bibliography at the end of the book), and trying out the exercises at the end of each chapter. We understand, however, that time may be limited, or that readers may wish to sample a chapter here and there, or make use of some of the checklists within various chapters for in-house training, or to supplement their understanding and experience in particular areas. For this reason, we have attempted to make each chapter stand on its own, with references to other chapters. Throughout the book we have included both theoretical underpinnings and practical applications that may be adapted or used

as they are in a variety of settings, in all types of libraries and information arenas, wherever librarians help people learn.

We have arranged these chapters of *Information Literacy Instruction:
Theory and Practice* in the order in which we feel those new to ILI should
learn about it. In Part I, Information Literacy Instruction Background,
we begin by discussing definitions in Chapter 1, and then the history of
library instruction/bibliographic instruction/information literacy in
Chapter 2. We also introduce in Chapter 2 the concepts of "synchronous" and "asynchronous" instruction used in many of the following
chapters to mean, respectively, simultaneous and in real-time, as opposed to non-simultaneous, any time/any place instruction.

We continue in Part II, Information Literacy Instruction Building
Blocks, with a solid grounding in learning theory and styles (Chapters 3
and 4), followed by in-depth discussion of library anxiety, mental models, and conceptual frameworks (Chapter 5), and then critical thinking
and active learning (Chapter 6).

Parts I and II provide an essential foundation for all instructional
planning and development.

With this foundation on which to build, in Part III, Planning and
Developing Information Literacy Instruction, we move on to needs assessment and goal-setting (Chapter 7), followed by general principles
for selecting instructional modes (Chapter 8). Also, in Chapter 8 we identify instructional modes as synchronous or asynchronous, and further
differentiate them as "remote" or "in-person," and "paper" or "elec-
tronic/electric."

Part III continues as we describe many forms of instruction in Chapter 9, listing pros and cons as well as tips for effective use. We do not,
however, recommend specific modes of instruction, or even combinations of modes, as many different factors may influence your mode selection decision. Instead, we recommend offering a range of modes to
meet a variety of learning styles and needs. We invite you to use the
interactive Web form and review the mode selection Web pages and
tables on the CD-ROM accompanying this book. The form allows you
to select parameters that describe your learner population, the time available for learning, preparation and delivery, and other factors, except cost,
and returns a list of instruction modes that match the parameters you
selected. We have not included cost as a factor because costs can vary
greatly depending on the complexity you wish to build into a particular
mode, and because developing technology may result in rapidly changing costs.

Part III of *Information Literacy Instruction* then moves on to Chapter
10, "Basic Copyright and Design Issues." Chapter 11 continues this theme

by focusing on design of specific instructional modes and materials, with the exception of synchronous in-person group instruction, which is covered in Chapter 13. The sample PowerPoint slide show and sample handouts on the CD-ROM supplement Chapters 10 and 11. Chapter 12 delves into the theories and practices of assessing, evaluating, and revising to round out the cycle of planning, designing, and developing ILI programs.

As Part III illustrates, planning, developing, assessing, and revising effective ILI programs takes time and effort. It also takes time and effort to prepare and deliver instruction for a variety of groups in different environments, and under different physical and technological circumstances. Part IV will help you do just that.

Synchronous, in-person group instruction is such a popular instructional methodology that we devote most of Chapter 13 to it, followed by four more chapters that are closely related: how to teach diverse groups (Chapter 14), how to develop instruction for particular library environments (Chapter 15), how to approach the teaching of technology (Chapter 16), and how to use technology in teaching (Chapter 17).

The final part of *Information Literacy Instruction*, The Future of ILI, is our view of what the future may hold for the topic (Chapter 18).

The CD-ROM offers a great variety of useful support material and information. Materials include: instructional mode Web pages and mode selector form, a sample PowerPoint presentation on distance education, tables providing an alphabetical listing of all the instructional modes listed in the Web pages, and a synchronous group instruction checklist. We have also included a "Read More About It" list for each chapter of the book. For a complete roster, please see The CD-ROM Contents List on page ix.

Information Literacy Instruction: Theory and Practice will provide you with a basic grounding in ILI. It is the first volume of the Neal-Schuman series *Information Literacy Sourcebook*s. In the next volume we will cover topics that will be of interest largely to those who have already had some ILI experience: the politics of ILI, managing technology for ILI, and teacher appraisal, stress, and burnout.

We may not have supplied answers to all of your ILI questions, but we hope we have provided sufficient background, support, and guidance so that you will be able to ask the right questions. We trust you will understand the range of instructional choices available, and be able to plan, prepare, evaluate, and revise ILI programs in any environment and for a variety of audiences.

We offer *Information Literacy Instruction: Theory and Practice* in the hope that it will serve as support and a stepping-stone to your success in information literacy instruction.

Acknowledgments

We are grateful to many people, institutions, and groups for their support—emotional, intellectual, and financial—without which this book would have remained in partial draft for many long years.

We thank the UCLA Library, particularly the College Library and the Louise M. Darling Biomedical Library, for their firm support of our book project through a three-month leave of absence with pay for each of us. We also thank the Librarians' Association of the University of California and the University of California Office of the President for grant funds to pay for reference desk replacements for each of us during our three-month leaves.

We thank our colleagues and the heads of our libraries for their good cheer, patience, and understanding during our respective leaves. Esther Grassian thanks her colleagues: Stephanie Brasley; Cathy Brown; Debe Costa; Alice Kawakami; Teresa Portilla Omidsalar; Lise Snyder; and the Head of College Library, Eleanor Mitchell. Joan Kaplowitz thanks her colleagues: Alan Carr; Janice Contini; Kathy Dabbour; Kay Deeney; Mike Fehr; Pat Steen; Rob Stibravy; David Yamamoto; Alison Bunting, Director of the Louise M. Darling Biomedical Library; and Judy Consales, Deputy Director. Special thanks to Cathy Brown who filled in for Joan while she was on leave from the Biomedical Library.

We also thank the Librarians' Association of the University of California, Los Angeles, the UCLA Library Administration, and Rita Scherrei, AUL for Personnel, for the funding to support our attendance at the 1997 LOEX Conference in Charleston. We owe thanks to Linda Shirato, LOEX Director, for graciously allowing us to conduct focus groups of our colleagues from colleges and universities in many parts of the country on the contents of this book and the next one in the series. We thank focus group participants, too, for their time and their many thoughtful comments.

Cerise Oberman deserves special thanks for writing such an excellent and thought-provoking Introduction, as does Mimi Dudley for her warm and eloquent Foreword. Thanks, too, to Trudi Jacobson for her comments on our manuscript, to Steve Rossen for his comments on

Chapter 17, and to Bill Childers for his patience and hard work on the Web pages and interactive form for the CD-ROM.

We also thank Farhad Novian, the attorney who helped us with our book contract, and David Berson for his indescribable help, and for referring us to Farhad.

Esther S. Grassian especially thanks her long-time love and favorite elementary school science teacher, the redoubtable Howard Cowan, for listening, for reading and making comments on one chapter after another, for many great dinners, hugs, flowers, and much love, all of which make him nearly as responsible for the existence of her portions of the book as she. She also thanks her wonderful sons, David and Daniel, and mother, Ann Stampfer, for putting up with a distracted and sometimes distraught mother and daughter, glued to her iBook, working endlessly on her book chapters and other materials. She thanks her good friends Mimi Dudley, Nancy Sevier, and Isabel Stirling for their unswerving support over many years of highs and lows, of yin and yang.

Joan R. Kaplowitz thanks Jenifer Abramson, Kurt Christiansen, David Harwell, Michael Hernandez, Robert Newlen, and Gary Tarver, who listened to her rantings, let her bounce ideas around with them, never stopped believing in her and her ability to complete this project, and amazingly remain her friends to this day. Thanks also to the faculty of ACRL's Information Literacy Immersion Program (Eugene Engeldinger, Craig Gibson, Deb Gilchrist, Randy Hensley, Sharon Mader, Mary Jane Petrowsi, Susan Barnes Whyte, Karen Williams, Beth Woodard, and Anne Zald), with whom Joan had the privilege of working during the 1999 and 2000 Immersion Programs. These are truly a gifted and generous group of information professionals, and their collective influence is reflected in this book. Thanks also to all the Immersion participants Joan met through this program. They all give us hope for the future.

Introduction

Information literacy has reached a new stage of importance in the professional consciousness of librarians. This importance is marked by a growing and shared recognition that all types of libraries and librarians—academic, school, public, and special—must be actively engaged in information literacy. There are also clear signs that K–16 educators, businesses, and organizations outside of librarianship are awakening to the importance of information literacy. Clearly, there is a growing appreciation for the skills and concepts of information literacy; clearly, there is a growing recognition of the centrality of information literacy skills for students, workers, and citizens.

In an increasingly complex information world, information literacy combined with the information needs of an array of users form a powerful synergy. This synergy marks the beginning of the twenty-first century as the most challenging time ever to be an instruction librarian. It is challenging because the body of information that a good instruction librarian must learn and apply has never been more plentiful. Not only do librarians need to know learning theory, pedagogy, technology, instructional design, politics, and management, but we also need to think about information literacy, not as a narrow and concentrated endeavor, but as a component of a cumulative process that begins in childhood and continues throughout life. It is challenging because it demands that we see our individual roles not only focusing on our immediate constituents, but also on the development of a holistic and integrated environment that is responsive to the needs of the larger community. It is challenging because we are only now just beginning to recognize that information literacy means different things to different people and we must meet the different needs of these varied constituencies.

The information literacy movement has grown and matured from a grassroots movement to a current wave of national professional initiatives and a heightened sense of the importance of information in our society. This has been a phenomenal change in a relatively short period of time. What is clear about this change is that a series of significant initiatives, both inside and outside of the profession, is catapulting information literacy from the periphery of the field to a professional core issue.

Perhaps the most visible sign of this change in librarianship is the emergence of information literacy as a national theme for the American Library Association in 2000–2001. As ALA President Nancy Kranich argues, "More information will not in itself create a more informed citizenry unless people know how to use information effectively to solve problems" (Kranich, 2000:7)[1]. To create a more informed citizenry, librarianship needs to work toward professional unity and toward community partnerships. In an effort to move this forward as a national agenda item, ALA's Special Presidential Information Literacy Partnerships Committee is working to define the long-term, nationwide goals of information literacy: 1) information literacy as the intellectual bridge for the "digital divide"; 2) information literacy as the work of all libraries and librarians; 3) information literacy as the basis for recognizing, celebrating and promoting the advantages of "information smart communities."

The ALA initiative brings together all types of librarians in a common cause for information literacy. This effort, not unlike the long-established ALA Library Instruction Roundtable (LIRT), is now fueled institutionally throughout ALA—reaching out to every division and section. In part, this is now possible because of the groundbreaking professional work that has preceded it. In particular, the American Association of School Librarians' *Information Literacy Standards for Student Learning* (ALA–American Association of School Librarians, 1998) and the "information power" movement have defined the importance of including information literacy in the K–12 curriculum. The Association of College & Research Libraries' *Information Literacy Competency Standards for Higher Education* (ALA–Association of College & Research Libraries, 2000) codifies both standards and outcomes for information literacy in higher education and underscores the universality of their importance and application throughout the academic curriculum. While no similar work yet exists for public librarians, there is a growing awareness that information literacy demands to be looked at anew in public libraries as the very foundations of library service shift in a more complex information environment. In many ways, the public library may be the "last frontier": nowhere else will information literacy realize the scope of impact and the breadth of demand than in service to the community.

If academic, public and school librarians can come together at the local and regional level to talk, discuss, examine and articulate the information literacy concerns of librarianship, it will be the first step toward building information-smart communities. This will not necessarily be an easy task. There is much stratification in our professional lives, reinforced by the types of professional associations and organizations to which we belong. Overcoming this stratification means reaching out toward a larger goal, breaking down barriers, creating a common language, and having the tools and strategies readily available to shape a common agenda. Collaboration among librarians will be the first step toward understanding the information literacy needs of a community and must be the first step in shaping the context for community involvement.

Community involvement in and support for information literacy takes us into uncharted waters. While there are examples of libraries and librarians creating information literacy partnerships with businesses or government around information literacy, they are, at the moment, quite limited. For information literacy to be recognized as an important and necessary set of skills beyond the educational milieu, librarians need to connect and work with the very institutions and organizations that can benefit from understanding the role of information literacy. For these connections to be successful, however, a new language of information literacy must be forged, the outcomes of information literacy must be made concrete, and an advocacy program for information literacy must be established. Above all else, librarians will need to listen. Librarians cannot assume answers without asking questions. Even more importantly, we must learn to ask the questions that will, in turn, allow us to reflect back on our assumptions about libraries and the proprietary control of information literacy.

There are a variety of voices currently saying something extremely important: librarians don't own information literacy and information literacy is not always described in the terms that librarians would use. Who are these voices? The National Forum on Information Literacy may be the oldest chorus of voices. This group, which has been active for over ten years, is a coalition of educational, business, and governmental organizations that embrace the importance of information literacy. The forum's focus is, in their own words, "the need to promote individual empowerment within the information society" (National Forum on Information Literacy, 2000). More recently, the Global Knowledge Partnership (GKP), made up of representatives from governments, UNESCO organizations, banks, and foundations, has expressed a commitment "to sharing information, experiences, and resources to promote broad access to, and effective use of, knowledge and information as tools of sustainable, equitable development" (National Forum on Information Literacy Overview 1999–2000 Report, 2000). These are allies waiting to work as partners in the realm of information literacy.

Regional higher education accreditation agencies are hearing the voices of librarians. Over the last ten years, a number of these accrediting associations have begun to consider the place of information literacy within the academic curriculum. Most notably, the Middle States Commission of Higher Education has already adopted information literacy as part of the accreditation standard and is now working on a project to promote campus-wide dialogue on information literacy, core disciplinary knowledge and general education. The next frontier in academe, as Middle States suggests, will be full integration of information literacy across the curriculum. This model, by its very nature, does not presume that librarians are the only purveyors of this information. In fact, it demands that information literacy also be the responsibility of teaching faculty, making the process of gaining proficiency in the concepts and skills embedded in information literacy an on-going and cumulative endeavor central to the mission of the academy.

In the business community there are also signs that information literacy is gaining attention. The Aspen Institute Forum on Communications & Society (FOCUS) is a group of chief executive officers that convene annually to address subjects relating to the societal impact of the communication and information sectors. In 1999 FOCUS held a meeting focused on information literacy. This meeting approached information literacy by posing two central questions: 1) What is the role of information in the lives of individuals, organizations, and institutions? and 2) How, if at all, is this relationship changing as new communications and information technologies take hold? FOCUS concluded that information literacy is a broad term that encompasses a range of other literacies including computer literacy (the ability to understand computing concepts and common software applications), technical literacy (the ability to use math and science concepts to problem-solve and create new products), and digital literacy (the ability to effectively maneuver in a digital environment in terms of expression and access). The conclusions of the Aspen Institute FOCUS seminar suggest that if information literacy is going to be recognized as an important component for workers, then librarians must understand the relationship of information literacy to the other identified literacies (*Information Literacy*, 1999).

Information literacy is no longer an isolated endeavor defined by type of instruction, type of library, or type of user. As a discipline within our profession, information literacy remains a young endeavor. Part of the maturation of this endeavor will be broadening our conversations about information literacy. Those conversations, whether they are with faculty, teachers, businesses, governmental agencies, social agencies, or all citizens, should be conversations that lead us to frame our roles more carefully and respond to needs more thoroughly. These conversations may mean broadening our current definition of information literacy, recognizing other areas of expertise needed in information literacy, or forming new partnerships and cooperatives.

All information literacy partnerships have the potential for transforming information literacy from a narrow and parochial term to an active theme that is woven throughout the K–16 curriculum, supported by public librarians, demanded by employers, extolled by governments, and recognized by citizens as a fundamental skill that improves their quality of life.

The pathway to this future begins with readers of this book. *Information Literacy Instruction* provides the critical foundation for understanding information literacy. This book is both a text and a reference tool, covering a wide range of subjects that instruction librarians must understand today. Moreover, it builds a common knowledge base and lays out a common framework that can assist librarians in speaking a common language. This book recognizes the need for all information literacy librarians to share a single vocabulary, explore similar applications in different settings, and encourages a broader, more inclusive, view of information literacy. This book is a baseline for both learning the craft of information literacy and giving librarians the tools to move beyond the current boundaries of information literacy. The next chapter in information literacy will be written by the next generation of instruction librarians—they will be well guided by the ideas and approaches in *Information Literacy Instruction*.

Cerise Oberman
Plattsburgh State University of New York
December 2000

NOTE

1. The Information Literacy for Community Partnerships initiative began as one of the goals of the ACRL Institute for Information Literacy; also see http://ala.org/acrl/nili/nilihp.html. Community Partnerships was adopted as an ALA Presidential initiative upon the election of Nancy Kranich in spring 2000.

Part I

Information Literacy Instruction Background

1

Information Literacy Instruction: What Is It?

The more I learn, the more I realize I don't know.

—Albert Einstein

A ROSE BY ANY OTHER NAME—OR IS IT?
WHAT IS INFORMATION LITERACY?

Welcome to the wonderful world of Information Literacy Instruction (ILI). In the following chapters we will introduce you to the various theories, methodologies, and techniques that will help you in your ILI endeavors. But before we begin, we need to ask (and answer) the question "What is Information Literacy (IL) anyway?" Until we have a good, working definition of the term, we will be hard pressed to figure out how to teach ILI.

The instruction part of ILI is easy. Librarianship has had a long history of instructing our users. Library orientation, library instruction, bibliographic instruction, and user education have been part of our vocabulary and our professional lives for many years. Does ILI differ from these predecessors? And if so, in what way? A seemingly simple question, but if the literature is any indication, it will not be an easy task to find a simple answer.

There are those who say that ILI is just a natural progression in the evolution of the field. To these professionals, ILI subsumes all previous concepts and adds additional nuances of meaning. Others resolutely state that ILI is just a new name for what we have always done. To these people, the only advantage of ILI is that it capitalizes on current societal and educational trends, and is perhaps more readily understood by those outside our field. Finally, there are those who firmly believe ILI is a new concept and that it represents a new way of thinking about our professional goals and responsibilities (Arp, 1990; Behrens, 1994; Rader, 1990, 1991; Snavely and Cooper, 1997).

What's In a Name?

Quite a lot apparently, judging by the proliferation of material published on the subject. Although some may feel the debate is just an exercise in semantics, defining what we mean by IL is crucial to our task as instructors. If we don't know exactly what IL is, then how do we teach it and even more importantly how do we know if we have succeeded (Arp, 1990; Bruce, 1997)?

Interestingly enough, the term Information Literacy is not as new as some might think. It was first coined by Paul G. Zurowski (1974). An IL individual, according to Zurowski, is anyone who had learned to use a wide range of information sources in order to solve problems at work and in his or her daily life. Zurowski's definition continues to have validity over 25 years later. But whether IL is an entirely new concept or just the most current favored phrase, IL seems to have gained legitimacy as the term to use in place of user education, bibliographic instruction, library skills instruction, and other previously coined descriptions. Professional organizations, such as the American Library Association and its division the American Association of School Librarians, as well as the Association for Educational Communication and Technology, have all produced documents describing this concept. Accrediting agencies such as the Middle States Commission on Higher Education (MSCHE) and the Western Association of Schools and Colleges (WASC), and various individual colleges and universities, have adopted or are considering adopting the term (ALA–American Association for School Librarians and Association for Educational Communications and Technology, 1998; ALA–Association of College and Research Libraries, 2000; Behrens, 1990, 1994). Many of these organizations and agencies have produced guidelines and standards for the concept. See, for example, ALA's Association of College and Research Libraries recently developed Information Literacy Competency Standards for Higher Education (ALA–Association of College and Research Libraries, 2000). So what is the problem? It seems that although the term IL seems to be accepted, what is meant by the term varies depending upon whom you ask. Even more than its predecessors, the term IL seems difficult to pin down.

What Are Some Typical Definitions of IL?

In 1985 Patricia S. Breivik describes IL as an integrated set of skills and the knowledge of tools and resources. IL is developed through persistence, an attention to detail, and a critical, evaluative view of the material found. Breivik also views IL as a form of problem solving activity (Breivik, 1985). The American Library Association's Presidential Committee on Information Literacy *Final Report* published in 1989 describes the IL individual as someone who has the ability to recognize an information need, and can locate, evaluate, and use information effectively. The emphasis here is on preparing people for lifelong learning.

"Ultimately information literate people are those who have learned how to learn" (ALA–Presidential Committee on Information Literacy, 1989:1).

Carol C. Kuhlthau agrees with Breivik on the need for persistence, attention to detail, and caution in accepting information. She points out that one of the most important aspects of IL is an understanding of the amount of time and work involved in information seeking and use. The IL individual must be aware that information gathering is not linear; it is a complex process in which questions change and evolve as new information is gathered and thought about (Kuhlthau, 1989, 1990). Susanne Bjorner contributes a few more attitudinal or personality traits to the mix. She includes not only recognizing but also accepting a need for information. The IL individual responds positively to the need for investigation, constructs a variety of strategies to reduce the information gap, evaluates and selects the most appropriate strategy and assesses the effectiveness of the chosen strategy. Finally, the IL individual not only uses the information now, he or she also stores it for future use (Bjorner, 1991).

[handwritten margin notes: Critical thinkers / Non-linear process]

Hannelore B. Rader discusses the IL individual as someone who can survive and be successful in a rapidly changing information environment. Being IL allows one to lead a productive and satisfying life in a democratic society and to ensure a better future for coming generations (Rader, 1991). The AASL/AECT standards also reflect this view. These standards define the IL student as one who accesses information efficiently and effectively, critically evaluates the information, and uses it accurately and creatively. There is an emphasis on independent learning and also an element of social responsibility. The IL individual is someone who contributes positively to the learning community and to

[handwritten margin notes: Model Democratic citizens]

society. Underlying this definition is the belief that an IL populace is the cornerstone of democracy (ALA–American Association of School Librarians and Association for Educational Communications and Technology, 1998).

Christina S. Doyle characterizes the IL person as one who recognizes an information need and acknowledges that accurate and complete information is the basis for decision making. The IL individual can formulate questions based on this information need, develop appropriate search strategies, and access information from a variety of sources. Furthermore, the IL individual must be able to organize information, and use it in critical thinking and problem solving (Doyle, 1996). Then we have Christine Bruce's description of an IL person as one who engages in independent, self-directed learning using a variety of resources (print and electronic). He or she values information and its use, approaches information critically and has developed a personal information style (Bruce, 1997). IL is described as a construct developed by the IL individual. Such an individual creates a specific relationship with information in which he or she interacts with it in a way that provides personal meaning.

So we seem to have no end to the descriptions of the term IL. We can even see some commonalties in the various definitions. In their examination of several descriptions of IL, Michael Eisenberg and Michael Brown identified six common themes. The IL individual recognizes a need for information, engages in information seeking behavior, explores, accesses and locates material, interacts with the information to formulate hypotheses, synthesizes, interprets and organizes the information, and finally evaluates the results (Eisenberg and Brown, 1992). Critical thinking, problem solving, and the ability to apply the information to the individual's life are also crucial elements that run through all the definitions.

HOW DO WE TEACH IT?

So if we have a definition, why all the controversy? The problem lies not so much in what we say IL is, but in how we might be able to teach it to our users. On one side of the debate are those who question the lack of operational definitions connected to IL. How do we recognize someone who is IL? Even more problematic perhaps is how do we tell if someone is information illiterate? One of the most basic tenets of IL is that the person has learned how to learn. But how do we know when that has happened? Can we identify competencies an individual must master in order to be IL? What kind of competencies does the person need to allow him or her to be IL now and also in the future (ARP, 1990; Bjorner, 1991; Foster, 1993; McCrank, 1991)? To be IL an individual needs to be flexible, versatile, open to new ideas, and must possess a high level of cognitive problem solving skills. The IL individual recognizes an information need, is able to address the need, and is a critical evaluator of the process. But are these measurable attributes? The Information Literacy Competency Standards for Higher Education referred to earlier in this chapter is an example of an attempt to answer this question.

To further complicate the issue is the body of literature that defines IL not as a conglomerate of skills, but as a phenomenological change in the individual's whole worldview. The idea here is that one does not just master a set of skills to become IL. The individual must change in some fundamental ways, the way in which he or she values, relates to, and interacts with information (Bruce, 1994, 1997). What characterizes these changes and how to measure them again becomes the issue.

So where does this leave us? Is IL an observable behavior or body of skills that can be seen and measured? Is it something more cognitive and internal and therefore more difficult to quantify? Or is it a combination of the two? The way that we answer these questions will determine what we select to include in our instruction. Our ability to write meaningful goals and objectives for our sessions, to identify appropriate learning outcomes, and to develop criteria by which we can measure if we have succeeded in reaching our objectives are all predicated on what we mean by IL.

One thing is clear, however. Information professionals are IL and our users are not. What do we know that they do not and how can we get them to know what we know? What skills, behaviors, and strategies have we developed that result in our being IL? Exploring answers to those questions will help us design IL programs that are more useful and meaningful than ever before. In the end, perhaps IL is more than a body of skills and a set of concepts. It is a way of knowing how to deal with information, a way of finding out about information resources, and a way of interacting with information that sets the IL individual apart. It is not just behavioral skills, cognitive problem solving abilities, or even humanistic attitude changes. It is all three and more. The issues of whether we are dealing with measurable observable behavior, cognitive thought processes, or humanistic attributes will be returned to in subsequent chapters, especially those dealing with psychology, teaching, and assessment. However, we need to adopt a working definition for the purpose of this book.

A Working Definition of IL

Our definition should include both the directly observable behavior and those less directly observable attributes, attitudes, and cognitive processes to see what challenges this definition presents to us. Instead of saying we cannot measure these things, let's direct our attention to the ways that we can. The field of qualitative evaluation may offer insight into ways to "operationalize" these less obvious characteristics of the IL individual.

At the core of the various definitions discussed throughout this chapter is the notion that an IL individual is able to identify, locate, evaluate, and use information effectively. Transferability seems to be another important aspect of the definitions. An IL individual must be able to effectively interact with information in a variety of situations and to address a range of information needs. Although these basic attributes can be seen as our working definition for this book, it is important to realize that there is really no totally agreed upon and standard definition of the term. IL means different things to different people and their definitions may even vary from situation to situation. One of the most important element of a needs assessment is to determine how the key players in your environment define the term. You can use their definitions both as a hook to get attention and approval for your IL initiatives, and as an opportunity to broaden their view of IL. See Chapter 7 for more information on needs assessments.

IS IL A NEW CONCEPT?

There remains the question of whether IL is really adding anything new to what we have always taught. Haven't we always tried to promote critical thinking in our sessions? When we introduced various different types of print resources, didn't we discuss when it would be appropriate to use them? Is our increased emphasis on critical thinking and evaluation merely the result of the proliferation of resources, especially via the World Wide Web, now available to the information seeker (Bruce, 1997; Breivik, 1991)? Admittedly the Web adds an additional wrinkle. In the past our users could rely on information professionals to some extent. We provided access to what we felt were reputable resources within the walls of our libraries. Now information is available everywhere and information professionals are rightfully concerned that the public may be unaware of the quality (or lack of quality) of the information they are accessing. So the need for enlightened, critical, and thoughtful information users has increased. The Web has upped the ante on the importance of being IL. But our goal has always been the development of thoughtful and selective information users (Candy, 1996).

Virginia Rankin in her excellent and inspirational article on the pre-search process, emphasizes the importance of critical thinking and analysis *before* the user ever sets foot into the library or begins to interact with any information resource (Rankin, 1988). Using reference material, print indexes, databases, and search engines are mechanical skills that can be disseminated through demonstrations, handouts, tutorials, and the ever valuable one-on-one interaction with the reference librarian. While these are all necessary skills for the IL individual, the underlying concepts of why this type of source over that one, the critical evaluation of the selected source, and the selection of resource material appropriate to a given topic are all components of IL.

MECHANICS VERSUS CONCEPTS

As discussed above, the idea of transferability is a critical part of what most people mean by IL. Teaching the mechanics of one specific system is useful in the short term and undoubtedly answers the individual's specific information need. But what if we teach them how to select an appropriate resource for a topic, as well as the underlying principles applicable to most databases, and a strategy for discovering how to find out the ways to use new resources when they are encountered in the future. Then we have provided the individual with a lifelong advantage in an information rich and complex world.

This brings us to the age-old question of mechanics versus concepts. It is obvious that mechanics are crucial. People must learn to walk before they can run. But how much instruction should be devoted to the "I need to know how to do it now" skills and how much to the strategies and concepts that will provide the user with lifelong IL abilities? With more and more resources being introduced, the pressure to introduce our users to everything keeps increasing. But the less-is-more rule applies now more than ever. If we are truly providing ILI, we need to concentrate on general, transferable strategies and concepts in our classroom presentations, our handouts, our computer-assisted instruction programs, and our instructional Web pages. We must de-emphasize the mechanics. We must pick and choose carefully among the vast number of resources available and highlight only the most crucial. Overkill is underlearning; the more you pour in the less will be retained. After all, you do not want your users to think that being IL is an unattainable task. Settle on one or two transferable concepts and illustrate them using the resources you have chosen to present. Then give them some sort of self-guided material for the mechanics (in print or virtually) and let them explore on their own.

"But that is not why they came to the session," you protest. "They came to learn how to use a specific set of resources. If I don't teach them the 'how tos,' they will go away dissatisfied." OK. Then just teach the mechanics. But don't pretend that you are helping people become fully IL in your sessions. Perhaps there is a time and place for mechanics and another time and place for full ILI.

FINAL REMARKS: IL, RELEVANCE AND PARTNERSHIPS

This leads to the idea of partnerships in your community. People learn when it is meaningful for them to do so. Trying to teach IL in a vacuum is frustrating and counterproductive. Your users do not care, and you lose credibility by trying to force feed them material that does not seem relevant to them (Eadie, 1990; McCrank, 1991). Clearly, IL concepts only become understandable when presented in context. Academic and school librarians have the advantage of being able to tie IL to classroom requirements. But IL should not be viewed in isolation. Nor should we treat it as something that belongs to us as information professionals. To really succeed, IL must be seen as valued by the community at large. That means not only getting attention and approval from faculty, administrators, teachers, and community leaders, it means having IL promoted as a necessity everywhere. IL abilities should be viewed as vital not only in the classroom, but also in the workplace and in every aspect of life (Breivik and Gee, 1989). When employers use IL abilities as part of the selection process, these abilities increase in value to the prospective employee.

How do we make this happen? Can we? The successful promotion of IL to our populations depends upon our success in developing collaborative partnerships in our institutions and in our communities. We need to be advocates for IL and show our constituents the importance of IL to the educated, responsible populace. We must share our expertise and develop ways for IL to permeate the educational process at every stage of life—in schools, colleges, and universities; in public libraries' continuing education programs; in the workplace; and in the home (ALA–Presidential Committee on Information Literacy, 1989; Behrens, 1994; Breivik, 1991; Harada and Tepe, 1998).

A seamless intertwining of ILI with all forms of instruction (whether taught by information professionals, classroom teachers, college/university faculty, employers, or community leaders) should be our ultimate goal. Can we do it? We can only try. Should we do it? We absolutely must if we are to call ourselves information professionals.

So how do we teach this somewhat amorphous, wide-ranging, and in some respects ambiguous concept called IL? In the end it is up to each one of us to decide. No matter what definition of IL you take as your own guiding principle, the material in this book will help you develop and possibly refine your skills as instructors. What you pick as your content, where you choose to present it, and how you decide to teach it, that will all be up to you. The following chapters will give you the framework. But you will have to provide the particulars.

EXERCISE

List three characteristics that describe an IL individual to you.

Describe how you would design instruction that would develop each of those characteristics.

Describe the ways in which print handouts, workbooks, guided exercises, Computer Assisted Instruction, and/or Web-based instruction could promote information literacy skills.

READ MORE ABOUT IT

ALA. Association of College and Research Libraries Task Force on Information Literacy Competency Standards. "Information Literacy Competency Standards for Higher Education" [Online]. Available: www.ala.org/acrl/ilcomstan.html [2000, November 11].

ALA. Presidential Committee on Information Literacy. *Final Report* [Online]. Available: www.ala.org/acrl/nili/ilit1st.html [2000, December 28].

Arp, Lori. 1990. "Information Literacy or Bibliographic Instruction: Semantics or Philosophy?" *RQ* 30 no. 1: 46–49.

Behrens, Shirley J. 1994. "A Conceptual Analysis and Historical Overview of Information Literacy." *College and Research Libraries.* 55 no. 4:309–322.

Bruce, Christine. 1997. *The Seven Faces of Information Literacy.* Adelaide, Australia: Auslib Press.

Snavely, Loanne, and Natasha Cooper. 1997. "The Information Literacy Debate." *Journal of Academic Librarianship* 23 no. 1: 9–14.

2

History of Information Literacy Instruction

A library is but the soul's burial ground. It is the land of shadows.
                                        —Henry Ward Beecher.

A circulating library in a town is an evergreen tree of diabolical knowledge.
                                        —Richard Sheridan, *The Rivals*

LIBRARIES AND LIBRARIANS: WHERE DO THEY FIT?

Happily, negative images of libraries and librarians are fading fast. Many now see libraries and librarians at the heart of the university, the college, the community, and even the corporation, organization, and research entity. Increasingly complex technology has placed the library at center stage as staff, faculty, administrators, students, and other user groups have begun to recognize the importance of being competent, literate, and, ultimately, fluent in information identification, location, evaluation, and use.

What does this mean for instruction in the use of libraries and library resources? For IL and for those who teach it—ILI librarians? In some ways it means too much for librarians—too much work, too much effort, too many demands, and too many classes and instruction-related products to design, develop, test, revise, redesign, implement, evaluate, redesign, etc. It means making tremendous efforts to work broadly from the top down, building IL into accreditation standards, raising consciousness about its importance among non-ILI librarians, administrators, and other higher-ups. It is a frantic world, quickly evolving, mutating—one blink, one breath, and it seems to have passed us by.

Some have questioned the end we are trying to serve (Gorman, 1991); others have questioned the means (Eadie, 1990). Let us look at the gifts the past offers us, acknowledge the long and difficult path to the current state of ILI and those who took it, and consider whether the end and the means are justified.

ROOTS OF INSTRUCTION AND INFORMATION LITERACY IN LIBRARIES

The modern library instruction movement began in academic libraries in the early 1960s, but library instruction is not new. At the first American Library Association (ALA) Conference in 1876, Melvil Dewey said, " . . . the library is a school, and the librarian is in the highest sense a teacher . . . " (1876). Surprisingly to some, " . . . between 1876 and 1910 . . . some twenty institutions gave credit courses in library research, and forty offered noncredit courses in library use" (Roberts and Blandy, 1989: 2). In an 1880 essay, for example, Otis Robinson firmly states, "So important do we regard a good library education, that special instruction is given on libraries and the method of using them." He goes on to say that he himself, " . . . is accustomed, as librarian, to give . . . lectures from time to time to freshman and sophomore classes, to make them understand the great advantage of the use of a library, to explain in general terms the nature and use of the devices for finding what one wants, to show how they may supplement their course of study at every point by reading the authors and subjects studied . . . But it is in the library itself that most of this instruction is given" (Robinson, 1880:21).

Tucker, Hardesty and Tucker, and Farber provide additional details on early library instruction efforts within the context of educational movements and historical periods since the nineteenth century. They note that libraries of all kinds have been involved in this effort for decades, and that academic librarians have been doing research and writing about the need for library instruction since the late 1880s, beginning with Justin Winsor (University Librarian at Harvard University in the 1870s and 1880s) and Otis Robinson, mentioned above (Tucker, 1980; Hardesty and Tucker, 1989; Farber, 1995a). They have tried to appeal to faculty and administrators at particular institutions, as well as the academic community at large, and have used a variety of technological means to do so, attempting to differentiate between "information" and "instruction," between service and education, between giving a man a fish and teaching him how to fish (Tucker, 1980).

School libraries in the U.S., first established in 1918, have been involved in library instruction since about 1938, when Alexander developed suggested library instruction for different grade levels, including checklists of skills for each grade (Bonn, 1960). Since then, school librarians (now called school library media specialists) have worked with teachers to plan, develop, and implement numerous programs for all levels of school children, from kindergarten through high school (Fargo, 1939; Kuhlthau, 1981; Craver, 1986). Public libraries and special libraries have traditionally focused on fact-finding and information delivery, many providing informal individualized instruction rather than formal programs or courses. Beginning in the 1980s, driven by a technological tidal wave and efforts to redefine "library instruction" as "information literacy," they have joined academic libraries and school libraries in developing and expanding more formalized instructional efforts for their users at all levels (Lubans, 1983). Where and how did this modern instruction movement begin in libraries?

Patricia Knapp's research at Monteith College Library in the early 1960s sparked the modern-day library instruction movement. Monteith was one of eleven colleges that made up Wayne State University. In the period from 1959 to 1962, Monteith College enrolled three hundred to seven hundred students and had fifteen to thirty faculty members. In this small college setting, Knapp conducted a research study to test out elements of Louis Shores's library/college concept (Knapp, 1966). Shores saw higher education revolving around the library, where increasingly students would learn by using what he presciently called "'wet' carrels," with increasingly higher tech products, individualized to each student's needs and interests (Knapp, 1966: 166). As he put it, "When a college is a library, and a library is a college, it is a Library-College" (Shores, 1970: 159).

Knapp envisioned the library as the center of the higher educational experience. She came up with a number of different assignments to help improve the quality of undergraduate research papers, including "Library Competency Testing," "Using Surface Clues to Evaluate Books," and "The Independence Assignment" (1966: 66). The latter combined workbook–type questions for 250 students related to specific reference tools with a pre-assignment visit to the class by a librarian and a post-assignment one-hour class discussion with the librarian. She noted then, as we do today, that "Students tend to be uncritical in their choices of sources of information . . . they tend to be content with 'something on' the subject, regardless of its validity" (1966: 41). To counteract this problem, she designed a number of assignments, one of which required students to select entries from the card catalog from among many on a single topic, and provide reasons for their selections. ILI librarians continue to reinvent critical thinking exercises similar to hers but with a technological twist, for example, "Hoax? Scholarly Research? Personal Opinion? You Decide!" (Grassian and Zwemer, 1999); see also Chapter 5.

DEVELOPMENT OF MODERN LIBRARY INSTRUCTION MOVEMENTS

Bibliographic Instruction

Knapp's efforts are at the root of the modern library instruction "tree," which first developed two main branches. One focused on intensive integration of library instruction into the entire academic curriculum, course by course, in a "synchronous" (real time) face-to-face group instruction mode (Farber, 1974). The other branch focused on an almost entirely self-paced, hands-on, "asynchronous" (any time, any place) approach (Dudley, 1978). Both Farber and Dudley launched their approaches prior to the existence of public access computers in libraries.

Synchronous and Asynchronous Instruction

"Synchronous" and "asynchronous" are terms commonly used in discussing distance education. *The Encyclopedia of Educational Technology* defines these terms as follows:

> Asynchronous communication is technology mediated and not real-time based. Teachers and/or learners are not tied to a common location or timeline (e.g., e-mail, etc.). In contrast, synchronous communication relies on real-time interactions between participants (e.g., Web cast). Although co-location is not needed, a coordinated timeline is required. (Schutt, 2000)

On the other hand, *The Oxford English Dictionary* (*OED*) provides more general definitions. It defines "synchronous" as "Existing or happening at the same time; coincident in time; belonging to the same period, or occurring at the same moment, of time; contemporary; simultaneous." It defines "asynchronous" as "Want of synchronism; non-correspondence in time" (1989).

For this publication, we will use *The Oxford English Dictionary*'s broader definitions, which include both in-person and remote instruction, and may or may not be technology-mediated. Synchronous instruction, then, is simultaneous, in real-time, and may be in-person or remote. Asynchronous instruction may occur any time, any place, and occurs remotely.

FACE-TO-FACE GROUP INSTRUCTION (SYNCHRONOUS, IN-PERSON)

Evan Farber developed a fully course-integrated model library instruction program beginning in 1964 at Earlham College, modeled on traditional in-person college courses (Farber, 1974). For 35 or more years,
Earlham College librarians and teaching faculty together have done an
outstanding job of integrating IL into the entire curriculum. Class by
class, teaching faculty and librarians develop syllabi and assignments
together in a synchronized, sequential approach to library instruction,
beginning with "placement tests" and continuing through increasingly
more complex instruction. In 1998/99 they reached all 1,100 students
("Earlham College", 1999). For many years Farber has also spoken, written, and held workshops describing this approach (1974; 1993; 1995b).
In 1987 he received the ALA Association of College and Research Libraries (ACRL) Instruction Section's (IS) "Instruction Librarian of the
Year Award" for his many efforts and achievements in promoting library instruction . This completely integrated and intensive approach
has succeeded at Earlham and in numerous other institutions primarily
because of their small size and higher ratio of librarians to students.
Faculty status for librarians is another contributing factor to the success
of this approach. Librarians who have faculty status are able to serve on
academic senate committees, especially curriculum committees. Even
in larger institutions, such curriculum committee service provides an
opportunity to raise consciousness about IL among faculty, and to lobby
for its inclusion, at least in undergraduate general education courses
(California State University, San Marcos Library, 1999).

However, librarians at many large institutions do not have faculty
status, have minimal contact with faculty, at least on the curriculum
development level, and have low ratios of librarians to students. Fully
scaling the Earlham librarian/faculty teaching model to large institutions seemed difficult, if not impossible in the 1960s and 70s. Instead,
another branch developed on the library instruction tree.

SELF-PACED WORKBOOKS (ASYNCHRONOUS, REMOTE)

In the early 70s, amid much resistance from administrators and reference staff, Miriam Dudley at UCLA developed a highly successful
learner-centered, self-paced library skills workbook (Dudley, 1978). This
simply designed, asynchronous workbook was utilized by thousands
of UCLA students over a ten-year period and mimicked by libraries and
librarians worldwide. It required students to use twenty different types
of reference tools in order to answer a series of questions. For example,
in the Almanacs section, students would need to find out who was Pope

in a particular year and select the correct multiple-choice answer. Each type of reference tool had its own "module" and students could skip around to different modules, or complete the workbook in the search strategy order in which it was printed. Workbooks were then corrected and students with wrong answers were coached and encouraged to obtain correct answers. This approach worked best for large institutions with low ratios of librarians to students, but also was adopted widely by smaller institutions with limited staff across the U.S. and in other countries.

Relationship to Reference

Dudley and Farber were farsighted pioneers, but many other pioneering librarians and organizations have written or edited significant library-instruction-related works over the past twenty-five or more years, including Beaubien, Hogan, and George (1982); Oberman and Strauch (1982); Mellon, (1987); Reichel and Ramey (1987); Svinicki and Schwartz (1988); Breivik and Gee (1989); Fink (1989); Roberts and Blandy (1989); Brottman and Loe (1990); ALA-ACRL-BIS (1991, 1993a, 1993b); and Shonrock (1996). These librarians and many others, documented annually in Hannelore Rader's *RSR: Reference Services Review* column on ILI publications, and LIRT's top twenty instruction articles of the year (ALA-LIRT, 2000), have defined and enhanced librarians' efforts to teach, introducing us to user-centered approaches, outreach, and learning outcomes assessment, as well as other education and instructional technology skills, concepts, and techniques.

The purpose of all of these instructional efforts was not necessarily to cut down on the total *number* of questions asked at reference desks, but to raise the level of complexity of questions that remain following instruction in basic IL skills. So, instead of getting fifty questions a day on how to look up a book using the online catalog, you might get ten of those questions plus another twenty on how to select among various electronic and print resources and how to construct an effective search strategy for the most appropriate ones. The more effective ILI is, then, the fewer basic reference questions you may encounter. Does this mean that reference librarians are less busy than they used to be? Actually, they are busier than ever, as the number, scope, and complexity of reference sources available even to the smallest, most isolated library has grown enormously. Stop-watch tests and statistics that keep track of the length of reference questions may be quite revealing to administrators who are used to relying on numbers of reference interactions alone to gauge reference desk workload. Furthermore, much of direct reference work with the public these days, in many types of libraries, has to do with teaching or helping people learn to make effective use of a myriad of sources, and not just finding the answers to their questions for them.

In the modern library instruction movement, beginning in the late 1960s and early 70s, instruction librarians were quite foresighted as they tried to raise awareness of the great need for user aid in the form of teaching. Since most librarians were not trained to teach, they struggled mightily to learn from each other, attending workshops, programs, and conferences, and devouring library instruction materials, articles, and eventually books. They fought a difficult battle for acceptance against those who felt that library instruction was a frill and was taking librarians' time away from their real work, answering reference questions at the reference desk.

Today there is much administrative and colleague support for ILI in all sorts of libraries. Interestingly enough, some are even recasting the workbook concept for the Web, particularly as interactive self-paced tutorials and exercises, but also as full courses. James Madison University's "Go for the Gold," for example, even begins with a tour of the physical library, just as Miriam Dudley's *Library Instruction Workbook* did (James Madison University, 2000). Bowling Green State University's "Falcon: An Interactive Web Tutorial" also follows the workbook model (1999).

On Beyond Farber and Dudley

Many other offshoots of both approaches have developed and grown over the years, notably workbooks or course-related or course-integrated one-shot sessions affiliated with a particular discipline or department, as well as independent standalone, library-initiated workshops or classes and various technology-based efforts.

The underlying goals of both of the Farber and Dudley branches were to help users learn about library resources and information tools, and to develop effective strategies for using them, for the purpose of lifelong learning. For example, Dudley's *Library Skills Workbook*, modeled by hundreds of libraries in the U.S. and elsewhere, was structured in a search strategy approach, beginning with basic sources such as dictionaries and encyclopedias and moving to more specialized sources later. Each segment was self-contained, so users could use the workbook in a linear or in a modular fashion (Dudley, 1978).

In the 1960s, 70s, and early 80s, little did instruction librarians know that their many efforts would one day sit at center stage in libraries as technology entered first the technical side of the library world and then the public arena. During the 80s and 90s, as technology made major impacts on libraries, faculty increasingly called on librarians to do "library orientations" or "library presentations" for their classes. Librarians began to emulate the teaching faculty's lecture mode, though often as guest lecturers who met with a class only once. During the 80s and 90s, many librarians enthusiastically researched and embraced educational theories and techniques as a substitute for the teacher training and education they did not receive in library school. After much research, study, and practice, library instructional theory matured and evolved. Some 30 years after Knapp's research, following the steady growth of both the Dudley and Farber branches, a new shoot developed that ultimately has encompassed all forms of library-related and information research-related instruction—information literacy (IL).

Information Literacy

In the 1980s, as technology was beginning to show its public face in libraries, Patricia Breivik reconceptualized the concepts and goals of library instructional efforts as "information literacy." She chaired the ALA Presidential Committee on Information Literacy, whose 1989 definition of the phrase is still widely in use today . This group saw IL broadly, not limited to library resources, but applying to all sorts of information sources. According to this view, if you need to know something for educational, personal, business, or any other reason, and if you can identify, locate, evaluate, and use that information effectively, then you are information literate.

National Forum on Information Literacy (NFIL)

Patricia Breivik has written and spoken widely on the issue of IL, and also established the National Forum on Information Literacy (NFIL), an organization of organizations devoted to spreading the word on the need for IL at all levels and in all environments. The NFIL encourages and lists important new developments in IL in a variety of organizations, including the American Association for Higher Education (AAHE) and the National Education Association (NEA). For example, it reported that AAHE " . . . created an action committee and now regularly offers programming on IL at its annual conferences" (National Forum on Information Literacy, 2000).

More IL Developments

As the NFIL helped this process along among organizations, Eisenberg and Berkowitz developed and pressed for implementation of "The Big 6™ Library Skills" approach for K–12 in 1990. In 1998, ALA's American

Association of School Librarians (AASL) published a critical and timely document, the first IL standards for K–12. These detailed and well-written standards have already had an enormous impact on school libraries and school library media specialists. As we have noted, however, debate has raged fiercely since 1989 over the meaning, application, standards, and, particularly, the expected learning outcomes of the concept of "IL" (Arp, 1990; Snavely and Cooper, 1997). ALA ACRL's "Information Literacy Competency Standards for Higher Education," and ACRL IS's "Objectives for Information Literacy Instruction by Academic Librarians," as well as ALA AASL's *Information Power* IL standards for K–12, will go a long way toward answering some of these questions. However, non-librarians have also begun adopting the phrase "information literacy," in some cases equating it with computer literacy or technology-based literacy (Shapiro and Hughes, 1996). This confusion of terminology is complicating matters for librarians who are struggling to define their own roles in the technological universe. We have to hope that it is not too late for librarians to seize and define the phrase IL in terms of learning outcomes and make certain it represents the unique role and contribution of the librarian—the skill, training, and ability to help people learn to take control over the information in their lives, evaluate it, and use it effectively. How do we get this message across to the public and work together to clarify and continue to define our role as well as expected learner outcomes for ILI?

Information Competency and Information Fluency

It has been a rather long and difficult process, as librarians and others have coined variant phrases since the phrase "Information Literacy" was first introduced, including "information competency" and "information fluency" (see Chapter 1). Maricopa County Community College was among the first to attempt to define IL competencies in what became known as "The Ocotillo Report" (2000). In 1997, WAAL (Wisconsin Association of Academic Librarians) developed an information literacy competency list and criteria for academic libraries in that state (1999), as SUNY (State University of New York) a year later did for that state (2000). The California State University system has also developed a major information competency initiative that aims to integrate IL into the curriculum of all 23 of its campuses (2000). California community college libraries have also been lobbying for an "Information Competency Plan for systemwide implementation, training and evaluation" (California Community Colleges–Board of Governors, 1998).

In 1999, the U.S. National Academy of the Sciences published an important document defining the concept of "information fluency." The report, "Being Fluent with Information Technology," posits three components of "Fluency with Information Technology" or "FITness":

- Contemporary skills, the ability to use today's computer applications, enable people to apply information technology immediately
- Foundational concepts, the basic principles and ideas of computers, networks, and information
- Intellectual capabilities, the ability to apply information technology in complex and sustained situations, encapsulate higher-level thinking in the context of information technology (U.S. National Academy of Sciences, Executive Summary, 1999: [online])

The *Report* describes similarities between IL and FITness, but also attempts to draw distinctions between them. For example, according to the *Report*, "Information Literacy focuses on communication and content. By contrast, FITness focuses on a set of intellectual capabilities, conceptual knowledge, and contemporary skills associated with information technology" (1999, Chapter 3, 3.2:[online]). The *Report* goes on to say that "in essence, [FIT] individuals need to form a conceptual map of information space. For example, they need to be guided in developing mental models of the relationships among documents on the Internet and in proprietary databases, library collections, and the like as a basis for learning to evaluate what information sources are likely to be most appropriate for their various information needs" (1999, Chapter 3, 3.2:[online]).

Does this truly differ from information literacy? Over the past thirty or more years, ILI librarians have excelled at teaching conceptual frameworks, mental models, and critical thinking, all designed to help people learn how to select the most appropriate information sources for their needs, and how to evaluate those sources, regardless of their format. ILI librarians have written many practical and theoretical books, articles, and Web pages on these topics as well. Examples include Knapp's *Monteith College Library Experiment* (1966), Frick's "Information Structure and Bibliographic Instruction" (1975), Oberman and Strauch's *Theories of Bibliographic Education* (1982), Reichel and Ramey's *Conceptual Frameworks for Bibliographic Instruction* (1987), Bodi's "Critical Thinking and Bibliographic Instruction" (1988), Alexander and Tate's "Evaluating Web Resources" (1999), and Grassian's "Thinking Critically About World Wide Web Resources" (1998).

Is information technology fluency on a higher plane than information literacy, as the *Report* implies? Not really. Although acknowledging that IL and FIT need to work together, the *Report* largely ignores this body of theoretical knowledge and practical expertise.

In fact, the primary differences between IL and FITness lie in the *Report's* focus on information technology and in the segments which deal with more technical skills. This focus is entirely in keeping with the group's admirable, but limited charge, of course, "to articulate what everyone needs to know and understand about information technology, an essential first step toward empowering all citizens to participate in the information age" (Preface, 1999:[online]).

However, footnote 4 in Chapter 4 of the *Report* clearly indicates that in some significant areas IL's lifelong learning goals regarding evaluative, effective, and ethical use of information in all formats go further than those of information technology fluency. In this footnote, the *Report* acknowledges that developing and maintaining FITness over one's lifetime requires "an adequate intellectual foundation" (1999:[online]), but also requires "access to the information technology infrastructure they used to develop FITness" (1999:[online]). It seems that we agree that access, in and of itself, does not guarantee continued FITness, as the technology infrastructure will continue to morph at a rapid pace for the unforeseeable future. However, not all information is computerized information, some will never be computerized, and some computerized information is not freely available to everyone. So, how do we help people maintain fluency with rapidly evolving information technology, and at the same time, learn new skills for identifying, locating, evaluating, and using all sorts of information effectively and ethically?

It seems clear that FITness is essential for successful information literacy competency in the technological age, and vice-versa. Rather than arguing over which concept is subsumed under which other concept, we need to acknowledge that IL and FITness share not only many of the same skills, but also much the same goals. That done, we need to work together to help people achieve these shared goals.

Whether or not you agree with this analysis, the FITness Report illustrates that the phrase "Information Literacy" has reached the national consciousness beyond librarianship. The IL approach seems to be growing stronger daily. It is a phrase and a concept that has become more familiar and more comfortable just as more and more complex technology has become familiar and comfortable to many librarians. Many of our users at all educational levels are also quite comfortable with new technology.

The U.S. government instituted a telecommunications discount program run by the Federal Communications Commission (FCC) as part of the Telecommunications Act of 1996. This "E-Rate" program, part of the U.S. government's Universal Service program, supports wiring for Internet connectivity and Internet access, as well as other telecommunications costs in schools and libraries. "Discounts range from 20 to 90 percent (based on the poverty level in the local community), and schools and libraries are required to pay the non-discounted portion of the bill themselves" (Bradley, 2001:324). In addition, there is a growing number of community technology centers in the U.S. In spite of these efforts, however, the digital divide documented in 1999 still exists, and is growing worse for the poor and minorities (St. Lifer, 2000; 3COM, 2000; U.S. Department of Commerce, 1999; Revenaugh, 2000; Cooper, 2000). In September 2000, the MIT Media Lab announced the "Creating Community Connections Project," which aims to make the digital divide a "digital opportunity," a means of empowering low- to moderate-income community residents both by training them in computer and Internet use and by helping them learn to collaborate in running the project itself. The U.S. Department of Education's Office of Educational Technology has also developed a "Tool Kit for Bridging the Digital Divide in Your Community" through community projects, which starts with coalition building, with an appendix to one chapter entitled "Partnerships with Local Institutions." MOUSE (Making Opportunities for Upgrading Schools & Education) is a non-profit voluntary organization in New York City that connects high-tech professionals and their resources with public schools. MOUSE also has a corporate partnership program (MIT Media Lab, 2000; U.S. Department of Education, Office of Educational Technology, 2000; MOUSE, Inc., 2001; Anthony, 2000; Digital Divide Network, n.d.; Haycock, 1999).

All of these groups emphasize coalition-building or partnering with others to help achieve universal access and computer literacy. These worthy goals are necessary but not sufficient in today's increasingly complex technology-based world. Libraries of all kinds should be natural partners of these groups, helping them expand their goals from access to effective identification, location, evaluation, and use—universal information literacy competency. ILI librarians and library organizations are already working within the ALA President's Information Literacy Community Partnerships Initiative and need only reach out to governmental and private groups like those mentioned above to have a major national and even international impact. In the interim, library organizations have developed ILI competency standards and are lobbying educational accrediting agencies in the U.S. to incorporate IL standards into the more traditional standards for school, college, and university accreditation. Where did this effort arise and what role have professional organizations played in the modern IL movement?

HISTORY AND ROLE OF LIBRARY INSTRUCTION ORGANIZATIONS, PUBLICATIONS, AND OTHER SUPPORT GROUPS

The ILI organizations we depend on and value so much did not spring magically to life. They developed in the early to mid–1970s due to a growing social consciousness and the grass-roots organizing efforts of librarians who were mostly on the front line of reference. At that time, increasing numbers of older returning students, international students, under-represented minorities, and other users labeled "non-traditional" were asking very basic questions at reference desks. Reference librarians were having a difficult time addressing their needs, as well as those of the populations that traditionally asked for help at reference desks. These problems were not limited to one portion of a country or even a single country, but seemed to be universal issues encountered in libraries worldwide.

Regional Instruction Organizations

In the U.S., librarians who were struggling to develop and deliver instruction banded together in the 1970s to talk and share ideas and approaches to teaching and learning. They mounted grass-roots efforts to establish organizations at the local, regional, and national levels that would support them with education, training, networking, and publications to keep them up to date (ALA–Association of College and Research Libraries–New England Chapter–New England Bibliographic Instruction Committee [NEBIC], 2000). For example, in 1974, under the impetus of Miriam Dudley and others, the California Clearinghouse on Library Instruction (CCLI) started life as a subcommittee of the California Library Association's (CLA) Reference and Information Services Chapter (RISC). In 1975, with over 200 members, CCLI dwarfed RISC, established itself as a separate CLA chapter, and broke into Northern and Southern Steering Committees. When CLA reorganized in 1991, both CCLI steering committees left CLA and became separate organizations in their own right. Since 1975, both CCLI groups' missions have been to serve as a forum for librarians interested in instruction, to share information and materials by means of a clearinghouse of paper, audio, video, and other materials, and to provide continuing education for its members by means of workshops, programs, a semi-annual newsletter, and other publications. To this day, both CCLI North and South continue these efforts, and have now extended them to the Web (California Clearinghouse on Library Instruction, North, 1999; California Clearinghouse on Library Instruction, South, 2000). Both organizations have been and continue to be wonderful sources of networking and aid for California librarians interested in instruction in all environments.

ALA ACRL Bibliographic Instruction Section (BIS)/Instruction Section (IS), and ALA Library Instruction Roundtable (LIRT)

Dudley was also instrumental in establishing the ALA's ACRL Bibliographic Instruction Section (BIS) and played a part, as well, in establishing the ALA Library Instruction Round Table (LIRT). It was a hard fought battle, as she went to three different ALA presidents trying to persuade them to establish instruction organizations within ALA. Finally, in 1975, at the same time that CCLI was started in California, ACRL agreed to establish BIS, and ALA established LIRT (Dudley, 2000). As a section of ACRL, BIS—now called simply the Instruction Section, or IS—is geared to the needs of academic librarians while LIRT serves librarians interested in instruction regardless of their environment.

Since 1975, IS and LIRT have put on ALA conference programs and preconferences, published semi-annual newsletters, as well as numerous other significant items related to library instruction, established and maintained highly useful Websites, and grown in stature and importance. As of late 1999, IS was the second largest ACRL section, with over 4,200 members worldwide. LIRT has 1,500 members and provides important linkages among instruction librarians and programs in widely varying school, academic, public, and special library environments.

IS has published both practical and theoretical works, including the 1983 *Evaluating Bibliographic Instruction: A Handbook*, the 1987 "Model Statement of Objectives for Academic Bibliographic Instruction," and a guide to its use, *Read This First: An Owner's Guide to the New Model Statement of Objectives of Academic Bibliographic Instruction*, published in 1991. The organization has also published other items to help novice and experienced instruction librarians alike, such as *Learning to Teach* and *The Sourcebook for Bibliographic Instruction*, both published in 1993, and *Designs for Active Learning*, published in 1998.

ALA's LIRT has published a number of highly useful instruction works as well, carefully designed to meet the needs of instruction librarians in all sorts of environments, including the 1989 *Case Studies in Library Instruction*, Brottman and Loe's 1990 *LIRT Library Instruction Handbook*, the 1992 *Evaluating Library Instruction Librarians and Programs: Case Studies*, *Information for a New Age: Redefining the Librarian*, put together by LIRT's Fifteenth Anniversary Task Force in 1995, and Shonrock's 1996 *Evaluating Library Instruction*.

Library Orientation and Exchange (LOEX)

1975 was truly an astounding and productive year in terms of library instruction-related organizations. CCLI, BIS, and LIRT were established, and so was another highly significant organization—LOEX (Library Orientation and EXchange). LOEX began as a 1971 conference at Eastern Michigan University. In the early 1970s, Eastern Michigan University received a grant from the Council on Library Resources and the National Endowment for the Humanities for a "library outreach" office, which was called LOEX for "Library Orientation and EXchange" (LOEX–National LOEX Library Instruction Conference, 2000). Its functions then, as now, were to serve as a national library instruction clearinghouse, a central depository for all formats of library instruction materials, and to educate instruction librarians. Under the able leadership of a number of directors, LOEX has surpassed all hopes to become a model depository and educational "institution." Its annual conferences are always overbooked with lengthy waiting lists, and have even been mimicked by others. Now there is a "LOEX of the West" conference every other year (1999), for example. These conferences are significant arenas for all of us to learn from each other about new and exciting developments in instruction. Annual LOEX conference proceedings are chock full of fascinating material, copies of handouts, and other useful information. For example, the 1996 conference was titled "Programs That Work" (LOEX, National LOEX Library Instruction Conference, 1997).

International Federation of Library Associations (IFLA)

The IFLA Roundtable on User Education was established in 1993 as a formal group, after three years as a working group of this international organization. The roundtable's purpose is "to foster international cooperation in the development of user education in all types of libraries." Among its goals, the roundtable aims to hold sessions on user education topics at IFLA conferences, disseminate information about user education projects and programs, and monitor education and training for user education librarians.

BI-L

Instruction librarians reached a major milestone in 1990 when Martin Raish established the Bibliographic Instruction Listserv, or BI-L, a moderated listserv for all librarians interested in instruction. Since that time, under his able direction, BI-L has played a significant role as an outstanding source of help, inspiration, communication, and even continuing education for practicing ILI librarians. It serves as a kind of current bibliography, cum help desk, cum ongoing conference of ILI efforts and queries, reflecting the unending creativity and dedication of ILI librarians. However, dedication and creativity in and of themselves are not enough to make for effective instruction. Basic background in instructional theory and practice, especially as related to libraries and information resources, are essential, with continuing education as an important follow-up.

ACRL Institute for Information Literacy (IIL)

CCLI, North and South, IS, LIRT, and LOEX are prominent institutions now, with lengthy histories. They publish important works—both theoretical and practical—hold conference programs, workshops, and other events, and generally provide and bolster professional development for instruction librarians. Since 1993, both the IFLA Roundtable on User Education and BI-L have served to raise consciousness about the importance of ILI in many countries. All of these groups and the BI-L community have thrived because they have filled a major need for community and continuing education among IL librarians.

Continuing education, of course, presupposes that a person has already learned something on which to build. This is not always the case when it comes to teaching IL. Library schools, pushed and pulled by many different constituencies and demands, both internal and external, have largely ignored the fact that almost all librarians teach and/or train users, staff and others. Few offer full-credit courses in library instruction or IL, and as a result, librarians new to instruction are still floundering, 25 years after the major library instruction organizations were formed in response to vast grass roots demand.

In 1996, Cerise Oberman decided that she had waited long enough for library schools to get around to the important task of preparing new librarians for instruction responsibilities. She proposed establishing IL immersion programs to help meet this basic need and to help prepare experienced instruction librarians to serve as IL change agents. ACRL heeded her call and generously funded development of the Institute for Information Literacy (IIL), which now has a three-pronged mission: to educate librarians for instructional roles via immersion programs, to support librarians, faculty, and administrators in leadership roles for IL programs, and to provide a forum for developing sequential IL partnership efforts among school, public, and academic libraries. IIL established a useful Website and mounted annual national, as well as regional, immersion programs, first offered in summer 1999. Applicants rate their institutions on the basis of an "Information Literacy IQ Test," which delineates criteria for evaluating where institutions lie on a continuum from "You Are Taking 'First Steps'" to "You Have a 'Model Program'" (Oberman and Wilson, 1998). Demand for the first IIL Immersion Program was great despite the cost (approximately $1,000), the length (4-1/2 days), as well as the fact that they are highly competitive with demand that far exceeds supply. Demand to host upcoming immersion programs has been so great that ACRL has posted a form for institutions and groups who wish to apply to host an IIL Immersion Program (1999).

These Immersion Programs promise to become a highly significant educational and continuing education venue for ILI librarians, both those new to ILI and experienced ILI librarians who hope to become "change agents" (Track 2 attendees). The IIL institutional "Best Practices in Information Literacy" initiative, spearheaded by Tom Kirk, has begun an ambitious and multifaceted effort to identify institutions that may offer model IL programs, and the characteristics of those programs that make them exemplary (2000c).

AASL's 1998 IL standards also promise to provide further impetus to IIL's third mission—supporting the development of sequential instruction programs for school, public, and academic libraries (1999).

ALA Information Literacy Community Partnerships Initiative

The IL "pot" is now coming to a full boil, as Nancy Kranich, ALA President for 2000–2001, has appointed a committee to pull together longstanding and new IL plans and activities among many different ALA divisions. Their goal is to work together to share information and efforts and to develop a plan for sequential IL education for lifelong learning, as part of ALA's "21st Century Literacy Initiative" (2000b).

WHAT ROLE SHOULD LIBRARIANS TAKE NOW AND IN THE FUTURE?

Where does all of this leave us? It leaves us in the tentative, yet exciting, position of defining our own future roles. What is it that ILI librarians do? What is or should be the role of the librarian in teaching or training for IL, and how does it fit with the role and activities of others in the teaching/training "food chain"? Let us venture forth and find out.

EXERCISES

    1.   What benefits and problems do you see with each of the three

major branches of the modern library instruction movement: Farber, Dudley, and Breivik?

2. What lessons have been learned, positive and negative, from past library instruction programs and individual efforts?

3. Which organizations (ILI, library and information science, accrediting agencies, community organizations), private groups, and governmental agencies should play a role in the evolving nature of ILI and in self-teaching and professional development for ILI librarians? How and why?

READ MORE ABOUT IT

ALA. "Information Literacy Community Partnerships Initiative" [Online]. Available: www.ala.org/kranich/literacy.html [2000, June 24].

ALA. Association of College and Research Libraries. "Information Literacy Competency Standards for Higher Education" [Online]. Available: www.ala.org/acrl/ilcomstan.html [2000, June 15].

ALA. Presidential Committee on Information Literacy. 1989. "Report." Chicago, IL: ALA [cited 2000, June 16]. Available: www.ala.org/acrl/nili/ilit1st.html.

Dudley, Miriam. 1978. *Library Instruction Workbook*. Los Angeles: University of California Library.

Farber, Evan Ira. 1974. "Library Instruction Throughout the Curriculum: Earlham College Program." In *Educating the Library User*, edited by John Lubans, Jr. New York: Bowker.

Knapp, Patricia B. 1966. *The Monteith College Library Experiment*. Metuchen, NJ: Scarecrow.

Shapiro, Jeremy J., and Shelley K. Hughes. 1996. "Information Literacy as a Liberal Art: Enlightenment Proposals for a New Curriculum." *Educom Review* 31 (March/April) [cited 1999, August 5]. Available: www.educause.edu/pub/er/review/reviewarticles/31231.html.

Part II

Information Literacy Instruction Building Blocks

3

A Brief Introduction to Learning Theory

A crank is a man with a new idea—until it catches on.

—Mark Twain

WHY PSYCHOLOGY?

What, you may ask, is a chapter on the psychology of learning doing in the middle of a book on IL instruction? Why should the information professional care about theoretical issues surrounding the field of educational psychology? How relevant are these discussions and disputes to our instructional endeavors? How does the broad field of educational psychology relate to our interests as information professionals?

The overall goal of this book is to help information professionals become better at the teaching and training aspects of our jobs. Although we may not often teach full-blown courses or deal with students on a continuing basis, we are still very much in the education/instruction/teaching business. To make the most of the time and resources available to us, we should have at least some familiarity with the established educational psychology principles that underlie effective instruction. It is not enough to know what to do. We must also have some basic understanding of the theoretical underpinnings that stand behind the methods and techniques we are using.

Clearly, reading one short chapter on the psychology of learning will not make anyone an expert in the field. Numerous books and articles have been written on the subject and this chapter can only scratch the surface of the material available. We hope to offer the reader a basic overview of the concepts, terminology, techniques, and important figures in the field. The emphasis will be on linking theory with practice. Knowing the theory behind our teaching techniques will enable us to improve our current material, and will help us develop new and effective instructional approaches that incorporate sound educational psychology principles. Chapter 4 will pay special attention to the research on individual differences in learning styles and will explore how our instructional endeavors can be modified to help all our students get the most out of their instructional experiences.

What—How—Who?

IL instructors must have a wide variety of skills at their fingertips. First they must have a thorough understanding of *what* they are teaching. That is, they should be completely familiar with the content that they are presenting. We can assume this familiarity as a given and will not be dealing with content issues here. Next, IL instructors must decide *how* to present that content. Decisions need to be made both about how to organize the content and about the formats to be used in the presentation of this information. Finally IL instructors must be aware of the possible range of individual differences in the way people learn. In other words, they must understand *who* their students are.

   This chapter will examine the psychological theories behind the "how" decisions. The next chapter will describe ways that our learners can differ and will offer suggestions on how to incorporate a variety of techniques into our instructional game plan so that we can reach people with a variety of learning styles.

   The most effective IL instructors are those who are familiar with a variety of learning theories and the teaching techniques that are based on those theories. Effective instructors remain flexible and are willing to mix and match various techniques as needed. The knowledgeable teacher can move easily between techniques, is familiar with a variety of options, and can select the technique or combination of techniques that is most appropriate for each situation. These teachers focus both on the content of what they are trying to get across and the differing needs of their learners.

SCHOOLS OF PSYCHOLOGY

There are probably as many different theories of learning as there are different researchers and writers in the field. However, each individual theorist can generally be placed within one of three main schools of thought: Behaviorism, Cognitive Psychology, and Humanist Psychology. Although there can be wide variations of the predominant themes within each school, the basic underlying principles remain constant. Keep in mind that no school can be considered entirely right or totally wrong. Each has made major contributions to our understanding of learning and teaching.

Behaviorism, or the Stimulus-Response Approach to Learning

In many ways Behaviorism was a product of its time and place in the history of psychology. Psychology in the late 1800s was just beginning to establish itself as an independent and more scientific discipline. The field was moving away from its parent discipline of philosophy, and was embracing the scientific method as a means to study and understand behavior. The publication of Charles Darwin's *Origin of the Species* (Darwin, 1859) postulated a continuum between man and the animal kingdom. This opened up the possibilities of using animals in experiments where the results could then be generalized to human behavior.

The first recognized laboratory specializing in the study of psychology was established in Leipzig, Germany, by Wilhelm Wundt in 1879 (Haynie, 1994). Human behavior was studied using a method called introspection that relied on human subjects describing their own personal experiences. Behaviorism as a theoretical school developed in part as a reaction to the subjective nature of these self-reports. Ironically it was the combination of Ivan Petrovovich Pavlov's work on the physiology of digestion (Pavlov, 1928, 1927) with principles from a philosophical theory called Associationism that really marked the beginning of this school of thought (Amsel, 1989; Aluri and Reichel, 1984; Bigge and Shermis, 1992; Elliott et al., 1996).

Based on Pavlov's work with the salivation reflex in dogs, the behaviorists developed a theory of learning that relied on the links or associations between stimulus and response. Many theorists and researchers are associated with Behaviorism—names such as Edward L. Thorndike, Edward Chace Tolman, John Watson, and, probably best known of all, B.F. Skinner stand out. Each contributed to the development of the school and its associated theories. Thorndike expanded Pavlov's work on conditioning and introduced the parameters that resulted in successfully learning such concepts as readiness to learn, the

value of repeating the behavior to be learned, and the relationship between the behavior and subsequent events (Thorndike, 1913). These
concepts have had direct applications to educational theory and practice (Elliott et al., 1996). Tolman's publication of *Purposive Behavior in
Animals and Man* (Tolman, 1932) identified the principle of reinforcement by postulating that activities that are followed by a successful outcome or some other reward are more likely to be repeated than those
that were not. John Watson expanded the notion of conditioning to human emotional behavior with his famous (or infamous) Albert and the
White Rabbit experiment. In this study, a loud noise was associated with
the sight of a small furry animal to create a conditioned emotional response in a young child (Watson and Rayner, 1920). Clearly. the concepts being discussed by the Behaviorists were not restricted to animal
behavior.

But it was B.F. Skinner, whose works span over fifty years, who did
the most to not only expand the knowledge base in this area but to develop links between his theoretical hypothesis and practical classroom
applications. It is through Skinner's work that the principles of active
learning, immediate feedback, programmed instruction, task analysis,
allowing students to learn at their own pace, and, of course, the value of
reward and reinforcement of desired behaviors have been applied to
education (Skinner, 1938, 1968, 1974, 1983). Skinner's emphasis on teaching to individual differences and allowing students to progress at their
own pace also has had great implications for the study of learning styles,
a topic we shall return to in the next chapter.

General Characteristics of Behaviorism

- Behaviorism tends to deal with observable behavior.
- Behaviorists view environmental factors in terms of stimuli and
  resultant behavior in terms of responses.
- Behaviorists attempt to demonstrate that every behavior is en-
  vironmentally controlled and is based on each behavior being
  externally rewarded or reinforced.
- Immediate reinforcement/feedback must follow desired behav-
  ior for the behavior to be learned.
- The reinforcement of improvements or steps in the right direc-
  tion, as well as reinforcing the final completed task, will help
  learners to proceed at a faster pace.
- Undesirable behavior should never be reinforced.
- Active participation is crucial to learning.
- Learners should be allowed to move at their own pace.

- Learners should be tested for mastery at each stage of learning and should not be allowed to proceed to the next level unless they have mastered preceding ones.

EDUCATIONAL APPLICATIONS OF BEHAVIORISM

Many practical classroom techniques have developed out of the Behaviorist theoretical framework. Here are some examples:

REINFORCEMENT

Activities that are followed by a positive outcome are more likely to be repeated in the future. In teaching a new task, reinforcement should occur immediately. Any delay between the behavior and the reinforcement increases the risk that some other behavior may be accidentally reinforced instead. In early stages of learning, reinforcement should occur following every correct response. As learning goes on, more correct responses should be required prior to reinforcement. A gradual shift toward intermittent reinforcement causes the behavior to be sustained over longer periods of time without having to continually reinforce each correct response. Do not insist on perfect performance on the first few tries. Reinforcing improvements or steps in the right direction speeds up the process. Monitor teacher behavior so that it never reinforces undesirable responses. The classroom troublemaker learns to be disruptive because the attention he or she gets from the rest of the class acts as reinforcement for the behavior. The withdrawn student may become reserved and silent if he or she feels that the environment does not reinforce gregarious behavior (Elliott et al., 1996; Skinner, 1953, 1968).

SHAPING

This technique relies on the behavioral principles of reinforcement and training through successive approximations to reach the desired behavior. The technique starts with identifying the end product and describing what you want the learner to ultimately do. Behaviors that resemble or approximate the final product are identified. Each successive approximation of the desired end product is then reinforced. In the early stages of learning very rough approximations are reinforced. The standard is raised as learning progresses until the complete task has been learned. The learner gets closer to the intended learning outcome with each successive attempt. It helps to reinforce improvement as well as perfection to encourage progress. Reinforcement should be used as a means to move the learner in the right direction toward the final desired behavior (Elliott et al., 1996).

TASK ANALYSIS

Task analysis relies on stating the learning task or objective in behavioral terms and breaking that objective down into prerequisite skills or sub-tasks. The relationship between the sub-tasks and the logical order in which they should be learned are then determined. Materials and procedures for teaching each of the sub-tasks are designed. Feedback (reinforcement) is provided to the learner at the completion of each sub-task and when the final task is performed. This procedure can be viewed as a form of shaping using successive approximations of the final task (Elliott et al., 1996; Mager, 1997a).

MASTERY LEARNING

Benjamin Bloom added one more layer to the task analysis idea. Material to be learned is still broken down into small units and instructional objectives are clearly specified for each unit. But learning of each small unit must be demonstrated before the learner can proceed. Diagnostic progress tests are administered at the end of each learning unit to determine whether each student has mastered the unit. Procedures to assist students who do not achieve mastery at any level are also developed. A final test is administrated after mastery has been exhibited on all the sub-units to ensure that the full task has been learned (Bloom, 1981; Bloom, Madaus, and Hastings, 1981; Elliott et al., 1996).

PROGRAMMED INSTRUCTION

Programmed instruction is a self-instruction package that presents a topic in a carefully planned sequence. It requires the learner to respond to questions or statements by filling in blanks, selecting from a series of answers, or by solving a problem. Programmed instruction packages can be presented either in print or via computer. This technique relies on many of the main principles of behaviorism. Students proceed at their own pace, are actively involved in the learning process, get immediate feedback on their responses, and receive reinforcement as they succeed with each step of the program. Those who advocate programmed instruction stress that it improves classroom learning by presenting even the most difficult subjects in small steps so that learners can proceed at their own rates. This technique builds on the concepts of task analysis and shaping by successive approximations (Elliott et al., 1996; Skinner, 1968, 1984).

MODELING

Modeling can be defined as learning through imitation rather than direct instruction. This type of learning seems to be based on what psychologists refer to as vicarious reinforcement: We observe the pleasure that a behavior gives to the model and we want that pleasure for ourselves. Advertising success is predicated on this principle. Much of our early learning is based on our parents' modeling of appropriate behaviors. Modeling is also a very useful technique to use when the task to be learned involves some kind of danger or risk. For example, modeling how to drive a car before actually allowing the learner to try is probably a much safer approach than just handing the learner the keys and letting him or her try to learn by trial and error. In teaching by modeling, the instructor demonstrates how to perform the task or skill. The learner observes the behavior and then attempts to imitate the instructor or model. Modeling enables the student to learn complete sequences of behavior in a much shorter time than by successive approximations and shaping (Bandura, 1986, 1977a; Elliott et al., 1996).

BEHAVIOR MODIFICATION

Behaviorists offer several methods for modifying inappropriate or undesirable classroom behavior. One such approach is the reinforcement of competing behavior. The key to this technique is the successful strengthening of a desirable behavior that will compete with and eventually replace the undesirable one. For example, selectively reinforcing the desired behavior of sitting still and raising one's hand to be called on while ignoring the inappropriate behavior of jumping up and speaking out of turn should decrease the instances of this undesirable behavior. In using this technique it is important to be consistent. Always reinforce the desired behavior and ignore the undesired ones (Elliott et al., 1996; Kazdin, 1994).

TEACHING FROM THE BEHAVIORIST POINT OF VIEW

1. Break material into small units. Teach each unit. Test for mastery at each level. If the material is not mastered at a certain level, offer help to reach mastery. Do not let learners proceed to the next level if they have not mastered preceding ones. Principles: Task analysis, mastery learning, moving at own pace.
2. Administer some kind of final check to ensure mastery of complete task. Guided exercises coupled with hands-on practice is a good application of this principle to IL instruction. Principles: Active participation, task analysis, mastery learning.
3. Provide for active involvement/participation in lessons by encouraging learners to respond to questions and problems. The addition of active learning exercises, hands-on practice, and in-

class problem solving experiences to IL instruction sessions offers the opportunity to apply principles and concepts to practical IL research situations. Principle: Active participation.

4. Provide immediate feedback to all student responses (quizzes, homework, in-class exercises, etc.). If your IL instruction session includes any of the active learning components described above, be sure to allow for time to discuss the results and respond to questions generated by the experience. Principles: Immediate feedback, reinforcement.

5. Praise students for correct answers, proper study habits, and other desirable behavior. Encourage involvement by supportive gestures, comments, and body language. Remember that if you want learners to become involved in the session you must not only offer them appropriate opportunities but you must allow them time to think and respond. Asking a question and then immediately answering it yourself will only discourage participation. Principle: Reinforcement.

6. Do not offer praise indiscriminately or it will lose its effectiveness. Be specific with your praise. Make sure the learner understands what is being reinforced by the praise. However it is not a bad idea to praise students who attempt to answer your questions as well as those who answer correctly. This will encourage your learners to continue to try and respond, and to become more actively involved in the instructional process. Principles: Reinforcement, shaping.

7. Offer the opportunity to do something the student likes to do as an inducement or reinforcement for learning some other task. In this day and age of recreational Web surfing, offering the learners some free time at the end of a session to search the Web for topics of their own choice may serve as an incentive for completing whatever other more structured exercises you have set for them to do. Principle: Reinforcement.

8. Model desired behavior. Set a good example for the learners in all your interactions with them. Respect their opinions and ideas and they will respect yours. The more you pay attention to their questions and comments, the more likely it will be that they pay attention to what you are trying to show them. Indicating by word and deed that you are interested in the learners' responses and respect their opinions will create an atmosphere that encourages full and complete participation from your learners. Principle: Modeling.

Cognitive Psychology

Just as Behaviorism was a reaction to the subjective and introspective approach to the study of learning that preceded it, the Cognitive Psychologists developed their theories in reaction to what they viewed as the mechanistic or simplistic view of learning described by the Behaviorists. Heavily influenced by Gestalt Psychology studies in perception, the Cognitive Psychologists were interested in how people perceive, organize, interact with, and respond to elements in their environment. They felt that people respond to patterns or whole situations not to individual stimuli. In addition, the Cognitive Psychologists called into question the Behaviorists contention that all human behavior, regardless of its degree of complexity, could be explained in terms of stimulus-response connections and the principles of reinforcement (Arp, 1993; Bigge and Shermis, 1992; Dembo, 1988; Driscoll, 1994; Elliott et al., 1996; Svinicki, 1994).

Many findings from these early Gestalt psychology perception experiments were difficult to explain in terms of accepted Behaviorist principles. For example, Max Wertheimer discovered that when two lights are turned off and on at a definite rate, human subjects report the perception of a single light moving back and forth. This report cannot be readily explained in terms of the stimulus-response model (Wertheimer, 1912). Known as the Phi Phenomenon, this behavior implies that when processing the stimulus input humans add something to this incoming sensory data that results in the perception of movement. Something is happening between the stimulus and the reported result; something that the Cognitive Psychologists felt needed explanation.

The Cognitive Psychologists point to the notion of insight as another example of behavior that in their view cannot be explained in terms of stimulus-response connections. Insight is the sudden perception of the relationship among elements in a problem situation. Often referred to as the "aha" or "now I see" phenomenon, insight is offered as an alternative explanation to the learning by trial and error (successive approximations and reinforcement of correct responses) principles of the Behaviorist. Learning in this view is seen as an insight into or the understanding of relationships, particularly the relationship between parts and the whole.

Wolfgang Köhler's famous experiment illustrates this point (Köhler and Winter, 1925). Monkeys are placed in a room with a bunch of bananas suspended from the ceiling just out of reach. The only other objects in the room are a couple of cardboard boxes. Monkeys in this situation tend to sit quietly for a time, looking around the room, and then quite suddenly get up and move the boxes under the bananas and pile them high enough so that the boxes can be used as a means of reaching the bananas. According to the Cognitive Psychologists, this behavior cannot be explained by the trial and error approach. There were no incorrect and thus unreinforced behaviors, and no possibility for reinforcement of successive approximations of the solution to the problem. There was, however, a sudden perception of the relationship between the boxes and the bananas that resulted in the solution to the problem.

Cognitive Psychologists view motivation to reduce ambiguity as the primary driving force behind learning. The learner is driven to organize the world and make it understandable. The degree of ambiguity that the learner perceives in a given situation does more to promote learning than either punishment or reinforcement. The learner is motivated to reduce ambiguity by fitting any new situation into the way the learner currently perceives his or her world. If that cannot be done, the learner must reorganize his or her perception of the world. Any new ideas or information that are not consistent with the learner's world-view must be somehow incorporated into that world-view. This may result either in an acceptance or rejection of the new idea and/or in a change in the learner's perception of the world at large.

Some Cognitive Psychologists have concentrated on how children develop the ability to modify their perceptions and form new world-views. Best exemplified by the work of Jean Piaget and his collaborators (Inhelder and Piaget, 1958; Piaget, 1952, 1954), these theorists studied the ways children think at various steps or stages in their development. Piaget's research was directed toward describing the components of these stages. To Piaget, the development of thinking represents a gradual shift from the concrete to the abstract. The sequence of stages is said to be the same for all children, although the ages when a child passes from one stage to the next can vary somewhat. Progress through the stages is one from concrete, irreversibility and subjective egocentrism (viewing everything from one's own perspective) to the ability to think abstractly, be independent of the here and now, and view the world through multiple perspectives—that is, to see the world as others see it. Furthermore, a person's stage of cognitive development sets limits for the type of learning that can take place. We will return to this idea when we discuss the concept of learning readiness in the Educational Applications of Cognitive Psychology section of this chapter.

Piaget studied the ways children extract rules from their interactions with objects in the world. They then build mental models that can be used to interpret, organize, and make predictions about future interactions. Once built, these models are assimilated or incorporated into the child's world-view and used to make sense of other experiences. The driving force behind this model building is accommodation. New experiences that do not fit into the old world-view create a feeling of disequilibrium or discomfort in the learner. This feeling of discomfort drives the learner to re-think his or her understanding of the world in order to accommodate the new information. Once new mental models are developed to account for the mismatch between current knowledge and new information, a new assimilation framework is developed that will be used until the learner experiences the next mismatch between knowledge and information. This continually recurring cycle between assimilation and accommodation accounts for the development of more complex modes of thinking (Piaget, 1952).

Studies beginning in the 1960s on how children think and learn have resulted in Constructivism, a variation on the Piagetian themes. Although retaining the idea of stages of cognitive development, the Constructivist theories stress experience over maturation as the impetus for moving through these stages. The Constructivist view, with its emphasis on learning in context, has called into question the Piagetian notion that cognitive growth is unidirectional moving from the concrete to the abstract (Ackerman, 1996). It does, however, owe much to another aspect of Piagetian theory: that of assimilation and accommodation.

Although both the Constructivist and Piagetian theorists agree on this cyclic nature of cognitive development, they disagree on what creates changes in the learner's ability to take advantage of this disequilibrium. To Piaget and his followers, the process is one of maturation. More complex assimilations occur at different stages in the child's growth and development. But to the Constructivist, change occurs solely as a result of interactions with the environment and can happen at any age or level of development. Knowledge is not viewed as simply passing from teacher to student; knowledge is actually constructed in the learner's mind, thus the name Constructivism. The learner does not get ideas; he or she makes ideas. Learners are thought to actively construct and reconstruct knowledge out of their experiences in the world (Driscoll, 1994). Constructivists propose that learners are particularly likely to develop new ideas when they are actively involved in making some kind of external artifact like a poem or a computer program that causes them to reflect upon what they are learning and share that learning with others.

Constructivists stress the role of affect or feelings as well as cognition in its principles. Learners are more likely to become intellectually engaged when they are working on something that has personal meaning to them. This idea also appears in the Humanist approach to learning that will be covered later in this chapter. The Constructivist and the Humanist approaches both contend that creating new ways of connecting to the material is as important as forming new mental representations of it. In addition, both these schools of learning emphasize diversity of approaches to learning. They recognize that learners can make connections with knowledge in many different ways and encourage multiple approaches to the presentation of the information so as to accommodate this diversity (Kafai and Resnick, 1996). The notion that variations exist in how people learn is also tied to the research into learning styles that will be discussed in more detail in Chapter 4.

GENERAL CHARACTERISTICS

- Cognitive Psychology deals with the organization of information.
- The Cognitive Psychologist delves into the internal processes by which an individual tries to deal with the complexity of his or her environment.
- The Cognitive Psychologist is interested in the ways a person perceives and conceptualizes his or her physical and social world.
- The Cognitive Psychologist organizes learning into patterns, not parts. He or she is interested in how various elements, ideas, and topics relate to one another.
- Behavior is based on cognition, which is defined as the act of knowing about the situation in which behavior occurs.
- Insight and the motivation to reduce ambiguity are viewed as underlying learning rather than the building up of stimulus-response connections proposed by Behaviorists.
- A subset of Cognitive Psychology deals with the development of thinking across the life span. Those working in this area stress that different types of thinking accompany different stages of development.
- The Constructivists counter that mismatches between new experiences and the learner's current mental models force the learner to develop more complex modes of thinking.

EDUCATIONAL APPLICATIONS OF COGNITIVE PSYCHOLOGY

READINESS
Readiness, an outgrowth of Piaget's work, proposes that learning cannot occur unless a person is at the appropriate stage of cognitive development. According to Piaget, children pass through four major stages of development (Piaget and Inhelder, 1969).

1. The sensorimotor period (birth to 18–24 months)
2. The preoperational period (2–7 years)

3. The concrete operational period (7–11 years)
4. The formal operational period (over 11 years)

Each child passes through these stages in order; however, the age at which a child enters a particular stage might vary. Particular types of thinking are associated with each stage of cognitive development. For example, the child in the sensorimotor period does not have a sense of object permanence; so, to the sensorimotor child, out of sight is really out of mind. That is why the peek-a-boo game works so well with very young children. When they cover their eyes and you are no longer in their line of sight, you actually have disappeared for this child.

The preoperational child has begun to use symbols but is not yet able to mentally manipulate these symbols. So, when water is poured from a tall thin glass into a short, fat one, the preoperational child believes that the amount of water has changed in some fashion. He or she is totally dependent on concrete examples and cannot extrapolate beyond these examples to alternative solutions to problems.

In the concrete operational stage, the child develops the ability to mentally manipulate symbols. But he or she can only do this with concrete, tangible objects. The child in this stage can put objects into order by size or sort them into categories by shape, and understands that the amount of water in the previous example remains constant regardless of the shape of the container into which it is poured. However, working with abstract concepts remains difficult. Thus, solving word problems is beyond the grasp of the concrete operational child.

The fourth stage, formal operational, is associated with the ability to think abstractly and is the beginning of adult thinking patterns. The child no longer is dependent on concrete manipulation of objects. He or she can use mental imagery and can consider a variety of possible solutions to problems, even those that may seem improbable or impossible. The formal operational child can now deal with the "what if" and is not totally dependent upon the "here and now." Children at this stage can try out various solutions in their minds, determine possible outcomes, weigh the relative merits of the solutions, and then select the best ones. A major characteristic of this stage is the ability to accept the fact that there can be multiple solutions to a problem and to deal with these options in a logical and systematic manner.

According to Piagetian theory, no amount of teaching will cause the child to change their perceptions and ways of thinking until they reach the appropriate stage of cognitive development. Teachers must take the child's cognitive developmental stage into account when attempting to present new concepts and ideas.

The Constructivist alternative to Piagetian theory states that there is really no qualitative change in children's ability to think and problem solve as they mature. What changes is their accumulation of experiences. Children simply acquire more and more information about the world through their interactions with it and as a consequence are better able to apply that knowledge to the problems at hand. Studies based on this experience view have shown that if children are shown simple versions of problems they are quite capable of the types of thinking that Piaget thought developed only at later stages (Fox, 1995). Although the means of developing more complex ways of thinking differ in these two approaches, proponents of both viewpoints agree that learning cannot occur until the child is in the appropriate state of readiness.

Regardless of how we define readiness, it cannot be ignored without great risk. Anyone who is pressed to learn something for which he or she is not ready will fail and thus lose interest in the process. Learners may even become so frustrated that they will avoid the subject in the future.

THE DISCOVERY METHOD

This technique, which is most closely associated with Jerome Bruner (Bruner, 1963; Driscoll, 1994; Elliott et al., 1996; Postman and Weingarten, 1971), presents learners with opportunities to discover the answer to problems on their own. Learners are allowed to try different solutions and possibilities. The teacher who uses this method acts as a catalyst, letting learners find their own meanings. By placing emphasis on discovery, the student learns to organize problems rather than attacking them in a hit and miss fashion. Discovery emphasizes intrinsic motivation (the learner's own desire to learn without the need for external reward). Self-fulfillment is the reinforcer here rather than any extrinsic or external reward from others.

Small group exercises and class discussions are especially suited to the Discovery Method. See also Chapter 6 for further discussion on this topic. The teacher sets the stage, describes the problem, and perhaps offers some possible methods for its solution. The learners, either as the entire group or split into subgroups, work on the problem for a set period of time. The teacher acts as a facilitator for these discussions rather than an expert who has all the answers.

Cerise Oberman and Rebecca Linton's work on the Guided Design Method is a good example of the application of the Discovery Method to the field of IL instruction (Oberman and Linton, 1982). This method uses an open-ended, problem solving exercise, consisting of seven stages that lead the students through the information gathering research process. A complete set of procedures for this Guided Design exercise is included in Oberman and Linton's chapter (1982). However, be warned if you plan to use this exercise with your learners, this Guided Design exercise can take over an hour to complete.

EXPOSITORY TEACHING AND MEANINGFUL LEARNING

Based on the work of David Ausubel (Ausubel and Robinson, 1969; Ausubel, 1977; Ausubel, Novak, and Hanesion, 1978) this approach applies Cognitive Psychology techniques to what Ausubel calls the reception learning process. Reception learning is best represented by the lecture and textbook approach of instruction. The key to successful reception learning is that it also be meaningful learning and not just rote memorization.

Ausubel believes that meaningful learning occurs when new material is related to material the students already know. Therefore, it is up to the teacher to organize and present this information in such a way that students are helped to make these connections. Information being presented either via the lecture method or in readings must be tied to what the learner already knows. Learning occurs when new information can be fit into the knowledge base the learner already has. This ability to relate new information to ideas already possessed by the learner is crucial for retention. The structure imposed on the information by the writer or the framework in which the instructor presents the information will allow the learner to make these crucial connections.

Expository techniques avoid the trap of rote learning by requiring learners to continually rephrase new ideas in their own words. One technique that can be used to check for comprehension and encourage the student's meaningful incorporation of new ideas is The Minute Paper. Using The Minute Paper, just prior to instruction the teacher tells the group they will be asked to respond to the following two questions at the end of the session: What were the main points of this session? What is your main unanswered question (Angelo and Cross, 1993)? This might be done verbally or in writing. The Minute Paper serves as a summary of the important points covered during the session and highlights what concepts seem to be most meaningful and relevant to the students. It can also serve as an informal assessment of the session. See Chapter 12 for more information on this technique.

ADVANCE ORGANIZERS

Advance Organizers are defined by Ausubel as abstract, general overviews of the information to be learned that is presented in advance of the lecture or actual reading (Ausubel, 1960; Elliott et al., 1996). Advance Organizers assist learners in their attempt to fit new information into context by providing a framework for the learning and presents relevant ideas to which learners can relate the new material. This introductory material is intended to help students ready their cognitive structures for incorporating potentially meaningful material. To help your students acquire meaning, identify relevant anchoring ideas that your students already possess. In other words, relate new, potentially meaningful material to some topic with which they are already familiar. In the case of IL instruction, comparing the similarities and differences between resources very familiar to the learner and the new ones being introduced can help provide a framework for the instruction.

Although Ausubel promoted the idea of introducing the Organizer before presenting new material, Organizers can be placed at almost any point in the session. Organizers can also be used as a way of pulling material together after it has been presented. The Organizer then serves as a summary of the material rather than an introduction to it. The placement of the Organizer has implications for learning styles theory. Learners who prefer getting the big picture first will appreciate an advanced look at the structure of the material. Those who like to build the big picture for themselves will prefer having the organization presented after the fact. See Chapter 4 for more information on learning styles.

Many Organizers have been developed for use in IL instruction. The idea of controlled versus natural language vocabularies, the publication sequence, primary versus secondary sources, etc. are just some examples. See Chapter 5 for examples of additional Advance Organizers useful in IL instruction.

METACOGNITION

The Cognitive approach places great emphasis on the process of learning. Students are expected to be able to manage their own learning. To be successful, learners must understand how they learn. To do so, they must acquire metacognitive skills. If students do not have the skills to manage their own learning, then teachers must incorporate ways to acquire these skills into the instruction itself. Teachers may wish to model the process or include some guided reflection during instruction (Driscoll, 1994). Learning is enhanced as learners become aware of their own learning strategies and begin to monitor the use of these strategies. Teachers should present examples of a variety of strategies and provide time during the learning experience for students to reflect on the process as well as the content of learning (Svinicki, 1994). Requiring students to write about the process in some kind of research journal can also help them acquire the necessary skills. See Virginia Rankin's 1988 article for an excellent example of incorporating a metacognitive approach to IL instruction (Rankin, 1988). See Chapter 5 for more on metacognition.

TEACHING FROM THE COGNITIVE POINT OF VIEW

1. The Cognitive teacher presents the learner with situations in which he or she can experiment in the broadest sense of the term. Allowing learners to examine new library material (print or electronic sources) on their own without previous instruction and then asking them to describe what they learned about the resource is a good example of applying the Discovery Method to IL instruction. Principles: Assimilation and accommodation to reduce ambiguity, constructing knowledge, developing personal meaning, Discovery learning.
2. The learner should be allowed to try things out to see what will happen, to manipulate symbols, pose questions, and seek his or her own answers. Again, free use of material and giving the learner the opportunity to select his or her own topic to explore will encourage this Discovery approach to IL instruction. Principles: Assimilation and accommodation to reduce ambiguity, constructing knowledge, developing personal meaning, Discovery learning.
3. The learner should be encouraged to compare experiences, to reconcile what is found from one situation to the next one, and to compare experiences with other learners. Once learners have explored on their own for a brief period of time, bringing the group together and asking for feedback from each learner about what he or she discovered will enhance everyone's learning experiences. Principles: Conceptualizing the world based on personal experience, organizing experiences into meaningful patterns, metacognition.
4. The Cognitive teacher pays special attention to the learner's state of readiness for a particular learning task. Learners will clearly exhibit interest in or frustration with a task. The Cognitive teacher persists only as long as the learner is interested and engaged in the task at hand and is making reasonable progress toward the desired goal. If the learner stops exhibiting these positive behaviors, the teacher stops and re-thinks what he or she is trying to do. Perhaps a different, simpler approach may be called for. At any rate, the disinterested learner is exhibiting a lack of readiness to learn that is not ignored in the Cognitive oriented classroom. Principle: Readiness.
5. This mode of teaching emphasizes the active role of the learner much as the Behaviorist style does. However, the Cognitive classroom de-emphasizes the transmission of information from an authority figure and places more emphasis on students learn-

ing through self-discovery. Principles: Assimilation and accommodation to reduce ambiguity, constructing knowledge, developing personal meaning, Discovery learning.

6. The Cognitive teacher acts as a catalyst or facilitator in the learner's quest for discovery. The job of the IL instructor in this type of environment is to come up with opportunities for interacting with the material that are unstructured enough to allow for self-exploration, but that have some specific goals so that the learner can have a feeling of accomplishment. For example, you can ask the learners to examine a resource and report back to the group what types of information are included in it, how it is organized, why they think someone would use it, etc. Principles: Assimilation and accommodation to reduce ambiguity, constructing knowledge, developing personal meaning, expository teaching, advance organizers.

7. Lecturing is de-emphasized in favor of self-exploration and discussion among learners. The teacher makes sure to allow for sharing of results from among the participants. Each learner/discoverer becomes an expert who then shares his or her new knowledge about the assigned resource with the rest of the group. Principles: Constructing knowledge, organizing experiences into meaningful patterns, Discovery learning, metacognition.

8. This is a student-centered approach that places as much emphasis on how people learn as on the content material they are studying. Students are encouraged to develop metacognitive skills through modeling, assignments, and self-reflective activities. Principles: Constructing knowledge, developing personal meaning, metacognition.

Humanist Psychology

Many aspects of the Humanist school of learning are closely related to principles discussed in terms of Cognitive Psychology. However, emphasis here is on the affective rather than the cognitive nature of learning. The Humanist Psychology offers an approach to learning that considers how a person feels to be as important as how he or she thinks or behaves. Furthermore, Humanist theorists insist that material must first have personal meaning to the learner or it will not be learned (Dembo, 1988; Elliott et al., 1996; Rogers, 1969).

The Humanist psychologist is also very interested in motivation and the notion of self-actualization (Driscoll, 1994; Maslow, 1987). Abraham Maslow hypothesizes a hierarchy of needs starting with the most basic physiological ones, such as thirst and hunger, and moving through more complex ones such as safety, love and belonging, and esteem, and finally ending with self-actualization. Self-actualization is the use of one's abilities to the limit of one's potentials. The learner cannot reach this final stage until all the needs represented by earlier levels have been satisfied. A deficit in any of these need categories will affect the learner's ability to function at his or her best. It has long been accepted that a hungry or sick person will not be able to function well in a learning situation. But the idea that the learner's emotional needs as represented by Maslow's love and belonging and esteem categories also play a part in the learning process is a newer concept.

Also related to the Humanist approach is Albert Bandura's work on self-efficacy (Bandura, 1977a; Driscoll, 1994). Self-efficacy is defined as the belief that one can produce a behavior regardless of whether one actually can. For example, there are many database searchers who believe that they are effectively searching the database when in fact they have no idea about how to construct a meaningful search statement. Humanists believe that everyone can learn if given the proper encouragement and stimulation. They encourage the development of self-efficacy in their students by offering students opportunities to succeed, and by creating a classroom environment where everyone's efforts are respected (Dembo, 1988). Humanist teachers believe in their students and so the students begin to believe in themselves and their feelings of self-efficacy grow. To develop self-efficacy in our database searchers, we could offer them opportunities to practice in a workshop setting with assistance and feedback from an instructor. As their search strategy develops, the learners can see improvement in their results. This type of teaching situation should result not only in better searchers, but learners who have gained more confidence in their own skills.

GENERAL CHARACTERISTICS

- The Humanist school is concerned with the affective side of learning.
- Feelings and concerns are as important as thinking and behaving.
- Basic needs must be satisfied before self-actualization or working to the learner's full potential can be accomplished.
- The educational environment should foster self-development and understanding, which will lead to self-actualization.
- The Humanist psychologist believes that people are determiners of their own behavior. They are not merely acted upon by the environment. People are free to make choices about the quality of their lives.

- Learning situations should be learner-centered and oriented toward developing self-efficacy.
- Material must have personal meaning or relevance for the students in order to be learned.
- Learners are felt to be intrinsically motivated rather than working for external rewards.

EDUCATIONAL APPLICATIONS OF HUMANIST PSYCHOLOGY

SELF-DIRECTED LEARNING, OR SDL
The Humanist-inspired Student Directed Learning, or SDL, approach to education empowers students to take responsibility for their own learning and to set their own goals for both the learning itself and for standards of achievement. Since students learn to please themselves rather than to earn external rewards, they acquire an approach to learning that can serve them throughout their lives. Instructors involved in SDL help learners use a variety of strategies and perceptual skills so that they may learn on their own. Learners become responsible for their own learning and gain the feeling of being in charge of their own intellectual growth (Areglado, Bradley, and Lane, 1996).

SDL stresses not only the acquisition of knowledge about the subject matter, but it also encourages learners to better understand their own work habits, perceptions, values, and potential. Under this process, the learner becomes motivated to have a better understanding of themselves and others, and to take control of their own lives and destinies. In some ways this is related to the Cognitive Psychology idea of metacognition. But the Humanists are interested in students developing a better understanding of their own feelings, attitudes, and values as well as their cognitive processes.

Self-directed learners exhibit initiative, independence, and persistence in learning. They accept responsibility for their own learning and see problems as challenges rather than obstacles. They are curious and self-confident and have a high degree of self-discipline. In order to succeed, self-directed learners must possess good study habits, be able to develop a rational study plan, and be goal-oriented in their approach to learning. Furthermore, these learners view themselves not as passive recipients of information, but rather as the owners of the learning process. They set their own standards for quality and perfection and, therefore, work to please themselves rather than for some outside, external reward.

The SDL approach builds on many of the basic tenets of the Humanist approach. The learners set goals and achievement standards themselves, so the material to be learned becomes highly meaningful and relevant to them. The instructor's role becomes one of support, offering suggestions about how learners can reach their goals in the most effective way possible. This can require a good deal of advanced planning and a high degree of flexibility in dealing with the learners. Instructors who wish to use this method must be willing to view situations through the learner's perspective. They must develop a high degree of empathy for their learners' feelings and points of view and they must always treat their learners with respect. SDL flourishes when both learner and instructor see one another not only as mutually helpful human beings with resources to share but also as self-reliant human beings who care for themselves and others. Educators who work in this type of environment act as models, coaches, and mentors who validate learning and encourage the development of self-confidence on the part of the learner. The educator in a SDL environment must have a tremendous faith in the ability of learners to both take charge of their own learning and to succeed in achieving their goals.

ARCS

John Keller's ARCS (Attention, Relevance, Confidence, Satisfaction) model for instructional design is another example of a Humanist approach to teaching (Driscoll, 1994; Keller, 1987). The ARCS methodology emphasizes gaining and sustaining attention, incorporating relevant and diverse examples into instruction, building confidence by creating positive expectations for success, and creating satisfaction by allowing the students opportunities to use newly acquired skills. The ARCS framework provides a way to incorporate Humanist principles into your instructional sessions. Starting your instruction with a thought-provoking quote or video as a means of gaining attention is one example of applying ARCS to the IL situation. Offering the students the opportunity to work on topics of their own choice adds relevance to the instruction as does the use of a variety of examples that reflect the diversity of your learners' backgrounds, cultures, ethnic groups, gender and age differences, and languages spoken. See Chapter 14 for more on teaching to diverse populations.

TEACHING FROM THE HUMANIST POINT OF VIEW

1. The Humanist classroom is student-centered with the teacher acting as a facilitator who advises students on how to develop to their full potential. Making sure that the learning environment is comfortable and that the instructor projects a warm and welcoming persona will go a long way to satisfy the learner's basic emotional needs and will allow the learner to progress

toward self-actualization. Principles: Importance of affective aspects of learning, learner-centered, self-actualization, self-efficacy.

2. The teacher is responsible for creating a safe educational climate that encourages the learning process. In the context of IL instruction, the desire to create a learning situation that will reduce library anxiety falls under the heading of Humanist Psychology. The idea that learners involved in IL instruction should not only acquire skills as a result of the instruction, but should also develop more positive attitudes about the library and their abilities to use library resources is a Humanistic one. Principles: Importance of affective aspects of learning, learner-centered, self-actualization, self-efficacy.

3. Humanists give students an important role in determining their own goals and objectives and in deciding when they want to work on certain tasks. IL instruction should be designed so that learners can have some freedom to explore on their own and to select material that is of interest to them. Although the IL instructor will have some overall goal and objectives for the particular instruction being developed, there are many places where the learner can be given some options in what will be happening. The learners can be given a list of topics that could be covered during a session and be allowed to decide which they would like to see included. Learners can be given options about which resources they will each be responsible for exploring during the session, and can also be allowed to select their own topics for either the instructor's demonstrations or their individual exercises. Principles: Learner-centered, student directed learning, relevance.

4. Students are also encouraged to participate in the evaluation of their own work under the principle that the students themselves are in the best position to determine what they have learned. Presenting the learners with self-paced, self-correcting exercises will allow the learners to determine for themselves when they have accomplished the designated task. Principles: Learner-centered, student-directed learning, intrinsic motivation, self-efficacy.

5. Goals in a Humanistic environment include helping the students learn more about themselves, helping them relate to others, preparing them for future society, and encouraging them to think for themselves and to make their own decisions. Principles: Self-actualization, self-efficacy, student-directed learning.

6. One of the Humanists' most fundamental beliefs is that every-

one has the ability to learn. The learner in the Humanist environment is seen as a creative and dynamic person who has the capacity to deal with all problems successfully. This positive outlook underlies all interactions in the learning situation. Sharing your own experiences in learning the material and showing what you personally went through can serve as an example of this positive attitude. It demonstrates that everyone has to start somewhere but that you believe that if you can learn it they can too. Allowing everyone to move at his or her own pace also reinforces this idea. Not every learner gets a concept instantaneously, but given enough time and effort everyone can learn any concept. Principles: Self-efficacy, learner-centered, student-directed.

7. Humanists believe that learning involves both the acquisition of new information and the individual personalization of this material. Since meaning is not necessarily inherent in what is being presented, the learners must instill this personal meaning into the subject matter themselves. Although it may seem self-evident to the instructor that what he or she is presenting will be of use to the learner, the instructor should demonstrate that relevance to the learners. Showing the learners how the resource can help them find a job, get into graduate school, or get information about recreational activities, as well as demonstrating its educational merit, can go a long way in capturing the learner's attention. No matter how well organized the material may be, learners will not learn it unless it has personal significance to them. The instructor can help students derive this personal meaning. Once the IL instructor shows the learners how what is being presented will be beneficial to them, it is up to the learners to decide whether or not they wish to acquire this knowledge. Principle: Relevance.

FINAL REMARKS

What this all means to you: All of the theories covered in this section have influenced the education process and how people approach instruction. No one single theory or theorist can be singled out as having the complete, right answer about how people learn. Each offers something for the IL instructor to think about and use. Once again we return to the notion of flexibility. A variety of practical techniques have been inspired by these theories. Some work better in certain situations than others. Some work better for different types of learners than others. If we approach instruction with an understanding of these theories and the many techniques that have evolved from them, we are better able to adjust our approach to instruction as needed. The most thorough and well-prepared IL instructor in the world can discover that what he or she had planned for a particular situation just does not work. Understanding why the plan is not working, and having one—if not more—back-up plans based on different theoretical approaches, allows the IL instructor to turn an unsuccessful situation into a triumph.

EXERCISES

1. Start with an IL instruction topic that you have been responsible for teaching. If you have not had this responsibility yet, use some situation in which you have been the learner.

     Analyze the experience by looking at all the different types of instruction that were used during the training. Some possibilities would be lectures, hands-on practice, self-paced workbooks or worksheets, readings, projects or papers, group work, journals, role-playing, brain storming, and so on.

     Match each technique that was used to one of the approaches to learning described above. Explain why that technique belongs in that approach and what principles the technique illustrates. If a technique seems to illustrate principles from a variety of theorists or schools, explain how the technique fits into all appropriate theoretical frameworks.
2. Think about training someone in some information literacy skill such as database searching or finding biographical information about a living person. Design an instructional experience that incorporates at least one example of the Behaviorist, Cognitive, and Humanist schools of learning. Explain how each example illustrates the theoretical principle associated with a particular theory or theorist.

READ MORE ABOUT IT

The material covered in this chapter was gathered from a wide variety of sources. Many excellent textbooks are available to offer more in-depth discussions on this topic. If you are interested in reading more about learning theories, the following items should prove useful.

Bigge, Morris L., and S. Samuel Shermis. 1999. *Learning Theories for Teachers.* 6th ed. New York: Harper Collins.

Bower, Gordon H., and Ernest R. Hilgard. 1981. *Theories of Learning*. 5th ed. Englewood Cliffs, NJ: Prentice-Hall.

Dembo, Myron. H. 1988. *Teaching for Learning: Applying Educational Psychology in the Classroom*. 3rd ed. Santa Monica, CA: Goodyear.

DesForges, Charles, ed. 1995. *An Introduction to Teaching: Psychological Perspectives*. Oxford, UK: Blackwell.

Elliott, Stephen. N., Thomas R. Fratochwill, Joan Littlefield, and John F. Travers. 1996. *Educational Psychology: Effective Teaching, Effective Learning*. 2nd ed. Madison, WI: Brown and Benchmark.

Gagne, Robert M. 1985. *The Conditions of Learning*. 4th ed. New York: Holt, Rinehart & Winston.

Hergenhahn, Baldwin R. 1988. *An Introduction to Theories of Learning*. Englewood Cliffs, NJ: Prentice-Hall.

Kaplowitz, Joan 1993. "Contributions From the Psychology of Learning: Practical Implications for Teaching." In *Learning to Teach*, edited by ALA, Association of College and Research Libraries, Instruction Section. Chicago: American Library Association.

Reigeluth, Charles M., ed. 1987. *Instructional Theories in Action: Lessons Illustrating Selected Theories and Models*. Hillsdale, NJ: L. Erlbaum.

Seifert, Kelvin L. 1991. *Educational Psychology*. 2nd ed. Boston: Houghton Mifflin Company.

Slavin, Robert E. 1997. *Educational Psychology: Theory and Practice*. Boston: Allyn and Bacon.

Theory Into Practice's *TIP database* [Online]. Available: *http://gwis2.circ.gwu.edu/kearsley* [2000, December 27].

Tighe, Thomas J. 1982. *Learning Theory: Foundations and Fundamental Issues*. New York: Oxford University Press.

4

An Overview of Learning Styles

If a man does not keep pace with his companions, perhaps it is because he hears a different drummer. Let him step to the music he hears, however measured or far away.

—Henry David Thoreau

WHO ARE OUR LEARNERS?

Of all the ideas discussed by current learning theorists, the notion that people learn at their own pace and in their own way has probably had the most profound influence on modern educational practice. These differences have been studied under the broad umbrella of learning styles. James Keefe (1987) defines learning styles as characteristic, cognitive, affective, and physiological behaviors that serve as relatively stable indicators of how learners perceive, interact with, and respond to the learning environment. Although the exact nature of these styles continues to be debated, the fact that people do vary in the way they learn has been widely accepted.

Just as there is no single all-embracing theory of learning, there is a vast array of studies that have identified a wide variety of learning styles. Controversies rage about the relative merits of these postulations, and numerous papers and books have been published that "prove" one or another of these learning styles paradigms. This chapter will attempt to summarize some of this research, and offer brief definitions of those behaviors that have been defined as learning styles. Whether or not you believe in the existence of each and every style, it will soon become apparent that there are many different ways that learners both interact with and process the information they are trying to learn. A better understanding of these differences will give the instructor a clearer insight into the *who* in our equation. Learning theories help us to decide *how* to present the information. Learning styles help us to better understand *who* our learners are and how they prefer to learn.

There is an additional implication to this research on learning styles. Everyone has his or her own learning style. This is important for our learners. It is also crucial to us as instructors. Regardless of the style under consideration, it is generally agreed upon that people are most comfortable working in an atmosphere that reflects their own style. It follows then that teachers may err on the side of their own personal learning preferences when presenting material. If this happens, then a number of students may be put at a disadvantage if there is a mismatch between the teacher's and the learners' styles. So, in addition to paying attention to our learners' styles, we must also be very aware of our own personal styles to avoid relying too heavily on what is most comfortable for us.

A SAMPLING OF STYLES

The following list of learning styles represents a cross-section of the research on this topic. It is not meant to be totally comprehensive. It should be used as a means to understand the various types of behaviors that have been labeled learning styles. For the purpose of this chapter, I will use Keefe's categorization of styles into Cognitive, Affective, and Physiological types (1987). Keep in mind that many of the described styles represent a continuum. People are rarely characterized as being at one or the other end of these ranges. Most people fall somewhere along the continuum, but are probably closer to one end or the other. Also keep in mind that there is no positive or negative end of any continuum. No style should be considered more "right" or valuable than any other. What follows are merely descriptions of possible variations in behavior. Some of the descriptions for individual styles may seem to overlap. The styles described have been compiled from a variety of sources and reflect several different approaches to the material. Some researchers have made attempts to gather styles together into broader categories in order to deal with these fine shades of difference. For references to material that discuss the following styles in detail and on research into categorizing them into broader groups, see the "Read More About It" section at the end of this chapter.

Cognitive Styles

Cognitive styles are information processing habits that represent the learner's typical mode of perceiving, thinking, problem solving, and remembering. These styles are the preferred ways that the learner perceives, organizes, and retains information. These preferences tend to be consistent across different situations and throughout the life of the learner (Keefe, 1987).

PERCEPTUAL MODALITY PREFERENCES

People perceive reality in three basic ways: visually through reading or viewing; aurally through hearing or speaking; and via the psychomotor senses through doing. As people mature their perceptual preference seems to evolve from the psychomotor to visual to aural. Although adults acquire the skill of using all three modes cooperatively, a preference for one of the three modalities tends to develop early in life and does not radically change throughout the life span.

FIELD INDEPENDENCE/DEPENDENCE

This style deals with the ability or inability to perceive things as distinct from their background. Field dependent people tend to be global problem solvers who view everything as related. As a result, they tend to be more socially oriented. A field independent person is not influenced by the surrounding context. They are analytical problem solvers and tend to be impersonal in their approach. They are not socially oriented. The field dependent person may appreciate an outline of the material in order to have a context for the information being presented. Field independent learners are able to isolate salient points on their own and will want to organize the material themselves.

CONSTRICTED/FLEXIBLE

The constricted versus flexible style deals with individual differences in susceptibility to distraction and distortions in tasks with conflicting cues. The constricted learner is easily distracted while the flexible one can concentrate on the task at hand in spite of outside influences or distractions. When presented with the word "blue" written in the color red, the constricted person has more difficulty responding quickly to this clue than the flexible person does.

Tolerance for Incongruous or Unrealistic Experiences

Differences in readiness to accept perceptions that differ from conventional experience characterizes this style. A person with a high tolerance style is willing to accept experiences that vary markedly from the ordinary. The low tolerance person exhibits a preference for conventional ideas.

Reflective/Impulsive

This style, also known as Conceptual Tempo, are characterized by differences in the speed and adequacy of hypothesis formation and information processing. Impulsives work quickly and tend to give the first answer they can think of even though it is often incorrect. They find quick accomplishments rewarding. Reflectives work slowly and with precision. They prefer to consider alternate solutions before deciding on their response. Reflectives seek to avoid error. Reflection tends to inhibit action while impulsiveness inhibits reflection and precludes the development of analytical thinking.

Abstract/Concrete

The abstract/concrete styles describe the ability or inability to grasp concepts readily without reliance on concrete examples or imagery. The abstract problem solver tends to analyze the "big picture," while the concrete thinker likes to start with specific examples.

Innovator/Adapter

This style looks at ways in which people deal with creativity and change. Adapters are resourceful, efficient, thorough, precise, and methodical. They are able to maintain a high level of accuracy for long periods of time. Adapters are especially good at detailed work. They tend to be the planners and apply structure to innovative ideas. They do not like change but are good at implementing it.

Innovators are unconventional, spontaneous, insightful, unique, original, energetic, independent, and inventive. They tend to be flexible, enthusiastic about change, and are not constrained by accepted theories of the past. Innovators tend to break new ground—they initiate change.

BROAD/NARROW

Differences in how learners group items fall under this style. Some people prefer broad categories containing many items. Others prefer narrow categories containing few items. When sorting examples into categories, broad learners will end up with fewer categories with lots of examples in each. Those with the narrow learning style will have lots of categories with only a few examples in each.

LEVELING/SHARPENING

This style describes ways in which learners deal with stimulus differences. Levelers ignore detail and blur distinctions between items. Fine shades of difference tend to be lost. Sharpeners, on the other hand, concentrate on detail and may even magnify differences between stimuli. When looking at a color palette, the leveler may fail to see any distinction between certain shades of a particular color. Sharpeners, on the other hand, will clearer see these differences and these changes will be meaningful to them.

CONVERGING/DIVERGING

Different methods of problem solving are described by this style. They deal with whether the learner uses narrow, focused, logical, deductive reasoning or broad, open-ended, associative, inductive reasoning when dealing with a problem. The converger would probably feel most comfortable using a database thesaurus to select terms before constructing a search strategy. The diverger would skip the thesaurus step and dive right in with keyword searching in an attempt to figure out the search strategy based on the results of these keyword searches.

SERIALIST/HOLISTIC

The serialist learner works through tasks incrementally, preferring to work through problems step by step. The holistic learner approaches problems globally, attacking the problem from several angles at once. The serialist learner would most likely enjoy some kind of guided exercise. Holistic learners would probably prefer to freely examine the system or resource to be learned on their own in order to figure out how it works.

Affective Styles

Affective styles are concerned with feelings or emotional aspects of behavior that represent the learner's typical ways of arousing, directing,
and sustaining behavior. These styles deal with attention, valuing, and
incentive. Motivation is included under this category. Affective styles
are relatively constant and remain stable over time (Keefe, 1987).

STRUCTURAL NEEDS

This style characterize how much structure a person requires in order to
learn. They relate to the person's ability to follow through on a task
without direct or frequent supervision. Providing outlines or guided
exercises would help the person who has high structural needs. Those
with low structural needs will be able to work without such guidance
and may even find the outline distracting.

CURIOSITY

Differences in attraction to the novel or adventurous aspects of the environment are represented by this style. Curiosity includes exploratory
behavior, reaction to change or the desire for change, and efforts to escape boredom. Some learners enjoy being presented with new resources
just because of this novelty aspect. Other learners are not automatically
interested just because it is something new.

PERSEVERANCE

Variations in the learner's willingness to labor beyond the required time,
to withstand discomfort, and to face the prospect of failure are listed
under this style. Low perseverance results in short attention spans and
the inability to work on a task for any length of time. Perseverance may
be related to, but not identical to, the mobility need under physiological
styles. Learners high in perseverance will stick with a complex resource
or database far longer than those who are low in this characteristic. Low
perseverance learners may require additional help or support as they
work through a complicated search process.

FRUSTRATION TOLERANCE

This style refers to how individuals differ in their ability to continue a
behavior in the face of conflict or disappointment. Learners who are
tolerant of frustration are more likely to extend efforts in a conflict situa-

tion and to accept the problem as a challenge. Perseverance and frustration can be seen as somewhat related to frustration tolerance. Those who are easily frustrated by the difficulties of what they are trying to learn may be unwilling to persevere at the task.

ANXIETY

Differences in the individual's level of apprehension and tension under stress conditions are described here. The high anxiety person is characterized as a tense and worried one. The low anxiety person is characterized as emotionally cool.

INTERNAL/EXTERNAL LOCUS OF CONTROL

This style relates to the individual's perceptions of causality. The internal person thinks of himself or herself as responsible for his or her own behavior, as deserving praise for successes and blame for failures. Internals may be too self-contained and withdrawn, failing to ask for assistance when it is needed. Internals may refuse to accept constructive criticism. The external person sees circumstances beyond his or her control, such as luck or other people, as responsible for his or her success or failure. Externals are more socially adept but may rely too much on the opinion of others

INTRINSICALLY/EXTRINSICALLY MOTIVATED

The ways in which people differ in their patterns of planning and striving for some internalized standard of excellence are described here. When learners are working to please themselves, they are said to be intrinsically motivated. When they are working toward some externally applied reward (grades, money, praise from the teacher), they are said to be extrinsically motivated.

RISK TAKING

This style deals with individual differences in a person's willingness to take chances to achieve some goal. Risk takers prefer low success probability situations with high payoffs. Cautious people like high success probability alternatives with low payoffs.

COMPETITION/COOPERATION

This style deals with individual tendencies to either be motivated by rivalry or by the sharing of experiences. The highly competitive person has a strong compulsion to win. The highly cooperative person has a strong need to agree and support.

Physiological Styles

Physiological styles relate to biologically based modes of response. These styles responses include the learner's physiological make-up and his or her reactions to variations in the physical environment. Physiological styles describe aspects of health and personal nutrition, reactions to light, heat, noise etc., brain laterality issues, and gender-based behaviors (Keefe, 1987).

GENDER-RELATED BEHAVIOR (FEMININE/MASCULINE TRAITS)

These traits or styles represent variations in typical learning responses for males and females. They may be innate or may be learned through socialization. Sensitivity to spatial (visual) relations and mathematical processes are said to be masculine traits. Skills in verbal and fine motor control tasks are said to be feminine traits.

HEALTH

This style looks at individual responses to variations to health-related situations such as hunger, malnutrition, lack of sleep, and illness. Poor health tends to make it difficult for the student to concentrate on the learning situation. However, some people tolerate these health-related situations better than others do.

TIME OF DAY RHYTHMS (MORNING/NIGHT PEOPLE)

The effect of time of day on the ability to learn is examined by this style. Some people perform better in the mornings, while others are at their best later in the day or well into the night.

MOBILITY NEEDS

This style deals with differences in the learner's need for change in posture and location. This dimension may be both age and gender-related. Younger learners and males generally require more mobility. However, this behavior could develop through socialization since we are less tolerant of fidgeting in older children. There is also some evidence that we are more inclined to expect females to sit still.

ENVIRONMENTAL FACTORS (LIGHT, NOISE, TEMPERATURE)

Individual preferences for, or responses to, varying levels of light, sound, and temperature are described by this style. Students tend to develop a favored level of light, temperature, and background noise that they feel is conducive to learning.

HEMISPHERIC PREFERENCES (LEFT VERSUS RIGHT BRAIN)

This style looks at information-processing behavior characterized by one or the other brain hemisphere. In processing information, the left hemisphere is thought to use an analytic, linear, rational, and sequenced approach. The right hemisphere is said to emphasize a more global approach to the perception, absorption, and processing of information, looking for patterns rather than details. Left-brain people are thought to be more verbal, while right-brain people are thought to be more visual.

ATTEMPTS AT CATEGORIZING THE STYLES

The vast number of different styles that have been identified, and the fact that many seem interrelated or even redundant, has had both practical and theoretical implications. On the practical end, teachers wonder how to apply this research to the classroom. Which styles should the teacher be concerned with? How many styles must be considered when designing instruction? Is it possible to design effective instruction that addresses so many differences? We will return to these questions at the close of this chapter. Meanwhile, researchers in this area are questioning whether each of these styles is unique and distinct. Several possibilities for grouping these styles into broader categories have been suggested.

The Wholistic/Analytic; Verbal/Imagery Dimensions

R.J. Riding and his colleagues have proposed an integration of styles into two cognitive style families: The Wholistic/Analytic and the Verbalizer/Imager. "Wholistic" is a term coined by these researchers in an attempt to differentiate it from the Gestaltist term "holistic." Although the terms are similar in intent, "wholistic" is used as a means to broaden the meaning beyond the perceptual or Gestalt aspects of the concept to a more cognitive or problem solving approach. "Wholistic" deals with how people process information, concentrating on the whole or the parts. Verbal imagery deals with whether thinking tends to be in pictures or words (Rayner and Riding, 1997).

WHOLISTIC/ANALYTIC

This dimension is concerned with whether an individual tends to process information in wholes or parts. Wholistics tend to organize information into loosely clustered wholes. Analytics tend to organize information into clear-cut conceptual groupings.

Styles that are thought to fall in this category include constricted/ flexible, broad/narrow, levelling/sharpening, field-dependence/independence, impulsive/reflective, converging/diverging, serialist/holist, and adapters/innovators.

VERBAL/IMAGERY

This dimension deals with whether an individual is inclined to represent information during thinking verbally or in mental images. Imagers are said to deal best with pictorial presentations, while verbalizers do better with written text.

Riding (Rayner and Riding, 1997) includes tolerance for ambiguity, abstract/concrete, and sensory modality preferences in this category. The work on hemispheric, or right-versus-left brain preferences, may also apply here.

Experiential Learning Model

Any discussion of learning styles would be incomplete without the inclusion of David Kolb's Experiential Learning Model (1984). Experiential learning emphasizes the importance of learning from experience. This approach differs from some of the other researchers in the field, most notably Keefe, who view a person's style preference as an inborn given (Keefe, 1987). The Kolb model describes how experience is translated into concepts, which in turn are used as guides in the choice of new experiences. Learners need to engage in four different kinds of behaviors. These are described as two pairs of polar opposites or dimensions. The first dimension has concrete experience at one end and abstract conceptualization at the other. The other dimension has active experimentation at one end and reflective observation at the other. The concrete/abstract dimension deals with how the learner processes information and the active/reflective with how he or she interacts with that information. Most individuals are seen as developing style preferences by selecting one of the two competing styles: concrete or abstract and active or reflective. Four possible combinations can result.

DIVERGERS

Divergers rely on concrete experience and reflective observation. These learners look at alternative solutions, seek background information before reaching decisions, investigate new patterns, and recognize discrepancies and inconsistencies.

CONVERGERS

Convergers learn best through active experimentation and abstract conceptualization. They are analytic and swift to make decisions. Convergers are always looking for connections, ways to tie things together.

ASSIMILATORS

These learners combine abstract conceptualization with reflective observation. Their strengths lie in planning and formulating theories. However, they may have difficulty applying their ideas in practical ways. Assimilators are skilled in inductive reasoning and can combine or assimilate various ideas into one integrated solution.

ACCOMMODATORS

Accommodators learn best through active experimentation and concrete experience. They are goal-directed but require frequent feedback to keep them focused on the task at hand. They tend to solve problems through intuition rather than analysis. Accommodators are excellent at setting objectives, describing all the possible solutions or opinions on a topic, and implementing decisions.

Kolb views the diverger and the accommodator as representative of a broad category called "lumpers" (1984). Lumpers are wholistic type learners who need to understand the "big picture" before they can deal with the details and facts related to the immediate problem. Convergers and assimilators, on the other hand, are the "splitters." These learners are analytics who concentrate on the parts or the specific details first before dealing with the whole concept.

THE EXPERIENTIAL LEARNING METHOD

This method builds on the fact that people fall into different stylistic patterns and the method creates an instructional situation that offers opportunities for each of the types to learn according to their favored style. The method consists of four stages:

1. Concrete Experience—During the concrete experience stage, learners must actively interact with the material to be learned. Immediate experience is stressed, as well as giving personal meaning to abstract concepts. Concrete examples are presented as the basis for formulating generalizations about the topic.
2. Reflective Observation—Students observe their experiences from a variety of viewpoints, reflect on what they have learned, and think about and interpret their experiences. The goal of this reflection should be the integration of these observations into some theoretical explanation of those experiences.
3. Abstract Conceptualization—This is the theory-building and problem solving stage. The learners are actively involved in analysis and synthesis of the material, and test out the ideas developed during reflective observation. Group activities can be useful at this stage to allow learners to test their ideas against those of their peers.
4. Active Experimentation—During active experimentation learners must apply their theories to reality-based problems. Practical applications of the theories developed during abstract conceptualization are tested during this stage.

Kolb's work has been very influential in education, probably because it offers practical suggestions about how to incorporate a variety of techniques within a single, instructional experience. A great number of the individual styles listed above can be accommodated by Kolb's four learning styles. Riding's Wholistic/Analytic and Verbal/Imagery dimensions also seem to be handled by this approach (Rayner and Riding, 1997).

Thinking Styles

Robert Sternberg and his associates take another approach to this topic of learning styles. Sternberg hypothesizes a category of styles, called thinking styles, to describe differences in how people learn (Sternberg, 1997; Sternberg and Grigorenko, 1997; Grigorenka and Sternberg, 1995). Sternberg (like Kolb) breaks with other approaches by proposing that thinking styles are not innate or unresponsive to the environment. Thinking styles are said to develop from experience and are viewed as fluid rather than fixed. An individual, who uses one style in a particular situation, may use a very different style as environmental demands change.

In addition, although individuals may exhibit preferences for particular styles at certain stages of life, they may show preferences for different styles at other stages. Thinking styles are based on a model of mental self-government. The major categories are reminiscent of types of government organizations and are described below. Whether or not you feel that the notion of thinking styles is a solution or just adds to the complexity of the situation, Sternberg has offered yet another way of looking at how individuals differ in the ways that they interact with and learn from their environments.

EXECUTIVE/JUDICIAL/LEGISLATIVE THINKING STYLES

This style looks at how people deal with rules. The Executive type likes structure and following already established rules. The Judicial type is interested in evaluating the rules. The Legislative type wants to come up with the rules.

MONARCHIC/HIERARCHIC/OLIGARCHIC/ANARCHIC THINKING STYLES

How people deal with goals is examined here. The Monarchic person is single-minded and does not let anything get in his or her way. He or she deals with one goal at a time. The Hierarchic person has a hierarchy of goals and recognizes the need to set priorities since not all goals can be reached at the same time. The Oligarchic person wishes to work on several projects at the same time. Oligarchic people tend to be motivated by several, often competing, goals of equally perceived importance. The Anarchic person takes a random approach to problem solving and tends to move among goals. Because Anarchic people tend to pick up a little from here and there, they often put together diverse bits of information and ideas in a creative way. They frequently see solutions that escape others.

GLOBAL/LOCAL

Levels of complexity preferred by the learner are described by this style. Globals tend to deal with relatively large and abstract ideas; they ignore or dismiss details. Locals like concrete problems and are very pragmatic; they tend to be detail oriented.

INTERNAL/EXTERNAL THINKING STYLES

This style looks at how people deal with other people. The Internal person tends to be introverted, task-oriented, aloof, and less socially aware.

They prefer to work alone and work out problems in isolation from others. The External person is an extravert who tends to be outgoing and people oriented. They are very socially sensitive and aware of what is going on with others. Externals prefer to work with others.

LIBERAL/CONSERVATIVE

The ways people relate to change are described by this style. Liberals relish change. They seek out ambiguous situations that call into question existing rules and procedures. They are easily bored and continually seek new stimulation and experiences. Conservatives like to minimize change, avoid ambiguous situations, and prefer the familiar. They like structured, fairly predictable environments.

SPECIAL CONSIDERATIONS

The identification and categorization of learning styles are just two aspects of the numerous controversies that swirl around this topic. The reliability and validity, as well as the predictive power of the instruments used to measure these styles, have also been called into question. Questions have been raised as to the relationship between styles and career choice, possible gender, ethnicity and cultural differences, and the notion of stylistic changes as one ages. Are people with certain styles more likely to succeed in certain careers, and are they drawn to those careers? Do men and women exhibit differing patterns of styles, and if so, are these differences innate or learned through socialization? Do different cultures and/or ethnic groups tend to rely more heavily on particular styles than on others? Are these patterns innate or learned through the value systems in place for that ethnic or cultural group? Is there a shift in the types of styles relied on as people develop across the life span? Do the styles used by the adult learner differ from those used by the child?

Measurement Issues

Generally styles are measured in one of two ways. In the first instance, some standard psychological test is adapted for this task. For example, Field Dependence/Independence is usually measured by the Embedded Figure Test (Witkin et al., 1977). Subjects are shown a figure and then asked to find that figure in a more complex drawing. The ability to succeed at this task is taken as a measure of the person's place on this continuum. The Stroop Test (Stroop, 1935), which measures reactions to inconsistencies between the written word and the color the word is written in, is used to test for the Constricted/Flexible style. The Rorschach Inkblot Test (Rorschach, 1942), which requires subjects to impose meaning on seemingly meaningless inkblots, has been used to measure tolerance for unrealistic experiences. The speed and accuracy of the subject's responses on the Matching Familiar Figures Test (Kagan, 1966), which requires the subject to find an exact match for a sample figure from a set of several similar figures, is thought to be a measure of the Impulsive/Reflective style.

In the second case, specific instruments have been developed especially to measure one or more learning styles. These include Kolb's Learning Style Inventory (1976), the Learning Style Profile (Keefe, 1988; Keefe and Monk, 1988), Riding's Cognitive Style Analysis (Riding and Cheema, 1991), the Swassing-Barbe Modality Index to measure modality preferences (Barbe and Swassing, 1988), the KAI for measuring the Innovator/Adaptor style (Kirton, 1976), the Sensation Seeking Scale (Gaines and Coursey, 1974), which deals with curiosity, and the Rotter Locus of Control Inventory (Rotter, 1950). The question here is can a test with the sole purpose of identifying a particular style be used as an indicator of a person's position on the continuum. In this case the same instrument is both being used to identify the characteristics that make up the style and also whether or not a person possesses that style. In some views this becomes a self-fulfilling prophecy (Sternberg, 1997). Whether any of the tests mentioned in this section accurately identify the styles in question has opened up an extremely fruitful area for future research opportunities.

Furthermore, the reliability of some of these specific styles' inventories has been called into question (Stahl, 1999). Some of the more commonly used inventories have been shown to have only moderate reliability (in the .60 or .70 range). If a test were truly reliable you would get the same result every time you administered the test. So the closer the reliability score is to 1.00 the more reliable the test. Most tests are only considered reliable if they have scores of .90 or above. These moderate reliabilities mean either that the test is not accurately measuring the concept or that styles are not really stable over time. In either case, these moderate reliability measures call into question the use of these tests for diagnostic purposes (Stahl, 1999).

Finally, many so-called learning styles inventories or instruments have been mounted on the Web. These are readily available to anyone with Internet access and usually include a scoring mechanism to determine the style of the person completing the inventory. While these may give some insight into a person's complex of learning styles, they should be used with caution. Each inventory probably is restricted to only a few of the styles parameters discussed in this chapter, so they may give only a partial picture of the learner's style. Furthermore, learning style inventories, just as any psychological or educational instrument, are meant to be administered and scored by trained professionals. They are not parlor games or popular magazine quizzes. So, although the results may be of some recreational interest, they are not to be trusted as a true measure of a learner's complex of styles.

Career Choice and Academic Achievement

Despite the questions about the reliability of the learning styles inventories, attempts have been made to use the various inventories to predict educational success, and as a means to identify potential career choices. Although research in this area has shown little uniformity or consistency of results, some studies seem to indicate that preference patterns do exist. Holists have been found to gravitate toward the humanities and social sciences. Serialists can be found in the natural sciences and mathematics (Pask and Scott, 1972; McKeachie, 1999). Kolb tried to relate his style categories to the various academic disciplines and found the following: People in the natural sciences tend to be assimilators. Those in science-based professions such as engineering are convergers. The social professions such as education and social work have large concentrations of accommodators. Divergers tend to specialize in the humanities and social sciences (Kolb, 1981).

Other studies have also found differences between students in the arts versus students in the sciences (Wilcoxson and Prosser, 1996). Nurses and teachers seem to exhibit similar styles (Sutherland, 1995). A relationship between style preferences and the choice of particular medical specialties has been found (Plovnick, 1975). In addition, medical generalists seem to prefer different styles than those who choose to specialize in a specific area of medicine (Kosower, 1995). More studies dealing with this issue are certain to follow.

Gender Issues

The question of whether certain styles are more characteristically associated with men versus women has been the subject of heated debate. Research seems to show that men and women exhibit different learning styles. Scores on Kolb's Learning Styles Inventory indicate that women tend to have the concrete experience orientation, while men tend toward abstract conceptualization (Kolb, 1976). Another study indicated that females are more likely to prefer to learn using the visual modality (reading and seeing) than males, and like to work in a quieter environment. Females are more motivated by authority figures such as teachers or parents than males are, and they are more persistent than males. In terms of time of day cycles, more males seem to prefer to learn in the later morning than females (Hickson and Baltimore, 1996). On the whole, women tend to be more field dependent and men exhibit more field independent tendencies (Anderson and Adams, 1992). See also the work on connected versus separate thinking (Burdick, 1996; Clinchy, 1994) described in Chapter 14.

Males do better in traditional educational settings that emphasize the abstract and the reflective since that closely matches the male preferred learning style. Females learn better in hands-on, practical settings that emphasize feeling and doing (Philbin et al., 1995). Are these gender-based stylistic differences innate or learned? Studies indicate that gender identity (the perception of one's masculinity or femininity) may be a better predictor of stylistic differences. If this is the case, then socialization, cultural, and environmental pressures may account for this differential (Severiens and Ten Dam, 1997; Weiner, 1995). See Chapter 14 for a further discussion of gender, socialization, and cultural issues.

Ethnicity/Culture-Based Issues

Just as research has uncovered learning style differences between the genders, studies indicate that different ethnic and cultural groups also show a variation in their preferred styles (Anderson and Adams, 1992; Dunn and Griggs, 1995; Gilton, 1994; Griggs and Dunn, 1996; Kolb, 1981). A brief summary of some of these research findings follows. Keep in mind that the research described below indicates a greater than average preference for a particular style in a particular group. They do *not* in any way indicate that all members of a group exhibit the exact same collection of styles. Great variation can and does exist among the members of each group. The most consistent finding among researchers in this field is that every person is an individual with a unique battery of learning-style preferences that distinguish him or her from other members of their family, culture, or ethnic group. Furthermore, the following represents only a sampling of ethnic or cultural groupings and does not deal with issues of mixed ethnic/cultural backgrounds or get into any subgroups that may exist within the groupings being discussed. For the most part, subjects of these research projects self-identified into each of the groups. So someone may have identified themselves as a member of a particular group even though they were of mixed heritage because they felt a stronger connection to that particular group. See Chapter 14 for further discussion of this topic.

NATIVE AMERICANS

Members of this group prefer cool temperatures and a formally arranged classroom. They exhibit low persistence or a tendency to need frequent breaks while completing a task. There is a marked preference for peer and team learning. Native Americans tend to be field dependent and reflective.

HISPANIC AMERICANS

These students also prefer a cool environment, formally arranged classrooms, and peer learning. They favor kinesthetic instructional resources and a high degree of structure. Role playing and modeling work well with this group. Hispanics tend to be field dependent.

AFRICAN AMERICANS

The majority of these students tend to be field dependent, wholistic in approach, and prefer brightly lit, quiet, warm environments. African Americans like an informally arranged classroom in which they can move around freely. These students tend to exhibit afternoon and evening time of day preferences and are visual-kinesthetic rather than auditory learners.

ASIAN AMERICANS

The members of this group prefer a formally arranged classroom with a high degree of structure in the presentation of material. They are analytic and field independent and concentrate better as the day moves toward late afternoon and evening. A strong preference for the tactual/kinesthetic modality is also exhibited.

EUROPEAN AMERICANS

These students prefer warmer environments. They like sound and bright lights when studying. Students in this group tend to have strong auditory preferences and favor analytic, rational, sequential, and inductive approaches. There is some indication that more European Americans are left-brain dominant than right-brain dominant. Members of this group like an informally arranged classroom that allows for free movement and mobility. They prefer to study independently and are strongly motivated by authority figures such as teachers and parents.

Again the question of the origin of these differences arises. Cultural values influence the socialization practices of all ethnic groups that, in turn, affects the learning styles preferences within that group. So these preferences may be handed down from generation to generation, as representative of what is normal within that group (Dunn and Griggs, 1995). A mismatch between a particular individual's cultural preferred learning style and his or her educational environment may lead to difficulties in the classroom, and may even result in the student being labeled as having a learning or behavioral disability (McIntyre, 1996).

The Adult Learner

This chapter started with the postulation that an individual's collection of styles is stable throughout his or her life span. If this is true, then there is no reason to assume that adults would differ substantially from children in the ways they prefer to learn. Individuals would differ from each other. But individual differences would be independent of the age of the learner. If, however, we follow some of the later interpretations by researchers such as Kolb and Sternberg, we must deal with the possibility that experience influences the ways a person prefers to learn. What follows then is that the mature, more experienced adult may indeed operate under a different body of styles than the young child.

The major proponent of this view of adult learning was Malcolm S. Knowles. Knowles's starting point was the work of Alexander Kapp, a German educator who in 1933 coined the term "Andragogy" to explain how adults learn (Knowles, 1978, 1980, 1984). Knowles describes the typical adult learner as one who is motivated to learn when faced with a specific need or interest. The adult's orientation to learning is typically life or work related. Adults are interested in practical application not theoretical issues. In other words, learning is problem-centered rather than subject-centered. Adults are motivated to learn only when they think the subject will have real meaning or relevance to their daily lives. Since the adult has a rich array of experiences to bring to the learning situation, he or she appreciates the opportunity to draw on those experiences and relate them to the current topic under discussion. Adults tend to prefer active participation rather than passive reception of information and want to be self-directed in the learning process. Furthermore, the adult usually submits voluntarily to the learning situation and will leave it if the situation does not prove to be relevant. For an application to library science see Sheridan (1986).

The adult, therefore, requires an educational environment that is mutually respectful, informal, and collaborative. The teacher in this environment acts as a facilitator between the learner and the information to be learned. The emphasis then becomes one not of providing information to the learner, but of supporting the learner's interaction with and assimilation of that information (Sims and Sims, 1995). The adult learner does better in a Cognitive-Humanist oriented classroom that promotes these principles of learning. He or she does not do well when faced with a typical child-oriented, pedagogical approach to learning that emphasizes the teacher as authority, is more formal and competitive, and in which the learner is given little or no responsibility for his or her own learning. In other words, adults do not do well when treated by the instructor as if they were children (Knowles, 1996; Hewitt, 1995). The adult learner fears failure, and is especially afraid of looking foolish before his or her peers. The instructor should emphasize the expectation that everyone has something important to contribute to the instructional experience. Adult learners must be encouraged to share their experiences and opinions, and be reassured that everyone's opinions will be valued and respected. This not only empowers the individual learner, but also promotes the idea of peer training and collaboration among learners.

The first step in successfully teaching adults, then, is the establishment of a climate that emphasizes openness, mutual trust, and mutual respect. The climate must be supportive, challenging, and exciting. Adults usually have clear-cut goals in mind when placing themselves in an educational situation and must be convinced that what they learn will have practical applications for them. Handouts and other material that offers explicit examples of possible ways to do things, as they relate to the topic being presented, are most helpful to the adult learner. Adults bring a great deal of experience and expertise to the learning situation and therefore have much to contribute. The instructor must create an atmosphere in which participants feel comfortable exchanging ideas and discussing issues. Students should be encouraged to and be rewarded for risk taking. Learners are empowered not only to take responsibility for their own learning, but to also challenge themselves and others in positive ways (Hewitt, 1995).

SO MANY STYLES—SO LITTLE TIME

Despite the controversies and debates that surround the study of learning styles, one fact remains clear. People are different. Our students, trainees, and learners are not homogenous in their approaches to learning. Regardless of what underlies these differences (heredity, experience, gender, culture, age), those we are trying to teach will differ in the way they approach the learning situation. So how do we as instructors cope with these differences? In most cases, those of us involved in IL do not have the time to test our learners to identify their styles, nor the opportunity to address the many possible styles that might be exhibited in a group. So what can we do?

First of all, instructors must understand how their learners might differ. The material in this chapter should help them acquire that understanding. Second, instructors must avoid the misconception that styles are value laden—that is, that some styles are "better" than others are. Rather, they should view styles as givens. Learning styles are part of the package that the learner brings to the instructional situation. Reaching learners by teaching to their preferred styles is the instructor's responsibility. Third, instructors must know themselves. The instructor who is familiar with his or her own style will avoid the common pitfall of only teaching in the way that they themselves like to learn. Instructors must be very sure to use methods that are different from the way they themselves like to learn as well as those that appeal to their own preferred style. The learners who are the most different from us are the ones we run the greatest risk of not reaching. Last, but definitely not least, instructors should vary their presentations so that they teach to the widest variety of styles possible.

MATCHING TEACHING AND LEARNING STYLES: DOES IT MATTER?

So our goal is to make sure learners are presented with material in the format or style most compatible with their own individual style. Or is it? Studies that attempt to examine the effects of matching versus mismatching teaching and learning styles have had mixed results (Barbe and Swassing, 1988; Ford, 1990; Frye, 1999; Spoon and Schell, 1998; Stahl, 1999). While some studies show improvements in achievement when learners are placed in style-compatible environments, others show little or no significant difference between learners in congruent (matched styles) settings versus incongruent (mismatched styles) environments. One explanation is that people (especially adults) have learned to cope. Although they may have preferences in the ways they like to learn, they have developed flexibility. In short they have learned how to learn in incongruent situations (Spoon and Schell, 1998). A second explanation may lie in what is being measured: achievement or efficiency. While people may eventually be able to learn something if it is presented in an incongruent manner, they tend to learn much more efficiently if allowed to process the information in the manner most congruent with their own style preferences. The more comfortable the learner is, whether we are talking about room temperature, time of day, or cognitive organizing principles, the better the learner can concentrate and the faster he or she will learn (Frye, 1999). So, do we need to offer people options in the way they can learn material? Although most people may eventually learn the material regardless of the mode in which it is presented, the matching of instructional mode to learner preference seems to speed up the process. So offering a variety of options may help our learners to be more efficient in their efforts.

DEALING WITH LEARNING STYLES

Our goal is to make learning comfortable for as many of our learners as possible. There are several approaches to doing so. We can provide multi-sensory presentations where each concept is presented simultaneously in a variety of ways. An alternative is the sequential approach where the same material is presented in a variety of ways. Both approaches offer the possibility of reaching learners with a variety of styles. But both have disadvantages as well. The multi-sensory approach can be overwhelming and distracting to some learners and may interfere with their ability to concentrate on their preferred mode of learning. In the sequential approach only part of the group is engaged at any one time. The rest may lose interest during segments that do not appeal to their own styles. Furthermore, if the same material is repeated in different modes, learners may become bored or even confused if they don't understand how the different presentations relate (Barbe and Swassing, 1988).

Another possibility for providing this variety is to build on Kolb's model of Experiential Learning. Different learning experiences appeal to different types of learners. For example, the use of logs or journals encourages reflective observation, while fieldwork or laboratory experiments appeal to those who prefer active experimentation. Having learners write research papers, engage in model building, or use analogies during discussions appeal to the abstract conceptualization mode. Showing examples or having learners work on problem sets offers concrete experiences (Svinicki and Dixon, 1987).

Sonia Bodi has developed a methodology that applies the principles of Kolb's work to IL instruction. Her instructional design illustrates how to vary experiences during a 50–70 minute freshman library instruction class in order to reach each of the four types of learners. The instruction includes a lecture accompanied by sample material. Students are then required to complete a worksheet and develop a partially annotated bibliography on a topic of their own choice to be completed following the lecture/demo. The students also meet with the instructors while they are working on this assignment to obtain feedback on their progress and to give them the opportunity to discuss and reflect upon what they now know about using library resources that they did not know before. Finally, the students must write a five-page research paper based on the material gathered using the worksheet. Each of the learning styles is addressed by these four experiences. The result is an increased likelihood that all students will have interacted with the material in a manner compatible with his or her learning style (Bodi, 1990).

The Myers Briggs Type Indicator is a psychometric instrument used to identify psychological type. The results are reported in terms of four dimensions: Extraversion/Introversion, Sensing/Intuition, Thinking/Feeling, and Judging/Perceiving. Sixteen different psychological types or styles can be identified using this instrument. Some grounding in the characteristics of these types can also suggest ways to vary instructional opportunities so there is something for everyone. For example, introverts appreciate a private place to practice new products or skills. Intuitive types like to explore on their own. Feeling types need a supportive, friendly climate for learning. Perceiving types enjoy comparing alternative solutions to problems (Moreland, 1993; Meyers and Jones, 1993).

Another approach is to offer a variety of learning options either within an in-person situation or as an alternative to in-person instruction. Web-based instruction with its built-in hypertext capabilities is one possibility. By allowing learners to move at their own pace, and to interact with the material in a way that is most compatible with their own styles, Web-based instruction provides opportunities for a wide variety of learners (Ford, 1990). Print handouts, guided exercises, and audio or video presentations can all provide alternative approaches. See Chapters 8 and 9 for a fuller discussion of a variety of instructional modes.

In-person instruction can provide some variety by incorporating free time within the session where learners can choose to engage in several different kinds of experiences: small group discussions, hands-on active experimentation, some reflective writing, etc. The type of in-person presentations can also vary with some offering demonstration and discussion while others feature workshop experiences that emphasize hands-on experience and offer learners the opportunity to practice and ask questions about their progress.

Keep in mind that the lecture approach meets the needs of only a portion of our learners: highly self-directed learners whose preferred approach is listening and reading do well. Those learners with other preferences often struggle under the lecture approach. Incorporating active learning techniques into instruction can provide opportunities for learners who prefer these other approaches. Active learning techniques and student-centered instruction can be designed to appeal to learners with a wide range of cognitive, affective, and physiological styles (Allen, 1995). See Chapter 6 for a further discussion of this topic.

Ultimately, the idea is to increase the possibility of reaching most if not all your students by varying your presentation approach or by offering some instructional options. Another way to approach this idea is to try to include examples of each of the following learning environments in order to broaden the way students are allowed to interact with the material being presented (Rainey and Kolb, 1995). Keep in mind that some of these opportunities could be presented electronically, in print, or via other alternatives to in-person instruction.

1. The Affectively Oriented Environment focuses on attitudes, feelings, values, and opinions generated from concrete, here and now, experiences. Free expression of individual feelings, opinions, and values are encouraged. Feedback is personalized and directly related to the individual's own goals. The instructor is a role model who respects everyone's ideas and opinions. Concrete experiences and active experimentation are stressed here.

2. The Perceptually Oriented Environment emphasizes appreciation and understanding of relationships between events and concepts. Students are encouraged to view topics from multiple perspectives. The process is emphasized rather than the solution. Students are therefore evaluated, not on getting the correct answer, but on the method of inquiry used to get to that answer. Abstract conceptualization and reflective observation are stressed here.

3. The Cognitively Oriented Environment emphasizes skill mastery and problem solving. Learner's solutions are evaluated objectively as either correct or incorrect. The teacher functions here as an interpreter of a field of knowledge against which the student's responses are being evaluated. Abstract conceptualization and reflective observations are the characteristics.

4. The Behaviorally Oriented Environment is geared toward the application of knowledge and skills to solve real-life situations. Activities are directed toward what is necessary to plan and complete a task. Learners are allowed to self-evaluate against criteria that they themselves establish. Teachers serve as coaches or advisors who leave the responsibility of problem solving to the students. This setting provides concrete experiences and active experimentation opportunities.

Finally, when dealing with learners either in a classroom setting or one-on-one, instructors should watch for those moments of confusion or lack of comprehension that may signal a learning styles problem. If one or more learners are not grasping what you are trying to teach, it might be a good idea to try and present the information in another way (Barbe and Swassing, 1988). Developing presentation alternatives that can be drawn upon in such circumstances is key. While you may not have to use them all in any given situation, having these options will allow you to switch approaches to one that might clarify the situation by appealing to a different mode or style of learning. This may also be the time to refer your learners to Web-based, print, or other instructional alternatives that might have a stronger appeal.

FINAL REMARKS

Flexibility, self-awareness, and open-mindedness are the keys to instructional effectiveness. Your willingness to try new approaches, especially ones that may not be compatible with your own style of learning, and your ability to take risks in your teaching will allow you to reach a variety of learners. And your capacity to change approaches even in the middle of a session if you sense you are losing your audience will increase the likelihood that each person regardless of his or her preference will have a positive learning experience.

An instructor who understands learning style preferences can arrange for flexibility in groupings, materials, and teaching styles. Pay attention to which learners remember better when reading silently, reading and listening, listening only, or engaging in activities. Do your learners rely on visual imagery, the spoken word, or behavioral action (gestures or other actions) to illustrate their points? Instructors who are sensitive to the types of activities that certain students prefer will be able to select activities that will engage a particular learner. For those of us who do not have a continuing relationship with our learners, making sure that we offer a variety of educational opportunities when dealing with any group should improve our chances of reaching most if not all our learners.

Allow for pacing alternatives that give students the opportunity to take breaks as needed and to move around if necessary. Provide for private, quiet space for those who prefer to work independently, and group activities for those who like a livelier environment. Do not allow the impulsive to dominate the group's discussions. Give the reflectives time to weigh alternatives before responding. If possible, let students choose from a variety of activities, some that benefit from quick responses and others that require more quiet reflection. Appeal to the visual, auditory, as well as the tactile learner by allowing for options in the way students are expected to exhibit competence and comprehension. Let students choose from a list of projects that might include developing a concrete, practical application of what has been learned, constructing an object that illustrates some point, writing a paper, or making an oral presentation in class.

Using only a limited number of techniques in teaching can disenfranchise many of our learners. Remember the Humanist credo that everyone is capable of learning. It is up to the instructor to present the material in a way that is compatible with the learner's style. Variety is the key. While we may not be able to identify the style of each and every learner we encounter, varying the techniques in our presentations increases the likelihood of reaching most if not all of our learners. Learning style preference research points out the ways people can vary. Learning theories and their practical applications offer us a variety of approaches that we can use in an attempt to accommodate these variations.

EXERCISES

1. What's Your Style? The following worksheet was developed primarily as a means for the teacher to become more familiar with his or her own style preferences. It can also be used to determine the variation of styles in your students. Obtaining learning styles preference information from your students in advance of meeting with them, or at the beginning of a series of meetings, might prove useful in selecting the types of material to incorporate into your session(s) with that group.

2. A Practical Application. Once you have completed the Self-Test below, select three of the styles on the test. Design an instructional situation that would accommodate people who differ within each of these three styles. For example, how would you incorporate material that would appeal to the visual, auditory, or psychomotor learners? What kind of material or activity would appeal to a reflective and what kind to an impulsive? How could you design your teaching environment to accommodate various responses to environmental factors? Keep in mind that many of our encounters with learners are limited to 50–70 minutes. However, you are not limited to these face to face experiences. Try to think of alternative modes of presentation that may not require in-person contact with the student. Many of our learners benefit from these on-their-own interactions with the topics to be learned.

Figure 4–1
Determine Your Style—A Self-Test

Learning styles are characteristic cognitive, affective, and physiological behaviors that serve as relatively stable indicators of how learners perceive, interact with, and respond to the learning environment. Determine your own personal learning style by using the definitions that are provided in Chapter 4 and then selecting how each style relates to you. Pick visual, auditory, or psychomotor as your modality preference and then circle where you feel you fall on each of the remaining continua.

Cognitive Styles

	Visual		Auditory		Psychomotor		
Perceptual modality preferences							
Field independence	1	2	3	4	5	6	Field dependence
Constricted	1	2	3	4	5	6	Flexible
Tolerance for incongruous or unrealistic experiences	1	2	3	4	5	6	Intolerance for incongruous or unrealistic experiences
Reflective	1	2	3	4	5	6	Impulsive
Abstract	1	2	3	4	5	6	Concrete
Innovator	1	2	3	4	5	6	Adapter
Broad	1	2	3	4	5	6	Narrow
Leveling	1	2	3	4	5	6	Sharpening
Converging	1	2	3	4	5	6	Diverging
Serialist	1	2	3	4	5	6	Holistic

Figure 4-1 (cont.)

Affective Styles

Needs structure	1	2	3	4	5	6	Does not need structure
High curiosity	1	2	3	4	5	6	Low curiosity
High perseverance	1	2	3	4	5	6	Low perseverance
High frustration tolerance	1	2	3	4	5	6	Low frustration tolerance
Highly anxious	1	2	3	4	5	6	Low anxiety
Internal locus of control	1	2	3	4	5	6	External locus of control
Intrinsically motivated	1	2	3	4	5	6	Extrinsically motivated
Risk taking	1	2	3	4	5	6	Cautious
Competition	1	2	3	4	5	6	Cooperation

Physiological Styles

Feminine traits	1	2	3	4	5	6	Masculine traits
Good health	1	2	3	4	5	6	Poor health
Morning person	1	2	3	4	5	6	Evening/night person
High need for mobility	1	2	3	4	5	6	Low need for mobility
High tolerance of environmental factors (noise, light, temperature)	1	2	3	4	5	6	Low tolerance of environmental factors (noise, light, temperature)
Left brain	1	2	3	4	5	6	Right brain

READ MORE ABOUT IT

The styles discussed in this chapter do not represent all the possibilities that have been hypothesized and studied. They do, however, include the ones that seem to turn up most often in the literature. A vast quantity of research has been performed to analyze the characteristics of each style and to validate their ability to predict behavior. In some cases, various similar styles are grouped into broader categories. If you are interested in reading more about learning styles, try looking at some of the following books and articles.

Barbe, Walter Burke, and Raymond H. Swassing. 1988. *Teaching Through Modality Strengths: Concepts and Practices.* Columbus, OH: Zaner-Bloser Inc.

Crozier, W. Ray. 1997. *Individual Learners: Personality Differences in Education.* London: Routledge.

Ford, Nigel. 1990. "Learning Styles, Strategies and Stages." In *User Education in Academic Libraries,* edited by Hugh Fleming. London: Library Association.

Keefe, James. W. 1987. *Learning Style: Theory and Practice.* Reston, VA: National Association of Secondary School Principles.

Rayner, Stephen, and Richard Riding. 1997. "Toward a Categorization of Cognitive Styles and Learning Styles." *Educational Psychology* 17 no. 1/2:5–27.

Sadler-Smith, Eugene. 1997. "Learning Style: Frameworks and Instruments." *Educational Psychology* 17 no. 1/2: 51–63.

Schmeck, Ronald R., ed. 1998. *Learning Strategies and Learning.* New York: Plenum.

Sims, Ronald R., and Serbrenia J. Sims, eds. 1995. *The Importance of Learning Styles.* Westport, CT: Greenwood Press.

Stahl, Steven A. 1999. "Different Strokes for Different Folks: A Critique of Learning Styles." *American Educator* 23 no. 3:27–31.

Sternberg, Robert. J. 1997. *Thinking Styles.* Cambridge, UK; New York: Cambridge University Press.

5

Library Anxiety, Mental Models, and Conceptual Frameworks

The Library defends itself, immeasurable as the truth it houses, deceitful as the
falsehood it preserves. A spiritual labyrinth, it is also a terrestrial labyrinth.
You might enter and you might not emerge. . . .
             —Umberto Eco, *The Name of the Rose*

LIBRARY ANXIETY: WHAT AND WHY?

Fear, unease, apprehension, panic—these are words long used to describe feelings about using libraries and library resources. Why? What
could be better, more useful, and more rewarding than using a library
and its resources to identify and locate information? Lots of things, as it
turns out, because library anxiety, melded into anxiety about computers and technology in general, are overwhelming to some.

Who or what is to blame for library anxiety, and what can be done
about it? The term "librarian" was first used in 1713 to mean "the keeper
or custodian of a library." That is, a "guardian," someone who watches
carefully over an item and may or may not let others near it (*Oxford
English Dictionary*, 1989). Today, IL librarians work hard to get across to
users that we are guides and helpers, and that libraries are incredible
gateways to knowledge. Contrast the positive image of Giles, the high
school librarian in the television show *Buffy the Vampire Slayer*, with

Malachi, the librarian in *The Name of the Rose* (DeCandido, 1999; Eco, 1983). Malachi was an extreme caricature of a book custodian. He alone knew all of the library's secrets, which books it contained, what was in each book, and where the books were located. It was in his best interest that few knew how to read and that he had the authority to decide who could read which books, for information was power then as it is now. Giles, on the other hand, is Buffy's protector. His job is to teach her what she needs to know in order to kill vampires and other creatures, and he figures out what to tell her by reading library books.

This is a major improvement in the image of the librarian. But even before technology "mutated" libraries, libraries still seemed like secretive, mysterious, and anxiety-producing places. As the detective, William of Baskerville, did in *The Name of the Rose*, the general public has had to locate a series of confusing codes, decipher them, and then wend their way through mazes, going around or backtracking when reaching "blank walls" or "mirrors." They needed a lot of help navigating the "system" even then, and often had trouble remembering underlying principles and structures. Users have encountered similar problems with card catalogs since Otis Hall Robinson first devised a model for them in the late nineteenth century, though they may not have realized what they were missing as they searched (Rochester, University of, Library, 1978).

Card catalogs were deceptively simple to use and seemed very similar to one another. As users saw them, they simply required the ability to read, to know the alphabet, to flip through cards, and to find either known items by author or title, or matches to topics (search by subject). One study of both academic and public library card catalog users found that " . . . almost half the users who failed in their first attempt [to find a known item] gave up the search" (Tagliacozzo and Kochen, 1970:375). About 75 percent of card catalog subject searches were successful, though the authors define "successful" as an exact or a partial match to the query term. This means that one-quarter of the time, users were not finding any matches and that some unknown percentage of the 75 percent success rate were only partial matches. Tagliacozzo and Kochen go so far as to say that " . . . at times the user's behavior appeared to be more the result of trial and error than of accurate planning" (1970:374). They also point out that " . . . almost half the users who failed in their first attempt [at a known item search] gave up the search" (1970: 375).These are good indications that while some may have grasped fully concepts such as controlled vocabulary and chronological filing of historical topics, for others it was blind luck that they were able to use a card catalog to identify desired library materials.

In her 1986 study of library anxiety, Connie Mellon stated that 75–

85 percent of library users she studied felt anxiety when using the library. She reported that library size, lack of knowledge of physical locations, and not knowing where to begin or what to do were significant factors in determining levels of library anxiety. Three key points emerged from her study:

1) students generally feel that their own library-use skills are inadequate, while the skills of other students are adequate,
2) the inadequacy is shameful and should be hidden, and
3) the inadequacy would be revealed by asking questions. (1986: 160)

Keefer's 1993 research reinforced Mellon's findings, indicating that "details" or physical logistics such as call numbers and stacks with rows of materials can also throw users and add to anxiety levels (1993: 336–37).

Relationship to Technophobia

Since Mellon's study, and increasingly since Keefer's study, technology has had an enormous impact on libraries, exacerbating the problem of library anxiety by making libraries much less standardized, much more complex in terms of navigating various formats of materials, and therefore even more anxiety-provoking than before. Difficult as the information-seeking process may have seemed at the time, few people suffered from "card-catalog-phobia," as card catalogs seemed fairly similar in most libraries. OPACs and other electronic tools, on the other hand, are more likely to seem different rather than similar, especially to naive users, and add the dimension of "computerphobia" to existing library anxiety.

In fact, computerphobia is a widespread phenomenon, even in the most technologically sophisticated countries (Weil and Rosen, 1997). It adds a layer of dread and distress to the angst many people already feel when attempting to use library resources in person or virtually, and can discourage library use more than ever. Now, in addition to the factors noted above, library anxiety can be caused by feelings of being overwhelmed by the size and number of information resources available via the library, feelings of inadequacy in knowing about likely sources of information to meet needs, and feelings of low self-esteem due to unintentional (or intentional) intimidation by library staff or being ignored because of low levels of computer skills. When the Web and technophobia are added to the library anxiety mix, when, as Clifford Lynch puts it, "The information seeker is faced with an assault by an overwhelmingly rich array of incoherent information and events" (1998), anxiety levels can reach a point of no return where users simply give up and leave the library or the system in frustration and/or despair. In these circumstances, it is not surprising that some former library users may turn to bookstores to meet their needs instead, assuming they can afford to do so and assuming that bookstores are located in fairly close proximity. This could be one explanation for the appearance of an *American Libraries* article in the late 1990s favorably comparing bookstores to libraries (Coffman, 1998). After all, when you need to find something in a bookstore, generally you do not look it up yourself. You ask at an information desk and someone else looks it up for you. Often a bookstore employee will also get the book for you or take you right to it, or order it for you, assuming the book is still in print. Of course you are quite limited in selection to books still in print and bookstores generally do not make efforts to acquire materials representing a variety of viewpoints. And the bookstore's primary goal is simply to sell as many books as they can, as quickly as possible. In order to do so, bookstores try to make their physical environment comfortable, attractive, and low-key. Shelves are labeled with large signs and materials are often grouped in broad general categories. Libraries, on the other hand, utilize call numbers to group like items together on shelves and require users to identify materials and call numbers on their own. This alone is quite anxiety-provoking and can be quite frustrating as well.

What Can We Do To Alleviate Library Anxiety?

Do you remember how it felt to be anxious about using a library and its resources? How can we help people feel empowered and less anxious about using libraries and library resources? Effective teaching requires an understanding of the state of mind (affective state) of the learners. It can be useful for ILI librarians to relive the insecure and fearful feelings common to those exposed to new devices, new technology, or new ways of doing things. Cerise Oberman's "Petals Around a Rose" exercise (1980), while intended to teach problem solving, can serve as a reminder of the feelings that arise when one does not know where to begin or what to do. Some people figure out where to begin or what to do quickly, while for others it becomes a panicky and embarrassing situation as they become stressed and anxious and see themselves as dumb or lagging behind everyone else.

These are the very same feelings users seem to have when they cannot figure out how to use libraries and computerized library systems. How do we help alleviate anxiety about using library resources and technology? Mellon's study of the literature indicated that "acknowledging the anxiety and its legitimacy, and then providing successful experiences to counteract the anxiety, is the most effective method for treatment" (1986: 163). Weil and Rosen affirm this recommendation by asking readers of their book to self-identify their "Techno-Type" and their feelings about technology and then exercising their own control over technology in their lives and how to make the most of it (1997: 15–17). An interesting 1998 research study showed that "Computer experience was . . . found to have a significant effect on computer confidence," and that this effect increased when users were exposed to computers both in school and at home. The same study found that people tend to become more self-confident and have more positive attitudes about computers when they are in control, when they can proceed at their own pace, and they can work from simpler to more complex programs (Levine and Donitsa-Schmidt, 1998: 139). This says much for the value of staged, sequenced, self-paced instruction; that is, providing anxious and less computer-savvy learners with the option of a linear approach.

Whatever the approach, the instructor's attitude and manner is all important. Intimidating trainers can have a negative effect on anxiety levels of computer users who are even slightly technophobic. It is important for technophobes to find friendly trainers, to work in pairs, not to be embarrassed about asking questions, and to be able to repeat tasks before moving on (Brosnan, 1998).

Keefer, too, states that it is important for the instruction librarian to acknowledge a library user's anxiety and make it clear that such anxiety is common. As she puts it, "Lectures and instruction programs that let students know that everybody experiences anxiety and that asking for help is an important part of the search process can go a long way toward making students' initial library experiences less stressful" (1993: 337).

In group instruction, one way to help decrease library anxiety is to use an overhead projector or a PowerPoint presentation to show the progressive stages that Kuhlthau says we all go through in performing library-related research: uncertainty, optimism, confusion/frustration/doubt, clarity, sense of direction/confidence, and relief/sense of satisfaction or dissatisfaction (1985). If you ask for a show of hands for each stage, and acknowledge having the same feelings yourself, learners will see that they are not the only ones who feel anxious about doing research. In fact, quite often learners will then visibly relax and seem able to absorb skills and concepts more readily. On a more basic level, a friendly smile, encouragement, and reassurance can also go a long way toward alleviating this sort of anxiety.

Signage, too, can have a positive or negative effect on library anxiety. Kupersmith suggests that positive, friendly signage with good use of graphics and color schemes can alleviate anxiety (1987). He also recommends a positive rather than a negative approach for example, instead of a sign that reads "No loud noise!" or "Shh," Kupersmith recommends using a sign that says "Quiet, please." In addition to relieving anxiety, this friendlier approach can also help in counteracting the negative image of the librarian as guardian of materials and the physical plant (Kupersmith, 1984). To extend this friendly concept further, libraries might consider labeling the beginning of each call number area in their book stacks with some broad subject categories, for example, "BF=Psychology." Libraries might also consider posting enlarged copies of the broad classification scheme in key areas in their book stacks. User-friendly point-of-use guides, handouts, tutorials, and self-paced workbooks or exercises can also help people feel more comfortable about using a library and its resources.

In general, our goal is to alleviate library anxiety, to make the library and information tools and resources more understandable so that the research process becomes more efficient and effective, and less frustrating. Another effective way to do this is to help learners discover the organizational structures underlying abstract concepts by using conceptual frameworks and analogies to draw parallels between previous concrete experiences and new abstract ones.

MENTAL MODELS AND CONCEPTUAL FRAMEWORKS

What do learners really know about information resources and libraries and how they operate? How much do they know about research strategy, and, in fact, how much do they need to know in order to make effective and efficient use of information resources in the search and evaluation process? What is the best way to help learners understand and assimilate abstract concepts and apply them to new situations? These perennial questions have bedeviled teachers and trainers at all levels and in many different disciplines.

As we noted in Chapter 3, there is evidence to support the Cognitive Psychology view that it is easier for people to learn something new if you relate it to something they already know (Ausubel, 1960, 1977; Ausubel, Novak, and Hanesion, 1978). Externally presented conceptual frameworks like controlled vocabularies can help explain what experts or designers had in mind in constructing systems and products. Mental models research can unearth users' internal views, the ways that users view the operation of these same systems and products. Sometimes this sort of research reveals that external conceptual and internal mental models for the same process can be worlds apart.

What are "mental models"? The phrase "mental model" is somewhat ambiguous, according to the *Encyclopedia of Psychology*, as the word "model" in this phrase can have two different meanings: " . . . a model as a miniature of a real-world object or system . . . and a model as a theory that generates predictions" (American Psychological Association, 2000: 191). Successful ILI can help people construct more accurate mental models of real-world systems such as "Cambridge Scientific Abstracts" or "Lexis-Nexis Academic Universe" in order to predict how other online systems will operate.

Altering Mental Models

Do people's mental models change, and if so, how difficult is it to help the process along? According to some researchers, mental models can and do evolve quite naturally, while according to others they may be quite resistant to change or even totally unaware of the fact that they should even consider change (Kruger and Dunning, 1999). For example, Donald Norman, a psychologist who has worked with the Apple Corporation on user interface design, states that, "A person, through interaction with the system, will continue to modify the mental model in order to get to a workable result" (1983: 7). According to Norman, it is fairly common for mental models to be technically inaccurate, and for people to forget the details of systems if they use them infrequently, to confuse similar devices and operations with each other, and to do extra physical work in order to avoid extra mental effort that would save physical work in the long run. It is not surprising, therefore, that ILI may not seem to "take" completely in group instruction, at a reference desk, or in remote learning situations.

Actually, concern about this problem is not limited to information literacy. A study of college physics students indicated that many had preconceptions about basic aspects of mechanics, such as the relationship between force and motion, and that these misconceptions often persisted following instruction. The author of this study saw this not as an obstacle, however, but as an advantage. He commended the fact that students had at least thought about the problem enough to construct their own "micro-theories" that actually worked in some cases, even though they were basically inaccurate. He saw this as an opportunity to get the learners to alter their theories on their own and accomplished this alteration in group instruction by posing questions asking students to predict the outcome of certain actions, or by pairing students to discuss and together make predictions (Clement, 1983). Clement's techniques for altering incorrect mental models such as this can be highly useful in ILI as well. (See Chapter 13 for detailed discussion of teaching techniques in group settings.)

Users of libraries and information resources operate under many misconceptions or incorrect mental models, and may even be unaware of their own lack of understanding (Kruger and Dunning, 1999). At the reference desk, for example, librarians encounter users who think that "RM" at the beginning of a Library of Congress call number stands for "Room" and that the number that follows is a room number. Other users may search for periodical articles in an OPAC (online library catalog), or in a separate list of periodical title subscriptions, rather than an article index. One user even asked a reference librarian, "Do you have a list of all the books I've ever read?" (Jeng, 2000). While you may discover some faulty mental models through reference questions, pre-testing prior to instruction can be more effective in revealing misconceptions and faulty mental models. For example, an objective-type pre-test question might ask where to look up scholarly articles on the topic of "interracial dating," with five alternative choices including "Sociological Abstracts" and the library's catalog. If learners pick the library catalog instead of "Sociological Abstracts," they probably think, incorrectly, that scholarly articles are listed in the catalog.

Once muddled mental models like this have been identified, the next step is to help users alter their misconceptions by focusing instruction on areas of greatest confusion. One effective approach is to identify broad stroke conceptual frameworks and use analogies to describe and explain them (Dagher, 1995). The research process lends itself quite well to this approach, for despite the red herring generated by massive and unfiltered Web information overload and other new forms of communication, basic IL research procedures and underlying structures and methods still remain remarkably similar to those used for decades.

Example: Basic Research Process

Generally, people conduct research for the purpose of scholarly investigation, creation of information, business, organization and government needs, or personal interest. Almost anything can be the subject of research. It can include: printed, computerized, audio, video, or daily life functions, music, animals, plants, physical structures such as sculptures, paintings, buildings, or cognitive structures, or activities including learning, thinking, memorizing, evaluating, writing, and speaking. Even garbage has been the subject of research (Cote, McCullough, and Reilly, 1985). Research "publications" can be divided roughly into original, primary works (including research studies, raw data, and personal "vanity" items), secondary studies or materials, or some mixture of the two. Different disciplines, of course, may define "primary" and "secondary" differently, and avenues of "publication" or creation of primary and secondary resources, as well as access, may differ. However they are defined, these materials now appear in a larger variety of formats, including print and electronic. Electronic materials themselves may be broken down into numerous subsets, such as CD-ROMs, streaming video and audio, static and interactive Web pages, databases, e-journals, and more. Whatever the format, the process of information literacy-related research still often follows these steps:

The researcher . . .

1. Becomes interested in and selects a topic, broad or narrow
2. Attempts to identify relevant information by using a variety of information resources, including people and citation trails, as well as other more traditional tools
3. Attempts to locate some or all of the information identified in step 2
4. May adjust or abandon her/his topic in favor of a new or modified one
5. Attempts to absorb, analyze, or review some or all of the information located in step 3
6. Again, may adjust or abandon her/his topic in favor of a new or modified one
7. Attempts to utilize some or all of this information to answer an information need
8. May present findings to others or utilize them for her/his own purposes

Using Analogies for Conceptual Frameworks

Understanding externally presented conceptual frameworks can help researchers save time and effort, and uncover important and relevant information. For example, when researchers understand what controlled vocabulary is and how it works in research tools, they can search more efficiently and effectively by making use of subject headings or descriptors and thesauri. How can the use of analogies help in this process?

In 1981, Kobelski and Reichel provided a brief history of the use of conceptual frameworks that helped learners understand underlying structures and identified seven types of concepts that would lend themselves to analogies useful in library instruction. In twelve chapters of Reichel and Ramey's 1987 book, contributors identified conceptual frameworks useful in teaching library instruction for specific disciplines. The goal was to teach at a higher level by focusing on underlying concepts both for reference sources and for research in various disciplines rather than what was commonplace at the time, teaching the mechanics of using reference sources, general and specific (1981).

In 1987, the idea of teaching conceptual frameworks and using analogies to do so was quite a revolutionary intellectual leap for the field of library instruction and has had enormous impact on ILI ever since, as analogies have increasingly been used to get these concepts across. Analogies are sprinkled throughout the ACRL Instruction Section's *Designs for Active Learning* (Gradowski, Snavely, and Dempsey, 1998). For example, Randy Burke Hensley and Elizabeth Hanson's "Question Analysis for Autobiography" uses "the analogy of human memory as a database . . . to teach students how to develop a controlled vocabulary . . . " (1998: 55–56). Loanne Snavely's "Teaching Boolean Operators in a Flash Using a Deck of Cards" is another good example of this technique (1998) , and BI-L messages on this topic generate much discussion (Murrell, 1996).

Most of the analogies described in these publications and in BI-L messages are verbal or written and describe concrete activities or processes, but effective conceptual models can be visual as well. The known item "research pyramid" is a visual representation of one approach that reference librarians use to help locate materials. They begin by searching the local OPAC or other licensed databases, then proceed to a broader regional library catalog (for example, the University of California's California Digital Library "MELVYL™ Catalog"), and from there to an even broader national catalog (for example, OCLC's "WorldCat"). The search strategy hourglass is another graphic representation of a concept. It starts with an unfocused topic, proceeds through the resource-filtering process to a narrowed topic, then broadens to examine selected materials more closely, and then broadens further to develop and communicate results (Kennedy, 1974). The hourglass depicts a series of steps in the research process, from topic selection, topic modification, and data collection, to synthesis and presentation, or submission of research results. Coincidentally, this hourglass diagram also meets Tufte's criteria for excellent graphic representation of data (see Chapter 11), as in and of itself the hourglass clearly conveys the message that research is a process and that it takes time to complete (Tufte, 1983).

Interestingly, analogies have been used in teaching all kinds of concepts in many different fields, especially in science education for children. For example, Mason's study used cake making as an analogy for photosynthesis (1994). Newby conducted two controlled studies of the use of instructional analogies in teaching advanced physiological concepts. Results of his first study of 161 college students " . . . indicate, first and foremost, that the use of analogies may significantly improve learners' ability to identify and comprehend the application of concepts" (1995:12), and also showed that recall and recognition of new concepts improved when analogies were used.

Components of Effective Analogical Reasoning

Teaching and learning by means of analogies, graphic or text, sounds like a quick, easy, and attention-getting means of helping people alter inaccurate mental models. There is more to this process, however, than first meets the eye. Researchers have identified seven independent components of analogical reasoning, most important of which are "encoding" (understanding the terms and attributes of "each end" of the analogy), "inference" (discovering the relationship between the main subjects of the analogy), and "application" (applying what they learned in the "inference" stage in order to "solve" the analogy) (Dagher, 1995). In other words, researchers caution us first to make sure that everyone understands what the supposedly familiar end of the analogy is and which features of it you will be focusing on before using it to explain a new abstract concept at the other end (Iding, 1997; Mason, 1994). So, for example, if you are using the analogy of original versions of songs as opposed to "cover versions" to explain the difference between primary and secondary sources, you will need to make sure that everyone understands that "cover versions" are songs sung by an artist other than the original artist and released at a later date.

Second, you need to be careful to help users understand the relationships you are trying to establish through analogies. For example, learners may need a bit of explanation or introduction before understanding the analogy of product grouping in supermarkets (produce, dairy, fresh meats, and fish) as compared to controlled vocabularies used in article indexes. If you use this analogy, you would ask the learners to tell you where supermarkets put yogurt and milk. The answer is the "dairy" section. Why? Supermarkets try to make it easier for customers to find products by grouping like items together so that you will not have to guess where items are and wander all over the store looking for them. Similarly, controlled vocabularies group like items together to save you time and to help you identify useful items on the same or related topics.

Third, research indicates that thinking about the process of using a concrete analogy to understand an abstract concept, and then discussing it in an interactive small group setting or "constructivist learning environment," can be highly effective. In other words, using metacognition, " . . . the inner awareness or ability to reflect on what and when, how and why, one knows" (Mason, 1994: 268), in a give-and-take synchronous environment helps learners understand how an analogy can help or hinder their understanding of a concept and can help them alter their own internal mental models, thereby integrating the new information. Hofstadter goes so far as to say that all human learning is based on analogy. Babies slowly build frames of reference, chunking experiences and comparing new experiences to older ones. Older people categorize or chunk experiences more quickly because they have more prior experiences with which to compare a new experience (Hofstadter, 2000).

In ILI, in fact, small- and large-group exercises constitute an important means of learning new concepts by analogy. Do conceptual frameworks still constitute an effective means of helping users adopt correct mental models about IL tools and approaches? What can we add to or take away from this list, and what are some effective means of utilizing a variety of conceptual models?

Examples of Analogies

PUBLICATION SEQUENCE

ILI librarians have used many of Kobelski and Reichel's concepts effectively since their publication in 1981. Some, like "Publication Sequence," have translated quite well to the Web. For example, the "Flow of Information" Website is based on Sharon Hogan's 1980 concept that describes how events are documented in stages through various forms of "publication," beginning with the first occurrence and proceeding through discussion, analysis, and summary or condensed reporting (Zwemer, 2000). You can teach the flow of information in an interactive large group exercise, in-person, and then refer learners to the Website for reinforcement. Only time will tell if this concept will continue to serve as a valid instructional approach, given the scholarly communication effort to bypass traditional journal publishers in favor of direct publishing on the Web by libraries and researchers. SPARC (The Scholarly Publishing and Academic Resources Coalition), for example, " . . . creates 'partnerships' with publishers who are developing high-quality, economical alternatives to existing high-price publications . . . [in order to] create a more competitive marketplace . . . ensure fair use . . . [and] apply technology to improve the process of scholarly communication and to reduce the costs of production and distribution" (SPARC, 1999).

TYPES OF REFERENCE TOOLS

The University of California, Santa Cruz's "Net Trail" offers another example of how to use the Web to teach an instructional concept. This site reflects Kobelski and Reichel's "Type of Reference Tool" concept using the analogy of a biking or hiking trail to take users to four modules that focus on specific types of Internet tools or uses. For example,

"Web Browsing," "Using E-mail," "Library Resources," and "Newsgroups" (University of California, Santa Cruz, 1998). Sites like this can be effective, especially if designed as independent modules where learners can "test out of" specific segments and can skip around, picking and choosing what they want to learn. Self-paced workbooks, both paper and electronic, often take a reference tools approach and also allow learners to skip around and select what they want to learn when they want to learn it. Again, Kobelski and Reichel's "Type of Reference Tool" concept may become less significant as Web-based information tools and resources merge, link with, and become more like one another—at least outwardly—just as many Web directories and search engines now have a number of common features.

Some wonder whether or not we should continue to teach information research as a linear process (Kobelski and Reichel's "Systematic Literature Searching") often described in terms of the following steps:

1. Define terms
2. Use encyclopedias to locate overviews
3. Use catalogs and bibliographies to find books
4. Use article indexes to identify and locate current information
5. Use Web search tools to find additional current information
6. Review materials, evaluate, and then write paper

Shippensburg University of Pennsylvania has created an overall Web-based interactive guide to the research process that does just this (n.d.). Will it appeal to all learners? Probably not, but as we discussed in Chapter 3, people learn differently. Some prefer to take a linear approach, while others like to skip around or just select the segments that interest them. The Web offers us the opportunity to help people see the linear approach, yet decide on their own where they would like to start and how they would like to proceed, particularly if Websites include site maps.

INFORMAL VERSUS FORMAL NETWORKS

ILI librarians have also applied a number of other important concepts in ILI. Greenfield's informal versus formal networks concept describes personal contacts and information shared at conferences, programs, meetings, and otherwise, as opposed to published materials that have been reviewed (1987). Informal "networks" that utilize e-mail, listservs, Newsgroups, chat, instant messaging, class discussion boards, and other Internet-based technology now constitute an important, though informal, part of the information development sequence. You can help people understand this concept by comparing it to gossip during coffee breaks as opposed to official announcements by administrators.

POPULAR VERSUS SCHOLARLY ARTICLES

Learners are still confused about the differences between popular and scholarly articles, another important teaching/learning concept (Greenfield, 1987). Bechtel suggests that we teach this concept by comparing academic communication to a series of conversations. In her powerful and eloquent article, Bechtel argues that the role of the librarian is, in fact, closely tied to the intellectual "conversation" that constitutes higher education. She sees ILI librarians helping learners understand what the various conversations are, who is participating in them, how to evaluate the quality of their participation, and how to "make a significant comment on the issue or problem" (Bechtel, 1986: 223). Using this analogy, popular magazine articles are then similar to an informal conversation between two people who simply express their opinions on a topic. Journal articles, on the other hand, have a particular structure and support their "conversations" or "arguments" with evidence in the form of research data, studies, and other publications. How does this translate to the Web environment? We often deplore the "mushpot" nature of the Web, but we can actually use the miscellaneous and unfiltered nature of the Web to teach this concept as well. You can draw analogies between vanity Web pages (popular material) as opposed to sites created, reviewed, and mounted by reputable publishers, institutions, or organizations, with research purposes in mind (UCLA College Library, 2000).

MECHANICS OF USE

In 1987, Lippincott identified a number of important conceptual frameworks for ILI, including mechanics of use. As we add each new information tool and upgrade to new versions of existing tools, teaching the basic mechanics of use increases in importance. The problem is that we are drowning not only in tools (and the information itself), but also in unique interfaces to those tools. We cannot possibly help everyone learn all aspects of every information tool, so we must step back and teach common features using a few examples of the bare basics. We must keep our focus on our underlying goal: helping people learn how to learn. What does this mean in practical terms? You must balance, balance, and balance again. Pare down until you reach the core of what people need to know in order to function at a minimal IL level. Teach concepts, but also mechanics, to illustrate those concepts and try to incorporate critical thinking throughout. For example, instead of helping people learn all of the different ways to search an online catalog, use the simplest approach that will get across an important concept. By using a keyword-to-subject search tactic, for example, users learn a practical approach to focusing a search, and at the same time gain a better understanding of the concept of controlled vocabulary.

The age and skill level of the learners, as well as the learning time they have available, may dictate what constitutes "the basics" in a particular environment. It may also influence your decisions about the best means of helping them learn as well. For example, very inexperienced computer users with just fifty minutes to spare may learn better in-person with one-on-one, hands-on instruction. Conversely, remote synchronous or asynchronous instruction via the Web may be most effective for those who are interested in and comfortable with technology, as well as those who want to learn it only when necessary to do so. (See Chapters 8 and 9 on selecting modes of instruction, and Chapter 16 on teaching technology.)

Learning to drive a car is an effective analogy for learning to use electronic information systems. If you want to learn how to drive a car, you have to drive it yourself. Watching someone else drive is useful, but you cannot learn to drive just by watching. Driving a car is really scary at first, but after a while it becomes second nature. In fact, it is very easy to forget how overwhelming and terrifying the entire process can be for a new driver. The same is true for newbies, those who are new to using computers. It really helps to remind people about these affective aspects of learning anything new.

SETS

Lippincott described four other useful teaching concepts: "Sets," "Bibliographic Record," "Controlled Vocabulary/Free Text Terms," and "Boolean Operators." Each of these concepts has grown in importance in the technological age, and you can use analogies to teach them all. For example, the concept of "Sets" helps people learn how to divide a topic into component parts in order to develop an effective search strategy, or to narrow or broaden a search. Useful analogies for this concept include:

1. Learning how to bake a cake by following a recipe that groups certain activities together—for example, sift the flour with the salt; cream butter and sugar together; add eggs to creamed mixture; measure liquid, and then alternate adding flour and liquid to egg mixture, 1/3 at a time (See also Grassian, 2000b, 2000c).

2. A set is similar to pasta with different kinds of pasta, such as linguini and elbow macaroni, as subsets (Guyonneau, 1996).
3. The "Building Blocks" approach breaks a topic into its parts, searches each part separately, and then puts various parts together to "build" a search that will provide the most relevant results (Markey and Cochrane, 1981).
4. The "Successive Fractions" analogy takes an approach opposite to "Building Blocks" analogy. You keep limiting a broad search until you end up with a "fraction" of your first search, which consists of those results most relevant to your topic (Markey and Cochrane, 1981).

MILKING THE BIBLIOGRAPHIC RECORD

Lippincott's "Bibliographic Record" concept helps people learn about the types of information provided about single items and how they may be "milked" in order to evaluate or filter for the most useful materials, as well as to find additional materials on the same topic.

A useful analogy for this concept is that you *can* tell some things about a book by its cover. Learners look at a list of citations for several items on the same topic and, simply by examining these citations, may be able to eliminate some or target others for closer inspection. For example, if you look closely at the author, publisher, title, and publication dates in a citation, as well as the length of an item, you may be able to identify which sources would be the most promising. If you open the book and read the introduction, you can probably shrink the number of promising results even further. In milking the bibliographic record, the equivalent would be reading the abstract for an item, if an abstract is provided. You can take this a step further by looking at the table of contents of a book, or by examining the subject headings in the bibliographic record to determine if the item is on target for your information need. You may also use these subject headings to focus your search, using the "TRACE" search tactic, an analogy to tracing your steps (Bates, 1979).

THE RESEARCH PROCESS

"Citation Pearl-Growing" and "Berry Picking" are other useful analogies for the research process. The former suggests that by utilizing descriptors of just a few useful citations as you search you can build a valuable "pearl" of search terms and additional citations relevant to your research topic (Markey and Cochrane, 1981). The latter describes real-life information searching as "an evolving search," similar to picking berries in a forest: one by one rather than in a bunch. When searching for information on a topic, users often shift their approach rather than finding and using only a single set of results that perfectly match their query within a particular system. Instead, researchers gather citations here and there as they go, and may use a number of other searching techniques and sources as well (Bates, 1989).

In the online world, doing research on the Net is like panning for gold—small gold nuggets and flakes are buried in rivers of mud. Like a gold prospector, to improve your take you can change location, tools, or techniques (Lawson, 1996).

Databases, Online Databases, Online Systems

Does your library subscribe to ten, twenty, or a hundred or more databases or systems, many with their own interfaces? If so, learning these search concepts can help learners become powerful information users, rather than people who are tossed here and there in the information gale. Put quite simply, a database is an organized collection of information, like the Yellow Pages or a baseball card collection organized by team. Placing the database's information into a computer's memory (with a means of searching and displaying results) turns it into an online database. Online systems are collections of online databases, like file cabinets with folders, which in turn may contain more folders. These folders, then, contain papers on specific topics. We often assume, quite wrongly, that these definitions are common knowledge, yet they are important for basic understanding of the electronic environment.

The Right Information Source/Tool for the Right Purpose

Picking among a myriad of Web search tools, licensed and unlicensed online databases, and print information sources can be an overwhelming task. Web search tools alone can differ widely from one another, particularly in their means of gathering, organizing, searching, and displaying data. They may also differ in terms of any behind-the-scenes relevancy ranking (algorithm) they utilize, as well as their commercial nature. For example, a *Los Angeles Times* article published in October 2000 revealed that AltaVista " . . . charg[es] fees for prominently displayed listings in search results . . . [and] has about 1,000 license agreements worth an average of $100,000 apiece" (Liedtke, 2000: 8). In discussing content—that is, what the search tool is searching—it is useful to draw a further distinction between Web search tool databases and licensed as well as unlicensed (free) databases. (See Chapter 16 for more detail on teaching technology.) This distinction goes hand-in-hand with an understanding of how Web search tools differ and also helps users distinguish among online databases and online systems. Useful analogies for this concept include:

1. Choosing the right index is like choosing a radio station (University of Arizona Library, 2001).

2. Selecting a database useful for a particular need is like shopping in a mall, where systems such as Infotrac and Firstsearch are the anchor department stores with a large selection of many items. Specialized indexes like Medline are like boutiques that focus on a particular type of merchandise or clientele (Guyonneau, 1996).

3. Online catalogs (OPACs) and databases with the same interface and search commands are like a well-functioning family whose members "talk" to one another. External databases (CD-ROMs, licensed databases available through other systems) are the "dysfunctional" family members. We must mediate between external databases and the OPAC, because they do not "talk" to each other (Riddle, 1996b).

4. McDonald's menu lists everything they serve in that location, while the Sears catalog lists some items available in stores and others available only through the catalog. Similarly, the OPAC lists everything available in the library, while article indexes list materials that may or may not be available in that physical library location, but can be ordered through interlibrary loan, if necessary (Riddle, 1996a).

5. Article indexes are like address books that include the "name of the building" (periodical title) and the "apartment number" (volume and issue number). The OPAC is the "street map" that helps you locate the periodical in the library (Nagumo, 1997).

6. Subject-specific licensed databases (for example, PsycINFO) are like specialty shops, while licensed general article indexes are like Wal-Mart, where you can meet a variety of needs in one store (DeArmond, 1999).

7. Using Web search tools is similar to using the Yellow Pages (or paid ads) to find a restaurant as opposed to using a restaurant guidebook like the Zagat Website (purportedly objective and more inclusive), which reviews and rates restaurants.

INTERNET VERSUS WEB

Internet use is increasing daily worldwide. What does this mean? Many people equate the Web and the Internet, yet the Web utilizes just one of the three main functions of the Internet: File Transfer Protocol (FTP). The other two main Internet functions are e-mail and telnet. A useful analogy for the Internet is a big highway with a variety of rest-stops, including fast food, truckers' joints, and home-cooking. "You approach these different stops using different off-ramps and you may even be required to dress differently at the different stops (using different software to access different types of servers)" (Fraser-Fazakas, 1996: [online]).

THE CAVEAT EMPTOR APPROACH

Empowering the learner is the essence of ILI, and what better way to achieve this goal than to help people become critical users of information and information sources. We need to encourage a healthy questioning attitude toward information products by helping them learn to pose a series of questions, such as: "Who is the audience?" "What is the purpose of the item?" "Who sponsored, developed, and wrote the item?" or "How accurate, complete, and up to date is it?" Buying a car is a useful analogy for this concept. Do you take the salesperson's word on reliability, drivability, and long-term value? Or do you do research ahead of time and then take it for a test drive before purchasing? Graves suggests using TV as an analogy. "I saw it on TV" provides too little information. Did you see it on a cable channel? When? Which show? Was it on *60 Minutes*? On a comedy show like *Friends*? Or on a network news show? (Graves, 1997).

Placement of Conceptual Frameworks

These suggested analogies are examples of conceptual frameworks and related analogies that can be used in whole or in part in various ILI situations, utilizing a variety of formats, and placed at different points in the learning process continuum. In fact, there has been debate about the point at which to introduce conceptual models such as these. Should they be used as "advance organizers" (prior to instruction), as "embedded activators" (during instruction), or as "post synthesizers" (following instruction) (Ausubel, 1960)? One large study of analogies used in textbooks found that a majority (76 percent) appeared as embedded activators during instruction, when the content became more difficult or abstract (Curtis and Reigeluth, 1984). Other findings from this same study included the fact that 84 percent of the analogies used were verbal only (used no accompanying pictures), 82 percent used a concrete vehicle to explain an abstract topic, and 81 percent used "enriched analogies" (stated the grounds for the analogy, and possibly the limitations). Questions arise here as to the effectiveness of analogies in learning, retention, and transfer, particularly in learning abstract concepts. According to Mayer, advance organizers "seem to have their strongest positive effects not on measures of retention, but rather on measures of transfer" (Mayer, 1979: 382). And the transfer of learning through learning how to learn is really what we are after.

The Cumulative Effect on Learning

In spite of these questions and the debate about where to place analogies within a teaching/learning context, learners at all levels seem to grasp new abstract concepts such as controlled vocabularies better when they are compared to well-understood concrete analogies. Moreover, when learners think about and discuss the analogies themselves as tools for understanding concepts—that is, when they engage in metacognition, or looking at their own thinking and learning process, especially in a small group setting—the effect can be multiplied (Hacker, Dunlovsky and Graesser, 1998; Unger, 1996; Mason, 1994).

Conceptual models like these, metacognition, and the use of analogies can help users construct more accurate mental models as they begin to understand the ever-more complex, information-laden world. They encourage learners to step back and think about the resources they use and various ways of searching for and organizing information. This sort of critical thinking helps make the information-seeking process a manipulatable tool under the control of the user rather than an obstacle to be overcome or even an end in itself.

FINAL REMARKS

Many people are still anxious about libraries and library resources. Some avoid libraries because they seem overwhelming and confusing, and are afraid to ask questions. We must continue to work hard to demystify libraries and alter mental models of information tools. We need to help people by simplifying and clarifying the information-seeking process, tools, and products. We have come a long way ourselves in learning to live with, if not anticipate, the new and changing face of libraries. Now we must work harder to help bring our users along with us.

EXERCISES

1. Think of some modern-day analogies you might use to help people learn new concepts, such as Web search tools versus licensed databases.
2. Review a Web-based tutorial that does not use an analogy—for example, Shippensburg University of Pennsylvania's "Ellis Skills Tutorial" (2000)—and come up with an analogy that would work with that site's approach.

READ MORE ABOUT IT

Keefer, Jane. 1993. "The Hungry Rats Syndrome: Library Anxiety, Information Literacy, and the Academic Reference Process." *RQ* 32 no. 3: 333–39.

Kuhlthau, Carol C. 1985. "A Process Approach to Library Skills Instruction: An Investigation Into the Design of the Library Research Process." *School Library Media Quarterly* 13:35–40.

Mellon, Constance A. 1986. "Library Anxiety: A Grounded Theory and Its Development." *College & Research Libraries* 47 no. 2:160–65.

Newby, Timothy J. 1995. "Instructional Analogies and the Learning of Concepts." *Educational Technology Research and Development: ETR&D* 43 no. 1: 5–18.

Reichel, Mary, and Mary Ann Ramey, eds. 1987. *Conceptual Frameworks for Bibliographic Education: Theory into Practice*. Littleton, CO: Libraries Unlimited.

Weil, Michelle M., and Larry D. Rosen. 1997. *Technostress: Coping With Technology @Work @Home @Play*. New York: Wiley & Sons.

6

Critical Thinking
and Active Learning

Let every eye negotiate for itself, and trust no agent . . . .
—William Shakespeare, *Much Ado About Nothing*

CRITICAL THINKING

Learning to think critically is one of the most important goals of undergraduate education, and indeed lifelong learning for all learners. Like
the term "information literacy," however, "critical thinking" has been
used for many purposes and to suit many different circumstances. Research studies abound on cognitive development (see Chapter 3), stages
in the development of reasoning skills, metacognition, and how to teach
critical thinking in various disciplines and at various educational and
age levels. In a frequently cited ILI-related essay, Mona McCormick re-
minds us that it is not the process of finding information that is important, but what people do with it once they have found it. She defines
critical thinking as the ability to distinguish fact from fiction, to notice
opinion, and actually to think about whether we will accept the "facts"
and agree with the opinions to which they may or may not lead
(McCormick, 1983). McCormick is referring to thinking critically at the
item level. However, critical thinking can be broader or narrower than
that, depending on the definition of the phrase and how one wishes to
apply it. In fact, the definition of critical thinking and how it is applied
lie at the heart of the debate over who should be teaching critical think-

111

ing, with some arguing for the ILI librarian and others for the content or subject matter expert—most often teachers or faculty at schools, colleges, or universities.

What Should Librarians Teach?

Actually, both ILI librarians and course instructors have important parts in the critical thinking instruction equation. Librarians can and should teach basic, even generic, critical thinking skills applicable to almost any form of information; while subject matter experts can hone those skills and focus them on the discipline at hand (Frick, 1975; Bodi, 1988; Rankin, 1988). For example, librarians can help people learn to examine information resources for sponsorship or authorship, timeliness, form of publication, and coverage or scope in comparison to other information resources in the same field. Once learners are sensitized to watch for these criteria, the subject matter expert can step in to provide her/his opinion as to the authority of the sponsor or writer, the reputation of the publication or publisher, and the depth and breadth, as well as accuracy, of the information itself. Educators have defined critical thinking, expanded on the notion of teaching it, and provided detailed practical frameworks for teachers (Beyer, 1985a, 1985b; Munro and Slater, 1985). These definitions help, and from the discussion above we may be able to agree that critical thinking is an essential element of IL. However, we still need to distinguish both critical thinking and IL from computer literacy or technology literacy.

INFORMATION LITERACY OR TECHNOLOGY LITERACY?

Does technology literacy include critical thinking, and is technology literacy distinct from and more important than IL? Shapiro and Hughes have tried to take the concept of critical thinking a step further by including the categories of "Critical Literacy" and "Resource Literacy" among the seven categories they list as elements of a prototype information literacy curriculum: "Tool Literacy," "Resource Literacy," "Social-Structural Literacy," "Research Literacy," "Publishing Literacy," "Emerging Technology Literacy," and "Critical Literacy" (Shapiro and Hughes, 2000).

Their thoughtful analysis is an admirable step in pinning down the slippery definition of IL, as it goes a few steps beyond computer literacy and includes a historical, social, and philosophical context. Unfortunately, however, in spite of the title of their article ("Information Literacy as a Liberal Art"), they define many of the seven categories primarily in terms of electronic resources. For example, "Critical Literacy" is defined as "the ability to evaluate critically the intellectual, human and social strengths and weaknesses, potentials and limits, benefits and costs of information technology." They also argue that "'Resource Literacy,' . . . the ability to understand the form, format, location and access methods of information resources, especially daily expanding networked information resources . . . is practically identical with librarians' conceptions of information literacy . . . ."

IL Encompasses Technology Literacy and More

Actually it is not. Shapiro and Hughes's definition ignores the librarian's role in helping people learn the basics of evaluating information resources and tools. It also ignores the librarian's knowledge of a range of information resources and her/his ability to weigh their relative value and uses. Shapiro and Hughes define information literacy as follows:

> . . . information literacy should in fact be conceived . . . as a new liberal art that extends from knowing how to use computers and access information to critical reflection on the nature of information itself, its technical infrastructure, and its social, cultural and even philosophical context and impact—as essential to the mental framework of the educated information-age citizen as the trivium of basic liberal arts (grammar, logic and rhetoric) was to the educated person in medieval society. (2000: [online]).

This definition is a lot closer to librarians' definitions of IL than Shapiro and Hughes would have us believe. Ultimately, their prototype curriculum is incomplete, as it falls short even of their own broad definition of IL by focusing too narrowly on electronic resources, particularly in their definition of "critical literacy." There is much more to the evaluation or critical thinking aspect of IL than this, and the librarian has a key role in helping learners understand its basics, particularly in this Web-based world.

IL Organizations Provide Direction

In 1989, the ALA Presidential Committee on Information Literacy stated that "To be information literate, a person must be able to recognize when information is needed and have the ability to locate, evaluate and use effectively the needed information . . . Ultimately, information literate people are those who have learned how to learn" (1989: [online]). "Evaluating" and "using effectively" comprise the critical thinking elements of this definition.

Building on this definition, in the early 1990s, ACRL IS's Model Statement of Objectives for Academic Library Instruction spelled this out in detail for academic libraries as a tool for instruction librarians (ALA–Association of College and Research Libraries–Bibliographic Instruction Section, 1991). The guiding principles of this document state that evaluation was incorporated into various sections of the document, as appropriate, to reflect the fact that evaluation should occur throughout the research process. The Introduction to the revised ACRL Instruction Section's "Objectives for Information Literacy Instruction by Academic Librarians" reiterates support for the librarian's role in helping people learn critical thinking and evaluation skills:

> Many of the outcomes from the *Competency Standards* that deal explicitly with evaluation are primarily the teaching responsibility of the course instructor in collaboration with the librarian. For example, the course instructor can address the quality of the content of an information source once it is retrieved; the librarian helps people learn how to interpret information in the sources that can be used for evaluating information during the research process. As reliance on Internet sources increases, the librarian's objectivity and expertise in evaluating information and information sources become invaluable. (2000:4)

In January 2000, ALA's Association of College and Research Libraries identified specific "competencies" that learners should have in order to become critical thinking information literate individuals. "Information Literacy Competencies for Higher Education" contains five standards along with detailed "Performance Indicators" for each standard, and even more detailed "Measurable Outcomes" for each Performance Indicator. For example, Standard Three states that "The information literate student evaluates information and its sources critically and incorporates selected information into his or her knowledge base and value system" (ALA–Association of College and Research Libraries 2000: [online]). The draft ACRL Instruction Section's "Objectives for Information Literacy Instruction by Academic Librarians" provides a number of possible objectives that librarians can address to meet Standard Three. For example, to meet Performance Indicator 3.2.c. ("Recognizes prejudice, deception, or manipulation"), you might want to address the following objective: "Demonstrates an understanding that information in any format reflects an author's sponsor's and/or publisher's point of view" (ALA–Association of College and Research Libraries–Instruction Section, 2001: [online]).

The ILI Librarian's Job: To "Save the Time of the Reader"

These important publications indicate that IL promotes self-reflective thinking about how to identify, locate, evaluate, and use information. As we have seen from Chapter 2, the IL movement's focus on evaluation and critical thinking carries forward Patricia Knapp's ideals. Yet for the most part, people really do not think much about how they search for information and often settle for whatever they can get quickly and without too much trouble. They may feel too shy or embarrassed to ask for help even when they cannot find the information they need. Often, undergraduates, for example, would rather find and e-mail or print out the complete text of articles or Web pages that are somewhat close to their topics than take the time to track down call numbers, locate periodicals in a physical library, and photocopy articles, even if they are much more suited to the topic or of higher quality. This natural tendency reflects a corollary to Ranganathan's fourth law: "Save the time of the reader, or the reader will save her/his own time by taking the shortest route to information, regardless of its quality" (Ranganathan, 1978). Mann expressed this corollary as "The Principle of Least Effort," meaning that users will do whatever takes the least amount of effort, even it means more effort later or if it means they end up with poorer quality information (1993).

Who Should Teach Critical Thinking?

It is the librarian's job to help the critical thinking process become a routine and natural part of each step of the information-seeking process. To do this effectively with various age and skill levels and in varying environments, we must focus on bare-bones basics and then provide additional evaluative criteria and detail for those who want it. What are the most basic elements of critical thinking from an IL perspective?

Critical Thinking Basics

- Audience & Purpose
- Content (Relevance To the Topic) & Accuracy
- Relative Value (As Compared To Other Information Sources)
- Sponsorship/Authorship, Authority, & Bias
- Recency

These broad-stroke evaluative criteria represent the unique contribution that ILI librarians have to offer. They can be layered on top of specific subject matter at any level and can be applied to all formats of information. Librarians are best suited to introduce these critical thinking concepts to learners, as librarians have been trained to keep track of a vast range of information tools and resources and to evaluate them objectively. Ideally, the librarian would help people learn generic critical thinking criteria first, followed by the subject expert who would help people learn how to apply these criteria to the topic under study.

What is the most effective means of helping people learn to apply broad critical thinking criteria and in so doing learn to change their internal mental models of information resources, as well as the information-seeking process? Active learning techniques, both in-person and remote, can be quite effective in this endeavor.

ACTIVE LEARNING

What and Why?

What is "active learning"? Allen points out that it is a concept that dates back to the Greek Socratic method, where a teacher poses questions, students respond, and learning takes place through a back-and-forth student/teacher interchange of questions, responses, comments, and new ideas (Allen, 1995). *The Encyclopedia of American Education* reports that John Dewey first developed this technique at the University of Chicago in 1896, and called it "indirect instruction." Children in his experimental program learned reading, writing, and mathematics indirectly as they played house and learned to cut and nail wood for furniture. According to the *Encyclopedia*, Dewey's belief that children learn best through activities that interest them eventually led the 70,000-member National Council of Teachers of Mathematics to adopt pedagogical standards for active learning in 1989. (Unger, 1996).

In libraries, "active learning" is a phrase often used to describe participatory learning activities that take place in a synchronous face-to-face classroom setting, though some instructional modes, such as exercises and workbooks, are also important forms of active learning instruction, and technological advancements now provide the means by which to incorporate active learning remotely as well as in-person.

Many definitions of active learning emphasize that, at its best, it engages learners, helps them discover conceptual models, and encourages them to learn by practicing various skills, especially learning how to learn (Svinicki and Schwartz, 1988; Fink, 1989; McKeachie, 1999). As Bruner put it, "If information is to be used effectively, it must be translated into the learner's way of attempting to solve a problem. If such translatability is not present, then the information is simply useless . . . Instruction is a provisional state that has as its object to make the learner or problem solver self-sufficient" (1966: 53). Chickering takes an important step further when he says "Learning is not a spectator sport. Students do not learn much just by sitting in classes listening to teachers, memorizing pre-packaged assignments, and spitting out answers. They must talk about what they are learning, write about it, relate it to past experiences, apply it to their daily lives. They must make what they learn part of themselves" (Chickering and Ganson, 1987: 5).

Indeed, the impact of learning often intensifies when learners can also practice skills immediately and get feedback, either by following along with an instructor or by doing an exercise during or after instruction. At its most basic level, active learning simply involves having learners do something, write something, say something, play games, get up, move around, interact, and take part in learning something, as well as in thinking about their own learning rather than passively observing demonstrations or listening to facts, theories, and information about how to do something. Examples of active learning include hands-on instruction, finding answers to exercise or workbook questions, and participating in small- or large-group exercises.

When and Where?

In-class active learning exercises can occupy one or more portions of a class, an entire class session, or can even stretch over more than one class session, but you do have to plan to include them or they may not occur (Warmkessel and Crothers, 1993). Active learning exercises can be designed for small groups, large groups, pairs, individuals, or a combination of any of these, for synchronous or asynchronous use. ACRL IS's *Designs for Active Learning*, for example, contains a wealth of active learning exercises geared primarily to undergraduates and meant to be used in a synchronous in-person classroom setting, but is also adaptable for other audiences and settings as well (Gradowski, Snavely, and Dempsey, 1998). In "Structuring a Session with Questions," for example, students pair up and have three minutes to come up with three questions they would like answered regarding libraries and research. Students tend to answer each others' basic questions during the three-minute period, the librarian writes their final questions on the board, groups them into categories, and then asks attendees if they have answers to any of the questions (Mestre, 1998). This exercise could be conducted as well via a discussion board over a week's time, with pairs of students first communicating with each other via chat, and then posting their questions on the discussion board. This combined synchronous (pairs communicating with each other via chat) and asynchronous approach (posting questions on a discussion board for individual reaction) might encourage shyer students to participate more than they would in an in-person group setting. It might also attract and hold the attention of more technologically sophisticated students who may wrongly believe that technology fluency is the equivalent of IL.

Fink's *Process and Politics in Library Research* also provides excellent in-class active learning exercises at the end of each chapter. For example, the class selects a topic and students discuss how it might be approached from the perspective of different disciplines (1989). Again, many of these exercises may be adapted for use with various kinds of technology.

On a more traditional note, Bonwell recommends an "enhanced lecture," which intersperses active learning throughout a lecture. For example, he recommends "The Pause Procedure," where the instructor stops lecturing every 13 to 18 minutes and has students compare and review their notes with a partner (1996). Walker calls this technique "Bookends" and also describes another useful technique, "Pairs to Squares," a variation of "Think/Pair/Share." Each student considers a problem individually: they make notes and then pair up with another student to discuss and come to agreement on a solution to the problem. After a given time period, two pairs team up and again must discuss and come to agreement on a solution (1998).

Tiberius and Silver provide additional highly useful active learning ideas that can be used during a workshop or class. For example, if your objective is to have learners get feedback while practicing using an article index to identify useful articles on a topic, you might want to try their "Helping Trios." Divide the audience into groups of three. One person searches an article index database while a second person provides feedback. The third person observes and takes notes and may use a checklist. After finding one useful article, the observer discusses her/his observations with the other two learners. Learners switch roles until each person has had a chance to take on each of the three roles (2000).

Bransford, Brophy, and Williams suggest a learner-centered active learning exercise for courses where you meet with the same group of learners more than once over a period of time. Students experience the same "event" when the course begins and then at one or two intervals later in the course, and analyze the event each time. For example, at three intervals during a term, the authors showed a 45-minute videotape and asked students to write down what they noticed and understood about it. As students learned more about the topic during the term, their analyses deepened and they became aware of their own learning (2000). In an ILI setting, at the beginning of a term, you could have learners compare and contrast a print and a Web-based resource on a particular topic. Later in the term, you could ask them to re-examine both resources and critique their own earlier analyses, adding a new layer of observations.

In synchronous in-person group settings, active learning exercises can also be used as icebreakers at the beginning of a class session, sprinkled throughout, or as a wrap-up at the end. Even assessment can be an active learning process. Angelo and Cross's "Minute Paper" is a good example of an active learning assessment exercise (1993). At the beginning of the session, the instructor tells the group that at the end of the session they will need to write down their answers to two questions: "What was the main point of this session?" and "What is your main unanswered question?" Learners then pay careful attention throughout the session, trying to figure out what the main point is and also make note of their questions as the session proceeds. This exercise works best when you will see the same group of learners more than once so that you can respond to their unanswered questions at the next meeting. However, you can ask learners to do the "Minute Paper" orally at the end of a one-shot session as well.

To What Degree Should We Incorporate Active Learning Exercises?

Active learning exercises can be used with almost any size group in-person, though very small groups of two to ten may respond better to individual, paired, or whole-group exercises instead. How do you select among so many active learning techniques, and how many of these activities should you include in synchronous as opposed to asynchronous instruction? Your goals and objectives or expected learning outcomes should be your guide. If you have a good idea of what you want learners to know, it will be easier to decide what you want them to do in order to learn (Bonwell and Sutherland, 1996). When there is limited learning time available, prioritize your goals and objectives or expected learning outcomes, and consider whether or not you can identify or develop an exercise that would help people achieve more than one at the same time. For example, using a "Flow of Information" exercise helps people think about how events are documented, the sequence of documentation, how to access documentation after the fact, and how to save time by using access tools appropriate for the type of information needed and the time period of an event. You can do this with a large group by drawing three columns on a board and asking how the audience first heard about a major newsworthy event. Radio, television, or the Web may be at the top of a list of types of sources that you can end with encyclopedias and other reference materials. These sources go in the first column. Next, ask the audience how long it took from the occurrence of the event until it was reported in a particular medium. This information goes in the second column. Use the third column to identify access—how you would get to this information in a particular type of source at a later time, for example, periodical indexes. Finally, ask the audience where in the flow of information they would start searching for information on a very recent event, and explain that setting an event in a chronological context can save them time and result in much more focused search results. You may also want to refer them to the "Flow of Information" Website for later review and refresher (Zwemer, 2000).

If learning time is not an issue, with asynchronous instruction, for example, consider offering a number of different active learning approaches to help learners achieve objectives or expected learning outcomes. For example, "Thinking Critically About World Wide Web Resources" offers a text-only list of criteria for evaluating Web-based materials. Learners could be asked to examine Websites of their own choosing with these criteria in mind (Grassian, 1998b). Or they may be directed to the "Who Dunnit: What Kind of Web Page is This?" or "Hoax? Scholarly Research? Personal Opinion? You Decide!" exercises on the same site, which provide pre-selected Websites for comparison and offers hints for figuring out correct answers (Brown, Costa, Grassian, Snyder, and Zwemer, 2000; Grassian and Zwemer, 2000).

Turn Your Teaching Into Learner-Centered Active Learning

If you have been involved in ILI for a while, you probably have outlines, scripts, and other tried-and-true materials with which you are comfortable. You have an idea of what you are trying to accomplish and some means of interacting with your audience. If you are new to ILI, you may have gone through the preliminary planning process, written goals and objectives or expected learning outcomes, selected one or more modes of instruction, and even prepared outlines and scripts and other materials. Or you may have borrowed or adapted your instructional plans and materials from others.

At this point, you may be wondering if you can increase participation and improve learning outcomes by involving the learners more. If you have never been involved in ILI you are probably wondering how to involve learners in the first place. As we have mentioned, there are a number of active learning exercises you can investigate and adapt for your own environment. You could also take a teaching segment, or expected learning outcome, and turn it into an active learning exercise. For example, instead of telling learners what the common features of databases are, you could have them complete exercises that require them to use two or three databases and then ask them to describe the common features of these databases. This turns a teacher-centered approach into a learner-centered active learning approach.

What is the process just described here?

1. You think about and write down your goals and objectives or the learning outcomes you expect the audience to achieve. In this case, you would want them to know how to learn that databases generally have common features (Barclay, 1995).
2. You list the learning elements you wish the audience to absorb.

In this case, you would want them to know that despite their apparent differences, databases have three common functions. You can search, you can display, and you can save, by printing, e-mailing or downloading.

3.   You figure out how you can get the audience to come up with these learning elements, rather than supplying them yourself. It helps to think of a practical, hands-on way that the learners can try something out first and then discuss what they discovered. If you prepare an exercise, try to use a topic of interest to the particular audience. For example, for an instruction session for high school students in a predominantly Hispanic area, you might want students to find magazine and journal articles on Latino doctors in a general article index and then in one or two specialized databases like PsycINFO, Ethnic Newswatch, or Sociological Abstracts.

4.   You plan to fill in any missing elements the learners leave out.

5.   You time everything and make sure you tell the audience how much time they will have before you start. It is easy to get off track and waste the limited time you have if you do not adhere closely to a timed plan, allowing, of course, for brief sidetracks and questions.

6.   You tell the learners in advance how you will let them know when their time is up (for example, by flicking the lights off and on), and then turn them loose to attack the assignment.

7.   You get their attention and then have them report back briefly.

8.   You check for understanding in-person by looking for body language, puzzled faces, yawns, or lack of participation. Online, you look for participation or lack of it. You ask the audience if they have any questions, then count seven to ten seconds silently and if there are no questions, ask if they are ready to move on to the next segment.

This is a self-help approach. If you want to help your colleagues incorporate more active learning into their instruction, you will need to work cooperatively with them in a trusting, non-judgmental manner. The best way to build trust and effect change is to use yourself as a model and open your own instruction to observation and constructive criticism. Ask your colleagues to observe you, teaching a live session. Give them observation forms and presentation checklists and ask them to describe what they liked and what they would teach differently. This is an excellent way to begin a discussion on teaching techniques and how to incorporate new techniques into in-person and remote instruction, both synchronous and asynchronous. The next step, peer coaching, is an excellent way to help build momentum. Here colleagues observe each other and provide constructive criticism designed to support individuals and improve instructional techniques. Keep in mind, though, that individuals differ, as do teaching styles, and that change does not always happen quickly or all at once. Patience, good will, and trust are critical elements in supporting and effecting change of any kind.

In-Person, Synchronous Active Learning

In synchronous in-person group settings it is important to note that small group work may or may not appeal to all learners, as learning styles and preferences can differ dramatically in any given group. If you do decide to use active learning techniques like the ones described above, there are four important logistical techniques that can help ensure success for any size group, but especially very large groups (40+).

GIVE PRELIMINARY INSTRUCTIONS

First, be sure to give very careful, simple preliminary instructions about what is going to happen and why *before* the learners break into groups. Preliminary instructions to the entire audience might be as follows:

> We are going to go through a topic selection exercise now that will take about ten to fifteen minutes. I'm going to ask you to count off from one to six, and then get into six small groups.

BREAK INTO GROUPS

Second, have some pre-determined means of breaking the large group into smaller groups. If there is extra time for moving around, have people count off in order around the room based on the number of groups. So, with six groups, for example, ask people to count one by one to the number six, and then start again with number one. Once everyone has counted off, tell them in which part of the room to meet the others in their groups. Also, with very large groups it will be necessary to allot more time to get into small groups, get back to the large group, and to report back. As for the size of small groups, a good rule of thumb is to aim for each small group to be composed of 10–20% of the large group. So, a large group of one hundred could have ten groups of ten, while a small group of thirty could have five groups of six. Sometimes fewer groups will be necessary because there are not enough flip charts, or other equipment, or because of a need to cut down on the time needed to report back. In terms of large group exercises in which the entire audience participates at the same time, an ideal number is around 30–40 to allow more of a chance that someone will come up with a response to any given question or discussion topic.

GIVE (AND DISPLAY) INSTRUCTIONS INCLUDING TIME LIMITS

Third, once everyone is divided into small groups or pairs, give the content instructions and ask them to look up at you when they are finished. Give groups an exact number of minutes for their group work and tell them how you will let them know that their time is up—by flipping the lights on and off, by using a timer, etc. Be sure to warn them a minute or two before their time is up, and when the time has expired ask if anyone needs another minute to finish up.

It also helps to have instructions and questions on a handout, on an overhead, on a board, on a flip chart page, or on a PowerPoint slideshow for reference during the exercise, in case anyone forgets or could not hear the instructions.

The content portion of the instructions could be:

> Each group has the same broad topic, "Hunger." In the next five minutes, I'd like you to use any or all of four limiters to narrow this topic and come up with a topic sentence. This timer will go off when your time is up, and then each group will need to report back to the entire class.

CALL GROUPS BACK TOGETHER

Call the groups back together by using whatever means were announced at the beginning of the exercise and ask for volunteers to report back for each group, again, making sure to stick to allotted time.

Asynchronous Active Learning

Simple active learning exercises like these can break up one-shot sessions or even repeated in-person group instruction, and make them more interesting by forming participatory "chunks." Of course, active learning and chunking are not necessarily restricted to classroom or other in-person group settings. Print library-skills workbooks, for example, were popular in the 70s and 80s and provided a prime and highly effective example of another approach to interactive learning. They utilized an asynchronous, learner-centered approach, which involved discovery and practice in the use of reference sources by means of a set of self-directed, self-paced exercises usually arranged in search strategy order. Workbooks were completed by individuals when they chose to do so, within a particular time frame. (See Chapter 2 for history of library instruction and reference to Mimi Dudley.) Learners would read instructions, find reference tools and the library catalog, and actually use them to answer a series of multiple-choice questions. Answers were corrected to provide feedback as quickly as possible. Effective workbooks were carefully constructed and written using captivating, brief, and clear language for descriptions and exercises. People who prefer to work on their own at their own pace are especially fond of the workbook approach, though workbooks have been disparaged by those who believed they were too simplistic, not relevant to immediate learning needs, too focused on mechanics of use, and lacking in the area of critical thinking and evaluation.

As a result, most paper workbooks fell out of favor during the late 1980s and the 90s in favor of synchronous, face-to-face group instruction, paralleling the lecture/classroom approach used in K–12 and higher education. Yet workbook-like approaches have come full circle now as they are being used more and more in a Web environment in the form of sets of interactive exercises and tutorials. Some are designed as a series of self-contained modules, with critical thinking, self-assessment, and immediate feedback at various points, for example, "Internet Navigator" (1999). (See also Chapter 9 for fuller discussion of various forms of instruction.)

Metacognitive assignments are also active learning projects, though often they are asynchronous. Examples include journal writing, search logs (see Chapter 11), and self-evaluations. Journals are sometimes called "I-Search papers," where students describe their research process, including the information tools they consulted, their evaluation of these tools, as well as the problems and successes they encountered along the way (Hinchliffe, 1999; Mark and Jacobson, 1995; Blakey and Spence, 1990).

Collaborative Learning

In some cases, entire class sessions or even entire classes can be comprised of a particular form of small group active learning called "collaborative learning," a popular educational approach for a number of years (Mallonee, 1981; Sheridan, 1990). Collaborative learning is really an extension of active learning. Its champions argue heatedly in favor of learning by doing and against the lecture method, which they almost invariably conceive of as a "tabula rasa" approach where the teacher "pours" information into the student's empty head. In contrast, collaborative learners often work in groups of two to five with shared responsibility for gaining knowledge. Groups can consist of students, students and teachers, colleagues, and/or other members of an institution. "Rather than having the teacher serve as a dispenser of facts and lower level cognitive information, constructivists believe that the teacher should serve as a facilitator who attempts to structure an environment in which the learner organizes meaning on a personal level; students and teachers should work in a collegial mode, often using small group procedures" (Cooper and Robinson, 1998: 386). So, with little or no instructor guidance, collaborative learning groups jointly investigate, discover, put together, and communicate the results of their information gathering and research. The key is that group members do not divide the work, but rather, share it and come to common agreement on the results (Brandon and Hollingshead, 1999).

The University of Washington's award-winning U-WIRED project, launched in 1994 as a collaborative effort of the University Libraries, Computing and Communication, and the Office of Undergraduate Education, is an excellent representative example of collaborative learning in practice in a large university environment (University of Washington, 2000). It may have been the first collaborative learning IL effort designed to meet the needs of undergraduates in learning community settings, though librarians at a number of colleges and universities in the U.S. are becoming more involved in this exciting new approach to undergraduate education. Librarians at five colleges and universities responded to a request for information on librarian involvement in learning communities posted on BI-L in June 1999 alone (Jackson, 1999). In June 2000, a separate listserv was established on the topic of higher education learning communities and IL based on interest expressed by participants in the ACRL Institute for Information Literacy's 1999 Immersion Program (Hensley, 2000).

Learning Communities

What is a "learning community" and what is its significance? DeMulder and Eby say that learning communities " . . . are interdisciplinary, collaborative, and participatory environments that foster the development of knowledge through multiple perspectives" (1999: 893). Others describe two types of "learning communities," apprenticeships in a discipline or profession (not limited to higher education) and school-based student/teacher learning communities that work on long-term collaborative and often multi-disciplinary projects (Gordin et al., 1996). Some learning communities offer "college survival" courses for credit. These courses often include some IL or research skills, and librarians are important collaborators in planning curriculum for these courses. At IUPUI (Indiana University, Purdue University Indianapolis), for example, this sort of course is run by an "instructional team" consisting of a faculty member, an academic advisor, a student mentor, and a librarian, each of whom contributes to the content of the course (Orme, 1999).

As these developments indicate, subject experts in various fields are having a hard time keeping up with information resources in their own areas of expertise. As it turns out, librarians too are having a difficult time keeping up to date on information resources in many disciplines that seem to multiply and mutate daily. However, we are doing a better job of it than our users, so it is not surprising that they turn to us for help. In the foreseeable future it seems clear that a librarian's guidance will be essential in helping users at all educational levels learn to identify, locate, and evaluate research materials needed for multi-disciplinary collaborative projects.

Collaborative Learning Backlash

In the humanities, such collaborative learning groups have really taken hold. Undergraduate English Composition instructors in some institutions, for example, may be told to place students in small groups within each class and from day one, provide the groups with sample high- and low-quality papers, letting the groups edit and grade each other's work.

However, cracks are now appearing in what seemed to be a marble fortress of collaborative learning advocacy. Some research seems to indicate that teams "usually do less well—not better—than the sum of their members' individual contributions" (Hackman, 1998: 246). In the sciences, collaborative learning approaches do not come naturally. In science education, for many years emphasis has been placed on lecture and individual mastery. Just adding small group approaches here and there has been a major step. Some scientists fear that when left completely to their own devices, collaborative learning groups may or may not be able to discover scientific principles and learn how to test theories in a scientifically valid manner. In some cases, learners may not be aware of dangerous circumstances or combinations of chemicals, for example. The main argument against a constructivist collaborative learning approach, in fact, is that " . . . there is a body of knowledge that is fundamental or foundational and that such content is best presented in more traditional instructional formats , such as the lecture" (Cooper and Robinson, 1998: 386).

Online Learning and the Web

This debate may continue to rage and increase in temperature as the Web becomes easier to use for instruction. As we shall see in Chapter 17, "Using Technology to Teach," the educational landscape is changing as full courses are now taught online, and other Web-based technologies are becoming more effective instructional tools. Some educators are even writing books on how to convert courses to wholly online courses (Ko and Rossen, 2001).

In fact, the Web's attraction lies partially in its interactivity, in the freedom it allows one to decide which way to go and what to do when. Clicking buttons with a mouse is both the same as and yet significantly different from using a television remote control device. Web users are not just picking a channel and then watching and listening passively. Deciding where to click, how many layers deep to go in a Website, and which of many possible branches to take requires some thinking and decision making. The question is whether we can influence the decision-making process by helping users become more thoughtful about it, more selective in where they go and on what they click, more skeptical about the information they retrieve, as well as the uses to which it is put, and more open to a continuous learning process throughout life.

FINAL REMARKS

We are just beginning to explore the use of the Web for instruction, but it does seem clear that people learn best by doing, by taking part in learning. Exactly how to bring about enhanced learning by doing and by thinking about what you are doing (metacognition) may be an individual decision on the part of the ILI librarian, or a joint decision between the ILI librarian and teaching faculty or other administrators. Nurturing collaborative relationships with others can help bring this goal to fruition.

EXERCISES

1. Design brief hands-on exercises that will help users learn:
   a. the mechanics of using their OPAC,
   b. how to evaluate information tools,
   c. how to evaluate individual retrievals, and
   d. how to distinguish between formats of information.
2. Come up with an active learning (participatory) technique to teach people how to think critically about information resources such as Websites and online databases.
3. Adapt a fifty-minute exercise from *Designs for Active Learning* (Gradowski, Snavely, and Dempsey, 1998) to fit a ten-minute time period.

4. In your own words, respond to the following questions:
    a. Is there a body of knowledge that ILI librarians should pass along to learners via the lecture method?
    b. Should we turn our synchronous instruction (in-person or remote) entirely into active learning exercises?
    c. How much guidance should the ILI librarian provide in synchronous and asynchronous instruction?

READ MORE ABOUT IT

Bodi, Sonia. 1988. "Critical Thinking and Bibliographic Instruction: The Relationship." *Journal of Academic Librarianship* 14 no. 3: 150–53.

Fink, Deborah. 1989. *Process and Politics in Library Research*. Chicago: American Library Association.

Frick, Elizabeth. 1975. "Information Structure and Bibliographic Instruction." *Journal of Academic Librarianship* 1 no. 4: 12–14.

Gradowski, Gail, Loanne Snavely, and Paula Dempsey, eds. 1998. *Designs for Active Learning*. Chicago: American Library Association.

Mellon, Constance A. 1995. "Library Instruction in the Information Age," In *Russian-American Seminar on Critical Thinking and the Library*, edited by Cerise Oberman and Dennis Kimmage. Urbana-Champaign, IL: University of Illinois.

Tiberius, Richard, and Ivan Silver. "Guidelines for Conducting Workshops and Seminars That Actively Engage Participants" [Online]. Available: www.hsc.wvu.edu/aap/aap-car/faculty-development/teaching-skills/conducting_workshops.htm [2000, November 4].

Part III

Planning and Developing Information Literacy Instruction

7

ILI Program Planning

Our plans miscarry because they have no aim. When a man does not know what harbor he is making for, no wind is the right wind.

—Seneca

HOW DOES INSTRUCTION GET INITIATED?

Where does the idea for instruction come from? What motivates us to begin the development process in the first place? In other words, what events in our environment trigger the idea that a new instructional endeavor is necessary? Something obviously drives us to feel we must take on the enormous effort of creating something new. We identify a need and feel that instruction is the answer to that need. In most types of libraries, the need materializes in three distinct ways. One way is that the staff working directly with clients, either at our reference desks or one-on-one, begins reporting a run of repetitive questions. A theme is identified in these questions that seems to indicate some kind of user need. One approach to deal with that need is to design an instructional response. Let us call this the reactive mode. User questions are driving the instructional development.

Instruction is also initiated a second way: when someone asks us to do it. This can be called the interactive mode. In this case you receive a call or a visit from someone who asks you to present some material, most often in a classroom setting. The requester usually has an idea of what he or she would like you to teach and you work with the requester to develop the presentation. So the requester is actually the driving force in this case.

The third way to initiate instruction is the proactive mode. Here *you* do the driving. You and your staff do some preliminary research and identify areas where your patrons could benefit from instruction. In the proactive mode, you, as an information professional, are in charge. The new instruction is neither a desperate attempt to deal with a situation that is already out of hand (reactive), nor a demand from an external source (interactive). The proactive approach is based on your professional judgment that instruction is needed.

THE PRELIMINARY PLANNING PROCESS

Regardless of how instruction gets initiated, or what your particular institutional environment might be, the steps for the planning process remain the same:

- RECOGNIZE the user need.
- DESCRIBE and ANALYZE the present situation, including available resources.
- DEVELOP instructional goals and objectives.
- DESIGN appropriate methods and materials.
- DELIVER the instruction.
- EVALUATE and REVISE. (This final step can lead to a re-working of some of the previous steps.)

This chapter will be dealing with the first three of these steps—recognizing the need, describing and analyzing the current situation, and developing goals and objectives. The rest of the planning process will be covered in subsequent chapters.

Obviously, the planning process can be time consuming. And in the reactive and interactive modes, you may not be able to dwell on some of these preliminary steps. But it is essential to the quality of your instruction that you pay attention to all the steps regardless of who was the initiator.

Needs Assessment

The first step is to find out what your population needs to know. This is called Needs Assessment. In the case of the reactive and interactive modes, the need is identified for you. You still may need to gather additional information on the exact nature of the information need, but for the most part this will be a very brief part of your planning process.

Doing a Needs Assessment, however, is really the heart of the proactive mode process. No one is identifying information needs for you. You are actively going out there and looking for them. During the Needs Assessment process, you gather information about what is currently happening in instruction and compare that to what potential library users would like to have happen. During this stage you gather data about your users, your community, your current programs and materials, your facility, staff, budget, etc.

Use your Needs Assessment to evaluate your library's actual world against the ideal (Loe and Elkins, 1990). This is the time to make sure the library is responding to real, rather than assumed, needs.

Needs Assessments don't have to be complex or complicated. Watching reference desk interactions or the behavior of users in the library can give you a good idea of what is needed. Talking informally to your colleagues or to library users can also help pinpoint problems that could be addressed through instruction. More formal approaches make use of surveys, interviews, focus group meetings, document analysis, usability studies, and so on (Loe and Elkins, 1990). Regardless of the approach you select, remember that your goal is to find out who your users are and what they need.

Basic to the Needs Assessment process is developing a clear and complete understanding of the characteristics of your population. Robert Mager (1997a, 1997c, 1997e) calls this describing your TPOP, or target population. What are the groups' attributes in terms of age, educational background, cultural and ethnic groups, previous library experience, language proficiencies, attitudes toward the library, ease of access, and preferred types of learning (Loe and Elkins, 1990; Roberts and Blandy, 1989)? Contact government offices for demographics and other types of census type data. Ask yourself, "Who would have this data in your own institutional environment?" In an academic setting try the registrar's office. Your local school board may be able to provide this information for a school library setting. City offices and library boards would be useful contact points for public library Needs Assessments.

Meet with administrators, faculty, students, community leaders, and members of local organizations and special interest groups to ask questions about population needs. How do they view the population in terms of make-up and needs? In a campus setting, check to see the balance between commuters and on-campus students. Look at course catalogs to see what kinds of classes are being offered that might have library assignments attached to them. Are both day and night classes offered? Are students generally full- or part-time? Are they coming to campus directly from high school? Are they community college transfers? Are they older, re-entry students? Or are your students a mix of all of these?

Study use patterns in your library. What time of day is the library most heavily used in person? Check on remote use as well. When are library resources most often accessed remotely? Do use patterns fluctuate over the course of the day for both in-person and remote use? For example, in a public library setting different age groups generally use the library at different times of the day.

Talk directly with your users. Try to develop a procedure to assess both library users and non-users. See if you can find out from non-users why they don't use the library and what would entice them to use it. Go out into the community and talk to people on the street. Or mail surveys to a representative sample of your population. Post interactive surveys on your library's Website, and other sites that your users frequent within your institution or organization.

If you use questionnaires or surveys, make sure they are clear, concise, and easy to return. Provide some kind of incentive for returning the surveys to increase your response rate. You might even consider administering some kind of pre-test to assess actual knowledge and skills. Making use of some kind of pre-test can further assist you in determining what your learners already know and pinpoint what they still need to learn. Pre-tests can be in the form of an objective paper and pencil test in which learners are asked to exhibit knowledge of resources and/or strategies, a performance assessment in which you observe actual research behavior, or a product appraisal (examination of papers, projects, or bibliographies). Once instruction has taken place, post-tests can be administered and compared to these pre-tests to help determine the success of your instructional endeavors. See Chapter 12 for further information on developing these types of assessments.

Remember to talk to your library staff. Get their impressions of the user population. Do they see particular areas where users seem to have a lot of difficulty using the facility and its resources? Check with your library administrators to see if any new information technology is on the horizon. If so, how will that new technology impact your user population? Keep an eye on what is happening overall in your institution regarding technology.

To be complete, your Needs Assessment must address institutional climate and politics. Any proposed instruction must fit in with the overall goals of your institution as well as those of your library. Review your institution's Mission Statement. Is IL included as part of the institution's mission? If so, how is IL defined? As we discussed in Chapter 1, IL can mean different things to different people. Interview key people in your organization to see what IL means to them. Finding out what your institution means by IL will help you tailor your initiatives to fit the goals of the larger organization. It will help you identify potential supporters and may even open lines of communication with and raise the consciousness of these key people. You may gain even more support for your programs as a result of these interactions.

Look at where the library fits into the overall organization. Who must be convinced of the merit of new instructional endeavors both within the library and in the broader organizational structure? Try to identify potential institutional partners and supporters. Media or computing centers can help with technology issues. Graphic designers and editors might help with handout and screen design. Research methods departments could help design surveys and so on. What does the library's Mission Statement say about instruction? What are the library's instructional goals? Who is the library mandated to serve? Are there stated user population priorities? Are there different goals for different groups and, if so, how would that impact your instructional program (Grassian, 1993a)?

Now look at your identified needs as they relate to what you are currently doing. What instruction is currently in place and how does it address (or fail to address) the needs identified by your assessment? Part of the planning process will be to identify which of your current programs and materials should remain, be modified, or actually be replaced by something new. You may also come up with non-instructional solutions such as better directional signs, screen design modifications, or re-organization of part or all of the collection to make it more accessible.

Finally, be realistic. Do an honest assessment of your facility, space, staffing, and budget. Do you have the space, the people, and the resources to undertake a big, new initiative? What you determine is the ideal instructional program may not be practical at first. Start small, perhaps with a pilot project, and hope you can build on your success. A Needs Assessment consists of two equally important parts—what needs to be done and what actually can be done. Nothing succeeds like success. So if you are forced by circumstances to make some compromises on your ideal, don't despair. Your success with the small stuff will provide a strong foundation for the more global program. Prove yourself competent, creative, flexible, and capable of delivering what you promise and your administrators may be willing to give you a chance to try something bigger (and more expensive) next time around.

Goals and Objectives

You have now completed steps one and two. You know all about your population and have identified their needs. You also have a firm and rational grip on what is possible given your current situation. The next step is to develop (in writing) your instructional goals and objectives.

Why bother? You would not start a long car trip without a map, nor would you start to cook a new or unfamiliar dish without a recipe. Goals and objectives are your guidelines, blueprints, or road maps for instruction. They show you where you want to go and how you plan to get there. They also help you determine when you have successfully arrived. Goals and objectives help focus your efforts and serve as markers for the evaluation process (Elliott et al., 1996; Linn and Gronlund, 1995; Mager, 1997e; Roberts and Blandy, 1989).

Quite a lot has been written on the topic of goals and objectives. If you pursue reading on your own, you will find many different approaches, some commonalties, and a plethora of definitions, terminology, and vocabulary—not all of which seem to match up. The following is one way to approach this topic. It is a way of coming to terms with the variations in the literature; but it may not work for everyone. In the course of your readings and research in this area, you may discover other approaches that suit your thinking better than the one presented below. As long as your approach clearly states your instructional intent, how you will get there in an observable, measurable way, and defines criteria for students to exhibit competence, you should be OK.

Goals describe the overall intent of the program in broad, general strokes. They describe what you would like to accomplish. They are general educational priorities and are frequently stated as global abstractions. Objectives on the other hand are more concrete. They indicate how you will accomplish your goals by identifying what participants will learn by completing the program. They describe, in a relatively specific manner, what students should be able to do, produce, and the characteristics students should possess once learning is completed (Bloom, Madaus, and Hastings, 1981). Furthermore, objectives describe behavior changes that occur when people learn. They are observable indicators of that behavior change (Tyler, 1976). Objectives are not abstract. They are actual behaviors teachers want to cause students to display. They describe what we want students to be able to do (Kellough, Kellough, and Kim, 1999). Objectives communicate our instructional plans and describe acceptable student performance for demonstrating the attainment of the objective. Objectives shift the focus from the teacher to the student and emphasize the product rather than the process of teaching (Linn and Gronlund, 1995; Mager, 1997a, 1997c, 1997e). Objectives identify those instructional and learning outcomes deemed worthy of attainment (Elliott et al., 1996).

Both objectives and outcomes are written in terms of behavior. Each seems to describe what we expect the student to be able to do at the end of instruction. It is sometimes confusing and difficult to tease these two ideas apart. According to Mager (Mager, 1997a, 1997c, 1997e), well-written and useful objectives include performance, condition, and criteria. An objective indicates what the student is expected to do, under what circumstances the behavior is to be exhibited, and how well the behavior must be performed. As such, an objective contains reference to the learning outcome. The objective describes the end product (your desire or aim for what students will be able to do). Outcomes are how the students exhibit that they got there and include criteria for determining how well they succeeded.

Both objectives and outcomes are written in terms of observable behavior. But the outcomes add specific performance indicators. A single objective could have multiple outcomes. Learning outcomes are what are measured to determine the success of the instruction. In other words, we look at the learning outcomes to indicate if the student has successfully attained the objective set for the instruction. Another way to look at this difference is that objectives describe what you expect the learners to be able to do, think, or feel as a result of the instruction; outcomes are what you measure to see if they achieved your expectations, and include some criteria or standard for success.

If our objective is that students can select the most appropriate database to search for articles on a given topic, then we need to develop a way to measure their success. We could give them a list of databases and a list of topics and ask them to match the topics to the most appropriate database. We could also set a standard of 90 percent correct as a criterion for success. Measuring the learner's ability to match topics to databases 90 percent of the time would be the learning outcome for this instruction.

Let's look at IL for example. Developing IL individuals is the abstract, global, broad, and general goal of our instructional program. We may wish to add some specifics to that in terms of audience or subject matter (i.e., freshman English composition students). But in general we are not describing any observable behavior. Our objectives then are dependent upon what we mean by IL in a particular situation. Let's say we are defining IL individuals as people that can identify when they have an information need, can develop strategies for finding the needed information, can evaluate the worthiness of the information found, and can apply these principles in a variety of real life situations. These characteristics are the basis for our objectives. But they need to be defined in terms of observable behavior. How will an outside observer know that someone has attained the attributes listed above? That is where the learning outcomes come into play. We take each of the characteristics listed above and expand on them so that they refer to measurable behaviors.

How would someone who is IL behave? For one thing, they would probably make more use of library resources than someone who is not

IL. They might approach the reference desk more frequently. And they would make more use of remote access opportunities. Could we measure these behaviors? Probably we could if we gave it some thought. So the objectives for our instruction are to produce students who identify an information need, develop strategies for finding information, evaluate material, and apply these principles in a variety of circumstances. The measurable behaviors are identify, develop, evaluate, and apply. The learning outcomes would further define the behavior by specifying the way we would measure the behavior and would indicate the exact performance, conditions, and criteria necessary to determine if the objective was met.

Let's say someone needs information about current research on a specific topic. After instruction, this person would be able to select the resource most likely to contain this information. He or she could generate a list of appropriate search terms, design an effective search strategy using the resource's special features and organization, and would successfully locate at least three relevant articles on the subject being researched. We could measure the performance by comparing what resources were selected to a pre-determined list of appropriate resources, and by examining the terms listed and strategies developed against some standard. Our criterion for success is the location of at least three relevant articles. A standard for relevance would also be included as part of this learning outcome.

Not every instructional designer separates objectives from outcomes. It is far more typical for the outcomes to be included in the objective statement along with conditions and criteria. There is a subtle yet important distinction between the two. The objective describes the behavior. The outcome deals with how the student exhibits the behavior. Whether you separate outcomes from objectives into different statements or you include your outcomes in the objective statement is up to you. What is crucial is that your statements contain a description of observable, measurable behaviors. They must provide a means for evaluating whether or not students have successfully attained the objectives set for them. Their successful performance of the desired behaviors will in turn serve as a measure of how well our instruction has succeeded.

WRITING GOALS AND OBJECTIVES

Although most IL instructors agree in principle that good instruction starts with the writing of clear, concise, and meaningful goals and objectives, in practice these crucial steps may be skipped or not given the attention they deserve. To those who have never written goals and objectives before, these preliminary steps seem daunting indeed. However, with some practical guidelines and a little practice, writing goals and objectives can become second nature.

First, remember that goals and objectives are *always* written from the student's perspective. Goals are general statements and may not even be complete sentences. They frequently start with the word "to" and identify what the teacher intends the students to learn. Objectives describe student performance. They are usually written in complete sentences and should contain an action verb that indicates what each student is expected to do as a result of the instructional experience (Kellough, Kellough, and Kim, 1999). Furthermore, they communicate your intent to your students. They let your students know what is expected of them and where their efforts should be concentrated (Mager, 1997a, 1997c, 1997e).

Writing the broad, global instructional goal is fairly easy. Teachers generally can verbalize the intent of their instruction. In our case our general intent is for students to become IL. Writing instructional objectives that describe the behavior of an IL individual, however, may not appear to be that straightforward. Instructors often find it difficult to describe how students demonstrate, in observable and measurable behavior, that they have learned what was intended for them to learn.

Let's start by looking at the overall format for objectives. Often referred to as the ABCD formula, it can serve as a framework for developing workable objectives (Armstrong and Savage, 1983; Elliott et al., 1996; Kellough, Kellough, and Kim, 1999).

> A = Audience for whom the objectives are intended
> B = Behavior that indicates learning
> C = Conditions under which the behavior is to appear
> D = Degree of competency that will be accepted

Another approach describes an objective as having three parts—tasks, conditions, and standards. Tasks are observable actions. Conditions are the situations within which the tasks are carried out. Standards are the criteria for performance success (Freedman and Bantly, 1982). These three parts can also be referred to as performance, condition, and criteria (Mager, 1997e). To see if your written objectives fulfill these requirements, check them as follows:

1. Performance or task—Does the objective describe what someone will do when demonstrating accomplishment of the objective?
2. Condition—Does the objective describe the condition that will exist when the student is performing?

3. Standard or criterion—Does the objective tell how to recognize the performance as satisfactory?

Goal analysis is a method for determining where you want your student to be at the end of your instruction (Mager, 1997a). It enables you to describe the performance that if exhibited would indicate you have achieved your goal and as such can be extremely helpful in writing the performance or task aspect of your objectives. To come up with a list of these relevant performances, try asking yourself how you would identify someone who had attained your goal when you saw him or her. (Mager, 1997a, 1997c, 1997e). What would you take as evidence (in behavioral terms) that your goal had been achieved? How would you separate a group of people into two categories, those who had achieved the goal and those who had not? Identify people you know have reached the goal. What characteristics distinguish these people as having attained the goal?

Once you have generated a list of performance or task behaviors, you are ready to begin writing your objectives. Each objective statement should contain verbs that are specific and indicate definite, observable behaviors—that is, responses that can be seen and assessed (Linn and Gronlund, 1995). Examples of such verbs can be found in Mager (1997c, 1997e), Roberts and Blandy (1989), and Linn and Gronlund (1995) and others. They include such words as "identify," "name," "distinguish," "define," "describe," "classify," "order," "demonstrate," "construct," "select," "write," "recite," "compare," "build," and so on. The meaning of specific behaviors can be further clarified by listing some of the tasks students are expected to perform to demonstrate achievement. For example, students can identify items by circling them, pointing to them, picking them up, touching them, etc. Returning to our distinction between objectives and outcomes, the verb "identify" would be part of the objective. But to circle the correct responses as a method of demonstrating identifying would be included as the measurable outcome. Don't forget to indicate any conditions under which the behavior would be performed and your criteria for measuring success. For example, let's say the objective is the following:

Given a specific research topic and the descriptions of several possible databases, the student will be able to identify the three most appropriate databases for locating articles on the given topic. Students will circle their chosen databases. Instructors will compare the scope and coverage of the selected databases to the topic being researched to determine the appropriateness of the selections.

The objective here is for students to be able to identify appropriate databases for a given topic. The conditions are that they are given a specific topic and the description of the databases. In other words, they do not have to come up with the databases out of their own heads. The criterion is the appropriateness of the selections. Note that a means of identifying appropriateness is also included in the above statement. While this statement may appear more convoluted and complex than you feel is necessary, it offers the advantage of identifying not only how the student will demonstrate competency, but also including a method for measuring that competency.

OVERT VERSUS COVERT BEHAVIORS

Proponents of the above strategy of writing goals and objectives say that if you want to teach something you should be able to describe performance (an observable action) that will indicate that the person has been successfully taught. However, others question this primarily Behaviorist view of learning. Referring to the Cognitive/Constructivist view of learning, they question whether performance-based instruction can result in higher-order thinking (Kellough, Kellough, and Kim, 1999). To make behavioral objectives valid, all learning must be defined in terms of observable, overt behavior. But some learning is internal and therefore difficult to define in these terms (Eble, 1988). These non-observable or covert aspects of learning are also viewed as valid objectives for instruction. How then do we write meaningful objectives to deal with these internal or covert behavioral changes? Furthermore, how can we tell when our students have obtained these objectives?

That second question is key to this controversy. If we cannot find a way to ascertain that a student has attained the objective, we have no way of knowing if we are successfully teaching. One way around this quandary is to describe performance that would indicate attainment of the covert objective. In other words, since we cannot directly see the covert behavior, we need to find an overt behavior from which we can infer changes in the covert behavior. The area where this becomes most relevant is in the arena of affective objectives. Frequently, we wish to include in our goals and objectives changes in attitudes and feelings about information, our resources, our facilities, and even ourselves as information professionals. But we can't see, hear, or touch these attitudes and feelings. You can, however, infer changes in an attitude toward something by how the person interacts with it. For example, a person who, as a result of our instruction, has gained a more positive attitude toward X, will be more inclined to approach or interact with X in the future. Conversely, a person who develops a negative attitude will try to avoid further contact with X.

Using this rationale, we can include covert objectives in our plan as long as we can come up with an observable behavior from which we can infer the attainment of the objective. Let's say one of our goals is for students to access information in all formats. Therefore we would like to address the problem of computer anxiety in our instruction. Our list of objectives would include something about students acquiring a more positive attitude toward using computerized databases. After having participated in our instruction, students' levels of computer anxiety will be reduced. Our objective, then, is a change in attitude. But since we cannot measure this directly, we must come up with an observable indicator of this change. What if we write our objective like this:

> Upon given the choice of using comparable print and computerized resources when researching their topics, students will select computerized databases at least as often as they do print resources.

Now let's try the performance, conditions, criteria test again. Our performance is selecting print or computerized resources. There are any number of ways that we could see and measure that behavior. For example, we could offer students equal access to these resources and observe the frequency of selecting one or the other format. Students could point to their selections, make a written list of the ones they would use, or we could actually watch them as they made their selections and used the resources. The conditions are that students have a specific topic to research and must select resources from the ones we have given them access to. The criterion is that students select computer resources at least as often as they select print resources. Choosing computerized resources as often as print ones can be inferred as a decrease in computer anxiety. In other words, students are now willing to approach computer resources as often (if not more so) than print ones.

Have we succeeded in writing an observable and measurable objective for this covert behavior? The answer is yes. Although it may be a bit more difficult to develop these types of objectives, they are well worth the effort. If we think something is worth teaching, then we must come up with a way for our students to demonstrate they have learned it. Whether we decide to assess the behavior through an actual performance test, some sort of interview, or by means of a written survey or questionnaire is the subject for another chapter. But our objective has been written in such a way that we know what behavior we need to measure in order to determine if our objective has been attained.

One more word on writing goals and objectives: While goals and objectives describe where you want to go with your instructional program and how you expect to get there, they must also be realistic, attainable, and appropriate (Roberts and Blandy, 1989). Your objectives must meet users' needs and should be consistent with the overall goals and objectives of your library and parent institution. Check to see if you have selected appropriate and rational objectives by looking at the following criteria (Linn and Gronlund, 1995; Mager, 1997e):

1. Completeness—Do the objectives include everything students need to know how to do in order to attain the instructional goal? If a person did all the things the objectives called for, would you be willing to accept that he or she had achieved your instructional goals? If not, what other additional objectives need to be added?
2. Importance—Is the objective trivial? Look at the consequence of not achieving the performance. If there is no significant consequence, then the objective is trivial and should be cut.
3. Appropriateness—Are the objectives consistent with the general goals of the institution and of your library?
4. Soundness—Are the objectives consistent with current educational practices and principles of learning?
5. Feasibility—Are the objectives realistic in terms of the abilities of the students and the time, staff, facilities, and space available?

Your Needs Assessment data will prove invaluable in helping you determine the answers to these questions.

As with any skill, writing goals and objectives becomes easier with practice. Your first few attempts may leave something to be desired. But you can learn from doing. If you write your goals and objectives and then discover that at the conclusion of instruction there is no way of proving students have attained them, you need to begin again. That is not to say that your instruction is a failure. It just means that you need to revise your objectives so that they include a means for your students to demonstrate attainment of your goals. Remember that the reason for writing goals and objectives is to communicate your intent, describe desired performance, and provide a way to demonstrate success. If you include all these components in your game plan, you will have succeeded in writing meaningful goals and objectives.

TAXONOMIES AND STANDARDS

Writing appropriate goals and objectives requires that we can articulate where we are trying to go and how we are planning to get there. This in turn means that we can identify standard definitions or descriptions for the terms we are using. Educators frequently rely on Benjamin Bloom's

Taxonomy of Educational Objectives (1956) as a starting point when writing their goals and objectives. In IL instruction, finding an equivalent starting point is not always an easy task. We are still struggling with our definitions of IL and the characteristics that identify an IL individual. In 1999, the ACRL Task Force on Information Literacy Competency Standards drafted a list of information literacy competency standards for higher education (Association of College and Research Libraries Task Force on Information Literacy Standards, 2000). The current version of these standards can be viewed at www.ala.org/acrl/ilcomstan.html. These standards may in fact turn out to be our version of Bloom's *Taxonomy*. They are certainly a place to begin when developing your own IL instructional goals and objectives. Keep in mind that these were written not in the language of goals and objectives, but rather in the terminology of educational competencies. However, they can be used to help us clarify our ideas.

ALA's Association of College and Research Libraries' *Information Literacy Competency Standards for Higher Education* (2000) are intended to provide a framework for determining whether or not a person is IL from a higher education standpoint. The 2000 revision built upon those developed for K–12 learners by the American Association of School Librarians Task Force on Information Literacy Standards (American Association of School Librarians and Association for Educational Communications and Technology, 1998), thus allowing for the development of a continuum of expectations for students of all levels. They include a definition of IL, a list of the characteristics or attributes that are viewed as the component parts of IL, and the behaviors if exhibited that identify a person as IL. As such, they can provide guidance for us when we write our specific goals and objectives. The competencies are broken down into five standards and twenty-two performance indicators. Each performance indicator includes a list of measurable outcomes for assessing student progress toward IL. Although the language used in this document varies somewhat from that used in standard educational practice, the standards, performance indicators, and measurable outcomes can be used as the basis for writing specific instructional goals and objectives.

Let's look at Standard One: The information literate student determines the nature and extent of the information needed. If our goal is to produce IL students, then this standard helps us determine how we can recognize someone who has attained the goal of becoming IL. One performance indicator for this standard is as follows: The information literate student identifies a variety of types and formats of potential sources for information. Clearly, this statement could be used as a learning objective. If we expand upon the measurable outcomes listed for this performance and include specific observable behaviors, as well as conditions and criteria for success, we would have identified how students indicate they had successfully attained the objective.

One such outcome listed for this standard is the student is able to differentiate between primary and secondary sources, and recognize how their use and importance vary with each discipline. If we expanded this statement to include how the student demonstrates this ability, we would have a workable and measurable learning outcome. So, for example, if we said that if given a list of resources the student could accurately separate them into two categories—primary and secondary resources—we have described a performance that we can both see and measure. If accuracy is our criteria, we also need to include some method for determining this accuracy, such as comparison to an authoritative list in the field or to a list that we have come up with in advance based on our experience and professional judgment.

Here again we see the separation of objectives from outcomes. The objective is for students to be able to determine the difference between primary and secondary sources. We determine if they reached this objective by creating an opportunity for the learner to demonstrate a learning outcome. The demonstration consists of having students accurately sort material into primary or secondary categories. Our criterion for accuracy is to compare their results to what we have pre-determined to be the correct result of this sort according to the standard definitions of primary and secondary resources in a given discipline.

If keeping these two concepts distinct in your own mind makes it easier for you to develop your own goals and objectives, go ahead. The idea is to do what makes sense to you. In the end, your aim is to come up with a workable guideline for your instruction. Your plan must clearly articulate where you are trying to go and how you are trying to get there. It also must include some way to tell that you have reached your destination. Regardless of the terminology you use to describe these component parts, as long as you have identified all of them, your goals and objectives will not only communicate what you are trying to do, they will provide the means for proving that you did it.

One final caution about using these competency standards. Use them as a starting point, but don't feel obligated to include every aspect of them in your own work. Documents like this are bound to undergo revision as people attempt to use them. The specific wording may undergo some change as a result of these attempted applications. The overall organization of the document itself may be modified as time goes on. The point is that these standards are an excellent place to look for ideas about your own instructional goals and objectives. They have been designed to guide you. Modify them as needed and make them work for you. To be most effective, the standards must be adapted to fit your particular institutional setting and the needs of your specific population. In other words, you must refine them until you can make them your own.

TRIMMING THE FAT IN YOUR PRESENTATIONS

There are lots of advantages to writing goals and objectives. They help guide you in your planning. They help communicate your intent to your administrators, colleagues, and students. They provide the means by which you can assess your successes. Finally, the process of developing goals and objectives causes you to think seriously and deeply about what is worth teaching (Mager, 1997a, 1997c, 1997e). In the course of thinking about how to address your students' needs, you may discover that instruction may not be the answer at all. Maps, signs, changes in screen design, etc., may all be ways of solving your students' problems. Many needs can be addressed by improving systems and removing the barriers that make using your facility and its resources more difficult to use. However, if instruction does turn out to be the answer, written goals and objectives can prove invaluable in selecting what to include in your sessions.

Look over your instructional plan and compare everything you do and say to your proposed objectives. Everything you plan to teach should support at least one of your objectives. Furthermore, every objective should be addressed by the content of your instruction. Each objective should be derived directly from the Needs Assessment. Teach only those things your target audience has identified as something they need or want to learn. Be ruthless. Cut out anything that is not essential to achieving one of your objectives (Loe and Elkins, 1990). Use your objectives to critique any active learning methods you were thinking of including. Activities that allow students to practice behavior associated with desired objectives are particularly valuable (Meyers and Jones, 1993).

FINAL REMARKS

By taking the time to perform a Needs Assessment and then writing appropriate, complete, important, sound, and feasible goals and objectives based on that assessment, you can develop an instructional plan that is both useful and effective. Furthermore, by placing your users' needs at the heart of your program and communicating your instructional intent to them through your goals and objectives, you are creating an instructional program that demonstrates your care and concern. Your students become partners in the development process. Thus, your instructional program becomes more relevant to them. In a very real sense, the students are part owners of the program. After all, you are only including what they have identified as important for them to learn. By word and deed you exhibit your respect for your students and their abilities. A student-centered planning approach such as this communicates your positive expectations. You have told them that by the end of the instruction they will be able to do whatever you have set out to teach them. Your students will leave your session with an enhanced belief in their own abilities, having been brought one step closer to becoming IL individuals.

EXERCISES

1. Preparing for a Needs Assessment. Make a list of the information you might wish to gather for a Needs Assessment. Be sure to include questions about your population, library, and institution. Divide your paper into two columns. List your questions in the left-hand column. Now use the right-hand column to identify where in your institution you could find the answers to your questions. Look for relevant documents such as Mission Statements, program descriptions, admissions requirements, etc. Determine which offices or agencies collect the information you need. If possible, find out the name of the person who could actually supply the data.

    Match each question in the left-hand column with a potential source of information in the right-hand column. You now have a plan for going about collecting the data for your Needs Assessment. Even if you are not planning to undertake the task at this time it is a good idea to go through this preliminary planning stage. It will make it possible for you to start a Needs Assessment with very little advance notice. You might also wish to update the information once a year or so to make sure your contact people are still correct.

2. Writing goals and objectives. Think about something for which you would like to design a class, or look at a session you already are teaching but which has no written goals and objectives at this time. Can you determine what the overall global intent of the instruction would be? That is, can you come up with a goal for the instruction?

    Once you have a goal (or goals), perform a goal analysis.

Answer Mager's question, "How will I know one when I see one?" (Mager, 1997a, 1997c, 1997e). Come up with a list of behaviors that if performed would convince you that your students had attained the goal.

Write an objective for each of the listed behaviors. Make sure to write them from the student's perspective. Describe what your students will be able to do (how they will perform) as a result of participating in your instruction.

Determine what the learning outcomes (in observable, measurable terms) would be for each of the written objectives. Make sure you have described the performance, conditions, and criteria of success for each one. What will the students do to convince you that they had attained each objective and thus had achieved the instructional goal?

Finally, check your objectives for completeness, appropriateness, importance, soundness, and feasibility. Use the data from your Needs Assessment to determine whether your objectives meet these criteria.

Congratulations. You have now written goals and objectives for your session. Test them out in a real instructional situation and revise as needed.

READ MORE ABOUT IT

Kellough, Richard D, Noreen G. Kellough, and Eugene C. Kim. 1999. *Secondary School Teaching: A Guide to Methods and Resources: Planning for Competence.* Upper Saddle River, NJ: Merrill.

Linn, Robert L., and Norman Gronlund. 1995. *Measurement and Assessment in Teaching.* 7th ed. New York: Macmillan.

Loe, Mary, and Betsy Elkins. 1990. "Developing Programs in Library Use Instruction for Lifelong Learning: An Overview." In *The LIRT Library Instruction Handbook,* edited by May Brottman and Mary Loe. Englewood, CO: Libraries Unlimited.

Mager, Robert F. 1997. *Preparing Instructional Objectives: A Critical Tool in Development of Effective Instruction.* 3rd ed. Atlanta: Center for Effective Performance.

8

Selecting Modes
of Instruction

He ten times pines that pines beholding food . . . .
—William Shakespeare, *The Rape of Lucrece*

AT THE INSTRUCTIONAL CAFÉ

Our teaching and learning smorgasbord groans heavily with an array
of choices—from simple signage to densely packed old-world-style lectures to workbooks, spa-like one-shot sessions and exercises, to full-
length credit courses—in a continuum that includes evolving approaches
such as interactive Web-based tutorials and online courses. Yet many
librarians find themselves starving amidst this sea of plenty, gazing long-
ingly at one after another teaching/learning confection wondering which
will delight and what the ingredients are for success. Which form of
instruction is best or most suitable for which situation? What factors
should one consider in selecting a mode of instruction, if, in fact, one
has a choice? How many modes of instruction and what types should
libraries offer? Which audience(s) should they serve, and which modes
work best with which audience(s)? How do budget, staffing, and preparation time limitations impact this decision? The list of questions goes
on and on and, given the many possible permutations of answers, instructional solutions may vary greatly from one environment or situation to another.

In an ideal world we would each offer a mix of different instructional methodologies and formats, allowing our users to select the ap-

proach that best suits their learning style and current needs. In fact, many of us do offer a variety of instruction in library-related resources, such as paper handouts, in-person library workshops, Web-based instruction, links to Web-based instruction created by others, course-integrated or standalone, in-person group instruction, and the reference desk. Some of these forms of instruction, like signage, are so basic to libraries that it is easy to forget the instructional role they serve. However, most libraries do not have unlimited funds or staff time to develop and maintain all forms of instruction, and circumstances may dictate your making a choice among the multitude of modes and formats. Some instructional projects, programs, or sessions also have pre-established formats that administrators may require librarians to follow, or that an instructor prefers, or that the staff feels represents the best approach (for example, course-integrated group sessions in electronic classrooms utilizing a strictly hands-on approach). Others may be more freeform where librarians volunteer or are assigned to deliver a project, program, or session, but are free to determine modes and formats on their own or in consultation with colleagues as long as the goals and objectives of instruction or the expected learning outcomes are met. Even with a set format, though, often there are ways to enrich instructional efforts by using a variety of techniques and methodologies within a single program, selected by IL librarians, or by offering a larger variety of programs or single-shot options—a cafeteria in a way, where the learners select modes and formats themselves to meet their own needs and preferred learning styles.

In this chapter we will identify categories of instructional modes and consider the factors you need to keep in mind when selecting a mode of instruction.

Which Form of Instruction for Which Situation?

SYNCHRONOUS OR ASYNCHRONOUS

In Chapter 2 we differentiated between "synchronous" and "asynchronous" instruction, using the *Oxford English Dictionary*'s broad definitions for both, with the intention of using these terms to refer to both remote and in-person instruction. Synchronous instruction takes place in real time. That is, the learner or learners participate and interact with the instructor and/or each other at the same time, either in-person or remotely. In academic libraries, most synchronous ILI has taken the form of in-person group instruction for a set interval, a mirror image of the most common form of undergraduate instruction, the class lecture. Public libraries and school libraries also hold synchronous in-person group instruction sessions for their users. Synchronous ILI includes formats such as one-shot, standalone group sessions, in-person guided tours, and guest lectures to classes. Fully course-integrated ILI, less common, includes librarian/instructor collaborative development of course curricula, materials, assignments, as well as some lectures or practical work conducted at the same time, such as synchronous hands-on exercises in an electronic classroom in the library. As technology has advanced, distance learning has become a viable alternative for many people. It has become possible to hold online courses where the learners and the instructor never or only rarely meet in-person. Portions of some of these courses may be conducted synchronously, where all of the participants are working or meeting together online at the same time, for example in a chat room, while others may be asynchronous, for example, where individuals discuss topics via a Web-based discussion board.

Asynchronous instruction takes place anywhere at any time. It does not require simultaneous activity or the physical presence of instructor or learner(s). Examples of asynchronous instruction include paper materials, such as self-paced workbooks and point-of-use guides, as well as electronic/electric materials such as Web-based tutorials and exercises or kiosks. Some online courses may be conducted entirely asynchronously by e-mail. Librarians are working hard to develop and mount attractive and useful Web-based versions of many types of asynchronous instruction in an effort to meet a real or perceived desire for remote or distance learning electronic/electric instruction.

As we shall see in Chapter 17, there are a number of different types of distance education interactions. These distance education interaction types apply to in-person as well as remote instruction, and both may be passive and teacher-centered or active and learner-centered. ILI librarians have often worked with formats such as paper or in-person group sessions. As we have seen in our discussion of learning theories and styles (Chapters 3 and 4), however, people prefer to learn in a number of different ways. To meet these needs, librarians are expanding both the variety and forms of instructional materials in many exciting ways, particularly as the Web both invites and facilitates easy mounting and updating of instructional materials.

Remote or In-Person

It is easy to get confused and to stereotype certain forms of instructional materials so that they seem to represent a single approach or fulfill a particular need. When a particular approach is out of favor or appears to be out of date, it may seem quite simple to decide to dispense with it in favor of another. For example, some libraries have decided to dispense with paper handouts and instead have put informational and instructional materials up on their Websites. Paper materials, however, have multiple uses: They can be used in many different settings, in group instruction, in-person or remotely, or by individuals.

"Remote" refers to instruction utilized asynchronously (any time, any place) by an individual *without* real-time contact with other individuals, or utilized synchronously (in real time) *with* one or more other individuals but at a physical distance from them. This definition would then include paper handouts or workbooks used independently at workstations in the physical library or from a distant location, for example, one's own home. It would also include Web-based discussion boards used by one individual at a time, as well as fully online courses, digital collaboration software, and chat rooms used simultaneously by groups of two or more people.

"In-Person" refers to instruction utilized synchronously (in real time) by one or more individuals, *with* real-time contact with one or more other individuals, face-to-face. This would include instructional modes such as guided tours, face-to-face group instruction sessions, flip charts, blackboards, non-electronic whiteboards used in synchronous group instruction, and reference questions that take place face-to-face within the physical library.

Paper or Electronic/Electric

"Paper" instructional materials may take the form of single or multiple sheets of various sizes, shapes, and colors, such as signage, posters, booklets, and so on. Paper materials may or may not have been designed and produced using some form of technology, such as word-processing or graphics software.

"Electronic/Electric" instructional materials require some sort of technology to use, including devices that require electricity in order to operate. Overhead transparencies fall into this category since you need an overhead projector in order to use them. This category also includes Web-based materials, as well as videotapes.

As we examine a range of instructional modes, keep in mind that we are listing each of these formats separately for the sake of describing their value and use, but they are not necessarily mutually exclusive. You may want to utilize more than one mode for a single instructional purpose or session, in-person group instruction in an electronic classroom, for example. However, you do need to be careful not to go overboard and get carried away with technology. You need to balance your use of technology by carefully considering the audience, the environment (including differing levels of access, hardware, and software), whether or not use of any given technology will help the audience achieve the learning outcomes you have selected, and how much time, effort, and money you have available to develop and maintain a particular type of technology. There are a number of excellent publications that may help guide you in deciding which technologies to use for instruction and how to use them. In *Teaching Online* (2001), Ko and Rossen offer very simple and clear explanations of various types of new technology that can be used in teaching, the benefits and disadvantages of each, and what sort of effort may be required to utilize them. For example, they describe "streaming media" as media files that are sent in a continuous stream to your computer, rather than in one huge file sent all at once (Ko and Rossen, 2001). The advantage of streaming media is that you will be able to see it as it "streams" or downloads to your workstation rather than waiting for the entire file to download before viewing the item. *Teaching the New Library* (LaGuardia et al., 1996) provides a unique perspective on ILI modes by comparing familiar formats, such as "Publications/help guides" with distance- or remote-learning formats for ILI, and by providing examples for each.

SELECTING FROM THE MENU

As libraries begin to understand and accept the fact that people learn differently (see Chapter 3), they may begin to take positive steps toward offering a wider range of instructional materials, sessions, and programs, and allow learners to pick and choose among them to meet their current needs and preferred learning style. It is our responsibility to focus on pedagogical goals in selecting instructional modes that will appear on the user's menu. In doing so, we should reexamine all the forms of instruction we offer with costs and benefits in mind, and not necessarily be tied to a single mode (Eadie, 1990). On the other hand, we must be wary of automatically tossing older forms of instruction such as paper and in-person modes in favor of exclusively Web-based instruction. If we teach only via the Web, we run the risk of assuming that everyone knows how to use the Web, a mouse, or even a computer, and thus may end up teaching only the technologically fluent while ignoring the people who most need to learn, often those at the lower end of the socio-economic spectrum.

Having said that, the Web does present enormous advantages to ILI librarians as well as learners. For ILI librarians, it turns the entire world into a wonderful, gigantic clearinghouse of materials for instruction and research, allowing them to pick and choose or link to a variety of ILI pages and sites, with permission of course. Let us hope, though, that these new primarily Web-based formats and methodologies will enrich the instructional cafeteria with many additional dishes rather than turning it into an "all-meat, all-the-time" establishment, even if all of our users have equal access.

The next chapter describes many different ILI methodologies, but the critical question for ILI librarians is still how to choose the proper modes for instruction. You might begin with some self-reflection. What is your teaching style? Do you like to lay out your instructional plan in detail or just have an outline and wing it on the spot? Do you like interacting with people on a personal level, or do you prefer to work behind the scenes? Would you rather work with groups or one-on-one with individuals? Your answers to these questions and others like them may help determine the instructional role you would like to play and the sorts of teaching techniques or methodologies you would feel most comfortable using. Never taught anything? Oddly enough, your preferred learning style (see Chapter 4) may be a good predictor of your preferred teaching style. Of course, as we have noted, you may not have a lot of choices, especially if you are assigned to work on a particular project. Assigned projects often come with pre-determined modes, while voluntary projects may allow for more freedom of choice. Even with assigned projects, though, you can make a case for experimenting with alternative instructional modes that may match your teaching style more closely.

A number of other factors figure into the selection of instructional modes, especially audience and purpose (goals and objectives or expected learner outcomes to be achieved), cost and budget, time constraints, staff help available, equipment, software, facilities, materials, preparation time, and learner time available. You will also need to consider impact on other staff and programs, personal preferences (your own, as well as those of the administration, other instructional staff, learners, or faculty), and the perceived effectiveness of some modes or instructional tools over others. For online instructional tools, you may be able to find evaluations and comparisons on the Web itself, for example, "Online Educational Delivery Applications: A Web Tool for Comparative Analysis" (Landon, Bruce, and Harby, 2000).

A librarian may be able to make individual instruction decisions on her/his own, though when it comes to establishing a new program or revising an existing one it is extremely important to include your colleagues in the process of selecting teaching modes, especially if they will be involved in the program in any way or if they will shoulder more responsibilities due to a revised or new program. This is true even if the plan is simply to propose a new or revised program to administrators rather than making full plans to implement, as more than one person may be teaching group sessions and/or assisting in preparing or updating instructional materials.

KEY SELECTION FACTORS

What are the critical factors one should keep in mind when selecting a form of instruction, if indeed, one has the luxury of choosing? As we explained in Chapter 7, you will need to begin by identifying needs and establishing or confirming instructional expectations (goals and expected learning outcomes), as well as the expected audience (type, skill levels, and size) and other key issues like staff, facilities, budget, and time constraints, both for preparation and delivery. BI-L, the library instruction listserv, is an excellent place to post queries to other instruction librarians if in-house advice is not available. Attending conferences and networking with others in instruction can also be extremely helpful. However, the following are generic variables that you should take into account when choosing among instructional modes. With the exception of cost and budget, each of these variables appears in the mode selection materials on the CD-ROM that accompanies this book.

Audience/Learners (Type, Age Or Educational Level, Skill Levels, and Size)

Who will the primary learners be, in what age group(s) or educational level(s) do they fall, and what is their level of information literacy expertise and computer literacy skills? How many learners do you need to teach at one time (synchronously)? Do space constraints limit the size of the audience, or is the size a given; for example, enrollees in a particular class? Can the size be limited if demand is great? Can people learn just as well asynchronously as synchronously, or remotely just as well as in-person? For Web-based instruction, the number of learners may not be a critical factor, unless you expect to provide personal feedback to each or if there are a limited number of ports available. However, you do need to determine your primary audience so that you can gear the level of instruction appropriately.

Computer literacy and IL skill levels may differ widely, even within groups that are fairly homogeneous in terms of age and educational background; for example, college freshmen. Yet these are significant factors in ILI, particularly in a period of rapid technological advancement and increasingly widespread access to information resources of all kinds, both information tools and the data itself. In Chapter 1 we delved into various definitions of "information literacy," and in other chapters we have discussed the differences between what computer trainers can do

---

Figure 8-1
Computer Literacy Skill Levels;
Information Literacy Skill Levels

Computer Literacy Skill Levels

None

Never used a computer or mouse; may or may not know how to type; unaware of what the Internet is and how it operates.

Novice/Beginner

May have used computer applications on a simple level, for example, Microsoft Word for basic word processing, or e-mail; limited mouse skills; demonstrates little or no knowledge or use of the Web other than for e-mail; may or may not type.

Intermediate

Has used two or more applications and at least one Web browser (for example, Netscape), and possibly more than one platform (for example, PC and Macintosh); demonstrates some knowledge and use of one or two general Web search tools (for example, Yahoo!); can check out most application capabilities via menus and online help; good mouse skills: can point, click, drag, and drop with ease; may use key combinations or macros in place of some mouse actions or keyboarding (for example, ctrl-C for "copy"); can describe software and hardware problems fairly well, but may not be able to troubleshoot on her/his own; good typing skills.

Advanced

Skilled computer user on one or more platforms, with a number of different applications; demonstrates knowledge of architecture of two or more Web search engines and directories; adept at mechanics of using two or more Web search tools; demonstrates full knowledge of Boolean operators, nesting, and truncation, as allowed by individual systems; troubleshoots many software and hardware problems; manipulates applications to make them perform desired actions, that is, gets around many quirks of an application; fairly quickly grasps architecture of various applications; demonstrates knowledge of standard menu items and icons, and often uses equivalent key combinations or macros; excellent mouse and typing skills.

[Note: At the high end of this continuum, the "Expert" level would include programming and other high-level computing skills.]

Figure 8-1 (*cont.*)
Information Literacy Skill Levels
None
Never used a physical library or an information tool, print (for example, *Readers' Guide to Periodical Literature*) or electronic (for example, Lexis-Nexis Academic Universe); unaware of Internet-related legal and ethical issues.
Novice/Beginner
Has used a physical library to identify and locate materials; may or may not have used an online library catalog (OPAC) or a licensed online database (for example, "Ethnic Newswatch"); demonstrates little knowledge of Web quality control or Internet-related legal and ethical issues.
Intermediate
Has used at least one OPAC and at least one licensed online database to identify and locate print materials in a physical library as well as electronic materials; evaluates the usefulness of print and electronic materials by applying general criteria including authority, accuracy, and recency; identifies some Web quality control and privacy issues; may or may not identify some intellectual property issues, plagiarism, and other Internet-related legal and ethical issues.
Advanced
Uses effectively more than one OPAC and licensed online database, as well as more than one print information tool, as necessary, to identify, locate, evaluate, and use print materials in a physical library, as well as electronic materials; has used at least one controlled vocabulary to focus information searches; demonstrates knowledge of limitations of Web search engines and directories, as well as their relative value in comparison to some other information tools and resources; through her/his usage patterns and information research activities or projects, demonstrates awareness of Web quality control issues, as well as intellectual property, plagiarism, privacy, and other ethical issues related to information and information resources.
[Note: At the high end of this continuum, the "Expert" level would include skills at the level of a librarian.]

and what ILI librarians can do. We have also mentioned the ACRL's "Information Literacy Competency Standards for Higher Education" and the ACRL Instruction Section's "Objectives for Information Literacy Instruction for Academic Librarians." Both of these documents help us define what we mean by "information literacy" in measurable terms. These are excellent contributions to the ongoing dialogue on this topic and will help ILI librarians design and assess instruction.

It may also help to have an idea of how to classify learners' general computer literacy and IL skill levels when you are trying to select modes of instruction. Figure 8–1 provides some working definitions that represent various points on a computer literacy continuum and an IL skills continuum. Both may be extended to the "Expert" level, which would include programming and Web authoring skills on the computer literacy side; on the IL side, it would include substantial expertise in systematic evaluation of information tools and items in a wide variety of formats, both print and electronic. We have extended the categories only through "Advanced" in Figure 8–1 and in the mode selection materials on the CD-ROM that accompanies this book, however, as these are the skill levels most frequently encountered among learners in ILI situations.

Many questions still remain, however—some of which may be addressed through self-reporting Needs Assessments or through pre-tests, post-tests, and other forms of assessment. For example, how do you determine your learners' IL and computer literacy skill levels? What methodologies can be used effectively for different sizes of audiences? What works best for different age and educational levels? Before we can answer these questions, we need to consider the purpose of our instruction.

Purpose

What are your goals and objectives or expected learning outcomes? Which instructional modes will help your audience achieve the learning outcomes you have selected? Are particular modes better suited to achievement of one learning outcome as opposed to another? The answers to these questions will vary from one situation to another and one environment to another. Remember that you do not necessarily need to develop learning outcomes completely on your own. Depending on the audience level, you may be able to select from or mix and match ACRL's "Information Literacy Competency Standards for Higher Education," and ACRL Instruction Sections "Objectives for Information Literacy Instruction for Academic Librarians" as you develop your own set of expected ILI learning outcomes. Which set of standards and which objectives or expected learning outcomes you choose may vary from one program to another, one session to another, or one audience to another, and may change over time. You may want to check with other ILI librarians and experiment on your own, within your budget, which is our next concern.

Budget and Cost

"How much will it cost?" is often the first question an administrator will ask about a proposal for a new or revised instructional program. To answer this question, you will need to do some advance research and find answers to the following questions.

Is there a separate budget? Who controls the budget and how is it allocated? Is there anyone to consult with in-house for advice on weighing costs and benefits of various modes of instruction? How much money will be needed for the entire program? Are administrators more amenable to a pilot project approach with lower initial costs before plunging headlong into a full-scale new or revised program? Are grant funds available, either in-house or externally? Is it necessary to write a detailed formal proposal requesting approval and grant dollars for each aspect of a new or revised program, or does the institution generally provide support for both revisions and new instructional enterprises? Is advance administrative approval necessary in general?

Once you have scoped out the financial environment, including procedures and the approval hierarchy, you will need to estimate both direct and indirect costs.

Direct costs include new or updated versions of software, hardware, outsourced design and development of materials or products, printing or photocopying, supplies, casual workers' time (for example, part-time student hours), materials, publicity, and marketing. Room and equipment rental, refreshments for special workshops or programs, and replacements or substitutes for time devoted to instructional projects are also direct costs.

Indirect costs include staff time needed for design, development, implementation, evaluation, and revision. These costs also include impact on other programs, departments, and staff, within and outside the library, equipment wear and tear, as well as increased demand for services of all kinds. It is tempting to assume that there is no additional cost when salaried staff create or adapt instructional materials. However, the time to do this must come from somewhere. Generally this means that other projects or responsibilities may take longer or may be dropped entirely, unless individuals are replaced by other staff or by temporary hires. Administrators will want to know how librarians are prioritizing their work and what projects or responsibilities will be delayed or receive less attention due to focus on new or revised instructional programs.

It is also important to acknowledge that tradeoffs often occur when it comes to budgetary matters. You may want to consider diplomatic negotiation by writing in-house proposals with goals that can be achieved by a higher cost option, as well as a lower cost one. For example, you may create a quick paper point-of-use guide to identifying and evaluating materials by using a new online system, such as Lexis-Nexis Academic Universe. Or you may want to develop a Web-based interactive tutorial to help users learn the same things. However, a Web-based interactive tutorial may cost more in terms of initial outlay, especially if professional Web designers must be hired to work on the project or if expensive software is needed to develop it. On the other hand, if administrators decide to create Web pages in-house, they may need to purchase software and arrange training for staff. It may then cost little or nothing for the library to provide access to the site, in contrast to the cost of reproducing paper products, and a Website may be more effective, easier to update, and may reach more users than paper handouts. Of course there are many other considerations to keep in mind, such as the cost of upgrading software as necessary, the need to update Web-based materials regularly, and the need to maintain and update staff skills in design and use of various forms of software and hardware needed to maintain the Website.

The interactive Web pages on the CD-ROM that came with this book may give you an idea of specific parameters to consider for each of a variety of instructional methodologies, and may help you select modes appropriate to your circumstances. However, they do not include a cost factor for each instructional mode for several reasons. First, it is difficult to project costs over time, particularly in light of the pace of frequent technological advances. For example, in the mid–1980s it cost about $1,000 per minute to produce a professionally created videotape and was uncommon for libraries to create amateur videos or films for instruction. Camcorders are now commonplace and, as of this writing, can cost under $300, so amateur videos can be created quite cheaply. Voice editing and video editing technology were not available to the general public prior to the 1990s. Now the iMac DV makes it cost effective even to edit videos without expensive professional help.

We have also not addressed cost as a factor because costs can vary depending on the staff time, effort, and level of complexity you choose to invest in a particular instructional mode. For example, you can create point-of-use guides with inexpensive shareware screen capture software, a simple paint program, and word-processing software. These guides can be photocopied on colored paper using an office photocopier. Alternatively, you may hire a graphic artist to create a professional-looking guide and have it printed by a printing service for a much higher fee. Websites too can be simple in-house creations or they can be quite complex, with extensive artwork and programming, requiring a large budget.

Basically, it costs money to design, develop, and implement any instructional mode, though sometimes these costs are indirect and therefore not obvious. Of course, cost and effectiveness do not necessarily go hand in hand, and there is no guarantee that a particular instructional mode will work well in a given situation. Often sufficient staffing is an important key to success.

Staffing: Planning, Preparation, and Delivery

Is this a single-person operation in terms of planning, preparing, and delivering instruction, or are others available to help? If one or more people can help, how much time can they put in, when, and will it be one-time help or on an as-needed basis? Keep in mind that clerical staff who work set schedules may not have the freedom to volunteer their help. In fact, negotiations with their supervisors or other administrators may be necessary, with focus on giving higher priority to information literacy efforts. If at all possible, it might be a good idea to request part-time temporary student help, or write a grant proposal to support some staff time, both clerical and professional, as the case may be.

If you take on a large project, however, even if it is supported by grant funds, you may need to drop or cut back on some shared duties, like reference. This means that someone else will need to take up the slack, and somewhere down the road something will not get done. The best approach is to discuss the pros and cons of all of this with your immediate supervisor and your colleagues. A wise administrator would then work with you and your colleagues to examine everyone's responsibilities, prioritize them, and then drop items off the bottom of the list or find additional resources (especially staff) to help out on a temporary basis during the time you will be working on a special project. Reassigning existing staff can cause problems if people begin to feel like chess pieces, but it may be difficult, if not impossible, to recruit and train temporary staff, especially librarians, unless you are fortunate enough to have part-time librarians on your staff who would like to increase their hours. You really do need to keep in mind the welfare of the institution and the library as a whole, as well as your colleagues, and be cautious about overcommitting without additional support, no matter how exciting a project may seem to you.

Time Constraints: Preparation and Development

How much time is available for preparation? Is partial- or full-release time an option? When new projects are added, what will staff push to the bottom of their lists of responsibilities or delegate to someone else? It is best to discuss this openly and agree upon it with colleagues and administrators before beginning a new project, or some responsibilities will drop off the bottom of priority lists by default.

Are there training manuals for existing programs or other efforts that can be adapted and utilized for this effort? It is a given that staff will need to spend time preparing and developing, as well as delivering instruction, but how much time does or should one person or a group spend on each facet? What impact will this have on other staff and programs, and how should one weigh priorities?

It is difficult to estimate how much preparation and development time may be needed for a particular form of instruction because people work differently and have different standards for acceptable products. In addition, some feel prepared to teach or to provide other instructional materials with minimal support, such as brief outlines of PowerPoint presentations, while others feel compelled to prepare each and every item in great detail. However, a good rule of thumb for preparing group sessions is to allow two hours of preparation time for each hour of in-person presentation time. When preparing interactive exercises for in-person group sessions, it may take many more hours per hour of learning time to develop goals and objectives for the exercise, come up with an interesting and usable format, as well as examples, test the exercise with naive users, and revise it. If it will be distributed as a paper exercise, you will need to allow extra time for printing or photocopying, stapling and collating, and then correcting. During the session, paper materials may be collated in a packet and distributed at the beginning of the session, or handed out at key points. There are time factors and other tradeoffs to all of these approaches, and, in the end, administrators may need to decide how much staff time to devote to a particular project.

Time Constraints: Learning and Timing

How much of the learners' time is available for instruction? You might want to experiment with different lengths of synchronous, in-person group ILI sessions—twenty minutes, thirty minutes, fifty minutes. Or you might just copy brief exercises and put them on handout racks or mount them on your Website for self-teaching, with links to the answers. When would it be best to provide instruction or instructional materials?

The answer: primarily when learners need to know. In colleges and universities, for example, most undergraduates work on research papers at predictable points in a term. They gain most from ILI and are most motivated to learn during these periods. On the other hand, all library users will be motivated to learn a new OPAC when it is first introduced.

Facilities (Space, Equipment, and Software) for Development

What sort of technology is available for developing ILI materials and managing the ILI program? Examples include word-processing software, screen-capture software, paint programs, presentation software, Web browsers, offline Web browsers, scheduling software, database management software, and spreadsheet programs for statistics. Do you have access to a workstation and other equipment (for example, a scanner) that may be used exclusively for development of instructional materials, or do you need to share equipment with others? Is a quiet space available for thinking, planning, designing, and developing materials?

Facilities for Delivery

What sort of space is available for ILI itself? If a classroom is available, how is it equipped? Are there outlets, phone lines, data lines, computers available for hands-on instruction, instructor's workstation, data projector, LCD panel, overhead projector, large screen, monitor, VCR, slide/tape machine, and an Internet connection? Do these rooms and equipment serve other purposes? If so, do they need to be scheduled for use in advance? If not, should they be? What size groups can they accommodate? Do you have control over scheduling them, over the kinds of equipment and software they contain, and how they are configured? Who maintains equipment, upgrades software, and does troubleshooting? If you must share facilities, or if you do not have computer troubleshooting skills yourself, you will probably need to rely on computer technicians or other computer center staff for help. Whether or not you find yourself needing their help, you should make every effort to establish and maintain a good working relationship with computing center and other technical staff. We have a lot to learn from each other as we all aim to help our user populations.

Paper versus Electronic/Electric

What are the advantages and disadvantages of paper as opposed to electronic/electric formats? Paper materials are portable, require no special equipment or software, are easily updateable, can vary in length from one sheet to a hundred or more pages, and can come in various sizes, shapes, and colors. In addition, paper materials are versatile. Groups may use them synchronously or individuals may use them asynchronously for initial learning or for later reinforcement. They may be simple or complex, both in terms of content and design. And depending on the design, learners may be able to skip around by looking through them quickly or by using an index to get to the sections that interest them. However, paper materials can be expensive to reproduce and can become outdated quickly. Most paper materials are designed in a linear fashion and take a single, simplified approach to instruction to save paper and to appeal to the lowest common skill levels.

Some electronic/electric materials may be easily accessible and available, any time, any place. Depending on their complexity, they may or may not allow for quick and easy updating. However, it can take a lot more time, effort, money, and expertise to develop electronic/electric materials than to develop paper materials. Which to choose? You can select paper, electronic/electric, or a combination of them in two ways. You can use the tables or the Web pages on the CD-ROM that accompanies this book to pick a format and look at all the available parameters, such as audience, purpose, and staff time needed. Or you can list your available parameters through the interactive form on the CD-ROM and then look at formats retrieved that match your parameters. The limitations of these parameters will help you determine how extensive or complex a mode you can provide. (See Figures 8–2 and 8–3 for an example.)

This example illustrates the fact that we can draw on a wealth of instructional materials and approaches and do not need to create all of these materials from scratch each time we want to arrange for ILI. Sometimes it just may mean putting together your own grab-bag of useful instructional Websites and materials that you or others have created. We can even draw on materials and approaches used in academic disciplines at all instructional levels, though we should all be aware of intellectual property issues, remember to give credit to others, and to take credit for our own work by putting our names on all the products we create (Schrock, 2000a, 2000b; World Lecture Hall, 2000).

PUTTING IT ALL TOGETHER

Many of the factors listed in the example above apply primarily to in-person group sessions, which represent only one form of instruction, albeit a popular one. Preparation and development time and many other factors may vary widely for other forms of instruction, depending partly on whether or not there are good models available that may be adapted

---

**Figure 8-2
Sample Teaching/Learning Parameters**

- <u>Audience</u>: Middle school students; two classes of thirty-five each
- <u>Purpose (goal)</u>: Help them learn how to evaluate the quality of Web pages
- <u>Staffing (for planning, preparation, and instruction)</u>: One librarian; one clerical staff
- <u>Time constraints: preparation and development</u>: Two weeks
- <u>Time constraints: learning and timing</u>: Thirty minutes learning time available for each of two class meetings, one during week three and the other during week five of the semester
- <u>Facilities (space, equipment, and software) for development</u>: Library office; one workstation with a Web browser, word-processing software, and paint software; printer; copy machine
- <u>Facilities for delivery</u>: School library and computer lab with fifteen workstations with Internet access and a Web browser

---

for different circumstances. No matter how well designed, though, instruction can work only if it meets needs, helps users achieve expected learning outcomes, and is actually used. It follows that those who develop ILI and those who work with learners must know about what is available and its value before they decide whether to use it or not. Knowledge of the range of possibilities will then guide you in making many mode selection decisions, including whether or not to establish an organized, structured ILI program, or to select instructional modes for a variety of situations as the need arises.

One way to publicize and promote your ILI offerings is to use a catchy hook to get learners' attention. For example, you might offer an "Information Literacy Cafe (ILC) & Cooking School," with three basic instructional modules:

1. For steady customers who dine at our cafe weekly:
   - One- or two-unit adjunct courses (collaborative with faculty; interwoven with course goals and assignments)
   - Term-long, stand-alone credit courses
2. For those who want to drop by for a quick meal without a reservation, during open hours:
   - In-person reference questions
   - Research appointments
   - Guided tours

Figure 8-3
Sample Instructional Modes and Process
for Figure 8-2 Scenario

---

1. Brief diagnostic pre-test for Needs Assessment to determine level of information literacy skills and computer skills.
2. Meet with teacher to develop goals and objectives for instruction, and come to agreement on content and supplementary materials, for example, point-of-use guide for Web browser (handout); may use existing guide (Schneider, 2000).
3. In-person synchronous group session to explain goals and process, and to do a small group Website evaluation exercise.
4. Use existing "Hoax? Scholarly Research? Personal Opinion? You Decide!" exercise, with learners partnering up during the class (Grassian and Zwemer, 2000).
5. Select appropriate examples for Web evaluation exercise homework.
6. Use Kathy Schrock's Web evaluation form as homework (2000a).
7. Use second in-person synchronous group session to debrief and collect homework.
8. Administer post-test.
9. Analyze homework and results of post-test, comparing them both to pre-test results.
10. Revise goals, objectives, and/or content accordingly.

---

3. For those who want "take-out":
   - Electronic reference (e-mail; digital collaboration)
   - Self-guided tours
   - Point-of-use guides
   - Paper exercises
   - Web-based exercises
   - Workbook
   - Web-based tutorials, interactive and passive (point-of-use guides mounted on a Website)

The "Cooking School" could be open to anyone interested: librarians, teaching assistants, faculty, and so on, and could be available at different levels: sous chef, assistant chef, pastry chef, or head chef. The idea is that in the Cooking School, attendees would learn how to use various techniques to help learners achieve particular learning outcomes. If you want to attend this school and learn to cook for yourself, an important basic element would be deciding what it is you want to cook and then picking and choosing ingredients or whole recipes or menus that would give you what you want. The Cooking School would also help you learn to develop and make use of assessment instruments to gauge both customer satisfaction and the technical quality of various dishes (effectiveness of instructional approaches in terms of achievement of expected learning outcomes).

There are several difficulties with this approach, of course, including how to get across the notion that some "meals" and "dishes" need to be developed collaboratively and need to support the "party" (academic course) theme. Also, a number of the modes listed above would require an enormous amount of initial work to develop, and then ongoing staff for maintenance, assessment, and revision. Some modes would require additional staff for delivery of instruction as well, while others would not. All of this would require much initial funding and ongoing funding as well. However, this is an example of a structure that might work, especially if you think of it as analogous to a cafe where the menu and servers may change, the menu may be limited to just a few items, and there may be specials, but the cafe and cooking school continue to exist with the goals of offering quality "food" and gently educating both customers and staff as to what actually constitutes quality and how best to achieve customer satisfaction.

FINAL REMARKS

In this chapter we have discussed various categories of ILI modes, offered general advice on picking and choosing among them for your users, and suggested a structure for offering an array of learning options to meet various learning styles and access needs. There are many different options for instructional modes and many different parameters to consider, however. In the next chapter we will examine specific instructional modes in detail.

EXERCISES

1. Identify a synchronous and an asynchronous instructional mode used in your environment (public, special, school, or academic library). Come up with a way to use the synchronous mode asynchronously, and vice-versa.
2. Find an instructional Web page that appeals to you and one that does not. Compare the two pages and identify the characteristics that you like and dislike in each.

3.   Come up with a way to build in-person interaction into paper and electronic/electric instructional modes.

READ MORE ABOUT IT

ALA. Association of College and Research Libraries. Bibliographic Instruction Section. 1983. *Sourcebook for Bibliographic Instruction.* Chicago: American Library Association.

Brottman, May, and Mary Loe eds. 1990. *The LIRT Library Instruction Handbook.* Englewood, CO: Libraries Unlimited.

Ko, Susan, and Steve Rossen. 2001. *Teaching Online: A Practical Guide.* Boston: Houghton-Mifflin.

LaGuardia, Cheryl, Michael Blake, Lawrence Dowler, Laura Farwell, Caroline M. Kent, and Ed Tallent. 1996. *Teaching the New Library: A How-To-Do-It Manual for Planning and Designing Instructional Programs.* New York: Neal-Schuman.

9

The Instructional Menu

"What food these morsels be!"

—Heinz fresh cucumber pickles, 1938.
The New York Public Library Book of Twentieth Century Quotations.

ILI MODES AND MATERIALS

Exactly what sorts of instructional modes do ILI librarians use? How does each of these modes work in the real world? What are the advantages and disadvantages of each? How can we make them more effective?

A number of library instruction-related publications published prior to 1997 listed instructional modes and methodologies, some with advantages and disadvantages of each (LaGuardia, et al., 1996; Hensley, 1993; Brottman and Loe, 1990; Roberts and Blandy, 1989; Svinicki and Schwartz, 1988; Beaubien, Hogan, and George, 1982). Since 1996, though, we have seen an explosion of Web-based sites such as Blackboard.com that allow you to try out an entire online course, or bits and pieces of it, for free; for example, a discussion board. Blackboard.com is just one example of a new form of "e-learning," Web-based sites that are leading us toward massive changes in the number, breadth, and depth of instructional modes we can use for ILI. Yet ILI librarians are still planning and developing other forms of instruction, including "wayfinding" materials, standalone or supplementary aids, usage guides and practice materials, and other individual and group interactive modes. Almost daily, Web pages and sites become more pervasive and more important in information-seeking and ILI. Many of the instructional modes that fall under the categories listed above may appear as Web pages or may be used through Websites. (See also the mode selection tables and the Web pages on the CD-ROM that accompanies this book.)

The Web as a Delivery Medium

It's glitzy, it's grandiose, it's often empty of significant content, and yet, when you hit that rich Web vein—"The English Server" at Carnegie-Mellon University, U.S. National Library of Medicine sites, or the University of California's "MELVYL™ Catalog"—you are instantly empowered. You hate it, you love it, you cannot live with it, you cannot imagine life without it, as it was in PW (pre-Web) days, before we could be anywhere in the world instantly, touring, shopping, learning, listening, discovering, reading, and printing out whole books, articles, government documents, and more. Is the Web simply a conglomeration, an indescribably tangled mess of pages and sites, unindexed, unregulated, and unreviewed? Yes, and yet this "mess" is an incredible tribute to human creativity and a marvelous delivery system, a way for people and groups to connect, to share information with each other. Some of that information is valid, authoritative, accurate, complete, and up to date, while some is not. Bias is apparent on some pages; it may be hidden or unintended on others. Individuals create some Web pages as personal statements, sometimes known as "vanity pages," or as "vacuum cleaner" sites that attempt to gather up all available information on a topic. Many sites are unreviewed, that is, no one looks them over to decide whether or not they contain accurate, reliable information. Others are subject to rigorous review by experts in a particular field or by sponsoring organizations, institutions, or groups.

For those unfamiliar with the Web, it seems like a quagmire, an easy place to get lost and an easy way to be misled. Should we use the Web for ILI? For those on the advantaged side of the digital divide, this is not even an issue. However, we cannot take it for granted that everyone we wish to reach will have easy access to a computer and an Internet connection. As we noted in Chapter 2, an increasing number of people are on the disadvantaged side of the digital divide. They do not have a computer at home and do not have an Internet connection. Because they are left out of the Web world, we need to consider carefully whether and how we will use the Web to deliver instruction, and what sorts of other alternatives or additional approaches we might use.

You can deliver many of the following modes of instruction through the Web. However, we have also listed "Web Pages/Sites" as a separate instructional mode both for consciousness-raising about the audience you may be able to reach with the Web, and because of its increasing pervasiveness as an informational and instructional tool.

Wayfinding Modes

SIGNAGE (REMOTE: PAPER; ASYNCHRONOUS)

Libraries use signage for many different purposes, including warning, direction, information, orientation, and instruction. Warning, directional, and informational signage appear most commonly in physical library locations, usually in paper and posted in conspicuous areas. Some libraries place simple instructional signs in areas where users may need help with mechanics of using simple equipment or hardware, such as a microfilm reader or a printer.

Pros:

- Can help identify and distinguish between service points in the physical library
- Available all open hours
- Can be handlettered or printed fairly quickly and cheaply with simple word-processing software, and then photocopied on white or colored paper
- Can serve as a welcoming, positive force, an aid in relieving library anxiety
- Professionally prepared signs are usually more durable and attractive

Cons:

- May need to be updated frequently
- Overuse can result in loss of effectiveness
- Professionally prepared signs cost more, take more time to prepare
- Can be confusing or ineffective and anxiety-provoking if poorly designed

Tips for Effective Use:
Try to make your signage consistent, clear, and simple. Signage that is phrased positively can be particularly effective. For example, instead of listing restrictions, such as "No Food or Drink," list what is allowable, for example: "Drinks in Sealed Containers Only" (Kupersmith, 1984,

1987). Remember to use signage at key points to avoid overwhelming users with too many signs.

MAPS (REMOTE: PAPER OR ELECTRONIC/ELECTRIC; ASYNCHRONOUS)

Many physical library users rely heavily on maps for self-help in locating materials, service points, and other locations within a single building, or in multiple buildings within a larger area such as a college campus.

Pros:

- Maps can save users time in locating specific areas or service points in the physical library
- A single paper page can have a map on one side and additional important information on the other, for example, hours, phone numbers, URL for Website
- Printed maps provide fairly low cost visual aids
- Web-based maps can become self-guided Web-based tours if there are links to descriptions of various areas of a building, along with guidelines or rules for library use, hours of service, etc.

Con:

- In order to squeeze in as much information as possible, the typeface or font may be so reduced in size that they are difficult to read
- Printed maps may be costly to reproduce and some information, such as hours of operation, may become outdated quickly

Tips for Effective Use:
Research on museum handout maps indicates that visitors need and want simple "wayfinding" guides. Research also shows that visitors are more satisfied with their visit if these sorts of maps are available (Talbot, Kaplan, Kuo, and Kaplan, 1993). You might consider mounting a library map on your Website, with links both to brief descriptions of what is available in a particular area and to related information. For example, if you have a map of the reference area, clicking on the literary criticism area might bring up a Web page with a selection of tips and tutorials for identifying, locating, and evaluating literary criticism materials.

SITE MAPS (REMOTE: ELECTRONIC/ELECTRIC; ASYNCHRONOUS)

"Site maps" are generally outlines of a Website that lay out its structure and content.

Pros:

- Site maps can save time by providing quick and easy entry to a specific page or path on a Website and at the same time can provide a snapshot of the site's scope, whatever its size
- They may appeal to learners who like to see the whole picture and then focus on specific segments, or who know what sort of information they want to find on a site but are not sure where the Website designer has put it

Cons:

- Website map labels (page titles) can be confusing if they are obscure or utilize jargon
- Site maps must be maintained

Tips for Effective Use:
Remember that site maps are supposed to mirror the structure of a site. Each time a page is deleted, added, or linked to from a different page on the site, the site map needs to be updated. Site maps should include each and every page within the site, but not links to pages off-site. Every page listed on a site map should link directly to that page to enable easy access. Text-only site maps work well both for the general public and for disabled users.

KIOSKS (REMOTE: ELECTRONIC/ELECTRIC; ASYNCHRONOUS)

Library kiosks are usually touch-screen, standalone workstations placed within some sort of stand near or within the entrance to a library building. They may have a map of the building layout or provide quick answers to a list of frequently asked questions (FAQs). Some kiosks are much more extensive. For example, Public Information Kiosk, Inc. has developed a kiosk that allows you to use a library's online catalog, apply for a library card, or become a member of Friends of the Library by filling out an application provided via the kiosk and faxing it using the kiosk's built-in fax machine. You can pay for your membership by using a credit card in the same machine, and much more (Commings, 1996).

Pros:

- Available whenever the area in which it is stationed is open
- Touch-screen kiosks do not require typing skill

Cons:
- Questions and needs are pre-determined, and may not meet or match all needs
- May require frequent updating

Tips for Effective Use:
Do a Needs Assessment of those who come to the physical library to find out if they would use a kiosk and what kinds of information they would like to get from a kiosk before spending a lot of time and effort developing and designing one. Make sure screens are simple and that users need to go down only three levels at most to get to the information they want. Provide good, simple signage regarding kiosk use and referral to live help as well as a URL or e-mail address for virtual help.

GUIDED TOURS (IN-PERSON; SYNCHRONOUS)

Tours generally provide orientation to a building and a library's services. In some cases, ILI librarians may combine a physical tour with brief instruction in the use of reference tools.

Pros:

- In-person guided tours provide personal contact and allow visitors to ask questions
- Tours can be a cheap and easy solution to an ongoing problem of erratic, unpredictable interest in physical orientation to a building and services
- Tours can serve as positive public relations for the library and help users feel more comfortable and less anxious
- Tours can reduce the number of directional questions at a reference or information desk

Cons:

- Staff need to spend time planning and conducting in-person guided tours
- In-person tours may reach relatively few users

Tips for Effective Use:
Research on museum tours indicates that guided (structured) tours result in significant increases in learning, while self-guided (unstructured) tours result in more positive attitudes (Stronck, 1983). The challenge may lie in how to increase both measures for all types of tours. For in-person guided tours, it helps to have a friendly, warm manner, match your walking speed to the tour participants, welcome questions, and be careful not to overwhelm people with too many facts and figures. It is important to cover the basics and to avoid providing too much detail in a guided tour, detail that could be conveyed better in a paper handout or on a Website.

SELF-GUIDED TOURS (IN-PERSON: PAPER; REMOTE: ELECTRONIC/ELECTRIC; ASYNCHRONOUS)

Some libraries provide self-guided paper or electronic/electric tours on audio tape or CD-ROM.

Pros:

- Tours can be a cheap and easy solution to an ongoing problem of erratic, unpredictable interest in physical orientation to a building and services
- They can serve as positive public relations for the library and help users feel more comfortable and less anxious
- Friendly pre-packaged, self-guided tours—in paper, on audio cassette or CD-ROM—can be useful substitutes when staff are unavailable, or for remote users
- Tours can reduce the number of directional questions at a reference or information desk
- Users can stop self-guided tours in order to take more time to understand a particular point

Cons:

- Tours of all kinds may need frequent updating
- It may be expensive to reproduce copies of paper self-guided tours
- For audio and CD-ROM tours, you will need to purchase equipment and replace it as it gets worn out or damaged

Tips for Effective Use:
For self-guided tours, it helps to structure the tour by numbering stopping points and providing corresponding numbers on a paper handout,

or by speaking numbers on a taped or CD-ROM-based tour as you come to a particular point. For virtual tours, be wary of using too many large images, which may slow down the speed at which a Web page loads.

Virtual Tours (Remote: Electronic/Electric; Asynchronous)

Tours may be mounted on a Website as static images or combined with text. Web-based maps and virtual tours may be linked together or may link to FAQs or to the instructional areas of a Website.

Pros:

- All of the positive points mentioned about self-guided tours also apply to virtual tours
- Virtual tours can help users figure out where they need to go before arriving at a physical location
- Web-based tours can serve as friendly and non-threatening entries to more complex areas of a library's Website, such as interactive instructional materials
- Users can meander here and there at their own pace with a virtual tour, picking and choosing which areas they would like to visit, and in which order
- Users can interrupt and return to a virtual tour at any time

Cons:
- The virtual tour may need to be updated frequently
- Software to create virtual tours and staff time to do the work can be expensive

Standalone and Supplementary Aids

Exhibits (Remote: Paper; Asynchronous)

Hand-lettered signs, glossy photos, professionally printed posters, blown-up sample Websites, sample research papers—any or all of these (and others) may constitute an exhibit or display mounted in the physical library.

Pros:

- Exhibits can be eye-catching and consciousness-raising, as well as instructional in the traditional sense
- Exhibits in the physical library can get across important points

briefly, often with visuals and other materials; for example, sample research papers

Cons:

- Exhibits can take much time and effort to design, develop, mount, and keep up to date
- Professionally printed or prepared exhibit materials can be quite costly

Tips for Effective Use:
Decide on a few simple objectives that meet critical user needs. For example, appeal to the undergraduate's desire to save time by focusing on basic steps to doing a research paper. Come up with an interesting hook that will get the attention of your learner community. Keep your focus on the basics or on a particular aspect of a topic, and distill words and ideas down to key phrases and images. Make use of existing instructional materials to constitute or to supplement the exhibit in the physical library. For virtual exhibits, you can also link to existing instructional materials on your library's Website or at other Websites.

FLIP CHARTS, BLACKBOARDS, WHITEBOARDS (IN-PERSON; SYNCHRONOUS; REMOTE: ASYNCHRONOUS)

Flip charts are large pads of perforated paper usually placed on a floor stand or tabletop stand. Blackboards, older technology than whiteboards, are made of slate and most often mounted on a wall. Blackboards require the use of chalk, though, as school teachers may tell you, thin paper items may also be attached to blackboards by using magnets. Whiteboards may be attached to walls, may be on a rolling floor stand, or may even double as flip chart easels. You write on whiteboards with special marking pens rather than chalk.

Pros:

- None of these technologies require advance design, training, or electricity to use and they can serve as handy backups for any sort of instruction that requires electricity-dependent technology
- All of them can be used both by instructors and learners, in synchronous in-person group instruction sessions, and require only simple writing tools
- Whiteboards and flip charts can serve as asynchronous, temporary informational signage or point of use instruction, can be

changed quickly and easily, and can be placed in strategic locations to attract attention to a particular information resource and
then provide guidance in its use
- Whiteboard and flip chart markers come in different colors, allowing the instructor or learners to increase interest and draw
attention to specific items
- Flip chart pages can be taped to a wall, moved around to different locations, and you can take them with you to transcribe at a
later time

Cons:

- If placed in public areas, flip chart, whiteboards, and blackboards
are subject to erasure and "creative annotation" by users
- Notes on flip chart pages may need to be transcribed and reorganized for later use or to share with others
- You can only save information on a blackboard or non-electronic
whiteboard by copying it down manually or with a word-processing program or other application

Tips for Effective Use:
These technologies help the audience keep track of where they are if
you number flip chart pages as you go along or use colored markers
consistently; for example, red for the most important points. Flip charts
can be quite handy devices for outlines and review because you can
stack pages on top of each other and cover them with blank sheets of
paper until you are ready to use them. You can do the same with blackboards and whiteboards, though you may need to erase and reuse part
or all of the space as needed. If you have a blackboard or whiteboard on
wheels or on an easel, though, you can also prepare partially completed
outlines, charts, or other supplementary materials and then hide them
by turning them around until you are ready to use them.

OVERHEAD TRANSPARENCIES (IN-PERSON: ELECTRONIC/ELECTRIC;
SYNCHRONOUS)

Transparencies are 8-1/2" × 11" clear plastic sheets onto which you can
write, draw, type, print, or photocopy in color or in black ink. An overhead projector enlarges whatever appears on the transparency and displays it by projecting the image on a wall or a screen. Special marking
pens allow you to write on transparencies at any time, even while they
are being projected.

Pros:

- Overhead projectors require only electricity and a projector light bulb to operate
- You can project images on a screen, a sheet hung on a wall, or the wall itself
- Overhead transparencies are quite versatile; you can use graphics and clip art or simply draw or write on them in advance or during a session
- You can create and print out course outlines to frame an instructional session or print enlarged computer screens on them in the order in which you will present them
- Overhead transparencies can also serve as backups in the event of unexpected problems connecting to a network or making a modem connection
- They can be used effectively for active learning exercises

Cons:

- You need an electrical supply in order to use an overhead projector and an area that can be darkened, as well as a wall or screen on which to project images
- Overhead transparencies are static, yet many learners are used to and expect motion, so it may be more difficult to keep their attention with overhead transparencies, especially if you turn off the lights so that they can be viewed more clearly
- It can be daunting to use an overhead projector for the first time, as it may be difficult to know which way to turn the transparencies, how long to leave them on the projector, and what to do if you drop the entire stack of overheads and they get all mixed up

Tips for Effective Use:
You can put overheads in plastic sleeves and number them so that you can manipulate them more easily, and so you can get them back in order quickly if you drop them. Timed "dress rehearsals" in front of an audience of one or two colleagues can also help in alleviating teaching anxiety regarding use of overhead transparencies and overhead projectors. It also helps to think about the fact that when you use overheads the audience is looking at the overheads rather than at you (Wood, 1995).

IN-PERSON PRESENTATION SLIDE SHOWS (IN-PERSON: ELECTRONIC/ELECTRIC; SYNCHRONOUS

Presentation software enables you to create slide shows that may include screen shots, captured images, clip art, motion, animation, and audio effects. You can insert movement, animation, sound, clip art, graphics, and captured images in these slide shows fairly easily because they are computerized. On a more basic level, these slide shows may just consist of simple text, closely resembling overhead transparencies or framed pages prepared with word-processing software. Slides may also be printed out on overhead transparencies or as handouts, and can be mounted on Websites.

Pros:

- The software is versatile
- The templates can help the teacher/presenter structure a session logically
- Hidden instructor's notes can accompany each slide
- If movement is incorporated into the slide show, the audience will pay more attention in group sessions
- The audience may be able to follow an instruction session better if it is outlined for them and if important points are noted on the slide show
- If learners have a printed outline of the session they are more likely to pay attention to the content rather than trying to take complete notes during an in-person group session
- Learners may visit a Website at any time to view a slide show shown in a group session or to see a slide show mounted as an additional form of instruction

Cons:

- Development and use of slide shows using presentation software requires electricity and a workstation with monitor
- You will also need some means of projecting the image (a data projector or an LCD panel with an overhead projector), unless you print the slides out and use them as overheads
- There is a learning curve for even simple, basic use of the software
- Instructors may overwhelm students by placing too much text on a slide, using too many slides, or using distracting backgrounds, animation, color, or movement, which make slides hard to read

- Instructors may become rigidly locked into the slide show sequence and find it hard to skip around or be spontaneous in response to audience questions
- Slide shows mounted on Websites may seem static and users often proceed through them in a linear fashion, though some Websites do allow you to skip around

Tips for Effective Use:
You will need to learn how to use the software, but you can speed up the learning process by partnering with someone else who is willing to coach you. You might even try trading presentation software lessons from a computer trainer for information research lessons. Presentation software often comes with templates to help you develop slide shows for specific purposes, such as presenting to, persuading, or educating an audience.

Remember to turn off the projector when the slide on the screen is no longer the topic of discussion. Turn it back on to continue with the show, or alternate between the slide show and other resources. For example, when teaching Web search tools, you might also want to show some examples of searches on the same topic in a licensed database or two and then explain the differences between these tools.

If you use PowerPoint, "Notes" pages can be a handy way to organize, from an instructor's standpoint, by allowing you to link topics, activities, and speaker's points to appropriate slides. You just type in your planned comments on hidden Notes pages, print them out, and have a session ready to go, with notes right under pictures of the slides to which they refer.

When used appropriately, especially in ten-minute segments, presentation software such as PowerPoint, RealSlideshow, and Quicktime can be an effective supplementary instructional tool (Ko and Rossen, 2001). Presentation software is particularly useful for introducing a synchronous group session, for providing an outline of a session, and for reviewing main points during and at the end of an instructional session. You can also support in-class exercises by keeping track of group topics, issues, and important points, when learners respond or report back from small group work. In addition you can illustrate concepts such as Boolean operators through the use of Venn diagrams, portrayed on a series of slides (see Figures 9-1 and 9-2). However, one research study seemed to indicate higher learner satisfaction in sessions where PowerPoint was not used (Bushong, 1998). Simplicity and judicious use are key to the effective use of presentation software. (See also Chapter 17.)

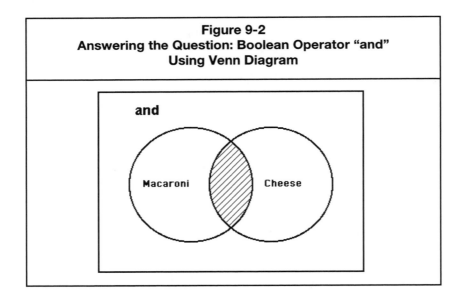

Figure 9-1
Posing the Question: Boolean Operator "and"
Using Venn Diagram

and?

Macaroni   Cheese

Figure 9-2
Answering the Question: Boolean Operator "and"
Using Venn Diagram

and

Macaroni   Cheese

REMOTE PRESENTATION SLIDE SHOWS (REMOTE: ELECTRONIC/ELECTRIC; ASYNCHRONOUS OR SYNCHRONOUS)

Presentation slide shows can be used in synchronous group sessions (in-person or remotely), mounted on a Website as a standalone instructional piece or as part of a larger instructional package.

Pros:

- The software is versatile
- The templates can help the teacher/presenter structure a session logically
- Hidden instructor's notes can accompany each slide.
- If movement is incorporated into the slide show, the audience will pay more attention in group sessions
- The audience may be able to follow an instruction session better if it is outlined for them, and if important points are noted on the slide show

Cons:

- Development of slide shows using presentation software requires electricity and a workstation with monitor
- You will also need to mount the slide show on a Website and perhaps do some editing if it is to be used asynchronously
- There is a learning curve for even simple, basic use of the software
- Instructors may overwhelm students by placing too much text on a slide, using too many slides, or using distracting backgrounds, animation, colors, or movement, which make slides hard to read
- Instructors may become rigidly locked into the slide show sequence and find it hard to skip around or be spontaneous in response to audience questions

Tips for Effective Use:
Same as the first and last paragraphs presented under In-Person presentation slide shows "Tips for Effective Use."

For synchronous remote sessions, you may want to use presentation software slides just at key points; for example, to display an outline of what you are planning to cover, to highlight one or two important points or questions, or to display at the end of the session a review of what was covered. You can illustrate concepts such as Boolean operators through the use of Venn diagrams portrayed on a series of slides.

Slides/Tapes and Videotapes (In-Person: Electronic/Electric; Synchronous; Remote: Electronic/Electric; Synchronous)

Simple slides/tapes and short (ten-to-twelve-minute) instructional videos with amateur actors, minimal live dialogue, and voiceovers require few instructional staff to produce. Prior to the advent of the Web, both media provided reasonably priced, effective means of providing instruction to masses of learners. Change occurred at a slower pace in libraries in the 1980s and early 90s when library instructional slides/tapes and videos were most popular, so they were not apt to need as frequent updating as they would today. Slides synchronized with an audiotape were also useful for baseline orientation and instruction. Slides and tapes can be produced independently and synchronized following production. Often, ILI videos have a story line that maps out or parallels someone struggling to find information, for example, "Searchin' Safari" (Smith, 1987) and "Navigating the Sea of Information" (University of Pittsburgh, 1997).

Pros:

- Both slides/tapes and videotapes can capture an audience's interest with movement and a variety of images and voices
- Some individual slides may be replaced with new slides as circumstances change
- Both may be developed on a fairly low budget, particularly now that camcorders are fairly inexpensive and widely available
- As software and hardware change in our current dynamic environment, it may become less costly to revise or replace all or portions of videotapes
- Digitizing slides preserves images and allows one to display them without the need for a separate slide projector or carousel

Cons:

- Both slides/tapes and videotapes take a rather large investment of planning and preparation time, and there are limitations to easy and cheap revision, especially of videos
- Professional videos require pre-production, production, and post-production time, money and effort, including rehearsals, actors, voiceovers, and professional filming—all of which may add greatly to production cost
- Video content needs to be carefully defined and limited in scope
- Streaming video requires much bandwidth and is not a practi-

cal option at present for remote use with dial-up connections, though increased bandwidth and newer technology may solve this problem before long

Tips for Effective Use:
An interesting ten-minute video can keep an audience's attention, but interest starts to drop off after that time. Both slides/tapes and videos can be used along with other forms of instruction, such as group sessions or exercises. Slides may be digitized and displayed using presentation software, such as PowerPoint (Ko and Rossen, 2001). Videos may be produced and screened for in-person group sessions or remotely on a loop in a public area. They may also be saved on a CD-ROM for later viewing or mounted on a Website and viewed remotely as "streaming video" (Ko and Rossen, 2001; Smith, 1987; French and Butler, 1988; Fidler, 1999).

Videotapes or video clips can be quite useful teaching tools when used in moderation. For in-person synchronous instruction, you might want to show part of a controversial video to illustrate a point about IL research or to start a discussion on how one might go about searching for information on a particular topic. You can even stop a video in midstream and engage the learners in questions about what will happen next and why. For example, in one scene in "Searchin' Safari" two undergraduates go to the reference collection to try to browse through reference books in an effort to find information on the topic of computer crime (Smith, 1987). You could stop the video just as one of the students picks up a volume of *The World Book Encyclopedia* and then ask your learners to predict whether or not this is a useful approach, and why or why not. Videos can be used passively or interactively, and, as bandwidth capabilities increase, we will be seeing more ILI videos on the Web. Videos shown remotely on a loop or streamed on the Web can stand alone as instructional tools.

Usage Guides and Practice Materials

POINT-OF-USE GUIDES (IN-PERSON: PAPER; SYNCHRONOUS; REMOTE: PAPER; ASYNCHRONOUS)

Librarians have been preparing step-by-step guides to the mechanics of using particular reference tools for many years. Usually, paper copies are placed near the tool. In pre-computer times, libraries could purchase one-page, point-of-use guides, which were designed to be photocopied and pasted inside the front cover of each volume of indexes like *The Reader's Guide to Periodical Literature* (Mountainside Press, Inc., 1980).

Point-of-use guides are quite popular, given the enormous and confusing array of reference tools currently available in various formats. Web-based, point-of-use guides constitute one form of "tutorial" (see below). Point-of-use guides may be used asynchronously by individuals or synchronously in face-to-face group instruction sessions for hands-on sessions.

Pros:

- Point-of-use guides provide simple, clear instructions to meet a learner's need to know how to use a particular tool, database, or system on the spot
- Paper versions are portable, suitable for note-taking, and can be consulted while utilizing the resource for which they are providing instruction

Cons:

- Point-of-use guides do not place a tool in context or provide a range of information sources available on a particular topic or in a discipline
- Often they focus on the mechanics of using a tool and do not include much information on research strategy or critical thinking
- Point-of-use guides may require frequent updating as well as expensive photocopying, both of which can be a drain on staff time

Tips for Effective Use:
Because there is not enough time in a one-shot session to teach everything we would like to cover, many librarians now try to teach basic transferable concepts during in-person group sessions and distribute paper point-of-use handouts to cover the mechanics of using electronic resources. You can use these guides as an outline for part of a hands-on session, and learners may take them away for later use. You can use them both for learning and for reinforcement (Turner, 1993). In addition, point-of-use guides can serve as substitutes for some one-on-one instruction at a busy reference desk and can be readily available when reference staff are not on duty.

PATHFINDERS (REMOTE: PAPER OR ELECTRONIC/ELECTRIC; ASYNCHRONOUS)

Pathfinders are brief, systematic guides to identifying and locating (and sometimes evaluating) material on particular topics. These topics are often multidisciplinary, difficult to track down, or frequently used for research papers. They are usually written in search strategy order and include key reference sources, as well as useful searching tips and subject headings. Most paper pathfinders are about one- to three-pages long; Web-based versions may be longer. As with signs and other paper instructional materials, paper versions may be prepared cheaply with word-processing software and photocopied, or they may be printed professionally at greater expense (Canfield, 1972; Stevens, Canfield, and Gardner, 1973; Thompson and Stevens, 1985). Some libraries still maintain some paper pathfinders, while others have mounted pathfinders on their Websites (Reichardt, 2000; Reusch, 1998).

Pros:

- Pathfinders can help library users who often do not know where to begin doing research
- They can serve as a quick way to instruct in a concept or approach to finding materials in a particular area—often hard-to-identify or hard-to-use materials
- Well-laid-out pathfinders can serve as search strategy models
- It may take just a one-time investment of intensive staff time to create a pathfinder template and lay out the basics
- Creating a pathfinder can be a good staff training project for a novice instruction librarian as an introduction to a more in-depth method of approaching research needs

Cons:

- The usefulness of a given pathfinder may be limited, as interest in various topics shifts
- They may require additional investment of staff time for updating and revision
- Some user feedback is essential to determine the continued usefulness of particular pathfinders and whether or not they should be updated or revised

Tips for Effective Use:
The shifting nature of information resources can make pathfinder development and maintenance difficult and time-consuming. However, pathfinders can be highly effective instructional tools, especially if they fulfill specific learning outcomes linked to courses, and are designed in collaboration with the course instructor or teacher. The pathfinder will then reflect both the content expert's and the librarian's view of the most important research tools for a given area or assignment. In addition, the

librarian can arrange the pathfinder in search strategy order and add searching tips and techniques, as well as recommended subject headings. In a more learner-centered approach, librarians teaching classes have asked learners to compile annotated pathfinders as a class assignment (Weaver, 1999).

EXERCISES (IN-PERSON: PAPER OR ELECTRONIC/ELECTRIC; SYNCHRONOUS; REMOTE: PAPER OR ELECTRONIC/ELECTRIC; ASYNCHRONOUS)

Exercises are practice materials that generally require people to learn by doing and can be designed for initial learning or for reinforcement following other forms of instruction. Exercises may be individual, standalone paper handouts, may be sequenced to form a workbook (see below), mounted on a Website, or used in participatory (active learning) activities that can take place in synchronous sessions, in-person or remotely. (See Chapter 6 for discussion of active learning techniques.) Exercises may be designed to be used on their own or in combination with other forms of instruction.

Pros:

- Exercises can be designed to teach the use of one or more tools (for example, "ERIC"), systems (for example, "Cambridge Scientific Abstracts"), or concepts (for example, controlled vocabulary)
- They may not need much revision over time, depending on the content
- Feedback can be provided by correcting exercises
- Users may be able to pick and choose the exercises that meet their needs

Cons:

- Exercises may need frequent updating, particularly for electronic resources
- If feedback is not provided, or if it is delayed too much, learning may suffer

Tips for Effective Use:
Brief exercises that focus on a particular skill or aspect can be highly effective instructional tools, both for group and for individual self-teaching. Many exercises are designed so that there is only one correct answer for each question, though in participatory (active learning) exercises there may or may not be a single right answer. In group participa-

tory activities, sometimes the exercise itself is an important learning experience. For example, Web-based exercises may be designed to teach critical thinking by raising more questions than answers. Quick feedback is important no matter which form of exercise you use. Gaynor's summary of BI-L responses regarding hands-on exercises for freshman seminar classes provided a wealth of useful ideas, arranged in categories such as "Tactics to encourage staying on-task" and "Exercise design/content" (1999).

Other Individual and Group Interactive Modes

WORKBOOKS (REMOTE: PAPER OR ELECTRONIC/ELECTRIC; ASYNCHRONOUS)

Paper and Web-based workbooks represent an important asynchronous "learning by doing" instructional mode. They usually consist of a series of brief explanations on the use of different reference tools followed by questions requiring students to use the tools to find answers. Workbooks often begin with a tour and are arranged in search strategy order. Dudley's *Library Skills Workbook* established a model for paper workbooks, and some Web-based tutorials follow a similar model (SUNY Buffalo, 2000a, 2000b).

Pros:

- Workbooks can help learners see that there is a structure and logical flow to searching for information on a topic, while at the same time exposing them to a wide variety of reference tools
- Exercises that require actual use of reference tools can help make a scary and overwhelming mass of reference sources seem much more manageable and understandable
- They can be tailored to any subject area (general or discipline-specific), any age or grade level, for any setting, and can teach the use of any format of material
- Workbooks provide a real-life experience, hands-on, which respects individual differences in learning style by allowing learners to proceed independently
- They offer users an opportunity for meaningful self-paced self-education
- Feedback is provided through corrected questions, but also may be provided virtually or in person
- Paper workbooks can be completely self-supporting in terms of staff help, printing, and purchase of extra copies of reference tools
- Some personal interaction can be built in by requiring students

to ask for materials at a reference desk or to consult with a librarian on incorrect answers
- Following initial development, workbooks can reach many students with a small investment of staff time
- They can cover many or just a few reference tools or subject areas, as desired

Cons:

- There may not be much personal interaction
- Both paper and online workbooks require much initial staff time to develop, though online versions require more time, skill, and effort for initial design and development
- Paper versions require staff time to update and supervise revision, printing, compilation, and correction
- They may be considered "just-in-case" instruction unless they are tied to a specific course or need

Tips for Effective Use:
Plan carefully for initial workbook development by determining and writing down goals and objectives or expected learning outcomes for the entire workbook and for each part of it. Make each segment self-contained and word each sparingly, yet with interesting and useful questions and ideas. Use multiple-choice questions for easy correction, and try to incorporate critical thinking throughout. Consider requesting grant funding to develop a first workbook as a pilot project, with pre-testing and post-testing and an expectation that it will take time and effort to develop the workbook as a measurably useful ILI product (Phipps, 1980). Staggered due dates can help ILI staff manage a large paper workbook workload, both in helping learners complete exercises and in correcting completed workbooks. Web-based assessment instruments can also speed the correction process and provide important immediate feedback to learners.

Tutorials (Remote: Electronic/Electric; Asynchronous)

Tutorials may be electronic versions of point-of-use guides, or holistic ILI guides or a conglomeration of pieces of both. Electronic point-of-use guides often take the learner through the mechanics of using a particular information resource, while holistic instruction guides and combined versions usually cover much more. For example, "RIO" contains a module on writing papers with a checklist/timetable for research papers to help students pace their time throughout a term (University of Arizona Library, 2000b). Tutorials may also include interaction, critical thinking and evaluation regarding a range of information resources, as well as guides to citation style, information about plagiarism, preservation, and the ethics of information use, and other topics. Interactivity, by definition, requires input from the user and feedback from the system.

Pros:

- Tutorials can provide "just-in-time," rather than "just-in-case" instruction
- They can be available 24/7 (24 hours a day/7 days a week) to anyone with an Internet connection
- Interactive tutorials can provide immediate feedback
- Tutorials for a specific information tool can be printed out and consulted while utilizing the resource that they attempt to teach
- Users may be able to test out of specific areas of a holistic tutorial, or skip around in it, learning the bits and pieces that interest them or fill their current information need

Cons:

- Learners may need to switch back and forth from the electronic version to the information resource itself if they are unable to print the tutorial
- If a tutorial is designed in many very small chunks, users may lose interest and feel they are not learning enough for the time they need to invest
- Maintenance and updating may require much staff time

Tips for Effective Use:
The Silverplatter "WebSPIRS Online Tutorial" is a good example of online instruction that is limited to the mechanics of using a particular product, and which could be designed by a computer trainer (2000). It utilizes Shockwave, a sophisticated presentation application, which requires the use of a "plug-in" (a small piece of software that you can download for use with a Web browser) to view the tutorial. The plug-in is free, but you must have a computer that has enough memory and processing speed to handle it, and you must have a fairly up-to-date version of a Web browser as well. Even with a high-speed network connection, the extensive graphics take some time to load. Simulations of searching included in this tutorial are helpful, but again, take so much time to load that users are likely to miss out as they simply click to continue with the tutorial, thinking that there is no more to be seen in a particular segment. Dial-up connections would make use of this tuto-

rial quite a lengthy exercise. On the other hand, by mounting this tutorial on the Web, Silverplatter has saved quite a bit in expensive costs of sending trainers out to sites that subscribe to their products. The tutorial can be reused again and again at no additional cost, other than the users' time, and can be updated fairly easily, when necessary. Interactivity in this tutorial seems to be limited to the users' ability to move between segments or modules and to click on an arrow to continue.

The University of Texas, System Digital Library has gone further, providing both a basic and an advanced version of their tutorial, "TILT" (2000). The advanced version of "TILT" also requires the Shockwave plug-in and is arranged in modules. According to Dupuis, the "TILT" tutorial incorporates "interactions throughout the entire tutorial that relate to various cognitive taxonomies such as evaluation, synthesis, analysis, and application" (1999c: [online]). "RIO," the University of Arizona's online tutorial, on the other hand, is simpler and more straightforward, requiring no plug-in software. Both of these interactive tutorials are attractive, seem to have well-defined learning outcomes, and have earned well-deserved praise. Many highly useful tutorials listed on key ILI Websites can stand on their own, or may be used in conjunction with courses (LIRT, 1999; LOEX, 2000a). However, as Dewald points out, we need to remember to apply the same instructional principles to tutorials as we do other forms of instruction. We need to establish expected learning outcomes, develop a plan for helping learners achieve them, prepare and provide instruction, and then evaluate and revise it as necessary. Beyond that, we need to be sure to offer personal help and as much active learning as possible (Dewald, 1999).

As Web-based technology has evolved, so has Web-based instruction, especially tutorials. You may want to read about the thinking, planning, development, evaluation, and revision process for ILI tutorials as you consider whether or not this sort of technological tool would be the best choice to provide support for your instructional goals (Johnson and Sager, 1998; Caspers, 1998).

COMPUTER ASSISTED INSTRUCTION (CAI) (REMOTE: ELECTRONIC/ELECTRIC; ASYNCHRONOUS)

CAI is software that is generally interactive, and is designed to instruct individuals in library research or use of information resources. For example, Ann Bevilacqua's "Research Assistant," an excellent early example of modular CAI developed with Hypercard, was used at various libraries around the country in the 1980s and early 1990s, including the University of California, Berkeley (Miller, Mari, 1999).

Pros:

- Use of CAI may decrease the need for in-person group instruction
- If properly designed, CAI may capture learners' interest
- CAI can be self-paced
- If constructed in a non-linear fashion, users may self-select segments of interest to them
- Immediate feedback can be built into the program
- It may help reduce library anxiety by providing positive reinforcement during instruction
- Learners may review or repeat portions or all of a program as often as they like, and on their own

Cons:

- Design, planning, and development may require a large investment of staff time, and may require expensive programming time as well
- The program may be difficult or costly to revise, or both
- Software used to create the program may become outdated or require expensive and frequent updating
- If the software is discontinued, or the vendor goes out of business, there would be little or no avenue for technical support

Tips for Effective Use:
Decide what you want to accomplish and get administrative approval first. This is particularly important for computer-based training (CBT), because direct, as well as indirect, costs can be quite high, especially if you want to include simulations. Check with colleagues and others on content, and storyboard your plan (Webb, 2000). If you can, test out your ideas and your storyboard or outline on learners. Research studies have concluded that computer-based training (CBT) takes less time for the learner than traditional classroom instruction, though there was "no significant difference in learning" between the two modes (Maul and Spotts, 1993; Kaplowitz and Contini, 1998; Richardson, 1997). Proponents of technology-based instruction see this "no-significant-difference" issue as a positive factor, while opponents see it as a negative factor (Russell, 1999a, 1999b, 1999c). The question remains whether or not CAI for ILI is a cost-effective instructional mode for most libraries (Kaplowitz and Contini, 1998).

REFERENCE QUESTIONS (IN-PERSON; SYNCHRONOUS; REMOTE: ELECTRONIC/
ELECTRIC; ASYNCHRONOUS OR SYNCHRONOUS)

Computerization in and of libraries has dramatically expanded the reference librarian's tools of trade. It began with computerized library catalogs, which provided ready access to lists of items owned by other libraries around the world. Prior to computerization, a fortunate user could consult an expensive book catalog or a wealthy user could identify and travel to libraries with collections in her/his areas of interest; or users might have tried to borrow materials through interlibrary loan. Now, users and librarians alike can search for information in library catalogs around the world, article indexes and other databases, as well as reference tools, common and uncommon, not to mention full-text materials and countless other Websites overflowing with information. Or can they? At the reference desk (physical or virtual), in-person, by phone, mail, e-mail, fax, or the Web, users get answers to their questions, but reference interactions can be instructional as well. Users may learn about the range of information sources that might answer their questions, how to evaluate and choose among them for specific information needs, and how to use them. The reference librarian has, of necessity, turned into a teacher, as well as an advisor and guide through the information morass. Reference librarians continue to do this in traditional ways, but are also experimenting with using new technologies for reference services.

   "CU-SeeMe" was one of the first digital collaboration methodologies to attract attention in libraries, largely because its videoconferencing feature allowed you to see the person with whom you were communicating (2000). Video cameras mounted on workstations took black-and-white pictures at intervals and then broadcast them to other Internet-connected workstations that had the same software and equipment. The system could handle up to twenty-five callers at once with a maximum of eight windows, one for each image projected by an individual video camera. In addition to the video images, the system projected a "talk window," where users could type in messages. Schools used CU-SeeMe to set up partner-classes or cooperative efforts between groups in distant areas. For example, a class helped professors and graduate students from Barcelona test a multimedia computer game, and in the process got to practice using Spanish in a real-life situation (Hodges, 1996). Academic libraries have also experimented with CU-SeeMe, especially for use in remote locations that are distant from the library and where students would otherwise not have access to live reference help (Lessick, Kjaer, and Clancy, 2000). The Singapore National Institute of Education (NIE) uses CU-SeeMe for "multipoint desktop videoconferencing" among schools and NIE researchers (CU-SeeMe, 2000). As Web-based technologies develop apace, some libraries have moved beyond desktop videoconferencing for reference.

The Library of Congress is currently investigating various digital collaboration software products and intends to work with partner libraries to offer this sort of "just-in-case" reference service remotely, worldwide (Kresh, 2000; U.S. Library of Congress, 2000). Public libraries are quite interested in digital collaboration software, which is quite understandable given their mission of serving all sectors of their communities, and their tradition of finding answers for individual questioners. In fact, many libraries around the world are experimenting with or investigating digital collaborative reference service 24/7 (24 hours per day/7 days a week) using many different software applications (McKiernan, 2000; Kerns, 2000; Lindell, Pappas, Ronan, and Seale, 2000; U.S. Department of Education, 2000; Coffman and McGlamery, 2000).

Pros:

- Digital collaboration reference and e-mail reference provide users with individual attention and help with answers to their specific questions
- Users may be able to learn how to use information tools from any location with Internet access, any time of the day or night
- Digital collaboration software provides access to a librarian for those in remote locations

Cons:

- Users may need help in-person when reference staff are unavailable, or when the physical library is closed
- E-mail reference service may require 24-hour or more turnaround time for answers or for further information because the reference interviewing process may require some back-and-forth responses
- Digital collaboration reference may not be cost-effective, as it can take quite some time to interact with individual users
- There may be too long a delay between the time a query is submitted and the time it is answered
- It may result in uneven or lower-quality service, depending on the skill level of the staff and their familiarity with and access to local or licensed databases and systems
- Librarians staffing digital collaboration reference "points" may not have easy access to print reference materials
- It may have a negative impact on staff working conditions unless it is implemented cooperatively across time zones

- There is a large learning curve for some digital collaboration software
- Users may need to have higher-end versions of software and hardware in order to make full use of more complex digital collaboration software
- It may take more staff time to answer questions using digital collaboration software, and users may not want to wait long for answers
- Competing digital collaboration reference services offered by local, regional, national, or even international library groups or institutions may waste scarce pilot project funds and end up confusing users with too many different types of software and means of using them

Tips for Effective Use:
Reference staff who use a "neutral questioning" approach present the questioner with a variety of potential paths to information, or information sources that may answer a question, as well as brief pros and cons of using each source. The questioner then chooses a source, or an "answer-path," to follow. Then the reference staff member guides her/him through the path and use of reference tools in a one-on-one teaching/ learning mode (Dervin and Dewdney, 1986). Some describe in-person reference as the ultimate "just-in-case" scenario, and therefore consider it dispensable in tight budget times. Yet for the many who utilize it, in-person and phone reference services are actually vital "just-in-time" services, often providing people with the information or one-on-one instruction they need when they want it (Kozlowski, 1995). Digital collaboration software is "just-in-case" reference service, as well, in a technological package.

In the original TV series *Star Trek*, crew members query the ship's "reference system" by asking questions preceded by the word "computer." A disembodied female voice responds almost immediately with data in answer to their questions. Any time/any place personal reference and instructional services seem to go far beyond the science fiction of the 1960s, but is digital collaboration software suitable for all ILI environments? Its one-on-one service structure and 24/7 staffing model, in particular, raise cost-effectiveness questions. What exactly are our users' expectations, and how realistic are they in terms of staffing? Do we have enough standardization across libraries to make this effort worthwhile at this time? With myriad restrictive licensing agreements and myriad database and system interfaces, are we ready to offer such individual help to a broad population spectrum? Will we build expectations for universal help any time any place that we may not be able to meet? Should we instead focus our energies on self-help with general reference tools, concentrated individual help for specific user groups, and, most importantly, on filtering (reviewing and recommending materials) and guided help for our primary user groups? We may want to consider targeting user groups and offering limited help during specific hours, or partnering with libraries in similar environments located in other time zones for fuller service, and cooperate with the Library of Congress to offer broader-based general reference help when it becomes available.

Libraries are experimenting with e-mail reference and a variety of digital collaboration software tools. Some digital collaboration software tools are much more complex than others. As these tools are developed and tested in pilot projects, we will probably see some shakeout and standardization. In the process, many of the questions posed above may be answered, new cost-effective tools developed, tools that incorporate a humanitarian across-time-zones approach toward staffing.

Remember, though, that like all sorts of technology, these are just tools, some glitzy and some simple. They will be useful only if people make use of them, and if by so doing, they achieve the learning outcomes we expect of them. The effectiveness of e-reference is being debated, even as libraries experiment with various forms of technology in the delivery of reference services. As Web services pop up that provide access to "experts," and commercial enterprises undertake "reference service," it will be interesting to see whether or not digital collaboration reference sponsored by libraries takes hold; and if so, if it replaces, supplements, or complements traditional reference services in libraries, as well as reference services offered via the Web by non-librarians, like refdesk.com and "Ask Jeeves."

INDIVIDUAL RESEARCH CONSULTATIONS (IN PERSON; SYNCHRONOUS; REMOTE: ELECTRONIC/ELECTRIC; ASYNCHRONOUS)

Often, research consultations are extended versions of reference desk interactions. Users usually make appointments to meet privately with a librarian and may indicate their areas of interest in advance. This allows the librarian to do some advance investigation and prepare a concentrated one-on-one instructional session, helping the questioner learn to select and use appropriate information sources, and evaluate their search results. This type of session is often broader in scope and more in-depth than can be handled at a reference desk or through virtual reference. On the other hand, some research consultations require little or no preparation because they involve helping users learn the basics about research, search strategy, information sources and their mechanics, and critical thinking (Herman, 1994).

Pros:

- Provides concentrated individual attention on a single user's needs
- Users can take their time in discussing their information needs and can learn in a more private setting, which can be less intimidating and less embarrassing than group settings

Cons:

- It may require a large investment of staff time to prepare for a single user's query or instruction
- Time invested in preparation or advance research may be wasted if the user does not show up for her/his scheduled appointment

Tips for Effective Use:
It helps to block out specific days and times for individual research appointments, and also provide an option for scheduling a mutually convenient appointment if none of the scheduled days and times work out for a particular person. Half-hour appointments often give users enough to get started. If not, you can always schedule additional appointments as necessary. It also helps to have some advance idea of the person's research question and their levels of IL and computer literacy. When conducting individual research consultations, it is best to be away from the reference desk in a more private area so that you can sit next to the user and encourage her/him to type and use other paper reference materials, with your guidance. If you have an idea of the user's research question in advance, you can also prepare a list of possible reference tools and approaches from which the user can then choose.

Course-Integrated or Standalone One-Shot Group Sessions (In-Person: Synchronous; Remote: Electronic/Electric; Synchronous)

One-shot instructional sessions may be simple or complex, may last for very brief periods (ten minutes), or for long periods (one-half to a full day), and may or may not be related to other instruction such as academic courses. In most cases, these sessions take place in-person and the librarian meets with the learners as a group just one time. However, some forms of technology, such as chat, may be used for remote one-shot group sessions as well.

Pros:

- One-shot, course-integrated sessions can reach learners when they are most interested in instruction, when some sort of assignment or other extrinsic motivation guides them; therefore, they are most likely to retain learning
- One-shot, course-integrated sessions require less preparation and presentation time than formal courses
- Personal interaction with a librarian can make the library and its resources seem friendlier and less anxiety-provoking

Cons:

- Some learners may be required to attend and therefore may not be ready to learn
- Learners may retain just a few concepts
- One-shot sessions may require a large investment of staff time to reach a relatively small number of learners
- Learners who are required to attend more than one of these sessions may find some of the information repetitive
- Standalone sessions may attract few learners and yet require much staff time for preparation

Tips for Effective Use:
Libraries may offer standalone, one-time sessions to meet instructional needs identified at a physical or virtual reference desk through users' requests or Needs Assessments. For example, reference staff may need to instruct users repeatedly in Web search tool use and critical thinking. At some point, staff may realize that a group session might cut down on repetitive one-on-one instruction and at the same time raise the bar of question complexity. On the other hand, some one-shot, standalone sessions may be aimed solely at library or other staff, for example, to introduce a new online catalog before it is released to the public.

Course-integrated sessions may be termed "guest lectures" by an instructor, and may take place in the physical library, a computer lab, an electronic classroom, or in the normal class meeting place. Both of these types of one-shot sessions require advance planning and preparation, including goal-setting, pre- and post-testing, timing, and careful attention to the amount of material presented. Incorporation of some active learning or collaborative learning techniques may also increase effectiveness (ALA–Association of College and Research Libraries–Instruction Section, 1998; Grassian, 1993a). (See also Chapter 6.)

FORMAL COURSES (IN-PERSON: SYNCHRONOUS; REMOTE: ELECTRONIC/
ELECTRIC; SYNCHRONOUS, ASYNCHRONOUS)

A formal course is usually a series of class sessions with the same students, synchronous (in real-time) or asynchronous (at any time, any place), in-person or remotely, for a term or a set period. Often, formal courses are offered for credit in higher-education institutions, either to regularly enrolled students or to those participating in outreach or extension programs.

Most people are familiar with traditional formal courses where learners and instructors meet in-person as a group at specified intervals during a term. However, an increasing number of fully online courses are now being delivered via the Internet, especially the Web. The World Lecture Hall lists and provides links to syllabi and other information about higher-education courses taught worldwide via the Web, from accounting to computer-mediated learning to library and information studies (2000). LOEX provides links to syllabi for many information literacy-related courses as well. The SUNY (State University of New York) Librarians' Association also has a long list of for-credit library courses (2000a). Some online courses are strictly available via e-mail, however, as text, though they may refer learners to other sources of information, such as Websites. For example, in 2000, the American Library Association conducted a fully e-mail course for librarians on the topic of copyright that was developed and presented by Kenneth Crews (ALA–Office for Information Technology Policy, 2000).

Pros:

- You will be able to cover more material in-depth
- You may be able to develop an ongoing relationship with your students that will allow you to do a better job of determining their IL needs and interests
- Pacing and structure of the course may vary somewhat, depending on the learners' skills, abilities, and interests
- You may be able to do diagnostic pre-testing in order to develop curriculum targeting weak areas, to test for learning, and to re-teach if necessary

Cons:

- Initially, preparation for formal courses requires a very large investment of staff time to reach small numbers of students
- Even more investment of staff time is required to develop and offer classes that are fully online

- Updating courses may take much time and effort
- Some courses may not be required and may be considered "just-in-case" rather than "just-in-time" instruction, thus attracting few learners

Tips for Effective Use:
Remember to write down the goals and objectives or expected learning outcomes you hope will be achieved by the end of the course, and then break them into manageable chunks designed to suit the audience, in terms of both age and skill levels. It helps to find out the learners' IL and computer literacy skill and experience levels prior to the start of the class. It is also important to have a course outline or syllabus arranged in modules that can be expanded, contracted, deleted, or replaced with other modules as the need arises. Teaching and learning are not cut and dry, and it is important to remember that each class is a unique entity with different needs and interests, so flexibility is important.

Remember, too, that if classes are lecture only then learners tend to retain little over time, so it is important to build in an appropriate balance of lecture, demo, interaction, and learner-centered exercises, assignments and hands-on work (Williams and Zahed, 1996; Dods, 1997). Online courses taught entirely over the Internet can be a boon to those who have difficulty attending in-person class meetings. However, online courses must be constructed carefully to insure a large amount of participation and interactivity as well as student feedback (Ko and Rossen, 2001). As a result, it can take an enormous investment of time and effort to learn appropriate technologies and to prepare these sorts of classes, and you would be well advised to consider this carefully before committing to teaching a formal course online (Stocks and Freddolino, 1998). Parise describes the Web-based course offered by Marylhurst University Library since 1993, describing the pros and cons of teaching a required three-credit online course and warns that "Online instruction, particularly Web-based classes, is not for everyone" (1998: 60). Hara and Kling have also studied and documented common problems students have with Web-based online courses, primarily in three areas: technology, lack of timely or sufficient instructor feedback, and "ambiguous instructions on the Website as well as via e-mail" (1999: [online]). (See Chapter 17 regarding the debate over the value of technology use in education.)

If you do decide to teach a formal course fully online in spite of these caveats, Ko and Rossen provide much excellent step-by-step advice on developing college- and university-level online courses, with real-life examples of various successful, fully online courses. One of the course-builder suites of software they discuss is WebCT (2000). WebCT and other course-builders allow instructors to mount online syllabi, set up discussion boards and chat rooms, and test learning and record and tabulate results.

Some people will prefer to take online courses personally taught or led by an expert in the field. Others may prefer fully self-paced and self-directed online courses, like Hong Kong University's "Foundations to Information Technology" (FIT), a computer literacy course developed using WebCT. The course is broken into modules and sub-modules, such as "Overview of Computer Hardware," "Principles of PC Systems," and Graphical User Interfaces" (2000). You may select any module or submodule or a self-assessment test from among the various segments offered. The DPEC Company goes further than FIT, offering more complex self-contained WBT (Driscoll, 1994). Learners take a "Skill Assessment" pre-test to find out what they already know. Check marks are placed next to the segments they have mastered, and they work on the remaining training modules in any order they choose. In order to receive a completion certificate they must demonstrate mastery of all the course modules by answering all module questions correctly or by passing the Skill Assessment (Rollison, 2000). This assessment is an extremely important feature, as there may be few clues regarding effectiveness of remote instruction and little feedback to designers unless specific forms of assessment are built into the product (Angelo and Cross, 1993). Personally taught online courses should also include assessment, especially self-assessment, at various intervals (see Chapter 12). Ideally, upon completion of the course and mastery of the material, learners should also receive some sort of recognition such as course credit or a certificate, or both.

DISCUSSION BOARDS (REMOTE: ELECTRONIC/ELECTRIC; ASYNCHRONOUS)

Discussion boards are electronic equivalents of bulletin boards, where people wander by and tack up individual messages for everyone to read. Many bulletin boards tend to look messy after a while, with messages tacked here and there, mostly in random order. Electronic bulletin boards are neater. Messages are still posted individually, but follow-up messages can be "threaded," or listed under the message to which they are responding. Your name and e-mail address accompany your posting so that someone can respond to you privately if they like. You can use discussion boards for public or private groups, like classes. Private discussion boards are usually password protected so that only members of a specific group can use them.

Pros:

- If your organization or institution does not or cannot provide or set up a discussion board for you, you can set one up for yourself for free, for a specified period of time, using course builder Websites like "Blackboard.com"
- You can specify the participants of a discussion board, their mode of access, whether or not they will need a password for use, and other features such as button colors
- You may also be able to set up smaller discussion boards for a class, so that smaller groups can work together remotely on group projects or can discuss topics covered in a class or through readings
- Shy students who do not feel comfortable speaking up in a group will probably be more inclined to respond to messages posted on a discussion board than they would in a group setting

Cons:

- If you require use of a discussion board, you make some assumptions about the learners' computer literacy skill levels and their access to a computer with an Internet connection (you are assuming that they know how to use a computer and a mouse, how to connect to the Internet, how to use a Web browser, and how to use a discussion board—if learners do not have these skills, someone will need to help them acquire the skills or they will be left out)
- Some shy students may feel wary of posting messages on a discussion board for an entire class to read rather than communicating directly and privately with the instructor or IL librarian

Tips for Effective Use:
Do some pre-testing to find out which learners have low computer literacy skill levels, and set up a special time to help them learn how to use a mouse, how to connect to the Internet, how to use a Web browser, and how to use the discussion board software you choose for the class. Post a welcome message and be sure to phrase all your messages in a friendly manner. If you are developing course-integrated instruction along with a faculty member, ask her/him if you can participate in the class discussion board to help answer information-research-related questions. If you are teaching a credit course yourself, consider requiring the students to post one or two messages to the class discussion board and respond to one or two of their classmates' messages.

CHAT (REMOTE: ELECTRONIC/ELECTRIC; SYNCHRONOUS)

Chat is discussion that takes place in a virtual "chat room" (often Web-based) to which two or more people logon. Chat participants take turns typing in messages to each other or to the entire group loggedin to a chat room.

Pros:

- People like chat because it is live, personal, and interactive in the sense that you send a message and may very quickly get a response from one or more other people interested in the same topics

Cons:

- People dislike "chat" because it is live, since it means you have to type in messages and then sit and wait for people at the other end to type in responses and send them back
- You may have to schedule several different instructional chat sessions in order to accommodate learners' schedules, as well as different time zones (Ko and Rossen, 2001)

Tips for Effective Use:
Ko and Rossen advise instructors to plan ahead by announcing the topic and chat conduct rules ahead of time (2001). You may want to proceed with the discussion in a particular way, posing questions and summarizing discussion at intervals or having students going off to look for something in the middle of the chat and returning with their reactions or discoveries. You may want to review standard "Netiquette" as well. You must be well organized and time activities and discussion carefully.

E-MAIL/LISTSERVS (REMOTE: ELECTRONIC/ELECTRIC; ASYNCHRONOUS)

E-mail, or electronic mail, is one of the most popular personal uses of the Internet, yet it can be used for instruction as well. Some online courses are offered strictly via e-mail, for example, a 2000 ALA copyright course created by Kenneth Crews (ALA–Office for Information Technology Policy, 2000). Listservs are subscription e-mail reflectors, designed to broadcast messages from one subscriber to all the other subscribers to the list. You may communicate with learners in an entire class through a listserv. This form of technology is called "push" rather than "pull" technology. "Push" technology sends or "pushes" information to the user. In this case, you push listserv messages directly to the learner's e-mail inbox. This is in contrast to "pull" technology, such as discussion boards where learners must take the initiative to go and get, or "pull," information from a particular place.

Pros:

- E-mail and listservs provide convenient means of communicating with groups, including an entire class
- Learners see messages in their e-mail inboxes, which may encourage them to read the messages more quickly and regularly
- Learners can save messages for later perusal or for review
- E-mail may make instruction available to those in remote areas, the disabled, or those who cannot meet during typical in-person class meeting times or in a particular physical meeting place

Cons:

- The number of e-mail messages in one's inbox can seem overwhelming
- E-mail instruction is one-way unless the learner chooses to respond
- E-mail instruction may assume that the learner's mind is a tabula rasa ("erased tablet") into which the instructor pours information and learning

Tips for Effective Use:
If at all possible, try to determine what the learners already know and what they want or need to know before you design instruction to be delivered via e-mail or listservs. Build in some interaction, even if it is only direction to the learners to try out a Web-based exercise or tutorial. You can create pre- and post-tests using licensed Web-based software like "WebSurveyor," which can be mounted on a Website. You can then e-mail the URLs for these tests to instruction participants.

Web Pages/Sites (In-Person: Electronic/Electric; Synchronous; Remote: Electronic/Electric; Asynchronous)

Web pages are simply files consisting of visual representations of text, images, and other items. These files may be stored by individuals on their own computers or on shared drives, computers called "servers." A server can be located right next to you or thousands of miles away, and allows other computers to contact it remotely in order to request copies of Web pages. You tell your Web browser software where Web page files are located by providing an address called a URL, or Uniform Resource Locator. The browser software sends a request to the server asking for a copy of the directions for displaying a specific Web page. These directions (written in HTML, or HyperText Markup Language) tell the Web browser how to display various elements of the Web page you wish to access. Web pages may be used synchronously in group instruction, in-person or remotely, or asynchronously by individuals, both for learning mechanics of use or for critical thinking exercises. On their own, or with the help of in-house staff, ILI librarians have created Web versions of many of the instructional modes listed above. Some of these pages are simply mounted as copies of paper materials, while others, particularly interactive Web-based tutorials, attempt to make use of the Web medium. "Signage" takes on new importance on the Web, as we see navigational buttons and warning or other directional "signs" on Web pages in the form of navigation bars, icons, and more.

Pros:

- Web pages present a distinct advantage, as it may be much less costly to mount a variety of modes and materials on the Web than to provide them in paper or to provide in-person instruction
- Web pages may be accessed any time or any place that a user has an Internet connection
- Updated versions may be mounted quickly
- Updates will be available to all who access the site, in the same words, and with the same graphic images
- Users may save or print out materials if they wish

Cons:

- Users must have a basic understanding of what the Web and the Internet are and how to use a Web browser
- Users must have access to a computer or other device with an Internet connection
- Designers may include features usable only to those with the latest versions of software, or those who have or can easily acquire "plug-ins," supplementary pieces of software designed for use with other software (for example, "Save With Images" is a plug-in for the Windows version of Netscape that allows you to save one or more Web pages easily, along with all of their graphics)
- Content providers may get carried away and include too many words or graphics, or too few

- Libraries may mount pages and sites without first conducting usability studies or checking for accessibility for disabled or "legacy system" users (those who use older equipment and/or software)
- Sites must be maintained and updated regularly
- Updates may be costly in terms of staff time, equipment, and software purchase and upgrades, as well as staff training
- We are just beginning to investigate the Web's potential for instruction, as businesses are, but need to be aware of the fact that without help in the form of extra staff and funding, our own library staff may not be able to keep up, especially if these responsibilities are added on top of already existing duties

Tips for Effective Use:
You can create many different kinds of Web-based instructional materials, simple and complex, to suit a variety of purposes. A prime concern for many ILI librarians, however, is how best to use Web pages and sites. How much money, time, and effort should we invest in designing and developing them? Should they be used in place of paper instructional materials? Should we create and mount solely Web-based materials, or modify versions of paper materials? How many learners are we reaching with Web-based materials? How effective are they in helping people achieve expected learning outcomes?

Learners at all levels appreciate simple, easy-to-understand, easy-to-use instructional materials that they can follow as they use one or another widely varying reference tool on their own However, we do not yet have universal home Web access. In addition, there is an enormous variety of information tools and resources, and we have certainly not attained sufficient standardization and simplicity so that learners can move easily from one system to another.

Furthermore, as we discussed in Chapters 3 and 4, people prefer to learn in different ways. So, in order to maximize learning for most people, we should try to provide instructional aid in paper and in some electronic format, preferably on the Web. If we provide printable copies of paper handouts on our Websites, we take an important step toward meeting the goal of providing a variety of learning tools to suit different learning styles and accessibility for those with older equipment and software, as well as to meet ADA (Americans with Disabilities Act) standards. Copies of paper materials can be converted into Web pages and mounted fairly easily, or scanned and mounted as Adobe Acrobat PDF files. To take the cafeteria or cafe approach presented in Chapter 8 a step further, you might want to consider a variety of means of making use of the Web medium to enhance these materials. Simple examples include

making live links to the online catalog within a guide to using the catalog. More elaborate enhancements might include breaking the paper
item into separate parts of the same page or separate pages, providing a
linked table of contents so learners can move around more easily, while
also providing exercises or "test yourself" links for each segment or even
linking to sites outside of your own institution or organization for other
approaches or additional information.

In addition to providing support for varying user learning styles,
this approach (paper-to-Web) can provide a comfortable and supportive transition for staff who have little or no experience designing and
developing Web-based instructional materials. However, it should not
preclude your taking an entirely fresh approach to creating strictly Web-
based instructional materials. The idea here is to start with the familiar,
transfer what you do well and feel comfortable with in one environment (paper) to a new environment (Web). As you go along, you can
learn the process and mechanics of creating Web documents so that later
you will feel more confident in designing and developing Web-only alternatives that are structured to make fuller use of the medium. For example, after you have gotten experience creating simple Web equivalents of paper point-of-use guides, you might want to try your hand at
creating Web-based exercises. You can simply post exercises on your
Website in the hope that they will help learners achieve expected learning outcomes. You may also incorporate these exercises into synchronous, in-person or remote instruction as active learning exercises
(Simkins, 1999).

This is all well and good, but, as some have pointed out, you must
be wary of using technology just for its own sake or because everyone
seems to be using it (Sullivan, 1998; Ruth, 1997; Ko and Rossen, 2001).
This is especially true for labor-intensive and expensive efforts to design interactive Web-based tutorials that are highly complex, require
much software on both the developer's and the user's end, and are not
tied to pedagogical goals or expected learning outcomes. Again, remember that asynchronous (any time, any place) learning does not appeal to
all learners, nor to all instructors and ILI librarians.

FINAL REMARKS

We have taken a close look at many different modes on the instructional
menu. Which you choose in the end may come down to cost, as well as
the current administrative culture, the risk-taking climate in your environment, and your ability to engage both your administrators and your
colleagues in dialogue and experimentation. As you go through this

process, you might consider asking learners to help construct at least part of the menu themselves so that you end up with a mixture of what you think learners should have and what they say they want. Openness to change is essential, as well as flexibility and a spirit of objective scientific inquiry into effectiveness within a given environment for a given audience, and under given circumstances.

EXERCISES

1. Compare and contrast a library-developed printed guide or pathfinder on a specific topic with an instructional Website on the same topic.
2. Examine a paper point-of-use guide and a Web-based tutorial for the same online database or OPAC. Come up with two arguments for and two arguments against each form of instruction.
3. Examine the online help provided for a commonly used piece of software and compare it to the online help available for an OPAC.

READ MORE ABOUT IT

Hensley, Randy Burke. 1993. "Teaching Methods." In *Sourcebook for Bibliographic Instruction*, edited by Katherine Branch. Chicago: ALA–Association of College and Research Libraries, Bibliographic Instruction Section.

Ko, Susan, and Steve Rossen. 2001. *Teaching Online: A Practical Guide*. Boston: Houghton-Mifflin.

LaGuardia, Cheryl, Michael Blake, Lawrence Dowler, Laura Farwell, Caroline M. Kent, and Ed Tallent. 1996. *Teaching the New Library: A How-To-Do-It Manual for Planning and Designing Instructional Programs*. New York: Neal-Schuman.

Ruth, Stephen. 1997. "Getting Real About Technology-Based Learning: The Medium is NOT the Message." *Educom Review* (September/October):32–37.

10

Basic Copyright
and Design Issues

"Is't not enough to break into my garden,
And, like a thief, to come to rob my grounds,
Climbing my walls in spite of me the owner . . ."
William Shakespeare, *King Henry VI, Part II*

GENERAL CONCERNS

Who owns graphics, design or structure, and text in media? Does it matter if media is print or technology-based? What can you use freely in designing and developing your own instructional modes and materials? Is that wonderfully designed point-of-use guide or interactive tutorial you've found available for the taking? Can you copy it wholesale and put your own institution's name and logo on it or just create your own instructions and link to it? What if you just copy parts of it and others like it, and simply adapt or mix and match to meet your own needs? How much can you use under "fair use" guidelines? Should you go for a linear or a modular approach? Synchronous or asynchronous? Remote or in-person? Paper or electronic/electric? Interactive or passive? Detailed or succinct? What about mixed formats? What sort of backup plans should you have in place?

Many copyright, design, and content questions can bedevil anyone planning or developing instructional modes and supplementary materials. Fair use may or may not be permitted for digital materials. Furthermore, well-intended but poorly designed modes and materials can waste time, money, and effort, can lower morale among staff and users, and increase rather than decrease the number of repeat, basic questions at a reference desk, help line, or an e-mail inbox.

COPYRIGHT, FAIR USE, AND INTELLECTUAL PROPERTY

Fair Use and the U.S. Digital Millennium Copyright Act (DMCA)

Any discussion of design in this technological era must begin with the issue of what is public domain, material that is freely available for the taking as opposed to privately owned. Copyright ownership and fair use pertain to the ownership and degree of permissible usage of an original work. The purpose of U.S. copyright law is to provide the creator of a work with exclusive rights to publish or sell her/his work, to prepare new works based on their own copyrighted work, and to perform or display her/his work publicly, during the author's life and for fifty years thereafter. The Copyright Act of 1976 includes an exception to copyright holders' exclusive rights, called "fair use," and lists four ways to tell whether or not your use of a copyrighted item without permission is legally acceptable (*West's Encyclopedia of American Law*, 1998). For ILI, the first factor, determination of educational as opposed to commercial use, is the most important part of the "test." The other three test elements involve the type of copyrighted item, how much of the entire item you are using, and whether the copyright holder will lose income as a result of your use of her/his work. In practice, judges try to balance these last three factors against the interests of the community, including scholars, who wish to have access to copyrighted works for research, education, and personal interest (University of Texas, 2000; New Mexico Junior College, 1999; Nimmer, 2000).

How does this work in the technological world? Some Internet enthusiasts, like John Barlow, one of the founders of the Electronic Frontier Foundation (EFF) (2000), believe that copyright has been applied to the "containers" in which information has appeared, though information itself is free. Furthermore, he believes that anything put up on the Internet should be free to everyone (Barlow, 1999a, 1999b). Others believe that copyright laws established for paper materials should be strictly applied to the Web and the Internet as a whole. "The Copyright Web Site" provides comprehensive information on Internet-related copyright issues such as those mentioned above (2000).

The truth is that copyright ownership is not clearcut, particularly with regard to technology. Artists spend time and artistic effort designing clip art for Websites. They make their living by designing art, so naturally do not want to give it all away for free. So what constitutes fair use of art on the Web? Faculty spend time and intellectual energy designing Websites for classes, some of which could be used for or viewed as research, as well. To whom do these Websites belong when faculty move to different institutions? This question becomes especially ticklish when the faculty member has come up with an idea for the content of a Website but the actual design and implementation has been done by the staff of a campus computing network; for example, "Fossil Flash Cards" developed and mounted by the UCLA Social Sciences Computing Network, with content developed by Professor Rob Boyd in the Anthropology Department (Boyd, 2000a, 2000b).

The DMCA, enacted into law in the U.S. in October 1998, was supposed to provide clear copyright and intellectual property guidelines for technology-related issues like these. However, major questions about this law have already emerged. Within a year after its passage, two cases were decided under the DMCA's anti-circumvention provision. The first, *Kelly v. Arriba Soft*, had to do with thumbnails of copyrighted visual images placed on a Website, which were then retrieved by a visual search tool (Arriba Soft, later called Ditto). The second case had to do with software available on various Websites that allowed you to get around copy protection on DVDs (digital video disks). In the latter case, eight movie studios wanted the software removed from the Internet (*Universal Studios v. Reimerdes*). Both cases tried to rely on the fair use principles derived from the 1976 U.S. Copyright Act. In the first case, the artist who had copyrighted his images and placed them on his own Website, lost to the defendant. In the second case, the plaintiffs won. Most importantly for libraries, the Special Libraries Association reports that in the second case, "The court held that there is no fair use in the DMCA; if there was such, then Congress would have said so" (2000: 37).

Unfortunately, instead of clarifying this situation for libraries, in October 2000 the Librarian of Congress took the same stance as the court did in the second case. He ruled that there would be only two fair use exceptions to the DMCA's anticircumvention provision, " . . . for malfunctions and to determine which sites are blocked by filtering software" (Bradley, 2000: 1,035).

Implications for ILI

In February 2000, the Pew Learning and Technology Program brought 14 higher-education leaders together to discuss and analyze the knotty issue of intellectual property rights for online courses and course materials, and to draw a clear distinction between these two categories. The symposium focused on online course and course materials for credit-bearing courses taught by full-time faculty. Participants acknowledged that potential financial gain may be at the heart of the intellectual property debate in these areas. They concluded that a faculty member "who invents a better way to teach online or learn through technology might be deemed as having fulfilled his or her commitment to the institution. Beyond the fulfillment of teaching duties for the specific course in question, he or she should be free to market the unique creation to others and reap the rewards" (Twigg, 2000: 24). They go on to recommend that " . . . the default policy should be that the faculty member owns the course materials he or she has created," though institutions may want to establish "trigger mechanisms" in their basic policy that would enact a second policy, for example, if outside interests seek to commercialize course materials (Twigg, 2000: 26).

How does this affect ILI? Questions still remain about intellectual property for which there are few answers and little definitive litigation as of yet. The Web world is quite a different place from the print world, and yet we must try to respect copyright and the intellectual creations of others. Instruction librarians have a long and admirable tradition of sharing their materials, their teaching methods, and even their course outlines and syllabi with others, but sometimes do not identify themselves on Websites as content developers or Website designers. Each of us should take credit for our creative work in all formats by including our names, dates of publication, and modification on each item we develop, along with our supporting organization's or institution's name. We should also credit institutions and organizations for providing direct and indirect support as well, but keep in mind that institutions and organizations do not create materials—people do, and people deserve credit for their efforts.

No one, however, wants to waste time and effort duplicating work others have done. So, if you find something you want to utilize, and if you are not sure whether or not you need permission to use all or part of it, or even to link to it, protect yourself and your institution by requesting permission from the author or sponsor. If you receive permission, be sure to acknowledge the original source. If you do not receive permission, you would be well advised to look for something else, or design it yourself or pay someone else to design it for you. The Web is a giant clearinghouse, a wonderful treasure trove of ideas where we can share our own work and build upon the good work of others, but only if they permit us to do so.

Until the courts can sort out and balance conflicting interests, a high-minded approach is best. It would be a simple and generous gesture to continue the ILI tradition of sharing by indicating that permission is granted freely for non-commercial use of the instructional materials you are willing to share. In order to create these "goods" in the first place, though, we need to look first at budget and administrative support, including hardware and software needed for design and development, and then at categories of instructional modes and materials. Finally, we need to consider general design issues, content, format, and general questions about software and equipment for design and development.

BUDGET, ADMINISTRATIVE, AND COLLEAGUE SUPPORT

Administrative Approval

As we pointed out in Chapter 8 ("Selecting Modes of Instruction"), cost is a critical factor in selecting an instructional mode. Design and development plans hinge on the direct and indirect costs your institution is willing to support, including hardware and software for design and development. So, you need to gain administrative approval before embarking on instructional projects. You should be prepared to defend your proposed design and development plans, and adjust them downward if necessary. It is important to keep in mind that instructional materials proposals that may seem wonderful, creative, and innovative are not always rewarded with approval and funding. There may be good or bad reasons for this rejection. Sometimes administrators may detect issues that have not been considered fully, such as staff time, equipment, software, or supplies needed for maintaining materials once they have been created, or the impact on staff time in other areas to compensate for the time you want to spend on this project. On the other hand, there may be more attractive competing projects for limited dollars, or political issues may interfere. Administrators often care about visible products that meet user needs, and they may be more amenable to experimental pilot projects before committing to new large-scale programs. If you want their approval for any sort of project, you will need to address the issues of money and staff time, your own and that of others. The more money and staff time you need for a project, the more important it is to get administrators' explicit approval in advance, and the more important it is to discuss your proposed projects in advance with your colleagues.

Software and Equipment for Design

Which basic software and equipment would be most helpful for creating instructional materials? The main considerations are:

1. What is already available for staff use?
2. What will the learners be using?
3. Which software and equipment would save time and help create more effective materials in a more efficient fashion?
4. Which would be essential for pilot projects?
5. How much would additional software and equipment cost, and can they be put to multiple uses?
6. What sort of training would be needed in order to utilize both new software and equipment, and what sort of learning curve should we expect?
7. Who should constitute the instructional development team, and how should it be put together?
8. How can we keep up with new technology and at the same insure access and effective use for those with legacy systems and software as well as those with devices for the disabled?

At the very least, ILI staff who design and develop instructional materials need to have the most up-to-date software and hardware the institution or organization can afford. At a minimum, you should have access to both Internet Explorer and Netscape Web browsers, word-processing software, a simple paint program, and inexpensive shareware screen capture software like "SnagIt." Some would argue that presentation software is essential as well.

In any case, designers need to have some time to explore and learn to use new software or new versions of software they may have already used. They may need to take classes and attend conferences and workshops to keep up with new or revised software and techniques. We can learn a lot from each other and from experimenting, but sometimes we need to turn to experts, so it is extremely important to remember that designers too have a learning curve and need training and support.

ILI material designers need up-to-date equipment as well. At a minimum, they should have one PC or Macintosh with as much RAM (Random Access Memory) and hard drive capacity, as well as megahertz (processor speed), as the institution or organization can afford, along with a CD-ROM drive, a Zip drive to store large graphic files, a high-speed Internet connection (T1 line, Ethernet connection, DSL, or cable modem connection), a large monitor, a sound card and headphones, and a color ink-jet printer. Equipment becomes outdated very quickly, though, so it would be best to replace workstations every two years. Older equipment can be passed on to other less design-intensive staff, while the highest-end equipment should be purchased for designers. Digital cameras are coming down in price, and digital images of staff or other locations within a physical library can be wonderfully humanizing additions to a library's Website.

Continuous heavy use of computer equipment comes with a physical, as well as a financial price. An ILI designer needs to have an ergonomically well-designed space, including a supportive chair at the proper height, foot rest, wrist rest, good lighting, properly operating mouse, a high-quality mouse pad, and scheduled periods of working away from the computer where eyes and body can move and focus differently.

Good instructional material design does not just happen at random. It is easier for talented people to design quality instructional materials, but everyone needs humane support and quality tools with which to design and develop materials. Institutions and organizations also need to provide support for training and release time to attend workshops and conferences, or just network with others working on similar projects. Organizations also need to provide support and release time for other staff who may be impacted by new projects, such as the ILI designer/developer.

Priorities

You need to provide realistic estimates of planning, preparation, implementation, and maintenance time needed for the project or program, as well as time constraints for learning and deadlines for designing and preparing instructional materials. Who is going to gather all of this? More often than not, it is the already burdened reference librarians who must gather the information, estimate the work involved, and then do the work of developing and implementing approved projects. How can reference librarians fit this in their schedule when they are already responsible for an endless number of other duties, which may include any or all of the following:

- Managing one or more Websites for their libraries, their institutions or organizations, or even for individual faculty
- Managing ILI programs in the library
- Teaching one-shot sessions
- Teaching credit courses
- Preparing instructional materials
- Working at a reference desk
- Training and supervising students and other support staff

Of course, reference librarians are very likely also carrying out other duties within and outside the library, including committee work and other organizational commitments. As David Tyckoson pointed out in *American Libraries*, the reference librarian's required knowledge base has grown enormously (1999). Even in the smallest institution or organization, librarians now have a world of information at their fingertips, and what a large world it is. The world of information now includes both filtered and unfiltered materials galore, licensed and freely available databases, vanity, commercial, governmental, military, and educational Websites, print materials, CD-ROM materials, and on and on. Given all of this, you must help administrators understand that staff at all levels have a finite amount of time, energy, and physical and emotional capacity, and that instructional projects usually take longer than estimated to complete. In fact, a good rule of thumb for creating or revising computer-based instructional products is to multiply your original time estimate by three.

Add a few sentences to each project proposal listing current priorities and suggesting reprioritizing to accommodate the new project, or some partial release time or additional budgetary support for clerical or replacement professional staff through special funds. This is particularly important for time-intensive projects such as developing standalone or supplementary instructional materials, but does not mean abandoning all other responsibilities. Rather, reprioritizing is a necessary means of temporary relief for the physical and emotional state of individuals and organizations, and an important aid to successful attainment of goals.

Even if a project receives approval in concept but does not receive funding from the institution, all may not be lost. You might consider applying for grants, like instructional improvement grants, U.S. LSCA grants available to states, or partnerships with others—staff, community, government, or academic. In the end, partnership may reap more rewards, especially if materials are designed for use in sequenced instruction in various types of environments. Whether or not you partner with others, you need to keep some caveats in mind regarding willynilly, ad hoc, temporary professional replacements. Identifying, hiring, training, and supervising temporary replacements can be difficult and time-consuming for the remaining staff. For all of these reasons, you should not go off and apply for grant funds on your own without full discussion and administrative approval, or you risk wasting a lot of time and effort for nothing, and alienating administrators and your overburdened colleagues as well.

However, even sustained time and effort, as well as administrative and budgetary support do not automatically insure effective instructional materials. We need to adhere to some basic design principles for all formats of materials in order to help our learners achieve expected learning outcomes.

CATEGORIES OF INSTRUCTIONAL MODES AND MATERIALS

Examining basic categories of instructional modes and materials and their design principles may help you select and design effective instructional modes and materials that suit your needs.

It is a truism to say that we live in a technological era. Nevertheless, it may be useful to categorize instructional materials on a continuum in terms of the level of technology needed to use them. At the low-tech end of the continuum are paper materials, including signs, maps, point-of-use guides, pathfinders, exercises, tutorials, and workbooks. They may or may not be designed using some form of technology, but the product itself is meant to be used without hardware, software, or other electronic equipment.

Mid-continuum materials may include overhead transparencies, audiotapes, videotapes, and presentation software used on a basic level. Most of these materials are designed using either specialized equipment or software and are meant to be used with electronic equipment, though overhead transparencies may even be handwritten or simply word-processed and printed out on transparencies or photocopied onto them.

At the high-tech end of the continuum are computer-based materials that include computer assisted instruction (CAI) software, Websites and pages, and multimedia. Websites and pages may be interactive or passive, and can include maps, guides, pathfinders, exercises, tutorials, and workbooks. High-tech materials are designed using computer hardware and software or other specialized equipment, and are meant to operate by means of a computer.

Some of these materials may be designed for synchronous (simultaneous) use, either in-person or remotely (for example, overhead transparencies or PowerPoint slide shows); others may be designed for asynchronous (any time/any place) use (for example, interactive Web-based tutorials). Or in some cases you may want to mix and match two or more types of instructional materials; for example, handouts and a presentation slide show. On a practical level, though, what are the basics of actually designing print and electronic/electric forms of instruction?

GENERAL DESIGN PRINCIPLES

A number of basic design principles are applicable to many different formats of instructional materials and cut across all age groups. We have already discussed copyright, budget, and administrative support. Four other major issues remain:

- Audience
- Instructional Needs (purpose)
- Content
- Format

Audience

The first and most important issues revolve around the audience and their needs. Who are the learners, what are their age or educational levels and skill levels, and do they need any of the instructional materials described in the previous section? (See Chapter 7 for various means of determining need.) If the answer to the last question is "No," then continue on to the next chapter. If the answer is "Yes," then the next question is "Why?" In other words, what is the purpose of the material? To what uses will it be put? For example, you need to design and develop ILI for 6,000 undergraduates a year, and you have selected expected learning outcomes, as well as modes of instruction and instructional materials. Now you need to decide how learners will make use of these modes and materials so that you can design them appropriately. You may want to design some as standalone items and others for support. The most cost-effective designs, of course, are multipurpose, such as paper point-of-use guides. They may be placed on handout racks for remote asynchronous use, or utilized in synchronous in-person group instruction as step-by-step guides for hands-on segments. Presentation slide shows may be used during in-person synchronous instruction, or may be mounted on a Website for asynchronous remote use.

Instructional Needs (Purpose)

Materials strictly used to support other forms of instruction will need to be designed differently from standalone materials. As accompaniments to other forms of instruction, support materials may address a particular instructional segment or may depend on an instructor's elaboration or explanation. Support materials can include simple printed instructions for in-person active learning exercises or very brief PowerPoint slides to help introduce or sum up a lesson or group instruction session. Effective standalone materials, on the other hand, designed to be used without "intervention," must meet much tougher standards. Self-paced workbooks, self-guided tours, and interactive Web-based tutorials will need to anticipate various ways of thinking and learning and include more content as there may be no one available to answer questions or explain complex concepts. The challenge of designing purposeful instructional material lies in balancing succinctness with clarity, as well as some means of maintaining the learner's interest.

How Much Content to Include

So often it seems that we all fall into the trap of trying to include too much content in instruction. In many cases, we seem to do this no less with asynchronous than we have with synchronous instruction. For example, in our sincere desire to help learners, we may try to introduce the library system and teach the mechanics of using the catalog, as well as two or three licensed systems and databases, Boolean logic, and critical thinking skills—all in one 50-minute synchronous session or in an asynchronous linear online tutorial. How do you decide how much to include in a single instructional experience, and how can you keep the learner's attention so she/he will complete it?

You might begin by determining the three most important things you want learners to take away from your instruction. Do you want them to understand that:

- There are many different online systems, interfaces, gateways, databases, and Web search tools
- There are similarities and differences among them, for example:
  — you can search, display, and save (by e-mailing, printing, or downloading) in all of them
  — subject matter, items indexed, and time period covered may differ from one online resource to another
- People have created all of them, and in doing so, have made conscious decisions about what to index, how to label materials, how you can search, how search results will appear, what time period will be covered, etc., and that these decisions may be politically motivated.

You may want to pick and choose even from the few items listed above and try to incorporate some larger concepts, such as learning to question all sorts of assumptions regarding interface design and coverage, and thesaurus selection.

MECHANICS VERSUS CONCEPTS

Similarly, it is important to question assumptions in information literacy. You might ask, for example, whether or not the mechanics of using various information tools could be handled through asynchronous, interactive modular tutorials or paper point-of-use guides or exercises rather than synchronous, face-to-face group instruction. What is it that can best be taught in-person, face-to-face, or in other synchronous approaches, and to whom? Consider, for example, that learner age or academic level, as well as IL and computer literacy skill levels, are important factors in judging how much content to include in instructional materials. Generally, the younger the age group, the fewer concepts may be absorbed at one time or through a particular instructional "piece." Adult learners will prefer practical learning, with real-world application as opposed to in-depth focus on theory and concepts. A prioritized outline of the most important points to get across can be extremely useful. Examples and exercises should be geared to the interests of a particular audience, but whatever the level of the audience, we should strive to teach complex concepts in simple, basic terms using common language and real-life examples. (See Chapter 5 for a discussion of teaching conceptual frameworks and the use of analogies in instruction.)

JARGON, COMPUTERPHOBIA, AND ACCESSIBILITY

In each issue, *Wired's* "Must Read" department includes a "Jargon Watch" section. *The Chronicle of Higher Education's* "Information Technology" section includes a "Jargon Monitor" (2000). Why? Learners can be sidetracked easily by jargon. When you use jargon, instead of concentrating on learning, they spend time trying to figure out what the jargon terms mean. The problem is that most people immersed in a topic or in a field tend to use thinking and speaking shortcuts ("jargon"). Sometimes we do not even realize that the terms we use quite frequently are mysterious jargon to a newcomer, for example, "search strategy," "online catalog," or "electronic resources." So, try to identify the jargon you use in instruction and then avoid using it unless it is essential for the concepts or skills learners will need. If you do use jargon, be sure to explain it in simple terms and check for understanding. Gear the material for the lowest common denominator, especially if a piece will operate by means of technology or involves learning any aspects of technology, and focus on what users need to know right away, the basics (Nahl, 1999).

We often take it for granted that all of our users know how to use a computer and a mouse. Yet research has shown that 25 percent or more of any given population (any age, male or female) can be computerphobic or can have low levels of computer skills, or none at all (Weil and Rosen, 1997). You will need to consider how to find out what your target user population knows and how to help them address this problem, either with computer literacy help or alternate forms of ILI, or both. Remember to design for maximum accessibility as well, including alternate versions for the disabled, no matter the medium. (See Chapter 11 for more on accessible Websites.)

KEEPING LEARNERS' ATTENTION

Attention, or "time on task," is a critical factor in successful instruction. How do you keep the learners' attention and get them to finish an instructional experience? To get and keep the learners' attention, find out what they most need or want in the way of help and give it to them. Do they simply want to know how to find a book by subject or how to get some articles at home at 2 a.m.? Ask your learners what they want to know and how they want to learn. Once you know what they want to know and how they want to learn, you may be able to get them to use your sites and complete your lessons. At that point you may be able to test for learning outcomes. These learning outcomes need to be based on standards or benchmarks like ACRL's "Information Literacy Competency Standards for Higher Education," as we have discussed in previous chapters. However, none of this careful planning and extensive effort will help if your sites and services are unused or underused because of "Web fatigue" or rebellion against an impersonal electronic world.

At least one Web-based training designer recommends that we "create a compelling instructional design . . . which will delight the learner, not just provide information" (Parks, 1999: 1). Compelling designs make you want to learn more and then provide content to meet your needs. Yahoo!'s directory structure, for example, is the core of its portal site that attracts visitors (2000). It is simply laid out in clear categories, has an attached search engine and provides substantial content. "The Librarian's Index to the Internet," on the other hand, has substantial authoritative content, but the top page design could use some improvement (2000). It is cluttered with many topic words that may put off a user who is unfamiliar with its outstanding content.

THE MINIMALIST APPROACH

You can apply a minimalist approach to ILI materials not only by trimming words but also by altering your approach. (See Figures 10-1 and 10-2 for examples of non-minimalist and minimalist documentation.) Research has shown that learners who use minimalist documentation developed with four principles in mind tend to complete tasks, recover from errors more quickly, and become more independent learners (van der Meij and Lazonder, 1993). The four principles are "action-orientation," "optimal use of text, "support error recognition and recovery," and "modularity." This and other studies have shown that learners prefer a problem-solving minimalist approach to instructional materials rather than more detailed materials that provide background and a very detailed step-by-step approach. When you use a minimalist approach to documentation, you use simple language, active commands, and questions rather than declarative statements, and you also provide error self-correction. A minimalist approach also presents prompts for learners to "get their hands dirty" as soon as possible by trying out procedures on their own rather than giving them lengthy step-by-step directions for many different uses or approaches. You design materials in a modular fashion, without referring people from one segment to another. This is a Constructivist or active learning approach that plunges the learner into a resource immediately, but also provides error-correction life jackets. However, a strict minimalist approach that includes techniques such as "fading," where you provide successively fewer instructions, relies on a linear approach, at least within a particular module. In other words, minimalist documentation assumes that learners will begin at the beginning of a segment and proceed through the documentation, learning incrementally and experimenting on their own as they continue. In the modular world we live in, where learners tend to skip around and glean a concept here and a thought there, you might think that this approach is not appropriate. However, people who learn from minimalist materials become independent users of the resources being taught more quickly than those who learn about these resources through more detailed conventional help (Carroll and van der Meij, 1996). Furthermore, the more independent learners become, the less anxious they are likely to be and the more willing to explore new resources. These are powerful advantages and may lead you to try a modified minimalist approach to all sorts of instructional materials, both electronic/electric and print.

HUMOR

Design of instructional materials is serious business, as it can impact learning in significant, long-lasting ways. But how many of us are so caught up with the seriousness of our instructional tasks that we forget to inject some comic relief into our instruction? As Black and Forro point out, humor in the workplace can be an important antidote to stress and can improve both morale and productivity (1999). A few well-placed jokes, even at our own expense, can also delight users. Humorous Web pages like "Thwart Not the Librarian" (Olsen, 2000) and "The Lipstick Librarian" (Absher, 2000) can help change the image of the librarian.

Humor in instruction, though, must be taken seriously. It can get the learners' attention and can help alleviate library anxiety, but it can be difficult to pull off and often is quickly outdated. "Searchin' Safari," an excellent instructional video created in 1987, relied on audience recognition of the humor in a well-known television commercial of that time (Smith, 1987). The Joe Isuzu commercials popular in the late 1980s showed a car salesman making very unrealistic claims about Isuzu cars,

---

Figure 10-1
Non-Minimalist (Text) Portions of Point-of-Use Guide

FOUR WAYS TO MOVE AROUND IN THE WEB

---

a. Click on a link (often highlighted, underlined, or colored).
b. Pull down the "Go" menu and select an item in your search history.
c. Use the "Back," "Forward," or "Home" buttons in the Toolbar.
d. Click on "Open" in the Toolbar, type the URL with exact punctuation and capitalization, and click "Open."

TO MANAGE BOOKMARKS

Begin by pulling down the "Window" menu and selecting "Bookmarks."

a. Find an item within your Bookmarks list.
- Go to the top of the window.
- Select "Find" in the "Edit" menu and type a word(s) in the box.

b. Edit a bookmark name
- In the "Item" menu, select "Edit Bookmark," and make desired changes.

c. View a bookmark list as a Web page
- Return to the browser window by clicking on the "Home" button.
- Click on "Open" in the Toolbar, then on "Choose File."
- Navigate to the folder that contains your Bookmarks file; highlight and click "ok."
- Click "Open" in the dialog box.

---

with words on the screen reading "He's lying . . . " followed by supposedly more realistic assertions about the positive qualities of Isuzu cars ("The 50 Best," 1995). Similarly, students in the "Searchin' Safari" video make claims orally, like "I know how to use computers. I use them all the time" while words appear on the screen contradicting the claim; for example, "She's lying. She's only used an ATM." Once the Joe Isuzu commercials stopped being aired, the humorous correlation in the "Searchin' Safari" video ceased.

Some studies indicate that humor can be distracting and even interfere with understanding, while others find that undergraduates believe they learn more from teachers with a "high humor orientation" (Sternthal and Craig, 1973; Wanzer and Frymier, 1999). That being said, humor, especially self-deprecating humor, can put an audience at ease, break

Figure 10-2
Modified Minimalist (Text) Portions of Point-of-Use Guide

FOUR WAYS TO MOVE AROUND IN THE WEB

a. Click on a link (often highlighted, underlined, or colored).

> Error correction message

Clicking won't work?
You may have moved the mouse while clicking.
Hold the mouse still and click again.

b. Pull down the "Go" menu and select an item in your search history.
c. Use the "Back," "Forward" or "Home" buttons in the Toolbar.
d. Click on "Open" in the Toolbar, type the URL with exact punctuation and capitalization, and click "Open."

> Error correction message

Did you get a "404 Not Found" message?
You may have made a typing error. Try again.

TO MANAGE BOOKMARKS

Begin by pulling down the "Window" menu and selecting "Bookmarks."
a. Find an item within your Bookmarks list.
  • Select "Find" in the "Edit" menu and type a word(s) in the box.
b. Edit a bookmark name
  • In the "Item" menu, select "Edit Bookmark," and make desired changes.

> User action directive with "faded" instructions.

Try it out: View your Bookmarks as a Web page
Your bookmarks are stored as a file.
Use the "Open" button to locate and see them as a Web page.

tension, and serve to humanize the instructor. Cartoons or comic strips can break the ice at the beginning of a session or soothe tension when interspersed throughout a session. Many library-related cartoons are available on the Web now ("Library Cartoons," 2000) and can be quite useful in establishing rapport with and relaxing an audience. Some instructors plan to make mistakes and ask a group to help problem-solve as a means of learning through discovery. Others laugh at their own poor typing or spelling skills as they quite naturally make these common sorts of errors. In any case, as long as humor is directed at an inanimate system or at oneself, it can go a long way toward relaxing learners and helping them absorb content. In no case, however, should an instructor single out a learner or their attempts to do research as a subject for humor in any instructional setting (Sarkodie-Mensah, 1998). One joke at the expense of a learner can harm the person and derail even the most carefully planned instruction. Remember, to the learner you are a powerful person. You are responsible for earning the learners' trust by treating them with respect and dignity, regardless of their age, education, or skill level.

If you feel comfortable with humor, try using it in different formats, but test it out on friends and naïve users before going to great lengths to incorporate it into instruction. As the famous satirist Stan Freberg put it, "Humor is such a fragile thing. . . . [It's] like a gun in the hands of a child. You have to know how to do it. Otherwise it can blow up on you" (Garfield, 1992: 52).

Format

INTERACTIVITY

As we have seen in this chapter and will learn more about in Chapter 11, IL instructional material designers now have a great number of format choices to make instruction modes and materials ranging from high- to low-tech, in a rainbow of colors, motion, sounds, and graphics. In addition, designers can build interactivity into many of these instructional options. What does "interactive" really mean in terms of instruction and instructional material? "Interaction is mutual action among the learner, the learning system, and the learning material" (Najjar, 1998: 314). What sorts of interaction can we build in and which instructional format(s) would be most effective to help our primary audience achieve expected learning outcomes? Interaction for ILI materials can include tutorials with Web-based quizzes that provide immediate feedback and exercises or workbooks that users have to complete and for which they receive feedback. Some interaction can occur, as well, without "graded" or "corrected" feedback. Just clicking buttons on a Web page can mean interaction of a sort, as the user makes cognitive choices about directions to take, further pages to view within a particular site, or links to external sites. What is the user learning, however? How can we focus our instructional efforts on user needs and design the most useful instructional modes and materials for our primary users? It all starts with the most important factor, the learner.

The Learner and User Input

Donald Norman recommends using the Apple Corporation's approach to designing and developing highly user-friendly products by consulting users about products at every step of the way, from design through development and implementation, and even afterwards ("Talking with Don Norman," 1999). One way to routinize this process for ILI would be to establish a working advisory board with representatives from user, staff, administrative, and other groups. This board could then provide regular feedback on all sorts of ILI projects and plans, as well as suggest new ILI initiatives and aid in goal- and priority-setting for the entire organization. If an advisory board would not work in a particular environment, ad hoc focus groups, surveys, or questionnaires are other means for learners to participate in deciding which formats would be most useful to them for ILI (Greenbaum, 1998; Quible, 1998; Morgan, 1997).

Whatever the form of learner participation, participants may need a jumpstart in terms of defining IL and coming up with ideas for ILI modes and materials. Examples of ILI materials from other locations can be helpful in this regard. Examine a number of different models of instructional materials and pick out the most appealing elements or segments to share with the participants, in order to get them started. In particular, look for models to emulate that have similar goals, no matter the format. School library media specialists can offer all of us good lessons in how to design instruction for different learner levels. What are the most basic concepts primary grade learners need to know and what should be added or reworded as age and skill levels increase? If the basics are simple enough for children, complexity can be added as the audience changes. For example, Kathy Schrock's Web critical thinking "tests" or "exercises" are designed for different levels, from primary to high school, and rise in complexity as grade levels increase (Schrock, 2000b).

Whenever possible, try to build into instructional materials some self-paced, individualized learner participation. Some even believe that this approach is the wave of the future as distance learning becomes more commonplace, at least in higher education ("The Future of Learning," 1999). It is interesting to note that from 1995 to 1998 the number of distance education programs offered in the U.S. rose by 72 percent, and continues to rise (Carnevale, 2000). In the United Kingdom, distance learning for higher education has been a reality since 1971. In 1997-98, the largest U.K. university was the Open University (OU), with over 200,000 students and customers, including 21 percent of all part-time higher education students in the country. Open University claims that its courses are "considered to be among the world's best distance education materials and are regularly awarded for their innovation . . . Nineteen subject areas within the OU have been recognized as producing research work with evidence of international quality . . . " ("Open University," 2000: [online]).

How individualized are these courses, and what proportion of their assignments and other activities are self-paced? Those who teach courses completely online recommend that instructors send students off regularly to complete brief, self-paced exercises or activities (Ko and Rossen, 2001). Do these recommendations include use of print materials in a physical library? It is difficult to know. In response to a request for information about how their students obtain and make use of print materials, or how they incorporate ILI into their curricula, the Open University indicated that they offer "complete modules on research methods and whole courses on aspects of information literacy such as You, Your Computer and Net which has a current [January 2000] enrollment of 18,000" (Prior, 2000: [online]). Do they license bibliographic databases and systems for student use, like "Historical Abstracts" and "Lexis-Nexis Academic Universe"? If so, how do students learn about their existence, their purpose, and coverage, and how to learn to use them effectively? Do distance learning enterprises like OU provide ILI remotely, or do they send students print materials (for example, point-of-use guides) to help them learn the mechanics of using information tools? Even more importantly, how do these students learn to evaluate information tools and individual items, and pick the ones that are appropriate to their information needs? How, in fact, can we best meet the needs of remote, as well as in-person learners, including those with low-end access, equipment, or software?

MEETING A RANGE OF NEEDS

In an ideal world with unlimited time, staff, and budget, we should provide a multiplicity of ILI formats to meet the needs and learning styles of most learners. Often, though, there is not enough time or money to develop and maintain a large number of different formats of instructional materials aimed at helping people learn the same things. At a minimum, you should try to meet the extremes of access to technology by providing a low-tech paper item and a corresponding electronic/ electric version, keeping in mind the following features:

- Interest level
- Freshness
- Simplicity
- Content-based
- Learner-centered structure

Continue involving users in the development process by testing materials on naïve users. Listen carefully to their comments, revise accordingly, and test again for ease of use. Remember to build in or separately design some means of testing learning outcomes, and ask the learners who used each format for user satisfaction feedback as well. (See Chapter 12 for more information about assessing instructional effectiveness.)

FINAL REMARKS

Copyright, budget, and administrative and colleague support all impact instructional mode/material selection significantly. You will need to examine these issues within the context of your environment, the user groups you are addressing, and their particular needs. You will need to do this before you can focus on specific instructional categories, decide on the balance of mechanics versus concepts, how you will keep learners' attention, the format, and many other design questions. If you give serious consideration to each of the preliminary design issues discussed in this chapter, you will be well prepared to consider design and development of specific instructional modes and materials.

EXERCISES

1. Take a one- or two-page paper point-of-use guide and determine its audience and purpose. Write a brief outline of the most important elements learners would need to know in order to use the resource. Highlight the most important elements provided in the handout. Were all of the elements in your outline included in the handout? Where would you place the missing elements? What would you delete from the handout in order to keep it the same length or make it shorter?
2. Make a paper copy of a point-of-use guide for an online article

index. Ask someone who has never seen the guide to read it and circle all the words on it that they do not understand. Which words did they circle? Would you consider these words to be jargon, or simply words that the person had never seen before? How would you revise the guide to make it more understandable and user-friendly?

3. Take a wordy or technical one- to two-page point-of-use guide and modify it so that it has some minimalist features. Describe what you changed, how you changed it (or them), and why.

READ MORE ABOUT IT

The Copyright Web Site. 2001 [Online]. Available: www.benedict.com/ [2001, February 19]

Ko, Susan, and Steve Rossen. 2001. *Teaching Online: A Practical Guide*. Boston: Houghton-Mifflin.

Nahl, Diane. 1999. "Creating User-Centered Instructions for Novice End-Users." *Reference Services Review* 27 no. 3: 280–86.

Sarkodie-Mensah, Kwasi. 1998. "Using Humor for Effective Library Instruction Sessions." *Catholic Library World* 68 no. 4: 25–29.

Schrock, Kathy. 2000. "Kathy Schrock's Guide for Educators" [Online]. Available: http://discoveryschool.com/schrockguide/eval.html [2000, November 26].

Twigg, Carol A. 2000. "Who Owns Online Courses and Course Materials? Intellectual Property Policies for a New Learning Environment." The Pew Learning and Technology Program [Online]. Available: www.center.rpi.edu/ PewSym/mono2.html [2000, September 17].

Van der Meij, Hans, and Ard W. Lazonder. 1993. "Assessment of the Minimalist Approach to Computer User Documentation." *Interacting with Computers* 5 no.4: 355–70.

11

Designing Instructional Modes and Materials

She comes in colors . . .

—The Rolling Stones, *"She's a Rainbow"*

Trainers, teachers, and librarians may not be trained in instructional or graphic design, yet often they must create a range of instructional materials to support both in-person and remote learning for many ages and skill levels. As we pointed out in Chapter 8, it is crucial to select modes of instruction and supplementary or standalone materials that best support your goals and objectives. Once you have selected modes and materials, how do you actually go about designing them? In Chapter 13 we focus primarily on designing and developing synchronous in-person group instruction. This chapter covers designing and developing many other instructional modes and materials as well as backup plans for inevitable glitches.

DESIGNING PRINT MATERIALS

What do you use to create print materials? Word-processing and paint software come to mind immediately, but you can still use a typewriter or even paper and pencil to design print instructional materials like handouts, guides, maps, pathfinders, exercises, and workbooks. Print is comfortable, static, and predictable, as well as easily portable. Learners can put paper materials down next to them, make notes on them, paper-clip them, and highlight or circle important sections. Some learners still value print materials to such an extent that they print off page after page of material designed for online learning. They may do so for all the reasons mentioned above, or simply because they prefer to see the whole picture before focusing on smaller elements. Whatever the reason, it is still important to provide print materials for those who prefer them, either as paper handouts copied and distributed by the library, or mounted on Websites in a format designed for printing. Paper point-of-use guides are also handy ways to reinforce learning in group sessions.

Well-designed print materials can help people learn more quickly and easily. According to Allen, in designing handouts we need to "make decisions about size, shape and stock, layout, typeface (or font), and color" (1993). We also need to consider structure, which deals more with content than with the look and feel of a piece, as well as the time available for preparation.

Structure

Often, users learn more quickly if they know where to look for specific instructions on how to use or interact with a reference tool. Instructional materials with a consistent look and feel, and a consistent content structure, can be a big help. Check to see if your library has a preferred template for print materials, and if not, consider designing one. If you do design a template, try to keep it as simple and uncluttered as possible. Templates often have a title at the top or bottom (header or footer), or even on the side. They usually include the library name and its logo, or that of the parent institution. The occasional odd piece that uses off-center, unusual, or even bizarre combinations of color, graphic design, images, layouts, and wording may get more attention than a standard template, but should be reserved for unusual or one-of-a-kind items, for example, a search log (Wehmeyer, 1996; see also Figure 11–1). Even these sorts of pieces can include a small header with a logo, and all instructional materials should be signed or initialed by the author(s).

There is debate about the advantages and disadvantages of linear, step-by-step instruction, particularly for electronic materials (Tennant, 1997). However, a logical linear structure can help learners orient themselves quickly, and is essential for learning and utilizing various features of electronic resources. For example, if a paper handout on using the Netscape browser includes the mechanics of e-mailing a page, it will need to list a series of steps, some of which must be completed in a linear fashion in order to mail the page. So, even with print materials, users could skip around and try printing pages or editing bookmarks but for each operation they will have a sequence of steps to follow. (See Figure 11–2.)

**Figure 11–1:
Sample Search Log**

Name: _____

Topic: _____

Date	Information Source (Database name, Web page title and URL, etc.)	Keyword, Author, Subject, or Title Search?	Search Words	Number of Results	Additional Subject Words

White Space, Graphics, and Layout

"White space" will speak more to users than most words you write, so allow plenty of it. As the well-known graphic artist Tufte puts it, "Erase non-data ink" and "Erase redundant data ink" (Tufte, 1983: 105). This means balancing the amount of content with the number of graphics and the number of pages permissible. Include appropriate graphics whenever feasible, but keep in mind that graphics can take up lots of space, and the longer the print piece, the more costly and time-consuming it will be to reproduce.

Graphics are important, however, and can be more effective learning devices than text alone for recalling and recognizing items. Often, though, they leave us in a quandary. How many should we include? How large? Should we use screen capture software like "SnagIt" for the PC or "SnapzPro" for the Macintosh, to "grab" part of a window or screen or all of it? How do we indicate or maintain context if we take a small piece of a screen shot rather than an entire screen or window? As Najjar puts it, and as the empirical research he cites indicates, "The information being presented in one medium needs to support, relate to, or extend the information presented in the other medium"(1998: 313). Research also indicates that though graphics are important, we must be quite cautious about how we use them. Including just any graphics or a large number of graphics will not necessarily improve learning. It helps to outline the main points, note where graphics may be needed, and include both words and graphics only as necessary. "The illustrations

---

Figure 11–2
Example of Linear Instructions

To e-mail a copy of a Web page (text only, no graphics)
while viewing the page in Netscape

- In the Options menu, select "Mail and News Preferences," then "Identity."
- Fill in your name and e-mail address and click OK.
- From the "File" menu, select "Mail Document."
- Type an e-mail address in the "Mail To" box and a subject in the subject box.
- Click on "Quote" to include the Web page (text only).
- For a clean, text-only copy of the Web page, click on "Attach" in the dialog box and then "Plain Text."
- Click "Send" to e-mail the message.

---

must help explain information that is presented by the verbal medium . . . [as] supportive illustrations allow learners to build cognitive connections between the verbal and pictorial information" (Najjar, 1998: 313).

The theory of "dual-encoding" may explain why this is so. This theory states that a person remembers a picture in two ways, as an image and also as a word or words, making for better recall of pictures than of words. According to Paivio, the same effect occurs regarding recall of concrete as opposed to abstract words (1973), which may also partially explain the power of concrete analogies used to explain abstract ideas (see Chapter 5). According to Tufte, the best graphic representations of data, " . . . are *intriguing and curiosity-provoking*, drawing the viewer into the wonder of the data, sometimes by narrative power, sometimes by immense detail, and sometimes by elegant presentation of simple but interesting data" (1983: 121). In other words, use graphics sparingly and primarily to support the goals and objectives of the instructional piece.

In addition, use the briefest and simplest context-setting language to describe where users should look for pieces of graphics—for example, "Scroll down and click on the box labeled 'go' halfway down the screen on the right-hand side." As Curtis puts it, "Your writing does not need to be 'interesting'; it needs to be invisible" (1995: 55).

Finally, make sure your graphics are easily readable, especially if your audience will include adult learners. The basic rule of thumb is: If a user cannot see a graphic clearly and completely, do not include it.

Figure 11–3
CDL "SearchLight" Point-of-Use Guide Example:
Too Many Graphics; Too Complex

3.   VIEW RESULTS (HITS)

- Results are listed in order of highest number of results within each category.
- Scroll down to view results or click on a category to go directly to it— e.g., Journal Indexes.

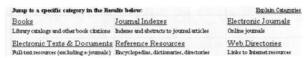

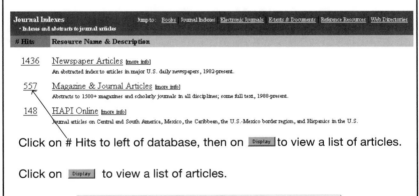

Click on # Hits to left of database, then on [Display] to view a list of articles.

Click on [Display] to view a list of articles.

	Search	Database	Items	Suggested Action
⦿	keyword **fidel castro cuba**	MAGS	557	[Display]	Find Fewer

4.   FOR EACH ITEM, VIEW...

☐ 5. Garcia, Maria Cristina **Hardliners v. "dialogueros": Cuban exile political groups and United States-Cuba policy.** Journal of American Ethnic History v17, n4 (Summer, 1998):3 (26 pages).
[Article Text]*
[Abstract] [Long Display] †
Print access:
(All, All UC, UCB, UCLA,‡ CSL, Greater Bay Area, Greater Los Angeles, Northern California)

* article text (if available):Entire article (words only).
† abstract (if available): Summary of article.
‡ library location: click on UCLA for campus library, call number & volumes owned.

The content, both textual and graphical, of systems provided by the California Digital Library are copyrighted by the Regents of the University of California unless otherwise noted. Permission was granted by John Obes, Director, Education and Strategic Innovation, CDL, Feb. 21, 2001.

Figure 11–4
CDL "SearchLight" Point-of-Use Guide Example:
Fewer Graphics; Less Complex

---

3.   VIEW RESULTS (HITS)

- Results are listed in order of highest number of results within each category.
- Scroll down to view results—e.g., **Journal Indexes.**

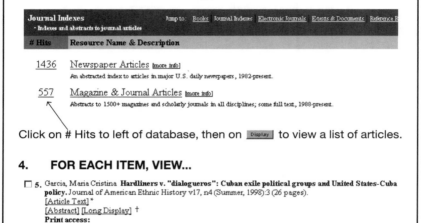

Click on # Hits to left of database, then on Display to view a list of articles.

4.   FOR EACH ITEM, VIEW...

☐ 5. Garcia, Maria Cristina **Hardliners v. "dialogueros": Cuban exile political groups and United States-Cuba policy.** Journal of American Ethnic History v17, n4 (Summer, 1998):3 (26 pages).
[Article Text] *
[Abstract] [Long Display] †
Print access:

(All, All UC, UCB, UCLA‡ CSL, Greater Bay Area, Greater Los Angeles, Northern California)

---

* article text (if available):Entire article (words only).
† abstract (if available): Summary of article.
‡ library location: click on UCLA for campus library, call number & volumes owned.

The content, both textual and graphical, of systems provided by the California Digital Library are copyrighted by the Regents of the University of California unless otherwise noted. Permission was granted by John Obes, Director, Education and Strategic Innovation, CDL, Feb. 21, 2001.

Share samples with users who may utilize these materials. Increase the size of graphics if necessary, and consider eliminating some to hold down the number of pages and, thereby, the reproduction costs. This is a delicate balancing act, though, since too few graphics may make a printed guide as useless as too many. As Tufte puts it so well, "Graphical excellence consists of complex ideas communicated with clarity, precision, and efficiency. Graphical excellence is that which gives to the viewer the greatest number of ideas in the shortest time with the least ink in the smallest place" (1983: 51). So pick and choose your graphics carefully, use a screen capture program to take the most essential portions of screens or windows, and use a paint program to adjust them to fit both the physical page constraints and to draw attention to specific points. Figure 11–3 shows a portion of a printed point-of-use guide with too many words and graphics that are too complex. Figure 11–4 shows the same portion of the guide, but with improved balance between words and graphics, adjusted with a simple graphics program to present the most important features.

In general, your pedagogical goals and objectives, and your bare bones outline, should serve as guides for both content and graphics. You can improve usability as well, if you share drafts with your colleagues (in your institution or remotely) and if you test drafts on naïve users.

Typeface or Font

One of the glories of word processing is being able to choose among a large number of typefaces, including picture fonts. Typeface alone can set a mood, suggest a content focus, tempt learners to read an item, or cause them to ignore it completely. Consider the following examples:

Verdana is a rather modern looking sans serif font—that is, it lacks the "little feet or appendages" that Allen claims improves legibility in print materials (1993: 19). Some people prefer this sort of plain font to serif fonts, for both print and electronic/electric instructional materials.

Palatino is a clean-looking serif font, a bit more modern than **Times New Roman**.

Comic sans mas is quite friendly and appealing for informal usage, even though it is a sans serif font.

Old English Text MT is too overly ornate or stylized for many instructional materials, but might be eye-catching for titles or headers in course-integrated art or history materials.

☜〰●○■◆□◆❖☒🗀✂✁📁📂🖘☺☹

Wingdings, shown above, is an example of a picture font that can be used for bullets or for illustration in place of clip art.

Try experimenting with different typefaces or fonts, but be a bit cautious about mixing different typefaces within the same document. Keep in mind, too, that words in italics are often ignored, and too much use of bold, underlining, shadow, and other special treatments can lessen their effect. If your audience includes adult learners, make sure the font size is easily readable by asking users to review samples.

Color

Color can invoke psychological reactions in many people. According to the *Encyclopedia of Educational Technology*, you can use color "to get attention, create a mood, enhance clarity, establish a code, label things in nature, and differentiate items" (San Diego State University, 2000). As the encyclopedia's detailed color table indicates, "gold" indicates a warm color like the sun, while "sky blue" is "philosophical and non-threatening." One does have to question its definition of "pink" as "lovely, sensitive, feminine," and the way it identifies the psychological treatment of pink as "It abandons logic for sensitivity." The encyclopedia does offer sensible advice on color use, including the use of hue and saturation in background and for contrast. For example, the encyclopedia recommends sparing use of pure, bright, or strong colors in backgrounds. This allows the strong colors to bring attention to a particular feature of a graphic. Most interestingly, color can be an effective instructional tool. Research studies indicate that

- Readers have color preferences
- Readers like additional color
- Color can facilitate learning
- Extra colors have to be used sparingly and consistently if they are not to confuse readers (Jonassen and Reeves, 1996; Dwyer, 1978; Deutsch, 1999).

Color is often used in advertising to entice people into buying particular products. For example, the color yellow is an "attention-getter," processed most quickly by the brain ("Supermarket Psych-Out," 1999). Color can even affect perception of drug effects. For example, one study found that " . . . a blue sugar pill made medical students drowsier than a pink sugar pill" ("Why Blue M&M's . . . ," 1997). A study of problem solving tasks showed that blue and white paper promoted better performance than red paper under low motivation conditions (Soldat, Sinclair, and Mark, 1997). Color can be an extremely useful tool both for handouts and for Web pages. For remote use, learners may come to expect particular colors of point-of-use guides for specific functions, databases, or systems. When a group has a large packet of handouts, for example, you can get them to focus on a specific one by saying, "Now, let's take a look at the blue handout." Garish and neon-colored paper may make materials difficult to read, however, and it may be hard to read dark-colored handouts in dim light. Try to save the most easily readable color or the item with the most contrast for the most important handout in a packet. Essentially, then, color can attract a learner's attention and, when used appropriately, can enhance learning. A good rule of thumb for color in instructional materials, though, is to use it sparingly and for a purpose, to avoid extremes, especially in paper and font colors, and *always* check for readability with naïve users.

Many of these print design criteria can be applied to other mediums midway and at the higher end of the instructional materials continuum.

Preparation Time Available

Time constraints for preparing or updating instructional materials can impinge on creativity, clarity, and comprehensiveness. When you have very limited time in which to design and develop instructional materials, write up your goals and objectives for the piece, make a quick list of all the points you would like to include, and then cross off all but the most basic. You can also pass your list among two or three naïve users and ask them to check off very quickly the three to five points they would most like to learn. Focus on explaining these functions clearly and concisely, with graphics inserted at the most critical junctions only. Try to weave critical thinking and evaluation into as many elements of the piece as possible.

DESIGNING AUDIO, VIDEO, AND PRESENTATION SLIDE SHOWS

Audio

In the 1970s, the most frequent use of audio for IL instruction took the form of self-guided audio cassette tours of the physical library. These audio cassette (or their present-day equivalents: CD-ROM) tours can be quite handy, especially when few or no staff are available to give in-person tours and where individuals or small groups tend to wander in unexpectedly. Audio cassette tapes can be produced fairly quickly and cheaply, and inexpensive personal cassette players can be checked out at a loan desk with a driver's license or other ID.

Mounting audio files on a Website or adding audio to a presentation software slide show and then mounting the entire show on your Website are possibilities. According to Ko and Rossen, the three most popular programs used for the latter purpose are "RealSlideshow" (RealNetworks, 2000), "Quicktime" (Apple, 2000), and "PowerPoint 2000" (Microsoft, 2000a). Using audio on the Web presents broader IL opportunities, as helpful comments or instruction may be added to instructional Websites, accommodating both learners with audio-preference learning styles and the disabled. Online catalog help should at some point offer an audio, as well as a text-only, alternative or accompaniment.

In any case, effective audio materials require simple and to-the-point content, spoken by a narrator who pronounces words clearly and distinctly. Professional narrators will raise cost and are not essential. Student or amateur actors or actresses may be willing to do narration for little or no fee, as long as they are given credit.

Video

Video production costs have come down dramatically with the wide availability of inexpensive camcorders, though professionally created videos can still be expensive. It cost $1,000 per minute to produce the ILI video "Searchin' Safari" in 1987 (Smith, 1987). Today, camcorders are common and cost under $1,000, so videos can be created quite inexpensively. Video editing technology was not available to the general public prior to the 1990s regardless of cost. It may be cost effective to film and edit videos created in-house using the relatively inexpensive camcorders and editing equipment now available.

Actors and actresses speaking dialogue can account for much of the expense of professionally created videotapes because dialogue often requires many "takes." Each take must be planned and set up in advance with proper lighting and equipment (both costly expenses), as well as accompanying personnel, whose wages must also be covered. One way around these particular expenses is to substitute as many "voiceovers" as possible for filmed dialogue. A "voiceover" is simply someone narrating off-camera while other items, people, scenery, or activities are being filmed. It is much easier and inexpensive to redo just the audio portion of a video than to keep reshooting people speaking their lines on camera. The fewer the takes, the less expensive the video.

Fidler offers many more excellent practical and succinct tips on educational video production in seven areas: production objectives, script and production design, editing scripts, planning camera angles, planning lighting, planning sound, and planning post-production work (2001). Though meant for psychiatrists, his advice is general enough to be useful in many different arenas. For example, he points out that "An elaborate production does not mean [that] teaching and learning will be better. Elaborate technical videotaping techniques may distract from learning ... " (2001: [online]). He also suggests posing questions and not answering them on the video in order to keep the content fresh and generate discussion by learners (Fidler, 2000).

There are many examples of good and bad ILI videos available to LOEX members. The most effective videos are short (ten to fifteen minutes or less), interesting, and to the point. The UCLA Office of Academic Computing, for example, prepared a captivating ten-minute video about the campus suite of software ("Bruin OnLine") by randomly asking students on campus to answer questions like "What's FTP?" You never hear the questions or see the questioner. Instead, most of the video consists of a number of cleverly edited clips of students giving impromptu and sometimes humorous answers, both correct and incorrect, all held together with title shots such as "E-MAIL" and "SCARED?" ("Bruin OnLine," 1995). "6 Ways to Ask a Reference Question," for example, is a classic proto-ILI video that uses gentle humor in six short minutes to illustrate the importance of asking detailed, explicit reference questions (Gould, 1977). The intent is to teach students to ask direct and complete questions at reference desks. In the process, though, it also teaches students that librarians are friendly and want to help. It also teaches librarians a variety of diplomatic means of interacting with users. The video is a kind of "proto-ILI" item because it was created toward the beginning of the modern-day IL movement and had two specific goals related to reference questions in general: to encourage users to ask questions at a reference desk and to be forthcoming about their reference needs.

As we mentioned earlier in Chapter 10, videos sometimes present humor that is widely understood only at a particular point in time. After the subject that the humor is based on has long been forgotten, the jokes can be lost on a new audience. Videos with themes such as library detectives may also be off-putting to more sophisticated audiences, especially adult learners, as they may seem too cutesy or condescending. On the other hand, eye-catching, ten- to thirty-second spots broadcast in a dorm, on a public access cable channel, or on the Web via streaming video may grab a particular audience that otherwise would not be attracted to ILI resources. However, streaming video does require lots of bandwidth and is not yet a viable option for most learners.

Overhead Transparencies

You can write, draw, or print out onto overhead transparencies in black or in color. They are called "transparencies" because an overhead projector shines a light through them and projects a magnified image onto a screen, a wall, a sheet, or any other object in front of it. A box of 100 blank overheads that you can write on costs about $20. Overheads that you put through a printer or a photocopier are heavier and cost more, about $25 for a box of 100.

The same principles apply to overheads as to print materials, with some added caveats. Be sure to make images and characters on overheads large enough so that those in the back of the room can read them clearly and easily. It is better not to use overheads at all if some of the audience will be frustrated because they cannot read the material—they will be thinking about your unreadable overheads during your entire session rather than the content.

You should also use as few bullets, words, and images as possible on a single overhead. If you write, print, or draw by hand on an overhead transparency, you need to use special pens and your writing should be extremely legible. In many cases when you use overheads, lights will be dimmed, so learners will only hear your voice and see what is projected on the screen. They may or may not see your body language unless you turn off the overhead projector and turn on the lights. Thus, your voice and your overheads will have to speak for you. Remember that overhead transparencies are a static medium, but you can get some movement by uncovering some portions of an overhead image a bit at a time, by circling or drawing arrows on a transparency, by switching transparencies fairly quickly, and by turning the overhead projector off from time to time.

To spruce up a session, you can use overheads to pose questions, state premises for discussion, or provide instructions for an exercise. You can also copy comic strips, graphics, or clip art onto overheads, though you do need to be aware of copyright issues if you are using these items in a for-profit situation. See Chapter 9 for more information on using overhead transparencies in instruction.

Presentation Slide Shows

Microsoft PowerPoint and other presentation software applications can be extremely seductive instructional tools, sometimes too seductive, at least for instructors. PowerPoint, for example, comes with a number of presentation outlines, including an especially useful "Training" outline. Presenters can choose from a large number of backgrounds and color schemes, insert clip art and other graphics, including screen captures, and even add all sorts of movement and sound effects to each slide. "Notes" pages are hidden from the audience, but when printed out allow the presenter to match notes to particular slides. You can also use presentation software to create a slide show and then print out the slides on overhead transparencies (Gribas, Sykes, and Dorochoff, 1996).

The key words here, however, are *"presentation* software" and *"presenter."* Although they are electronic, many people use presentation slide shows in a passive manner. Learners sit and watch as an instructor talks and shows slides, attempting to pour information into the tabula rasa of the learner's mind. As we saw in Chapter 5, though, learners really do not have empty minds. Often they have mental models of what we are trying to teach, sometimes incorrect models or other thoughts or motivations that may or may not have anything to do with our instruction.

To get their attention and improve learning and retention, you should aim to make presentation software shows as interactive as possible, even if slides are created online and then printed out onto transparencies for use with an overhead projector. For example, you can show a slide with two intersecting circles called Venn diagrams and ask the audience to predict which parts of the diagrams should be filled to represent various Boolean operators. The next slide or overhead can then show the correct answer. Also, at various points, instead of just letting a bulleted point appear on the screen, ask the learners to guess what it will be. If you are using overheads created with presentation software and printed onto transparencies, you can uncover points one by one as you come to them, or overlay transparencies with the correct answer.

Even if you increase interactivity, though, other pitfalls may confront you. Presentation software often unduly captivates instructors in many fields. Once you have learned how to use it, you will be sorely tempted to overuse it because it is fun, you can make words move, insert cute graphics and clip art, and you can have each slide "transition" to another slide by wiping right, uncovering left, dissolving, and so on. You may also end up trying to dump too much information into the learner. The most common error is to convert to slides almost every word in your notes or every word you would speak. It is difficult and unnecessary for learners to sit in a room and read slides on a screen when you could just as easily have handed them a bunch of photocopies of your slides and told them to come see you if they had questions. You must work hard to resist this temptation. Keep words that represent key concepts only, bullet them, and consider enlarging the font size. Use color to highlight important items, but check to see if colors will be clearly visible from the back of the instruction room, or via Web browsers if mounted on a Website. Use clip art and graphics in place of words whenever possible to illustrate points or for humor, but be careful to allow for white space on each slide. For example, instead of creating a slide that reads "Does anyone have any questions?" you might just have a slide that looks like Figure 11–5.

Dimming previous bulleted points can give the illusion of white space even on a crowded slide. Movement attracts attention, so make use of transition options for slides and points on particular slides. Too much movement and highly detailed, cluttered, and deeply colored backgrounds can be quite distracting, however, so choose colors carefully. Test out the entire slide show first by yourself and then with a colleague or a naïve user.

**Figure 11–5
Sample PowerPoint Slide**

Above all, keep in mind that presentation software is just another tool, one that can turn learners off as easily as it turns presenters on. Use it sparingly.

COMPUTER-BASED INSTRUCTION (CBI)

Computer-Assisted Instruction (CAI)

Computer-assisted instruction (CAI) has a number of advantages over other formats, but as a standalone tool it can be a quicksand approach to ILI, at least for the designer and the developer, drawing one into a potentially enormous and costly project (Kaplowitz and Contini, 1998). Some CAI programs promise interactivity, color, movement, and the ability to utilize a simulation for parts or all of the material to be learned. For example, in 1998, the University of California contracted with CBT Systems to provide full downloading and access to over 400 computer-based training (CBT) courses, including "Understanding and Using Newsgroups" and "An Overview of Java" ("Online Computer Training," 2000). These downloadable courses were training simulations designed to teach the mechanics of using the Internet via Netscape, Microsoft Word, networking systems, and much more. They were modular, which means that users could skip around and take any segment of a course they liked in any order. Users could also test out or receive individual feedback on specific modules or entire courses.

These courses were designed and produced using authorware (software) that could be utilized for ILI purposes as well. However, it takes much time and effort to develop CAI programs. If the authorware is fairly complex it may mean additional expenditure and time for programmers and instructional designers to develop a fairly professional looking product and for librarians to review it for content. Meanwhile, the product being taught may have changed dramatically in the interim, especially if it is Web-based. For all of these reasons and more, many instructors now rely on Web-based instruction instead of CAI.

Websites and Pages

The technology behind Web pages seems especially mystifying and magical to many, yet it is based on three quite simple principles:

1. Decide what you want to appear on a Web page
2. Write instructions for what you want to appear on the page and how it should look
3. Save the page and view it with a Web browser

Once you understand these three principles, the steps to creating a Web page are simple (see Figure 11-6).

Granted, many of us are not artists or instructional designers, and do not have extensive knowledge of or skill with detailed HTML programming. However, there are many Web design books and Web pages you can consult, classes you can take for instructions, and tips and tricks about creating new Web pages or revising existing pages to build your own pages; for example, the NCSA guide to HTML for beginners (University of Illinois, 2000). Hartnett's brief article, "Tag, You're It!," is also an excellent introduction to HTML (2000). This brief lesson may help you see, though, that logic rather than magic is behind the Web page "curtain." But if you still do not want to learn how to use HTML to create Web pages, you may be able to build on the work of others rather than creating Web pages entirely from scratch. You can identify elements of pages you like, view the page source, and then copy and paste it into your own page or examine the source code to see how the page elements were designed. Be careful, though. It is all too easy to do this without much thought, but you do need to consider copyright and intellectual property when you copy text, images, forms, or any other portions of Web pages. Even small items you may think of as "clip art," like Web page buttons, may be an artist's source of income. A Google search

Figure 11–6
How to Create a Simple Web Page

1. Decide what you want to appear on a Web page—text in various colors, sizes and formats, graphics and other images of various sizes and types, backgrounds of various colors and types, and other features such as tables and frames.

2. Write instructions for what you want to appear on the page, and then how items on the page should look. To do this, you may write your own Hypertext Markup Language (HTML) tags, or you may write a document in Microsoft Word and save it as an HTML file, or you may use Web page authoring software that does this for you, like Netscape's Web page editor, "Composer." For example, if you want to have a Web page that has a very large headline on it called "How I Learned to Stop Worrying and Love the Web!" the HTML version of it might look like this:

   <H1>How I Learned to Stop Worrying and Love the Web!</H1>

   The HTML tag "<H1>" stands for "Header 1," the largest size you can use on a standard Web page.

   If you want to create this page in Netscape Composer (version 4.72), rather than typing in the HTML tags yourself, you simply pull down the "File" menu, click on "New/Blank Page," pull down the menu on the top far left and change "Normal" to "Heading 1." Then type "How I Learned to Stop Worrying and Love the Web!" Or, type the words first, then highlight them and change "Normal" to "Heading 1."

   Save the Web page: Click the "File" menu, then "Save," select where you want to save the page (for example, on your hard drive), give the file a name, and click the "Save" button. Then if you click "View/Page Source" you will see that Composer has put the HTML tag <H1> at the beginning and end of your headline.

3. You can then use Netscape Communicator or some other Web browser to view your Web page. When you do, you will see that the <H1> tags do not appear on the page. These HTML tags simply tell your Web browser how to display the page.

You have just created and viewed your own Web page!

under "free clip art" will retrieve many sources of freely usable graphics.

There are also many Web page templates and other freely available Web items and tutorials you can use fairly easily. For example, Walden University has three easy-to-use templates, one for a standard Web page, one for a page with a table, and one for a page with an image. "Nuthin' But Links" lists many sites that offer free buttons, bars, clip art, Web page templates, and more. "Carlos' Forms Tutorial" is a simple, engaging and friendly way to learn how to create Web-based forms (Pero, 2000).

There are many advantages to using Web pages for instruction, including the ability to provide updated information in a timely fashion, the ability to include interactivity for feedback and to maintain interest, and the ability to reach your learner audience at any time and in any place where they have an Internet connection. On a political note, using Web pages for instruction places us in the same position as teaching faculty, businesses, and other groups and individuals who are learning as they go and trying to make the best use of new technology to help and/or appeal to existing or new users. It also places information literacy and the ILI instructor in a logical and supportive position: We are able to relate to others in this world and draw attention to the need for IL skills at all levels.

On the negative side, you need to remember that users must have access to a workstation or other device with an Internet connection in order to view your pages. They must also know the basics of Web browser use, or someone will need to teach them.

You as the Webpage creator must have a workstation or other device with a Web browser in order to develop and view Web pages, and you must be ready to invest some time in learning. How much time? It depends on what you want to do yourself, how quickly you tend to learn software, how complex, artistic, or glitzy you want your site to be, and how much time you can spend on maintenance once your site has been created. You may also want to invest in a Web authoring program like "Dreamweaver," as well as additional equipment such as a digital camera and a scanner. While it is not necessary to have Web authoring programs, graphic programs, and additional equipment in order to create simple Web pages, their use can provide a more professional look and feel to your Web pages. For more complex Websites, like interactive Web tutorials, you may very well need to purchase all or some of this ancillary equipment.

If you decide to create your own Web pages, or if other library staff will create them, they must be aware of some common pitfalls. For example, it is quite simple to view the HTML code for a Web page and then copy and paste it into your own page. You can copy graphics quite easily as well, but for text, design, or graphics, you must be wary of using the intellectual property of others without their permission. It is also very easy to get carried away and put too much material on a single Web page. You need to consider, too, how much time and effort you can afford to invest on your own to learn Web page creation skills. As we have seen, it is not difficult to create a simple, basic Web page. You can even insert a few public domain clip art images and some links without too much difficulty. If you want to include forms for interactivity, animation, and more complex graphics, though, you will need to learn much more, such as how to use software like Adobe "Photoshop," a complex graphics program. Just designing and putting together a set of simple Web pages can take many hours of planning, storyboarding, and actually preparing and testing the pages on naïve users. It might be more worthwhile for you to come up with the learning outcomes objectives, an outline, a storyboard, and other content and then hire a professional or a skilled student who will actually prepare the Web pages or Website for you.

Of course, there is no guarantee that anyone will actually use your Web pages, no matter who prepares them or how much time or money you spend on creating them. Your pages will be competing for attention with many hundreds of thousands, if not millions of others. To get and keep users' attention, you or someone you hire will need to put some time and effort into ensuring its quality. You will need to maintain your Web pages, updating links that die or move, revising content as instructional tools change, learning new Web development skills, and always striving to simplify and standardize. It is a never-ending process and you may very well tire of doing it on your own, especially if you are responsible for maintaining a number of pages. CGI (Common Gateway Interface) and PERL scripting for Websites are beginning to get around the problem of keeping up with mutating software. In the future we may very well see CGI and PERL scripts available in more user-friendly forms, built into easy-to-use Web editors. In the meantime, students of many ages who have grown up with computers and are Web-savvy may be a wonderful source for technical aid in developing Web-based ILI programs.

Web Page Design Principles

In a number of respects, guidelines for instructional Website design are very similar to those for print materials. For starters, if "content is clearly king" for Websites, both in terms of accuracy and completeness, then *need* is surely "emperor" (Stover and Zink, 1996). Do the primary learners need the site and why? What are the expected learner outcomes for the site and for each page? Storyboarding and brief outlines for each page and site maps diagramming site layout and structure can be very helpful in this regard (Hogle, 2000; Fryer, 2000).

LAYOUT AND TYPEFACE

Like print materials, once the need and content of a Web page have been identified and described in writing, important decisions remain, especially concerning layout, font, color, and other design considerations specifically for the Web. Websites cry out for a consistent look and feel, for buttons and navigation bars that appear in the same place on each page within a site, for similarly styled graphics (cartoon-like, photographs, drawings, and so on), and for consistent use of fonts and colors (NCSA, University of Illinois, 2000). Jakob Nielsen recommends improving usability by standardizing and simplifying, for example, by using a shopping cart icon and concept for personalized selection (2000b). When you search an OPAC or an online article index, for example, you could "put" items in your shopping cart. Instead of saying you are saving a "list" of items, just call it a "shopping cart." Instead of buying what's in your shopping cart, you get to save it by downloading it to a disk, printing it, or e-mailing it.

Nielsen also recommends standardizing on the Yahoo!-style directory interface with search capabilities. Libraries could provide a Yahoo!-like subject heading directory—Library of Congress, Dewey, Medical Subject Headings, and so on—with a default keyword search box and a link to advanced search options. Google's approach is simpler still. The word "Google" appears at the top of the screen. Under it is an empty search box that allows single or multiple word searches, or even phrase searching by means of quotation marks. Near the search box are links for a Yahoo!-like subject directory and an advanced search option.

COLOR

Color choice is extremely important for Websites, especially in backgrounds and for links and graphics. Dark or heavily patterned backgrounds can be distracting and annoying to the point where users will avoid them if at all possible. Red lettering should be used sparingly on Web pages and combinations of link colors and backgrounds should be checked for readability thoroughly on a variety of platforms and browsers before finalizing.

Differing browser displays add to the complexity of designing Web pages. No matter how hard you work at designing pages that have graphics of just the right size and color, in just the right position, and the most readable fonts for your page, learners may use browsers that display colors, graphics, fonts, tables, and other items in different ways, or in some cases, not at all (Kreunen, 2000). Older versions of browsers may not be able to display tables. The images on your page may display when you use Netscape, but not when you use Internet Explorer. Users may also change font size, colors, window size, and other features on their own.

There is hope, though. Baysinger's site, for example, will teach you how to use consistent color in designing pages for all Web browsers (2000). There are also basic, simple, getting-started guides to designing Web pages that include both techniques and tips, written with respect for the intelligence and dignity of the beginning adult learner. Deanna Nipp's "Innovative Use of the Home Page for Library Instruction," for example, suggests an excellent approach to designing Web pages and Websites, along with numerous examples (1998). Her many practical and useful ideas can be applied to many types of Websites, not just library homepages. Although not the newest of publications, *The HTML Manual of Style* (1994) and *Web Publishing with Netscape for Busy People* (Crumlish and Humes, 1996) both provide an excellent grounding in the basic mechanics of Web page creation and design. Jakob Nielsen provides excellent, common-sense advice on Web design in his monthly Alertbox essays, for example, "Differences Between Print Design and Web Design" (1999a) and "The Top Ten *New* Mistakes of Web Design" (1999b).

USABILITY AND ACCESSIBILITY

Now that you know what goes on behind the Web pages that you see, even if you put in much time and effort in designing and developing your ILI Website, can you be sure that people can and will visit and learn from it? There are no guarantees, of course, especially since you will be competing with professional Website designers and programmers developing hundreds of thousands of pages and sites trying to get people's attention.

In addition, you need to be aware of important Website accessibility issues to meet ADA (Americans with Disabilities Act) requirements. For example, Web browsers utilized by those who are vision impaired cannot read tables or frames properly, so it is important to meet ADA standards by providing additional non-frames, non-tables, or text-only versions of Web pages, as well as alternative text for graphics. Alternate versions will also allow easier access by those with low-end hardware and software. Links labeled simply "Click here" do not provide useful information for the vision-impaired person using a reader, so make it a habit to use key words or phrases as links instead.

The Minneapolis Community & Technical College's (MCTC) "Information Literacy Tutorial" is an example of how you might provide alternative versions of your Web page. MCTC's tutorial offers both a "Standard Version" and an "ADA Version." The former uses HTML tables, while the latter does not (Minneapolis Community & Technical College, 2000). TILT, the award-winning University of Texas IL tutorial, offers a choice between "Full TILT" and "TILT Lite." "Full TILT" requires the use of the Shockwave plugin, while "TILT Lite" does not (University of Texas Digital Library, 2000). Jakob Nielsen discusses the World Wide Web Consortium's 1999 "Web Accessibility Initiative (WAI)" in a chapter of his excellent book, *Designing Web Usability* (2000a). Based on the WAI, Nielsen recommends strongly that we provide text-only versions of Web pages for those with visual problems who use software that reads Web pages out loud. Graphics need to include "alternative text" (words that describe the graphic in the background), or the reader software will simply say "image." Screen readers will also read tables line by line, from left to right, and read "Click here" links on a page literally as "click here," both of which are meaningless to the person using reader software (Casey, 1999; Microsoft, 2000a; Coombs, 2000). The WAI's Website itself is a treasure trove of links to Web-accessibility-related sites, including news, technology, tools, and means of becoming involved in this area. A Website called "Bobby" will even check your Web pages to see if disabled people can use them without problems (CAST, 2000) .

What is the answer? Should you just put up your Web page as it is and then see if anyone uses it or has problems with it? Nielsen describes this as the mud-throwing approach, " . . . throw it at the wall and see if it sticks!" (Nielsen, 2000c). As he points out, this is a tactic that may very well backfire, as anyone who even happens upon your poorly designed site and tries it may be so turned off they will not come back to it even if you make major improvements later (Nielsen, 2000a; Cunningham, 1999).

Will throwing money at your Website help? Maybe, but remember that the most important design factors for Websites are usability and accessibility. Checking for accessibility using sites such as CAST's and doing usability studies with your primary learner group(s) are essential because you will find out what your users value and which areas you need to fix to improve ease of use (Nielsen, 1999c; ALA–LITA–Human/ Machine Interface Interest Group, 2000). If you want design ideas, you might try Nielsen's common-sense advice and look at the sites that get visited most often (1999d). What are they doing right? Can you identify any common design elements or approaches? For example, how many times does a user have to click on links before she gets to desired content? How does the site provide help? How successful are these sites in achieving their goals? For instructional sites you will need to test for learning outcomes as well if you want to find out how effective your site is.

Many of these design considerations are similar to those for printed materials. Unlike print, however, the Web offers many advantages, but also some sandtraps. For those with Internet access, many Websites are available whenever and wherever there is a Net connection. Time and place are of little or no consequence for the Web user. This is a significant advantage for instruction, as, theoretically at least, users can get help when they most need it. The question remains as to whether the kind of help they can get is best suited for their needs.

Web-Based Courses

Are Web-based courses worthy alternatives to in-person instruction? Ko and Rossen recommend trying out online courses by using sites such as "Blackboard.com," as do various BI-L messages from librarians (Ko and Rossen, 2001; Smith, 1999; Bell, 1999). It is important to note, however, that there are a number of popular online course builders that perform the same or similar functions, most notably WebCT. The University of British Columbia Library, for example, uses WebCT for its IL tutorial (2000). The "Web-Based Instruction Resource Site" provides a list of links to Web-based instruction sources (Harvey, 2000). Keep in mind that many creative people are developing Web-based instruction materials, so it may not be necessary to create everything from scratch. If there is an excellent Web page or site that meets the needs of the primary learner group, no matter the level or purpose for which it was originally designed, why not request permission to link to it. Just make sure to provide some kind of indication that this link will take the user off-site. It would also be helpful to indicate how to return, especially if the link opens a new window, as it is easy for a person to feel lost when this situation occurs—that is, when they try to go back to a previous page by clicking on the "Back" button and nothing happens because the new page does not retain the search history from the original page.

There are other ways to feel lost or left out when using Web-based courses, as well. Access to the Net, in and of itself, does not always equate to access to a particular site or specific information on a site. The disabled and those with older hardware and software or low-end dialup connections may not be able to utilize the snazziest and newest features, such as video streaming, Java, instant messaging, chat rooms, and the like. Be wary of frames and tables because some users may not have hardware or software capable of displaying these features or may be visually handicapped and relying on a reader for content. If you use some of these more advanced features, be sure to provide text-only alternative pages as well. Also, remember to use alternative text for any graphics included on a Website, again for the benefit of the visually impaired. This will certainly mean more time in the planning and development stage, but it is essential to provide these easily accessible alternatives to high-tech Websites both for equal access at the lower end and for adherence to ADA regulations.

Even if they can navigate your Web pages, visitors to a site can feel lost in "verbiage." Given the fact that there is little or no cost to providing lengthy, wordy materials on the Web, there is a great temptation simply to transcribe the contents of an oral presentation or lecture to a Website. As a result, some Website content providers fall into the trap of using overly wordy expositions or lengthy conversational-style discourse when simple instructive language would do. A good way to avoid this problem is to pretend that each Web page is a print handout with very limited space and sparingly use only those words essential for basic understanding.

If your Website consists of multiple pages, carefully examine every sentence and every word on each Web page, keeping in mind the goal of each page. Try to delete as many words as possible and still maintain the integrity or core of the Web page, using graphics or icons in place of words if possible. Break long pages up into smaller chunks or provide a table of contents at the top or side of the Web page, and also provide an easy way to get back to the table of contents once you are deep into the page. If Web pages are broken into smaller chunks, though, try to provide content that is no more than three easily navigable steps or clicks away.

Visitors may get annoyed and frustrated when images load slowly, and may abandon a site rather than wait to see the images. If text is located well below a large image, visitors may not even realize that scrolling down will provide them with some information while they are waiting for images to appear. One solution is to define the height and width of the image, using HTML tags. The browser then recognizes the size of the image, sets aside space for it, and continues to bring in the rest of the page without waiting for the entire image to download first.

Some Website visitors may enter a site at a level below the homepage, which would be like receiving only the middle page of a multi-paged paper handout. The visitor is once again lost, wondering where this page came from, what its purpose is, and how to get to the starting point. Tennant recommends that we avoid this problem by abolishing "linear thinking" since we really cannot know how a visitor may arrive at or use our site (1997). He says that it is important to design all pages so that each can be used or understood independently of the remainder of the site.

While avoiding linear thinking is a worthy goal, linearity still has its place on the Web. This is particularly true for instructional Websites where the goal is to help users learn the mechanics of using a system or database, as we have seen, for example, with paper handouts. However, you do need to be wary of creating lengthy, linear exercises that require the user to continue answering a specific series of questions in order to progress through each segment of an exercise in order. Users may feel lost and helpless, and may end up abandoning the exercise completely rather than go through every part of it. Whatever the goal of the site, it is important to allow users the option of skipping around within a site in order to self-select for their individual learning needs. Learning modules offer a compromise solution, and resemble the concept of in-person group instruction modules. For example, learning use of a new OPAC may be broken down into basic and advanced searching modules, as well as other modules on saving and e-mailing results. Again, following the rule of three can helpful here. Try to have no more than three linear steps in an exercise before allowing the user to proceed to whichever segment of the exercise she/he would like to try next.

How much content should you include? What is the maximum number of instructional "chunks" for effective learning? How many separate pages should one have on a single site, and how much content is too much for a single page? Tennant warns against "chunkitis," where a site contains many small pages, each with very little content; as well as "linkitis," where designers include too many links on a single page (1997). Stover and Zink recommend a maximum of about seven links on a homepage (1996). Determining a happy balance in terms of text, numbers of pages, modules, graphics, and other features can be difficult, just as it may be difficult to determine balance in all sorts of instruction. Again, this is where user input, examples of effective and well-designed instructional Websites, as well as some publications on Website design created especially for libraries, can be extremely helpful (ACRL, IS, 1998; LIRT, 1999; Schrock, 2000a, 2000b; Grassian and Clark, 1999; Grassian, 1998b). For example, Stover and Zink's appendix, "Points to Consider When Constructing a Home Page," is still extremely useful and quite applicable to instruction Websites, although published in 1996—an aeon ago in Web terms (1996: 19–20).

What about Web-based interactive materials? Effective Web-based exercises and tutorials, at the very least, should meet the standards we impose on these materials in other media. They need to fulfill important purposes in an interesting or even captivating way. The learners need to have a good chance of succeeding if they try the exercise or tutorial out, and they need to get as much immediate feedback as possible. Ideally, Web-based material could be utilized either with groups, or by individuals, and they would be available in different forms, depending on the audience size, experience level, age, or other characteristics.

Graphic design, backgrounds, fonts, images and other artwork, as well as layout present additional dilemmas for Website designers, both from a design- and from a copyright/intellectual-property point of view. General Website design publications can be helpful, both those published in print and Web-based (NCSA, University of Illinois, 2000). Tufte's five basic data graphics principles can be applied quite usefully to the Web as well. We have already mentioned two of them—"Erase non-data ink" (eliminate irrelevant or needlessly elaborate information) and "Erase redundant data-ink" (eliminate repetitive information). The remaining three are:

- Above all else show the data
- Maximize the data-ink ratio
- Revise and edit. (Tufte, 1983: 105)

"Above all else show the data" translates to identifying the key points you wish to get across and highlighting them unmistakably. The University of Arizona Library's "RIO" is a good example. (University of Arizona Library, 2000a). "Maximize the data-ink ratio" is a call for simplicity and clarity. The BUBL Information Service's homepage and the UCLA Young Research Library's "Reference Collection Online," for example, look simple and clean (BUBL LINK, 2000; UCLA, Young Research Library, 2000). "Revise and edit" seems self-evident, and yet there is so much we would like our users to know, so much help we would like to provide them. With few space and size restrictions, we may use overly elaborate words, too many words, too many repetitive instructions or descriptions, too small a font size, too many graphics, too many frames, too many glitzy features like blinking or rotating images, and so on.

Personalized Websites

How can we, much less our users, sort through all of this? Some BI-L listserv messages suggest that personally customized instructional Websites similar to "My Yahoo!" or UCLA's "MyUCLA" would allow each user to pick and choose the kinds of help she/he wants to use or revisit. Personalized Websites are popular, but they do have drawbacks, some of which may not be immediately obvious. For one, users will have to pick and choose among the kinds of help we have to offer, which may or may not be a good fit. It may be some time, in fact, before users have the option of selecting "stripped-down" minimalist help, the equivalent of an entire course, or something in-between.

Once a user has selected items to include, she/he may not go back at a later date to see if other options have been added. As a result, the user may become complacent, relying on her/his personal site, believing that it contains or links to whatever she/he may need. Given the pace of change and the number of added and deleted information resources, users may be depriving themselves of access to information sources and help in using them.

Librarians tend to be highly enthusiastic about personalized library Websites, according to one study, while users generally are not (Ghaphery and Ream, 2000). However, the same study found that both learners and librarians make good use of class Web pages created by ILI librarians to meet the needs of particular courses, especially in colleges and universities. Learners greatly appreciate the time-saving shortcuts, including recommended databases, tutorials, and links to reference materials like citation style guides. ILI librarians appreciate having a template where they can fill in all of these items easily, without having to learn and use HTML. As the authors point out, however, these pages receive high use during the term when the course is offered, and little or no use thereafter (Ghaphery and Ream, 2000). Furthermore, few users go to the trouble of creating and then continuing to make use of their own personalized library-related Web pages, even though learners are encouraged to do so in ILI sessions.

It seems logical, then, to capitalize on the features of this approach that most interest learners: focused pages created by librarians for particular groups at specific times. These pages need not be limited to higher education needs. For example, in spring or summer each year, public libraries might want to develop Web pages for parents considering schools in which to enroll their children or online courses for home schooling that go beyond a list of links or links with descriptions. ILI librarians might consider developing a page listing points to consider when selecting a school or an online course and a link to AASL's IL standards. High school library media centers might do the same for colleges and universities, with a link, instead, to the IL Competency Standards for Higher Education on the ACRL Website. Academic libraries and high school library media centers might link to consumer health information suitable for their user populations, highlighting the need for caution in relying on Web-based health sites, and linking to Web evaluation criteria and other IL skills. Special libraries might consider offering workbook-type ILI tutorials during new employee orientations, and academic libraries could do the same for new faculty and Teaching Assistant orientations, as well as for new students. All sorts of libraries might consider reaching out to potential students, parents, and employees at critical times of the year with information, helpful links, and recommended, evaluated information sources suited to specific needs of that population group.

DESIGNING MIXED OFFERINGS

A mix of ILI formats is often interesting and appealing to learners used to sound bites, video games, motion, and "performances." Learners can take control of their own learning if they are able to pick and choose from a variety of instructional materials and approaches. We can offer separate paper, Web-based, or other AV instruction from which learners can pick. Multimedia instruction, on the other hand, can offer a mix of electronic materials within a single framework, and asynchronous (any-time/any-place) online multimedia instruction, in fact, may soon be commonplace. Najjar's excellent review article offers many valuable recommendations regarding effective multimedia interfaces based on characteristics of the materials, the learner, the learning task, and the test of learning. Two of his recommendations are especially noteworthy and can be applied to many instructional material formats:

> Use the medium that best communicates the information (1998: 311).
> Make the user interface interactive (1998: 314).

He concludes by observing that verbal and pictorial information should be used together and that we should incorporate activities that will help learners digest and understand information.

How many different kinds of instructional materials should you use to meet the same pedagogical goals for the same audience? For in-person synchronous group instruction, you may want to use a presentation slide show to present an outline of the session, illustrate a couple of points, and, at the end of the session, do a review. In-between, you might lecture a bit and do a demonstration, with the learners following along on workstations. Then you might have them do a paper exercise, show a short video clip, and set up small or large group exercises. All of this requires careful planning, timing, and pacing to avoid losing learners with a scattershot approach. This is especially important for sessions that are scheduled for specific lengths of time, often a single 50-minute to two-hour guest session. Remote instruction, too, may work best with a mixed approach. For example, Patricia Knapp held preliminary and then debriefing sessions for learners in-person before and after they completed exercises on their own (remotely). Mimi Dudley built in-person reference desk interaction into her workbook program, also completed by individuals on their own (remotely).

Today, some online courses require that students meet in person for the first and last sessions and successful online courses utilize a variety of approaches, including chat, exercises, discussion boards, and group and individual assignments. Even traditional in-person lecture-type courses to large numbers of students may include discussion board interaction and group chats, as well as guest lecturers live in-person or via chat.

Similarly, in addition to passive and interactive tutorials, ILI Website designers may want to offer chat rooms for synchronous online classes or instant messaging for individual research consultation. "Instant messaging" is software that allows one to send messages in real time. If the recipient is online at the time and has activated the instant messaging software, these brief messages then pop up on the recipient's screen in a small window. The recipient can then respond, in essence, having a synchronous—at the same time—live "conversation" with the original sender, but without waiting for a response. In other words, both sender and recipient can send messages to each other simultaneously, in real time. "ICQ" is an example of a popular free instant messaging software. This may or may not work out for instruction in every case, since for instructional purposes the sender would have to understand that there may not be an instant response. If the recipient is not online or has not activated the instant messaging software, messages will be stored for future viewing. However, both chat and instant messaging present different options with which we should experiment.

With all of these modes, you may also want to provide printed point-of-use guides and search logs. In an ideal world, of course, learners would pick and choose the forms of instruction that would appeal to them most, but sometimes we may have to simply give them a variety of materials in the hope that one or more may appeal and sink in.

BACKUP PLANS AND PROCESS

"If anything can go wrong, it will," most definitely applies to instructional materials (Bartlett, 1992). Handouts become outdated; presentation software ceases to function or will not open at critical junctures; Web servers go down; Web-based interfaces change at a moment's notice or with no notice at all; and network connections fail. These are just facts of life in the technological age, so instead of panicking when they happen, you may as well expect them. Backup plans are essential, especially if you may have just one chance to teach or help someone learn.

Salvaging Outdated Handouts

It may be possible to use portions of outdated handouts, even if there have been drastic changes in what you are trying to teach. Perhaps you can still use a handout to teach users how to mail Web pages, even if you suddenly have to use a new version of a Web browser. Like encyclopedias, not all portions of software are automatically changed with each upgrade or new version. At the very least, you might be able to use the handout to structure your session or to help users learn how to approach a piece of software or a reference tool. For example, you might draw their attention to the fact that the handout begins with the top of the window and works its way down from there. Then they might begin exploring a new piece of software by pulling down each menu and exploring the options listed and continue by experimenting with buttons and other icons. Or you might point out that the handout has some specific goals in mind, for example, to help you learn the basics of searching, displaying, and saving information retrieved from a database.

Preparing for Non-Functioning Presentation Software

It is always a good idea to prepare a "Speaker's Outline" listing the main points you are planning to cover in a presentation software show. The outline helps learners see the structure of the session and eliminates the need to take extensive notes. When the software fails, the outline can serve as a reminder of what you were planning to cover and parts of it could be used without the software. You might have some in-class exercises ready to go in case of a software failure, and then ask the group which they would like to try out. Remember that you do not need to have a live connection to the Internet to use Microsoft PowerPoint or some other presentation software packages. In fact, you can download a presentation to a disk and take with you a separate free copy of the Microsoft PowerPoint Reader software that allows you to view and display PowerPoint slide shows even if you do not have Microsoft Office software or if your Office software is not functioning properly.

What To Do When the Web Server Is Down

Offline browser software like "WebBuddy" (Mac) and "WebWhacker" (PC) allow you to download and save copies of Web pages with their associated images and view them even when you are not connected to the Internet. You can restrict the saved files to the same site and indicate how many levels of linked pages to save. So, when the Web server goes down in the middle of a session, you can switch over to a "canned" set of pages. Or, if you will be teaching without a live Internet connection, you can still display a series of linked Web pages, though you will not be able to alter the pages or do a live search. You may also be able to alternate between these pages and a presentation software show (for text-based information using clip art and other features, such as slide transitions), just as though you had a live connection.

Preparing for Unexpected Changes in Web Interface or Content

This is one of the most interesting and challenging "teaching emergencies" you may face. It takes some nimble footwork and requires diplomacy and a good sense of humor. Depending on the extent of the changes, you may be able to recoup and continue instruction by quickly scanning menus and buttons to locate the most critical functions you were planning to teach. Ask the learners to help, but spend as little time as possible fumbling around while a large group watches. Patience is thin when the instructor does not seem to be in charge. You may be able to turn this situation into an important teachable moment, though, as it will give you the opportunity to remind learners to print copies of important and useful Web pages. Printouts will provide them with URLs and Web page titles, and document what the learner saw when doing Web-based research. If all else fails, have some active learning activities or exercises with you and use them if necessary, or simply skip over this portion of the session and go on to something else, after explaining to the learners that sometimes that is just the way it works with the Web. You must be patient and flexible, and allow lots of extra time for connection, distraction, and unexpected pitfalls.

What To Do When the Network Connection Fails

Failed network connections can make us all realize how much we have come to depend on computers for teaching and learning. It is important to note, though, that teaching and learning can go on and pedagogical goals can be met without computers. When network connections are down, you can teach with overheads or a whiteboard and paper handouts. This does not mean you have to draw complete copies of Web pages on the board, but you can pose questions to a group, for example, asking which commands they would type or which buttons they would click in order to do a keyword search. You might pose a couple of command options and ask what each would retrieve. Or you might just draw some Venn diagrams on a board and teach Boolean operators; go through a small group topic selection exercise; mind-map topic words; etc.

   No matter what the computer glitch happens to be, or how many of them there are, just try to keep cool, maintain a sense of humor, and connect with the learners any way you can. They will feel a lot better about their own computer glitches if they see you handle these almost inevitable problems with aplomb.

FINAL REMARKS

This chapter has focused on the practical aspects of designing print and electronic/electric instructional materials that you have presumably selected based on your pedagogical goals and objectives or expected learning outcomes. Some of these design guidelines may be familiar to you, while others may be new. Many may, in fact, seem straightforward and over-simplified. It is often the case, though, that the clearest, most simply designed materials can take enormous time and effort to develop. When they are completed and ready for use, learners and teachers alike may take them for granted or may consider them simplistic or too elementary, yet they can make an enormous difference in insuring that significant learning takes place. After all, is that not our ultimate goal?

EXERCISES

1. Locate an instructional Website that is not interactive. Come up with one simple and inexpensive way to make it interactive. What mechanisms could be utilized for feedback to the learners?
2. Identify a paper handout that has a Web-based equivalent. In what ways are they the same? What is lost or gained by each format?
3. Compare your institution's OPAC help to that of a Web search tool of your choice. Which features were most essential for each? Which features need improvement, and how would you improve them?
4. Compare three instructional Websites. What, if any, features should be included in all of them? Do they suggest a standardized approach in terms of help, navigation, icons. approach, etc.?
5. Compare and contrast an IL video and an IL Website that have the same or similar goals and objectives.
6. Analyze accessibility (usage capabilities for the disabled) for an interactive and a passive instructional Website. How could they be improved?

READ MORE ABOUT IT

Allen, Susan M. 1993. "Designing Library Handouts: Principles and Procedures." *Research Strategies* 11 no. 1: 14–23.

Fidler, Donald. 1999. "Producing Educational Video" [Online]. Available: www.hsc.wvu.edu/som/tsp/video/video-producing.htm [1999, July 26].

Nielsen, Jakob. 2000. *Designing Web Usability*. Indianapolis, IN: New Riders Publishing.

Nipp, Deanna. 1998. "Innovative Use of the Home Page for Library Instruction." *Research Strategies* 16 no.2:93–102.

Tufte, Edward R. 1983. *The Visual Display of Quantitative Information*. Cheshire, CT: Graphics Press.

12

Assessing, Evaluating, and Revising ILI Programs

Self-knowledge and self-improvement are very difficult for most people. It usually needs great courage and long struggle.

—Abraham Maslow

WHY ASSESS?

You have done your Needs Assessment, developed an instructional plan, written your goals and objectives, selected appropriate modes, and delivered the material. You breathe a sigh of relief and congratulate yourself on your accomplishments. But wait! You are not quite done yet. How do you know students have learned what you set out to teach? To find out, you must complete the final stages in ILI program planning—assessment, evaluation, and revision.

Why bother? We assess, evaluate, and revise because we want to find out if our instruction has been effective. In other words, we need to find out how well our goals and objectives have been met. Furthermore, we want to highlight areas where our efforts might be improved for the future. Developing instruction is an iterative process. We plan. We develop. We deliver. We assess and evaluate the results of the assessment. We revise, deliver the revised material, and assess and evaluate again. Perfection is always just out of our reach; but continually striving for perfection contributes to keeping both our instruction fresh and our interest in teaching piqued.

Recent trends in education are contributing to a renewed interest in assessment among IL instructors. In an era of financial retrenchment, institutions everywhere are taking hard, long looks at where the money is going. The expense of ILI programs must be justified to the parent organization or the programs may no longer be supported (American Association for Higher Education, 1992; Bober, Poulin, and Vileno, 1995; Dolphin, 1990; Gibson, 1992). Assessment lends credibility not only to the program, but to the library as well, especially if the programs can be shown to support national mandates such as IL and lifelong learning.

The presence of a strong institutional mission statement provides an invaluable starting point for the assessment/evaluation/revision cycle. When questions about educational mission and values are skipped over, assessment may become an exercise in measuring what is easy rather than what is meaningful (American Association for Higher Education, 1992; Banta et al., 1996). Worthwhile assessment can only take place when there is a clear sense of what matters in the library, and to the parent institution as well. In order for assessment to lead to improvements, it must reflect on what is valued in that environment. The process of transforming the institutional mission into specific goals allows us to link assessment efforts to improvement and to collect useful data that informs our parent organization about the value of our instructional endeavors.

The political context of assessment should not be taken lightly. Keep in mind that administrators will be using the results to make decisions about the fate of your programs. However, IL instructors should also never lose sight of the second reason for assessment, that of program improvement (Loe and Elkins, 1990). While positive assessment results can be used to promote the value of the program and increase its support base, even negative results can be helpful. If an assessment indicates that the program is falling short of expectations, that information can be used to pinpoint problem areas where improvements could lead to a better, stronger program in the future (Corcoran and Langlois, 1990). Furthermore, it could highlight where additional financial support might enhance the program and can be used as an appeal to administration to gain that support.

Increased interest in the process of learning has also contributed to the growing emphasis on assessment. Teachers everywhere are concerned not only with what their students are learning, but how they are learning it. The goal here is not accountability to some outside agency; the goal is to find out about the learning process itself in order to improve the experience (Cross, 1998; Gilchrist, 1997). These ongoing assessments, some of which occur during the instruction itself, contribute to the revision and improvement of methods, techniques, and materials. Assessments can be used to provide information on the effectiveness or efficiency of new or existing programs; compare the outcomes of two or more methods for teaching the same content; and identify areas in which staff needs training. Assessments such as these are primarily developed to provide internal feedback to ILI instructors or coordinators themselves. However, they can also be used to promote ILI programs to people outside the library. Results should be communicated to administrators as a means of bolstering budget requests and to provide data that could expand political support for your programs (Kellough, Kellough, and Kim, 1999; Linn and Gronlund, 1995; Loe and Elkins, 1990; Svinicki and Schwartz, 1988; Westerbrook, 1993).

THE ASSESSMENT/EVALUATION/REVISION CYCLE

Although assessment and evaluation are often used interchangeably, they actually refer to two different things. Assessment encompasses the collection of data and the analysis of that data. Data may be collected in any number of ways, both formally and informally, and is a relatively neutral process. Evaluation, on the other hand, involves judgement and places a value on the data collected. The goal of evaluation is to make sense of the collected data. Evaluation is said to occur when data is examined to see if identified objectives have been achieved and that information about the adequacy and effectiveness of an instructional endeavor is provided. The results of evaluation contribute to decision making about the fate of the instructional endeavor under review (Elliot et al., 1996; Kellough, Kellough, and Kim, 1999; Shonrock, 1996). Revision is the final step in the cycle. It occurs after you have evaluated the data and have made a decision based on those results.

Effective instructors are always engaged in assessment, evaluation, and revision. They watch for signs of boredom and confusion while they are teaching and, if possible, make on-the-spot adjustments to address any problems. But as valuable as this fine-tuning is, it is not sufficient to completely address the question of how effective our instruction might be.

Assessing instruction and evaluating the results of that assessment lets us know what has happened after we have acted. It provides information about whether or not we have achieved what we set out to do. Although the assessment/evaluation/revision cycle takes place after instruction has been developed and delivered, attention should be directed toward these stages much earlier in the planning process. As a matter of fact, developing an assessment/evaluation/revision plan should occur in conjunction with writing instructional goals and objectives. There is a direct, almost reciprocal, relationship between instructional goals and objectives and the assessment/evaluation/revision cycle. Assessment looks objectively at what was or was not learned. Evaluation compares that data to our original instructional intent; that is, to our instructional goals and objectives. Deciding how best to assess the learning while writing goals and objectives makes both endeavors more effective and meaningful.

When the assessment/evaluation/revision cycle is built into the planning process from the beginning, it allows us to determine how well we have reached our instructional objectives (Loe and Elkins, 1990; Shonrock, 1996). The importance of writing clear, concise, and meaningful goals and objectives cannot be over-emphasized. The goal of assessment and evaluation is to determine if your objectives have been met. Thinking about how to provide the evidence that the instructional objectives have been reached while you are developing those objectives will not only force you to write more precise objectives, it will help you make decisions about what methods and techniques to use during the assessment phase. You will know what type of data you need to collect in order to answer your assessment questions and you will have identified the criteria for success that you will need to use when you are evaluating this data. Determining assessment and evaluation methodologies at this point in the development process will help ensure that you will be collecting the most appropriate data and will be analyzing it in the best possible fashion for your purposes.

STEPS IN THE ASSESSMENT PROCESS

1. Decide what you are trying to teach. In other words, determine your instructional goals and objectives. Make sure your goals are learner-centric. Focus your goals on the learner and structure those goals in terms of ability and performance. Rather than asking "What are we trying to teach?" ask "What do we want learners to be able to do when they are finished with the instruction?" (Alverno College Faculty, 1994; Gilchrist, 1997; Iannuzzi, 1999).
2. Decide how participants can exhibit what they have learned. These are your learning outcomes and criteria. These will help you select your assessment methodology based on the data you are trying to collect. See Chapter 7 for details on developing goals, objectives, outcomes, and criteria.
3. Provide the learners with an opportunity to exhibit what they did or did not learn from the instructional experience. This step can take a number of forms that will be discussed in a section

later in this chapter. During this step you will gather data about what has actually been learned.

4. Evaluation is the next step. It is during evaluation that you determine how well the objectives have been met. Depending upon why you undertook the assessment in the first place, you can use the results as a means to justify your instruction to others, to improve your own program, teaching technique, or methods, or to identify those learners who might need additional help.

5. Prepare and report your findings. Data should be summarized and analyzed. The information can then be incorporated into annual reports as a way of sharing instructional objectives, trends, and accomplishments with everyone who need to be kept informed. This includes administrators, faculty, the public, and other community and user groups. State the implications of the data clearly. If the results indicate that some of your efforts need improvement, use this as an opportunity to explain what you have learned, and, more importantly, how you will apply that learning to the improvement of your instructional endeavors (Loe and Elkins, 1990; Shonrock, 1996). These reports should aim to produce evidence that relevant parties (internal or external) will find credible, suggestive, and—above all—applicable to decisions that need to be made. The challenge is not collecting the data, it is using the data to effect change (American Association for Higher Education, 1992; Banta et al., 1996).

ASSESSING ILI

Do librarians involved in ILI regularly engage in assessment? Although assessment and evaluation is frequently discussed in both the education and library/information science literature, rigorous assessment studies are not often practiced in the IL field (Bober, Poulin, and Vileno, 1995; Dolphin, 1990; Ensor, 1998). Many factors contribute to this situation. Assessment takes planning, skill, time, and often money. IL instructors develop and deliver instruction under considerable constraints in all those arenas. They may feel they lack the expertise to do it properly. In addition, they may be reluctant to siphon off either development time or money for this purpose. IL instructors may also be unwilling to include assessment in their sessions because it reduces the amount of material that can be included in the limited time available to them.

A 2000 review of the literature, done for this publication, using ERIC, Library Literature, and LISA, showed little evidence of any in-depth rigorous assessment studies. If information professionals are engaged in these types of studies, they are not often reporting it. A few studies reported using a pre- and post-test design based on objective test items such as multiple-choice or fill-in questions (Colborn and Cordell, 1998; Fry and Kaplowitz, 1988; Germain, Jacobson, and Kaczor, 2000; Kaplowitz, 1993; Kaplowitz and Contini, 1998; Vander Meer and Rike, 1996). Trudi Jacobson and Janice Newkirk (Jacobson, 1996) used both questionnaires and an examination of search strategy printouts to measure the impact of instruction. But for the most part, when assessment is reported, it is most often of the "feel good" variety. There is a tendency among ILI instructors to rely on attitudinal measures to determine the overall success of a program (Bober, Poulin, and Vileno, 1995; Colborn and Cordell, 1998; Ragains, 1997). We ask participants if they liked the program, and us. But rarely do we delve any deeper into the question of whether or not they had actually learned anything.

Admittedly, reducing library anxiety and increasing students' confidence in their own research skills are valid and important goals of ILI. The attainment of these more affective goals are often measured by participant satisfaction with the instruction (Stamatopolos and Mackay, 1998). However, when teachers use student satisfaction as a criterion for instructional success, they should be aware that these reports can be highly influenced by the enthusiasm of the instructor, the students' expectations about what constitutes "proper" instruction, and a variety of other extraneous circumstances (McKeachie, 1986). These "how did you like it" or "happiness" scales also tend to err on the positive side. People are inclined to say they liked the experience because they do not wish to hurt our feelings.

Attitude or opinion assessments, though valid in their own right, do not provide all the necessary information to be used for either accountability reporting or a means of improving instruction. What we are really doing is asking learners for their opinions about whether or not they felt they learned anything of value. Even if your instructional goals are mostly affective, i.e., you wish to increase your learners' comfort level in using resources and decrease their library anxiety, asking learners if they feel better is not the same as having them demonstrate this change in some real-life situation. Learners may think they feel better about it all, and may really believe they have acquired some new skill or ability, but when faced with their next information need, they may still be uncertain, anxious, and unable to apply what they thought they had learned.

SELECTING A METHODOLOGY

Who Wants to Know?

Selecting a methodology depends upon why you are doing the assessment, the audience for whom it is intended, and how the results will be used. As we have already discussed, there are two overall reasons why we assess our ILI programs: accountability and improvement. In the first instance, assessment is initiated because someone, usually an administrator-type, wants to know how effective our programs are and whether they are worth the time and money involved in maintaining them. In the second instance, we assess our programs to make them better. We want to determine if our goals and objectives are being reached. We are interested in examining the effectiveness of our methods. And we are trying to identify ways in which to improve our instructional endeavors.

Accountability assessments are usually required at particular intervals. For example, ILI statistics may be requested as part of the library's annual report. Budget constraints may also influence the library's decision to assess ILI programs. The amount of money expended on a program may need to be justified. New programs are especially susceptible to this requirement particularly if significant expenditures of funds are involved. The "Are we doing a good job?" assessments, however, should be ongoing. These assessments may be formal or informal in design, but they are necessary to insure that our instructional efforts are successful and to provide us with information to help improve our programs.

If the assessment goal is to provide feedback to the teacher regarding instructional methods and materials, timing, or relevance of the material, then the information should be collected informally and often—perhaps each time the material is presented. The data should be gathered during, not at the end, of instruction, and be sufficiently specific to alert the teacher to strengths and weaknesses in the instruction. If, on the other hand, the assessment is being used to justify the high cost of a program and/or the equipment involved, a more formal assessment process may be needed (Dolphin, 1990; Avinicki and Schwartz, 1988).

Assessments designed to improve the learning process itself should attempt to answer some or all of the questions listed below. Data from these types of assessment may also be used to report effectiveness to administrators and can be included in accountability reports.

- Have the students learned the intended content?
- Have program objectives been attained?

- Have participants improved their research skills?
- Was the instructor effective?
- Were the instructional methods effective?
- How effective was the support material?
- Have participants' attitudes toward information, libraries, and librarians been modified?

What Type of Data Do You Need?

Establishing the reasons for the assessment and determining to whom you will present the findings are two very important pieces of the puzzle. But you still need to decide what kind of data will be required to achieve your goal. Who will see the final results? What will be done with these results and how will they be used? How precise must the data be? How much detail is needed? How quickly do you need the data? Are you being asked for hard, numerical data or will more descriptive reports based on participant comments be sufficient? If the data being collected will be used to improve instruction, you might be as interested in participants' attitudes and opinions as you are in learning outcomes. The purpose of an assessment will obviously influence the type of information you need to gather and the format in which it is presented (Dolphin, 1990). The bottom line is that the choice of an assessment method will depend upon how you ultimately intend to use the information being gathered.

Practical Considerations

One more factor goes into the methodology decision. In choosing an assessment technique, there is the educational ideal for measuring instructional success and then there are the practical constraints such as time, money, and available expertise that may require a compromise with that ideal. IL instructors operate under special educational circumstances. With the exception of full semester IL courses, we generally have little or no authority over our learners, have limited contact time with them, may never get the opportunity to see how they might perform in real life, and probably won't have the chance to examine the products of their learning. So most ILI assessments must occur on the spot in parallel with the instruction itself.

An alternative to these on-the-spot assessments is to develop a post-test, questionnaire, or survey, either in print or on the Web, and ask your learners to complete assessment at some later date. If your learners have a required assignment, this post-instructional assessment could be turned in along with the course assignment. The advantage here is that the learners would have had the opportunity to apply what was presented in the ILI when completing their assignments and would, therefore, have a better idea of whether or not the instruction seemed to help them in the research process. Asking people to describe what they learned about the research process and/or themselves as researchers can not only supply you with valuable information, but it encourages them to think about the process and self-assess the experience (Gilchrist, 1997).

Assessing learning outcomes and the success of your instructional efforts should not be restricted to face-to-face instructional situations. With more and more instructional material being provided virtually via the Web, teleconferences, CD-ROMs, computer-assisted instruction software, and so forth, it is important to include this "virtual" distance instruction into your assessment plans. Fortunately, many types of assessment can be adapted to this virtual environment. Learner satisfaction questionnaires or surveys, as well as tests that measure learners' progress, can be distributed via e-mail or interactive Web forms. Many course-management software packages actually come with built-in assessment modules for the instructor's convenience (Dewald et al., 2000). Whatever your mode of delivery, including assessment should be a fundamental part of your instructional planning process.

ASSESSMENT PARAMETERS

Assessment methods should be selected because of their relevance to the learning outcomes or performances to be measured. Comprehensive assessments frequently require a variety of procedures. Selection is also dependent upon knowing the limitations of each method, the type of information that will be provided by each, and how well a method can answer the questions under review. Furthermore, the method must provide information in the form that will meet the needs of the identified audience for the final report (Linn and Gronlund, 1995; Woods, Burns, and Barr, 1990).

Assessment techniques vary along several parameters. They can be formal or informal. They can result in numerical data (quantitative assessment) or descriptive information (qualitative assessment). They can differ in how closely they simulate real work experiences. Assessments can take place during the development process (formative assessment) or once the instruction is implemented and in place (summative assessment)(Scriven, 1973). They can rely on recognition, picking out the correct answer from a given number of choices, or on recall, when students must supply the answer to the question from memory. Scoring can be either norm-referenced in which student scores are compared to each other, or criterion-referenced in which scores are measured against some standard or criteria. Furthermore, different techniques vary as to their reliability, validity, and usability. Let us take a closer look at some of these concepts and how they affect the selection of an appropriate technique for a particular purpose. An understanding of these principles will be useful when we examine the individual techniques later in this chapter. The information used to create the following five sections was drawn from a variety of sources (Adams, 1993; Bloom, 1981; Dolphin, 1990; Elliott et al., 1996; Frick, 1990; Kellough, Kellough, and Kim, 1999; Linn and Gronlund, 1995; Mager, 1997d; Shonrock, 1996; Svinicki and Schwartz, 1988).

Formative and Summative Assessement

Formative assessment is used to provide feedback to the instructor. It is intended to guide instructional planning, implementation, or improvement. This type of assessment tends to be done during development stages of a new program or product. It can also refer to the on-the-spot or spontaneous assessments teachers make during instruction itself to monitor the effectiveness of a presentation, method, or technique. In either case, the reason behind doing formative assessment is to provide information about where instruction needs modification and improvement. It addresses the questions "Which parts of the instruction went well?" and "Which parts of the instruction need improvement?" Formative assessment frequently relies on informal assessment techniques such as observing verbal or nonverbal behavior during instruction itself, how well students succeed on in-class exercises, or noting participants' questions and comments as instruction progresses.

Summative assessment is meant to determine the overall impact or outcome of a program or product after it has been implemented. It is administered once the instruction is complete and the results may be used to determine if some standard or educational mandate has been met. Summative assessments tend to use more formal assessment techniques and findings are frequently summarized for accountability reporting. They most often involve a single comprehensive study of an entire program as a final product. Summative assessments usually answer the question "Should the instruction in its present form continue?"

Reliability, Validity, and Usability

While the difference between formative and summative assessment refers to the timing of the assessment, both require the selection of data collection methodologies. The type of assessment tool chosen will depend in part on the goal for the assessment. However, any method must be judged on three criteria: reliability, validity, and usability. Reliability refers to consistency. The same student taking the same test at different times should obtain the same or similar scores. Validity, on the other hand, refers to meaningfulness. Does the assessment method actually measure what it is intended to measure? For example, does the assessment tool accurately measure if a student can pick an appropriate database for a particular topic? Usability refers to practicality. It is determined by examining the ease with which the tool or instrument used for the assessment can be constructed, administered, and scored. An instrument that is high in both reliability and validity may still be worthless if the cost (in time, effort, and money) makes it impractical to use.

Norm-Referenced versus Criterion-Referenced Assessment

Reliability, validity, and usability refer to characteristics of the assessment method itself. The criterion against which the results of the assessment are judged is a characteristic of the evaluation. When participants' performances in searching an online catalog, for example, are compared to each other and the relative position of each student is given a score as a result of this comparison, evaluators are using what is called normative-referenced evaluation. Often referred to as grading or evaluating on the curve, it is not always a good measure of instructional success. The students who rate the best in this method will get a high score regardless of whether or not they learned anything. Those who perform more successful searches than the average of the group would be said to have learned the task even if they only managed to find three of the ten items being searched for.

In criterion-referenced evaluation, judgments are made based on a comparison of a measurement to an objective standard. In the previous example, only those students who could find eight out of the ten items being searched for would be considered successful. Criterion-referenced evaluations are appropriate when we want to know whether an expectation, objective, or criterion has been achieved. We are not interested in whether one person scores higher than another does. We want to determine who has and who has not attained the instructional objectives originally set for the instructional endeavor (Linn and Gronlund, 1995; Mager, 1997d).

Control versus Relevance

A further consideration when selecting an assessment method is the issue of control versus relevance. The most common example of a high control method is the multiple-choice, objective test. Control assessment methods are concerned with ensuring comparability between students. Assessments that rate high on control rely on objective techniques and are designed to be identical from student to student. The goal here is to minimize the possibility of extraneous influences. Test situations are kept as uniform as possible when control is the uppermost concern. Therefore, all learners would be tested in the same place, at the same time, and on the same questions or problems.

Relevance deals with how well the skills being tested relate to the actual performance of the task in a real-life situation. Assessments that are high in relevance tend to include some kind of simulation or performance assessment. The goal here is to have the assessment situation as closely approximate the real-life behavior as possible. Watching learners actually performing database searchers or an examination of database search logs could be used for this type of assessment. While both control and relevance are desirable criteria for an assessment, they tend to be difficult to combine in a single task. Tests high in control tend to be low in relevance, and vice versa (Wergin, 1988).

Quantitative versus Qualitative Methods

The type of data provided by a particular technique is of crucial importance in deciding whether or not it is appropriate to the task at hand. Quantitative techniques provide data in numerical form. It deals with questions of how much or how many. How many searches were successful? How many times did the learner select the correct resource for a particular information need? These techniques are based on deductive reasoning and are strongly associated with methods used in the natural sciences. In this approach, a hypothesis is formed about the effect of a particular intervention (in this case, instruction) and then data is collected and analyzed to see if the hypothesis is proven or unproven. Possible outcomes are predicted in advance and are limited in number.

Qualitative data is more descriptive. It is usually reported in the form of words and results from interviews, observations, open-ended questions, self-reports, and analysis of written material. The research journal in which learners write about the experience of doing research would be a qualitative data collection method. Learners discuss what they felt were successful approaches and useful resources, and why. They also indicate where they felt they could have done things differently and how they would handle similar situations. Qualitative techniques are based on inductive reasoning and are strongly related to the naturalistic type of inquiry seen in the ethnographic discipline of anthropology. Results are not slotted neatly into pre-set categories; as a matter of fact, categories are often not determined until after the data has been collected and reviewed to reveal these possible categories. Qualitative assessment permits (and may even encourage) responses not anticipated by the evaluator (Carspecken and Apple, 1992; Frick, 1990; Patton, 1980).

The form of information required or expected is key to deciding between using quantitative or qualitative methods (Frick, 1990). Qualitative assessment is to be preferred when the nature of the program or its aims can be best (or adequately) measured without the use of numbers or when detailed descriptions provide the best data for altering, judging, or continuing a program. They are also preferable when the evaluator wishes to gather opinions without imposing preconceived notions or categories on subjects that could interfere with their responses. Quantitative measures may be required when data must be reported in numerical or statistical formats.

It is important to note that the choice of using quantitative or qualitative data does not reflect on the rigor of the assessment. Both types of data can be collected, counted, analyzed, and interpreted. They can both be used in pre- and post-test experimental designs in which data collected prior to instruction is compared to that collected after the instruction has taken place. A change in this data can be used to decide if the instruction had any effect. Furthermore, both quantitative and qualitative data can be collected from learners who have had instruction (the experimental group) and compared to a similar group comprised of students who did not receive the instruction under review (the control group). Quantitative versus qualitative issues refers only to the type of data (numerical versus descriptive) that is being collected, not to the assessment design used to collect that data.

Although quantitative assessment is still in widespread use, interest in qualitative assessment techniques as an alternative to these so-called objective measures seems to be on the rise. Many factors contribute to this change. Objective or quantitative measures tend to look at the product of education. They view individual behaviors in isolation and have been criticized as not being representative of real behavior. Quantitative approaches tend to rely heavily on objective tests that may or may not provide a clear indication of learning. People who score well on objective tests may only be showing that they are good at taking objective tests. But these high scores do not necessarily mean that learners can actually apply what they learned in a real-world situation (Courts and McInerney, 1993). So, while they may have been able to select the correct search strategy for a particular topic from a list of possible strategies, when faced with researching their own topic, the student still cannot formulate an appropriate strategy.

Qualitative methods stress a holistic approach to assessment. People using these methods strive to understand the complete phenomena. They believe that if the whole is greater than the sum of its parts, then a description and understanding of a program's context is essential to determine the effectiveness of any instructional endeavor. It is insufficient simply to study and measure parts of the situation by gathering data about isolated behaviors (Patton, 1980).

Qualitative methods seem particularly suited to assessment of Cognitive/Humanist approaches to teaching and learning. The Cognitive/Humanist teacher is interested in exploring the process of learning. They wish to uncover what is going on in the mind of the learner (Steadman and Svinicki, 1998). Effective assessment of Cognitive and Humanist teaching methods, with their emphasis on self-directed learning, critical thinking, active learning, the importance of content relevance, and so on, seems to require qualitative rather than quantitative assessment methods. See Chapter 3 for more on Cognitive and Humanist theories of learning and their applications in the classroom.

Qualitative methods also address the learning styles issue (see Chapter 4). Since people learn in a variety of ways, it seems only logical that assessment techniques should offer some flexibility in how that learning is exhibited. Quantitative methods, with their emphasis on numbers, norm-referenced scoring, and competition, force students to all perform in one standard, uniform manner. They reinforce the teacher-centric approach to learning that requires rote memorization and exact repetition of what has been presented. Qualitative approaches, on the other hand, reinforce student-centered teaching approaches. They acknowledge diversity of styles, backgrounds, and behavior in the classroom. If assessment ignores the "voice of the other," then it is forcing students to follow one style of learning and performing and ignores deeply embedded cultural practices of many of the test takers (Belenky et al., 1986; Courts and McInerney, 1993). Again, this may not be a true measure of achievement. If there is no overall "best" way to teach everyone, what does a single assessment score mean? Poor results may result from a mismatch between the learner's style and either the teaching mode and/or the assessment technique, and therefore may not be a true indication of the learner's accomplishments (Kaplowitz, 1995). For example, Western educational methods have been known to emphasize competition (as in norm-based assessment). However, many other cultures emphasize cooperation and collaboration over competition, and learners from those cultures are uncomfortable when their results are judged against those of their fellow students. See Chapter 14 for more about diversity issues in ILI.

Assessment provides information about both the process and the product of instruction. Whether we use this information as formative feedback to improve the process itself, or summative evidence that justifies the value of our efforts (the product of our instruction) to outside agencies, the point of assessment is to provide answers to our questions. Is our instruction successful? Are our students learning? Are goals and objectives being met? Are our methods appropriate? Is the program cost-effective? If the evaluation of the data indicates the instruction is not meeting expectations, then that instruction needs to be examined and revised.

Assessment/evaluation/revision is an ongoing process. It points out the strengths and weaknesses of instruction and almost always leads to some sort of change. As the newly revised program is developed, the cycle of assessment/evaluation/revision is incorporated into it, and the cycle begins once more.

TYPES OF ASSESSMENT TOOLS

Deciding how to assess is not determined only by the "why you are doing it" and the "who wants to know" questions. Selecting an appropriate technique depends on having a thorough understanding of the strengths and weaknesses of the various techniques. This allows you to match your assessment needs to the best technique for your intended purpose. In other words, you need to know enough about the various techniques so that you can determine what type of information will be provided by that technique and how that information can be tabulated and presented.

An assessment method is neither good nor bad in its own right. The problem arises when an inappropriate technique is used to answer a particular assessment question. Mixed data collection and triangulation (the use of both qualitative and quantitative methods) is increasingly the norm (Frick, 1990; Morse and Field, 1995). In triangulation, a combination of methods is used to explore a single situation, including product and performance assessment along with skills and attitudes. The strengths and weaknesses of individual methods are balanced to produce a more complete picture of the situation (Banta et al., 1996; Colborn and Cordell, 1998; Morse and Field, 1995; Westerbrook, 1993).

Keep in mind when you are making your selections that the distinction between qualitative and quantitative techniques refers to the format in which data is collected—it does not refer to how that data is analyzed and presented in your final report. While quantitative data is obviously easier to manipulate statistically, qualitative data can be organized in such a way as to allow for its statistical manipulation as well.

For example, the essay examination, which has been used for many years to assess student success, seems on the surface to be a qualitative method. But in most cases a numerical score or grade is assigned to the essay according to some pre-selected criteria. These grades can be used in quantitative statistical data analysis. So the seemingly qualitative nature of the essay can be deceptive.

The more descriptive data that is usually collected from such qualitative methods as interviews, open-ended questions, or focus group transcripts can also be organized in such a way to result in numerical data. Descriptions can be grouped into like categories and the number of people responding in each category can be then manipulated and compared. Do not dismiss the use of qualitative data collection methods just because you need to report your assessment findings in terms of numbers and statistics. Such statistical analysis is possible whether you have used quantitative (numerical) or qualitative (descriptive) methods of data collection. What you do with that data after it is collected is up to you and will depend in large part upon whether those for whom this assessment was undertaken require narrative or numerical results

Discussing the individual assessment techniques is beyond the scope of this book. See the "Read More About It" section at the end of this chapter for suggestions about sources that can supply this information as well as samples of instruments at use in many library settings. But remember, trying to find an already developed instrument that will suit your specific needs may not be easy. While it is comforting to use an instrument that has already gone through some field testing for reliability, validity, and usability, it may be difficult to find one that really suits your purposes. Very few instruments have been developed in the field of ILI and those that have tend to be very context specific. These instruments may not be directly transferable to your particular environment. They can, however, be used as models and guidelines for developing instruments more directly suitable for your institution and specific assessment needs (Shonrock, 1996).

The following seven sections provide a brief discussion of the advantages and disadvantages of some of the more typical types of assessment methods. Whenever possible connections will be made to the principles under reliability/validity/usability, control/relevance, etc., discussed earlier in this chapter. Material contained in this section has been drawn from many sources (Adams, 1993; Bloom, Madaus, and Hastings, 1981; Brottman and Loe, 1990; Dewald et al., 2000; Dolphin, 1990; Pappas, 1998; Roselle, 1997; Steadman and Svinicki, 1998; Steward, 1998; Svinicki and Schwartz, 1988).

Objective Tests

Objective tests may also be referred to as fixed-answer or select-answer tests. The most common type of items are multiple-choice, matching, or true/false questions. Objective tests, therefore, test recognition rather than recall. They are excellent for determining the acquisition of facts. But they are less valid for testing higher-level cognitive skills such as analysis, synthesis, and evaluation, or to determine process learning and the acquisition of concepts. As such, they may not be appropriate for many of our ILI needs. Objective tests are frequently criticized for setting up an artificial situation that does not really test how the learner would react in a real-world situation. They tend to be reliable but vary in validity. Objective techniques can be useful for gathering demographic information and usage patterns, however.

Fixed-choice assessments (multiple-choice, true/false, matching) are high on control but are difficult and time-consuming to construct. They require a good deal of specialized training to develop and analyze. Outside expert assistance may be needed. Objective tests are easy to administer and grade and the results can be readily quantified. One major advantage of objective tests is that they allow you to collect a lot of data in a relatively short period of time. They lend themselves nicely to a pre- and post-test comparison research design, or comparisons between groups exposed to different instructional methods. However, their strength lies in the measurement of specific facts and principles, so they cannot be relied upon to measure changes in complex behavior or actual performance success.

Furthermore, using a pre-, post-, or between-groups test design contains its own pitfalls. It is difficult to attribute any change in behavior totally to the instructional intervention, even when a control group that does not receive the instruction is used as comparison. Outside influences such as the innate abilities of the groups, the instructor's attitudes and behavior, the amount of library work done in other classes, or availability of outside help can all interfere with the results. Although objective tests may be easy to administer, score, and quantify for statistical analysis, the interpretation of the results is not always simple and can be open to debate (Burton, 1977).

Open-Ended Questions/Essays

These are sometimes referred to as supply questions since the student must supply rather than select answers. In other words, they test recall rather than recognition. Supply type assessments are higher in relevance than select ones since students are given more freedom to express themselves. Students are encouraged to demonstrate their understanding of complex concepts and the interrelation between them. Supply assessments tend to be a better measure of process learning and higher cognitive skills. They are also useful for gathering data about attitudes and opinions. The nature of these assessments, which offers students more flexibility of response, also results in a decrease in control. Responses are often difficult to score consistently, and results can be hard to quantify and compare. These assessments are fairly easy to administer, but need to be developed with care. Questions must be clear and unambiguous; at the same time they need to be written in a neutral voice that gives all possible responses equal value.

Open-ended questions are considered a better indication of real world behavior since respondents supply answers rather than select from fixed options. But people are still describing the subject rather than doing it. Predicting real behavior from these written responses may not be entirely valid. Assessments using open-ended questions often lead to unexpected (and therefore frequently very interesting) results. Since people vary in how much they might respond, it is often hard to predict the amount of data that can be collected during a given period of time. Adding one or two open-ended questions to more objective-type assessments, however, can enhance the quality of information gathered.

Questionnaires/Surveys/Rating Scales

These instruments tend to be used primarily to assess attitudes and opinions. They can contain open-ended questions, fixed-response objective type items, or a combination of both. In rating scale situations, respondents are asked to select their responses to statements along some continuum, such as "strongly agree" to "strongly disagree." Usually referred to as Likert scales, they generally employ a five-point scale in order to allow for a neutral response (Anderson, 1988). One potential drawback of allowing for this neutral position is that respondents tend to cluster around the center option.

Designing instruments of this sort takes a great deal of time, skill, and expertise. They are fairly easy to administer. Scoring ease and reliability depends on what types of items are included (open-ended or fixed-response) and share the characteristics of each type. Amount of data that can be collected per unit of time also varies depending on what kinds of items are being used in the assessment. Validity can also suffer since once again people are responding about what they would do rather than actually doing it. In addition instruments of this sort sometimes suffer from the politeness factor. People may be less than truthful because they do not wish to hurt our feelings.

Interviews

With their more relaxed and personal approach, this type of assessment can provide valuable information about what people really think and feel. In addition, jargon can be defined and any confusion about questions can be clarified. Interviews can provide extremely relevant information about how people are reacting to instruction. Success in using interviews for assessment is highly dependent upon the skill of the interviewer.

Interviews can either consist of a fixed set of questions with no deviation from the pattern permitted or a more open structure with only a few fixed questions with the interviewer having the latitude to follow-up in whatever direction the interview is leading. Fixed questions obviously result in a more standard set of responses that may be easier to quantify. But the more open approach allows for the collection of information in more depth and detail. Although the interview shares the problem of talking about something rather than doing it, the interview setting does allow for a discussion of process as well as an examination of skills acquisition. However, people may be reluctant to be critical in a one-on-one situation. Having a neutral interviewer (someone not directly involved in the instruction) can encourage more honest responses. Keep in mind that interviews also carry some public-relations value and provide the opportunity to offer additional and individually targeted instruction. So, depending on what you want to gain from the process, you might wish to conduct the interviews yourself.

Data collected from interviews can be difficult to quantify. Interviews share many of the disadvantages of open-ended questions. In addition, since they are verbal in nature, it is sometimes hard to transcribe the results accurately even when the interviews are taped. Furthermore, interviews are a very time-consuming assessment method since data is collected on an individual basis. Using focus-group interviews can counter this factor somewhat. In focus groups, interviews are conducted with four to ten people at the same time. While this enables the interviewer to obtain more data per unit time, the accuracy of the data collected may suffer. People may feel uncomfortable responding in this more public setting. The interviewer must also take care that everyone is given an equal opportunity to speak. However, even the most skilled interviewer may not be able to overcome the problem of one or two people dominating the group. Although everyone may be asked to respond to each question, some may be reluctant to express an opinion that seems counter to the more vocal members of the group. On the positive side, focus groups can be excellent opportunities to test-market, though they do require some careful preparation.

Performance Assessment

Performance assessments and simulations (sometimes known as authentic assessment) are on the other end of the spectrum from fixed-answer types. Performance assessments and simulations are extremely high in relevance since the student demonstrates the skill or concept that was taught. However, performance assessments are extremely low on control because the performance environment is hard to manipulate or standardize. Evaluators interested in Cognitive psychology issues and higher-order thinking tend to favor performance assessment. These methods more readily address the question of how people learn rather than what they are learning. Performance assessment views all responses as important and looks beyond the right or wrong parameter. Questions about why students make the incorrect choice are examined as well as why students answer correctly.

Performance assessments are the most difficult to grade or quantify. They are subject to a variety of rating biases. These biases include the halo effect (rating a specific skill based on the overall impression of the student), the contrast effect (using oneself rather than an external criteria as the standard of evaluation), and leniency (giving the student the benefit of the doubt on skills not adequately exhibited). Furthermore, no matter how closely the test situation simulates reality, it is still not the real thing and may only be testing a narrow range of skills. Relevance can still be an issue.

Performance assessment depends upon direct observation. It is a particularly useful way of assessing process learning. Performance assessment tends to rank high on validity because the behavior or skill is actually being observed. It tends to be a very time-consuming form of assessment since, like interviews, it must be done on an individual basis. Performance assessment can also be tricky to score since it is not always obvious how the student is performing the process or solving the problem being observed. In addition, if students know they are being observed, the very act of observation can affect the results. Students may become nervous and perform badly. On the other hand, they may exhibit behavior that they think you want to see rather than show you what they would really do when on their own. Just because someone demonstrates that he or she knows the steps to a process does not guarantee that the process will be applied in another situation.

Unobtrusive observations that are conducted without the knowledge of the person being observed can counter some of these problems. However ethical issues of privacy and confidentiality then come into play. These unobtrusive observations can be even more difficult to score than obtrusive techniques. Although providing the advantage of being able to observe actual, real-world behavior, all control over the situation is lost. Unobtrusive observations can be a useful way to informally assess the success of your programs. Asking reference desk personnel to report on the types of questions people are asking and what difficulties they seem to be having in researching their topics can provide useful feedback and may highlight potential areas for improvement in the library's instructional program. Another approach could be to analyze search logs for the most commonly occurring errors.

Product Assessment

Product assessment involves the examination of papers, projects, bibliographies, or other research products against some standard or criterion. This type of assessment generally requires cooperation from whoever assigned the task (teacher, professor, or supervisor). It can be a useful way to determine what students have accomplished; but it does not indicate how they got there. We make the assumption that a good product means that the process was followed in the way that we taught it. However, we cannot be totally certain of that fact. Even if we could be sure that the process was followed, it remains unclear whether it was our instructional intervention that contributed to the end product or some other influence. Students may have gotten help from reference desk personnel, teachers, or fellow students. They may have had other instructional opportunities. Finally, we cannot be totally sure that they did the work themselves.

Classroom Assessment Techniques

Although many assessment methods require the development of formal instruments, questionnaires, and surveys, many less formal approaches are available. As a matter of fact, the most informal approach is probably the one that ILI instructors use the most, that of observing behavior of our students during instruction. Good teachers are always monitoring verbal and nonverbal cues as a way of keeping our instruction relevant, appropriate, and on-track. The use of in-class exercises, worksheets, and hands-on practice can also serve as assessment devices. Although their primary intent is to offer the students active learning opportunities, classroom assessments can clearly pinpoint any instructional problems. As students attempt to practice what you have shown them, questions, confusions, and problems can arise. This offers the teacher the opportunity to modify instruction on the spot and provides information about how to restructure the session in the future.

Classroom Assessment Techniques, or CATs, are of particular interest to the ILI instructor. CATs are teaching and assessment methods that require students to stop and think about what they have learned, to synthesize and articulate an important piece of that learning, and to think actively about what they did not understand. They offer learners the opportunity to monitor their own progress, reflect upon it, and possibly take some corrective measure.

The Minute paper is an example of this type of assessment. It is simple to use and provides immediate feedback to teacher and student about what is being learned (and what is *not*) (Cross, 1998). This technique can be used at the end of any session. Learners are asked to respond to two questions: "What were the main points of the instruction?" and "What unanswered questions do you still have?" Although the Minute paper is frequently done in writing, it can also be done orally. This is most appropriate in one-shot sessions when you do not expect to see the learners again and therefore will be unable to offer them constructive feedback. By doing the Minute paper orally, responses can serve as a review of the session and the instructor can answer questions as they occur. If learners are told ahead of time that they will be required to do this at the end of the session, they may reflect on what they are learning during the session and become more actively involved in trying to sort out what is important about the instruction.

CATs involve the learners as collaborators. They reinforce the idea of learning as a shared responsibility and offer people the opportunity to gain insight into their own learning. The use of CATs during instruction encourages learners to reflect on and develop the academic and life-long learning skills of inquiry and analysis. For further examples of CATs, see the "Read More About It" section at the end of this chapter; see also Chapters 6 and 13.

FIELD TESTING

Once you have selected the assessment technique you will use to collect your data, and have designed one to fit your particular situation, you still need to thoroughly field test it in advance of using it for your actual assessment. Make sure that you try your methods out on a sample group that as closely approximates your target population as possible. Check to make sure that the directions are clear, questions are unambiguous, the language is at an appropriate level, and your scoring method is accurate. Objective tests, questionnaires, surveys, and rating scales are particularly tricky to develop. If you have adequate funding, either from your institution or a research grant, it may be useful to enlist the assistance of test construction and design experts if you wish to use these types of tools. Talking to experts in educational assessment may also be useful if you are developing assessments using open-ended questions, interviews, performance, or product assessment. These experts can provide advice not only about how to develop these assessments, but also the best way to both score and analyze the resulting data.

FINAL REMARKS

The shift toward process over product in education, and the current emphasis on life-long learning skills and information literacy, promotes a re-examination of how to measure educational competencies. The relative merits of qualitative versus quantitative modes of assessment, as well as issues of control versus relevance, are becoming more critical than ever. ILI professionals must become even more versatile and flexible in their use of assessment techniques. They must be willing to embrace the notion that different methods are valid under different circumstances. They must be knowledgeable about the strengths and weaknesses of each technique. And they must be willing to mix and match methodologies so that the assessment results in the greatest amount of usable information possible (Kaplowitz, 1995).

Our learners can also gain from the assessment process. As they reflect on the instruction, what they have learned, and how that information has been useful to them, learners begin to explore the learning process itself, thus engaging in the metacognition process. They delve into how they interacted with the information being presented and consider how they might do this more effectively in the future. A well-designed assessment not only provides useful information for the instructor, it actually benefits the learner and helps to reinforce the material that was taught. Research has indicated that people who become aware of themselves as learners—that is, those who are self-reflective and analytic about their own learning process—become better learners. They move from being "surface learners" who merely reproduce information provided by others to "deep learners" who not only understand the information, but can apply it appropriately in a variety of settings (Corno and Mandinach, 1983; Cross, 1998). As a result, thoughtfully designed assessments can enhance the students' abilities to become life-long learners. Assessment, therefore, contributes to the over-all goals of ILI. It enhances the learners' experience by allowing them to examine how they learn and to develop more efficient and effective IL strategies and skills.

EXERCISE

Step 1.   Select an instructional session or support material that you wish to assess.

Step 2.   Assume that you are assessing in order to provide feedback to the instructor or developer about the effectiveness of the instruction. What sort of assessment tools would you use to provide that information? Why did you choose it?

Step 3.   Now assume that you must justify the instruction method or material to the appropriate people in your parent organization. How would you modify the assessment to produce the appropriate results and why?

Step 4.   Compare the methods used in Steps 2 and 3. What are the advantages and disadvantages of each?

READ MORE ABOUT IT

For further information about individual assessment techniques:

Bloom, Benjamin Samuel, George F. Madaus, and J. Thomas Hastings. 1981. *Evaluation to Improve Learning*. New York: McGraw-Hill.

Brottman, May, and Mary Loe, eds. 1990. *The LIRT Instruction Handbook*. Englewood, CO: Libraries Unlimited.

Elliott, Stephen N., Thomas R. Kratochwill, Joan Littlefield, and John F. Travers. 1996. *Educational Psychology: Effecting Teaching, Effective Learning*. 2nd ed. Madison, WI: Brown and Benchmark.

Shonrock, Diana, ed. 1996. *Evaluating Library Instruction: Sample Questions, Forms, and Strategies for Practical Use*. Chicago: American Library Association, Library Instruction Round Table.

Svinicki, Marilla, and Barbara Schwartz. 1988. *Designing Instruction for Library Users: A Practical Guide*. New York: Marcel Dekker, Inc.

For further information about Classroom Assessment Techniques (CATs):

Angelo, Thomas A., and K. Patricia Cross. 1993. *Classroom Assessment Techniques: A Handbook for College Teachers*. 2nd ed. *The Jossey-Bass Higher Education and Adult Education Series*. San Francisco: Jossey-Bass.

Cross, K. Patricia, and Mimi H. Steadman. 1996. *Classroom Research: Implementing the Scholarship of Teaching*. San Francisco: Jossey-Bass.

Steadman, Mimi Harris, and Marilla D. Svinicki. 1998. "CATs: A Student's Gateway to Better Learning." *New Directions for Teaching and Learning* 75:13–20.

Part IV

Delivering Information Literacy Instruction

13

Teaching: Preparation, Performance, and Passion

Education is not filling a bucket, but lighting a fire.
—William Butler Yeats

WHAT MAKES A GOOD TEACHER?

Why are some teachers more effective than others? How do we forge connections with our students? How do we put the learner in the center of our teaching? Are good teachers born or made? For many of us, getting up in front of a group is a frightening and intimidating experience. We frequently have little training or experience in teaching, yet we are told that instruction is a primary part of our job responsibility. We are expected to stand in front of a room full of people and know how to capture their attention, engage their interest, and communicate appropriate information.

Can we learn to be effective teachers? Of course we can. Many fine books have been written on the subject. But to become effective takes a commitment to change, willingness to experiment, and the courage to face, and hopefully, conquer some personal demons. Furthermore, we need to accept that we will never reach perfection. Effective teachers are self-reflective (Brookfield, 1995). They review their presentations for what worked and what didn't go quite right, and use that information to improve their teaching skills. Teachers are forever destined to be works in progress. But in many ways that's what makes being a teacher fun, exciting, and always challenging.

Good teaching, whether it is in-person or remote, consists of planning, presentation, and passion. We must plan our content and determine our methods. Our presentation must capture and hold our students' attention. Finally, we must model our passion for the information so that our students are motivated to learn both during and after our time with them. Although many of the topics discussed below can and should be applied to remote learning situations in which teacher and learner do not share the same physical space, the bulk of the material that follows will be directed toward the in-person, face-to-face type of learning situation.

PREPARATION

Let's assume you have already done the essential preliminary work. You have completed a Needs Assessment. You know who your audience is and have identified what needs to be taught. Based on this information, you have articulated your game plan by writing clear and concise instructional goals and objectives. Think of the goals and objectives as your road map for the instructional planning process. They help you determine and prioritize what needs to be communicated. A good approach is to work from the student's perspective. Think about what they need to know, do or feel at the end of your instruction. What kinds of experiences will enable them to do so? What will make your session relevant to them? Like any good book, a well-constructed instruction session has a definite beginning, middle, and end, all of which require planning and preliminary effort.

You are now ready to develop your full-fledged lesson plan. Everyone has his or her own idiosyncratic method of doing this. But here are some things to consider:

Get Their Attention

Though librarians may teach full-credit courses, more often than not they meet with students only once or twice, at best, and for limited periods of time. In addition, they are often guests on someone else's turf. Regardless of your role, what you do in the first five minutes of a session will determine how effective your session will be. Use this time to capture the students' attention and build a rapport. Most people will pay attention for the first few minutes of a session. Holding on to their attention for the long haul can be a bit more problematic (Lowman, 1995).

What can you do in those first five minutes to ensure instructional success? If you have done your homework, you already have a lot of information about your audience and what they need to know. Capture their attention by showing them the relevance of what you are about to cover. In other words, use those first five minutes to let them know what's in it for them. There are a lot of ways to do this. But keep in mind that this opening segment is crucial to your overall success.

It is a good idea to get learners engaged as soon as they walk in the door. Make sure you get to the room before they do and chat with them as they come in. Plan an activity for people to do as soon as they enter the room. Some people call these sponge activities because they "soak" people up as they arrive and immediately make them part of the learning process. You can give out small file cards and ask them to write some questions they may have about the topic. They can also use these cards to describe a previous experience (good or bad) they have had with the material. Place a thought-provoking quote or question on the board and ask students to describe their reactions to it. Give a brief quiz that will help point out what people do (and do not) already know about the subject. Have a list of topics on the board and ask students to vote on what interests them. Tell them you will use the list to structure your session. Ask students to self-select into particular categories or break the class into groups you have pre-determined and then use this selection to generate discussion or debate. Using a sponge activity puts you in control from the very start of the session. It sets the tone and lets students know that you are interested in what they think. Furthermore, you can gain a lot of useful information about the group, their background, and previous experiences.

Obviously, the exercise needs to be well thought out and planned in advance. It must be relevant to the topic at hand and be connected to your instructional objectives. If it is viewed as busy work, you will lose rather than gain respect and credibility. This type of exercise also builds rapport. From a stranger talking at them, you become a person who is talking with them. Dealing with their responses in a warm, non-threatening, and accepting manner creates a classroom atmosphere that is conducive to learning.

Have a Big Finish

Designing the sponge activity is only one part of developing your lesson plan. How you close your session is also crucial. Many presenters suggest that you develop your opening and closing before you work on the content that occupies the middle of the session. Just as you win or lose your audience in the first five minutes of a session, you can undermine the entire session by the way you end it. The last five minutes or so should be used to summarize important points, as a check for comprehension and/or to encourage participants to apply what you have taught (Davis, 1993; Mager, 1997b, 1997c). Try a game show approach where participants are asked to match resources with particular research topics. Or present a topic and ask participants to come up with a search strategy for a particular database. Compare and discuss the different strategies that might be suggested. Trying to cover a few more points as people are rushing out the door, or just dwindling off into nothingness when you run out of things to say, can defeat all the good you may have done during the session (Lowman, 1995). Make sure you plan an upbeat and appropriate finish and that you leave the proper amount of time for it.

What Goes In-Between

You have an attention-getting opening and a smash closing. What goes in the middle? Here is where you have to make the tough decisions about what to include and, more importantly, what to leave out. To help make these decisions, return to your goals and objectives. What do you expect your students to know, think and/or feel at the end of the session? Are any of these goals more important then others? Are you being realistic about how much you can accomplish in the time allotted to you? A good teacher emphasizes the important material, deletes the unimportant, and can tell the difference between the two. The overriding rule should always be less is more. It is far better to present two or three important items in a clear, thorough, and memorable fashion than to attempt to quickly cram a dozen items into the session with the hopes that the students will remember some of it. They won't, and you will have set them up for failure. The topic will seem overwhelming, and your students will get the impression that it is impossible to learn. This is definitely *not* what we want to have happen in our instruction. We want our students to become engaged and have them leave feeling confident and competent in their abilities to use what you presented.

TIPS FOR PLANNING SESSION LENGTH

- *Consider the length of your session carefully*—You may be restricted to the length of a class session, or you may be able to negotiate for a longer chunk of a session than the instructor originally planned on giving you. Generally, though, our contact with learners is brief and our content is huge. The decisions about what to include and what to leave out can become very painful indeed. Furthermore, in cases where we are limited to only one or two interactions with the learners, we are tempted to pack a lot into our brief encounters. We may not be able to slip over into the next session, as there rarely is a next session. Making sure we prepare the correct amount of material to fit the timeframe is crucial, and one of the more difficult tasks that faces the IL instructor.

- *Develop flexibility*—Remember that once you get into the presentation situation, anything can happen. So be prepared for the unexpected. Try developing only enough to fill about two-thirds of the session's length. That leaves time for questions, unexpected student-generated topics, technical difficulties, late arrivals, and other acts of God and nature.

- *Have something extra up your sleeve*—Most students will be happy to leave early if you run out of material before the time is up. But if that really bothers you, try developing a tiered approach to your outline. Prepare three levels of material. The first contains the crucial material they have to know. Next comes the "it would be nice if I could get it in" stuff. The third level contains the bonus information that they really don't need to know but might be of some interest to them. Highlight the notes, using three different colors, to indicate the three levels and make adjustments as you go along. Put timing notes on the edge of your outline to indicate when you need to move on to the next segment. Have a clock or watch with you so you can stay on track.

- *Think like a novice*—To determine what goes into each of the three levels, think back to when your were first learning the material. What did you need to know to get started? Those are your main points that must be presented or the learner will be unable to function. What did you want to know once the basics were conquered? This will be the material for your second layer. Finally, what extra (bells and whistles) features/skills/strategies did you pick up after you had developed some expertise? These can be added as your third level and are usually special tips and techniques that only make sense once you have had some experience with the material. If you don't get to this material (and you might not be able to), it won't stop your students from functioning successfully.

ESSENTIAL ELEMENTS OF A LESSON PLAN

Whatever you decide to include as your content, here are some segments that should be part of your lesson plan:

- *Introduction*—The introduction sets the stage for the presentation. It follows the previously discussed sponge activity and should be used to place your material into a meaningful context for the group. To ensure their attention, appeal to the "what's in it for me" factor during your introduction. Try to cover the essentials, but be as succinct as possible. Remember, you are just giving hints about what is to come, you will be expanding on the details later on in the session itself. Finally, use the introduction to set up the conceptual framework for your presentation and to provide the group with whatever facts or background material they may need to understand the information.

- *Active learning experiences*—These can be distributed throughout your session. They can follow a more formal, lecture-type segment or can be used as a means for self-discovery. In any case, each activity should be a method for illustrating and reinforcing important points and concepts. Use your session objectives as a guide to determining the usefulness of an activity. Will the activity help the students reach the instructional objectives? If the answer to the question is "Yes," then use it; if not, delete it. Such an activity might be fun, but in the end it is only busy work and can detract from the overall effectiveness of the session (Allen, 1995).

- *Checks for understanding*—You should end each segment with some kind of comprehension check. Do not go on to the next segment until you are sure that the learners are ready to do so. You can ask specific content-related questions or ask learners to summarize what has just been covered. If you decide to go with "temperature-taking" questions, make sure you use the kind that cannot be answered by "yes" or "no." For example, instead of asking, "Do you have any questions?" ask "What questions do you now have about what we just did?" Remember that you can (and should) include such comprehension checks in your Web-based, remote instructional endeavors as well as in your in-person ones. In the case of remote instruction, you will have to provide a means for the learner to determine if their answers are correct. This can be done by having self-correcting mechanisms built into the comprehension check or by having these checks e-mailed to the librarian for feedback. See Chapter 17 for more on this topic.

Asking for learner input in the face-to-face instructional setting should not be a pro forma exercise. Whenever you ask for learners' responses, make sure you give them enough time to actually do so. Most people are uncomfortable with silence and teachers are no exception. But if you do not hold firm and wait for them to respond, they will think you really are not interested in what they have to say. Show them you mean it by waiting for the reply. If you find yourself jumping in too soon to fill the silence, force yourself to count very slowly and silently from one to ten. If you still get no reply, try re-phrasing the question and then count to ten again. You will be surprised at how often people will respond when given an appropriate amount of time.

There is one last thing to do before you are ready to go on. Follow the theatrical model and do a dry run and time it, if possible with a trusted friend watching and providing constructive feedback. Are you being realistic about what you plan to include? Will it fit? If you start to feel rushed, look for places to cut. Rehearsal helps you smooth out the rough spots and alerts you to where you may run into trouble with a segment or an activity. Be especially cautious when including student activities in your session because they always take longer than you think they will. If students need to move around to form groups, be sure to factor in the time it will take to do so. Remember, it generally takes some time to get everyone out of the groups and back to their seats. Develop some attention-getting signal that will get their eyes back on you. For example, flick the lights on and off or use a timer that makes a loud and obvious noise.

Planning a group instructional session takes practice but no matter how much you practice, you may not get it right every time—no one does. Learn from your experiences. If you run into problems, try to do some post-session analysis to see what went wrong. Even more importantly, see if you can figure out what you could do next time to make it better.

For more preparation advice see Brookfield (1995), Davis (1993), Eble (1988), Elliott et al. (1996), Hagle (1990), Mager (1997b), McKeachie (1986), Palmer (1998), Smith (1991).

PRESENTATION AS PERFORMANCE

You have prepared your material and are ready to present. Or are you? You certainly know what you want to communicate to your learners, but are you ready to sell it to them in the classroom? The best material in the world is worthless unless you are ready and able to present it in a dynamic, enthusiastic, and effective manner. Teaching is performing and, as such, teachers are a lot like actors. For one thing, both professions must deal with stage fright. Getting psyched to teach is not an easy task. Even experienced teachers will tell you they still get the jitters before having to present. They may love to teach when they are doing it, but they still dread it when they are preparing for it and waiting "to go on." Sound crazy? Well, most performers will say that they feel the same way. In the *Confident Performer*, David Roland interviews athletes, musicians, actors, and other performers who all agree that if you are not nervous you should not be performing. Being nervous is part of caring about doing a good job (Roland, 1997).

Stage Fright

Being too nervous, of course, can interfere with your ability to present at all. At that point, panic sets in and you may be unable to think, speak, or move. You may make mistakes or rush through the session leaving important points out. But being totally relaxed could be detrimental as well. You may not be alert and may appear disinterested in the material. If you look like you do not care, why should your audience? What you need to develop is your personal level of optimal anxiety. One way to do this is to learn more about the physiological aspects of anxiety.

What happens when you are feeling threatened? Your heart beats faster, your mouth gets dry, you may shiver or sweat, and your breathing may become shallow. These are all normal reactions to stress and they signal your body's readiness for dealing with it. Now think about what happens when you are excited about some challenge. The symptoms are the same. So what does that mean in terms of dealing with anxiety? If you can view these physiological signals in a positive way, as the body preparing you to meet a challenge rather than urging you to run from a threat, you will have a much more positive attitude about the upcoming experience. There is nothing wrong with some honest sweat or palpitations as you enter the classroom. Just view these bodily changes as symptoms of your concern and commitment to doing a good job. It means you are excited about the upcoming experience and are ready to do the your best (Roland, 1997).

Relaxation Techniques

- *Personal tension points*—If your anxiety gets to the point where it interferes with your performance, there are ways to keep it under control. Learn some relaxation techniques and use them just prior to your session. Do whatever works for you. Some people feel tension in their necks. Others feel it in their shoulders or their backs. Concentrate on relaxing your personal tension points. Books on acting, sports psychology, yoga and meditation can all offer suggestions. Some basic techniques include rotating your neck, raising and lowering your shoulders, and shaking your arms and hands. Do not forget to warm up your voice by humming or sub-vocalizing.

- *Breathing*—Pay special attention to your breathing. Place one hand on your chest and the other on your abdomen and take a breath. Which one moves? The healthiest, deepest breathing is from the abdomen. Chest breathing is shallower and quicker and reduces your oxygen intake. When you are feeling anxious, try to consciously monitor your breathing and focus on abdomen rather than chest breathing. Doing so will result in a decrease in anxiety-related physiological symptoms and will calm you down. Roland's *The Confident Performer* includes some excellent examples of breathing exercises and relaxation techniques (1997).

- *Rehearse*—Know your stuff. Practice your material thoroughly in advance so that your presentation is smooth and unflustered. In addition to the benefits we have already discussed, rehearsal helps reduce performance anxiety. It alerts you to where you may run into trouble before it happens for real. Try to identify potential logistical problems. If possible, go to the classroom ahead of time so that you are familiar with the layout and any equipment you will be using. You might have to modify some of your activities depending upon the physical arrangement of the room.

- *Practice positive self-talk before the session*—You are the expert on this material. You have practiced your material and know what you want to say. Tell yourself that you will give it your best and that you are good at what you do. Pump yourself up just like athletes do before competing. Visualize doing an excellent job and expect to succeed.

- *Focus on the content you are trying to present*—Once you start teaching, try to concentrate on the points you are trying to make and what the audience needs to know. Remember to include comprehension checks to make sure you are succeeding. If you get caught up in getting your ideas across, you will become less self-conscious and nervous.

- *Deal rationally with mistakes*—Everyone makes mistakes, do not let them throw you. Remember that you will notice your mistakes much more than your audience will. Acknowledge and correct your errors and the audience will empathize. There is a benefit to making mistakes: If you can make mistakes, it is OK for your learners to do so and still expect to succeed at the task.

Put your mistakes in perspective. Do not dwell on them. Take pride in what went well. View your successes and your mistakes as learning opportunities. Concentrate on emphasizing what went well and improving what did not. Your goal is to learn from the experience in order to do it better the next time.

- *Be prepared for anything*—Another way to alleviate anxiety is to be prepared for any contingency. Terry Smith's *Making Successful Presentations* (1991) includes some useful pointers about getting ready for your presentation. First, develop a speaker's checklist that includes everything you should consider in advance about the setting, equipment, logistics, your handouts, and material (Smith, 1991). Keep in mind that all the advance planning in the world will not help if the projector light bulb blows out, the extension cord is too short, or any number of random acts of chaos that can plague a speaker. Terry Smith's answer to this is to create a personal speaker's emergency kit (1991). His basic kit includes such standard items as tape, push pins, chalk, markers (regular and erasable), clips, scissors, flashlights, and so on. Most people add to the basic emergency kit as a result of being faced with some unexpected situation that they wish to be prepared for in the future. For example, some people include a couple of night-lights in their kits. You can use these for some ambient light during the lights-out portion of your presentation. Paper towels are good to include in case of spills. You might want to have cough drops in your bag to help with dry mouth. Manila file folders make great emergency charts. Swizzle sticks can be used as pointers in a pinch. Post-it pads can be used as highlights on overheads or can be used in learning activities for sorting ideas into categories. File cards of all sizes are also useful; learners can use small or mid-sized ones to record questions or comments for discussion, larger ones can be folded in half and used as place cards. Include whatever you can think of that will help you deal with unforeseen circumstances, and then continue to add to it as you experience other unforeseen circumstances.

Whatever methods you use to deal with stage fright, remember that getting yourself up for the task of teaching is crucial. You must prepare yourself emotionally as well as intellectually for your "performance" (Lowman, 1995). Try and set aside some time, even just a few minutes, before you have to teach to prepare yourself psychologically for the task ahead. Use this time in whatever way that can both calm you down and get you motivated and energized. Breathing exercises, meditation techniques, positive self-talk, stretching, and humming are all useful ways to use this time. Come up with a routine you like and make time for it. Doing so will make you more relaxed and primed to teach and your enjoyment and that of your students will be increased because you are in the right frame of mind to "go on."

Stage Presence

Now you are fairly calm, or at least know how to make your anxiety work for you. You are equipped with a logical, well-thought-out lesson plan. You have gone over your pre-presentation checklist and have your emergency kit handy. What else goes into getting ready to perform? You need to know how to use your instrument to put the material across. The instrument in question is not your overhead projector, microphone, or computer. The instrument in question is your voice and your body. Verbal and non-verbal cues can make or break a presentation. You need to know how to use your voice and your body as emphasis and as a means of motivating your students.

- *The first and most important rule is to be comfortable*—You may read a lot of advice about what clothes to wear, how to move, gesture, talk, and behave in front of a group. Pay attention to what makes sense to you. Work on what you can do to improve your presentation, but do not make yourself crazy. Do what feels right to you. If you like bright, cheerful colors, wear them. If flashy jewelry makes you feel confident, go for it. If you tend to make wild gestures to emphasize a point, do it (as long as you do not poke anyone's eye out in the process).
- *Adopt an easy conversational tone*—Prepare your session for the ear rather than the eye. Listen to yourself as you practice. Do you sound like your are chatting to a friend or lecturing to a group of strangers? You have a better chance of connecting to the group if you talk to them rather than at them.
- *Use your voice for emphasis*—Changing the speed at which you are talking, pausing after a point, and adjusting your inflection (up or down) can highlight your points. If something is important, repeat it. Many presenters actually give a verbal cue. Say "This next point is crucial," or "You really need to remember this next point." Tell people that if you were going to remember anything at all about the session, this is it!
- *Articulate clearly*—No Professor Mumbles allowed! Practice volume and pitch control and learn to project. Lower pitches seem

to go further. If you are having trouble being heard in large rooms, try lowering your pitch. Always make sure you can be heard in all parts of the room. Ask for feedback from the group right at the beginning of the session.

- *Do not maintain the same pitch throughout your session*—A voice that exhibits a range of pitch is much more interesting to listen to than a monotone (Lowman, 1995). Think about using your voice as a musical instrument. While you probably do not want to try singing your material, you do want to keep the sound interesting. Shifts in pitch can work to hold your listeners' attention. Pitch shifts can also be used as emphasis and to mark changes from one topic to the next.

- *Speak at a comfortable speed*—Do not speak so fast that students are unable to keep up with you or so slow that it sounds like you are playing a recording at the wrong speed. Stop every so often to allow students who are taking notes to catch up.

- *Try moving around a bit to add variety to the presentation*—If you are illustrating varying viewpoints on a subject, try changing your position when you switch sides. Or change your position to indicate that you are moving to a new topic or are changing activities. Move closer to the group during interactive question and answer or discussion segments. Lean toward a student who is speaking to convey interest in what he or she has to say. Use appropriate and meaningful gestures to emphasize your points (Lowman, 1995).

- *Maintain eye contact with the group*—Never, ever speak to your notes or talk with your back turned to the group. If you are writing on the board, flip charts, or pointing to the screen, make sure you turn toward the group before you begin to speak. This takes some practice, but it is crucial not only so you can be heard, but to keep your connection with the group.

- *With-it-ness*—Speaking of connections, a good teacher is always aware of the atmosphere in the room. Jacob Kounin (1970) calls this "With-it-ness." Watch your students' body language and facial expressions. Are they engaged or bored? Are they listening attentively or are they restless and disinterested? Use these cues to gauge your effectiveness. If they start to loss interest, maybe you are dwelling too long on a particular point. Move on. You may have reached the "too much of a good thing" point of your session (Elliott et al, 1996; Mager, 1997b). Change the pace, introduce something new. If they look confused, repeat or restate your point or add a few more examples. If they are excited and enthusiastic, build on that energy. Take a moment to congratulate yourself on doing a good job of getting them involved and engaged.

- *Do not read verbatim from your notes*—Use your notes to keep yourself on track; but if you were just going to read to the group, they could have stayed home and read it themselves. Remember that you are there to add value to what they could learn on their own. Your job is to summarize, synthesize, emphasize through examples, and make sure they understand the material. Develop your own cue card technique. Some people use over-sized cards (5" × 8") with just a few important cue words on them. Others outline the whole session (usually in large point type) and then highlight the key phrases. Whatever you do, make sure your notes are easy to follow and that you can find what you need when you need it.

- *Be positive, upbeat, and enthusiastic*—Discussions of master teaching frequently include references to how teacher's attitudes affect student learning. You need to care about what you are teaching and to show that you care. If you are not enthusiastic about what you are doing, it will show. Students will pick up on your attitude. If you are not interested in what you are saying, why on earth should they be?

- *Finally, do everything you can to create a warm, supporting and encouraging learning environment* (Brophy, 1987)—Welcome questions and comments. Look at your students when they speak. Respond to their comments with smiles and nods. Do not be judgmental or critical of what they think or say. Treat your students with dignity and respect. Do not lecture to or talk down to them. Engage them in the exploration and discovery of new ideas. Make learning a shared responsibility.

For more hints on presentation skills see Eble (1988), Elliott et al. (1996), Hagle (1990), Kroenke (1984), Lowman (1995), Mager (1997b, 1997c), McKeachie (1986), Palmer (1998), and Smith (1991).

Teacher-Student Interaction

How you structure your session plays a large part in creating your classroom environment. What you do communicates your attitude toward the students as much as what you say. You have a range of format options for your session. In general, formats fall into one of two categories, that of teacher led (direct learning) or student directed (indirect or active learning) (Elliott et al., 1996; Mager, 1997a, 1997c; Svinicki and Schwartz, 1988). The direct "sage on the stage" lecture format has long been the model for teaching, especially in the higher education arena. Defenders of this format insist that it is the only way to present large amounts of information in brief periods of time. While this may be true from the presenter's point of view, the question remains whether the learners can gain anything by being bombarded with this type of information overload. A major advantage of the direct format, however, is that it offers the teacher the opportunity to summarize, synthesize, and pull together information from a variety of sources. It also models the intellectual process involved in this sort of analysis (Eble, 1988; Frederick, 1986; Kroenke, 1984).

Current educational thought seems to be moving away from the straight lecture to a more mixed presentation format that includes a variety of modes and formats such as lecture, group activities, hands-on practice, multimedia presentations, and so on (Elliott et al., 1996; Jacobson and Mark, 1995; Mager, 1997c, 1997d; McKeachie, 1986). There are several advantages to this mix of direct and indirect techniques. For one thing, it helps deal with the variety of learning styles that will be represented in your class. For some, listening to you talk will be just fine. Others may need to see and/or actively interact with the material in order to absorb what you are trying to teach. Mixing formats also seems to keep attention and motivation high. Finally it ensures that a variety of voices are heard. Indirect learning techniques show the students you care about what they think and feel. It allows them to relate to the material in a personal way and it addresses issues of learning styles and cultural diversity by letting everyone put the information into a context that is individually meaningful. See Chapter 4 for additional information about learning styles issues and Chapter 14 for a discussion of ILI for diverse populations.

If students are to become IL they must have the opportunity to incorporate IL strategies, values, and concepts into their own mental models. According to Piaget (Piaget and Inhelder, 1969) people can become uncomfortable when presented with new information. They may even exhibit hostility if the experience is perceived as threatening to their current mental model. If information cannot be easily assimilated into their understanding of the world, it may be rejected. However, if people are allowed to interact with the material, they can construct a modified mental model that accommodates the new experience (Allen, 1995; Meyers and Jones, 1993; Nelson, 1994).

To facilitate this accommodation, students must analyze, evaluate, and synthesize the new material themselves. William Perry (1981) theorizes that people tend to think in absolutes when confronted with new information. They believe there must be right and wrong answers if only the teacher would just tell them the "truth." Perry refers to this stage of thinking as dualism. As people learn more about the material, they begin to realize that authorities can differ. There seems to be no definitive truth, so everyone has a right to his or her opinion. This mode of thinking is called multiplicity.

The idea of multiplicity requires that students accept uncertainty. Once they have accepted that there are multiple possibilities, they are ready to move on to the final stage, that of evaluating their options and making selections based on their own values, experiences, and beliefs. Learners at this stage question the material and view it as relative and context specific. At this point, learners can make informed judgments based on what is personally valid to them (McKeachie, 1986; Nelson, 1994). Learners are now capable of making decisions based on a critical examination of the material. Knowledge is constructed, not merely absorbed. These students question authority—including that of the teacher. They are flexible, adaptable, and open to new ideas and they are prepared to deal with an uncertain, complex, diverse, and often confusing world.

Incorporating some indirect, learner-controlled activities into your sessions can encourage this final stage of thinking (Allen, 1995; Eble, 1988). It allows the student to experience, reflect, construct, and understand the material for his/her self. The new information is now a part of the learner's own mental model. Since the learner has organized the material in some meaningful fashion, and has stored it in a personally relevant and logical way, there is a greater likelihood that it will be retrievable in the future.

Many teachers are reluctant to include indirect methods in their sessions. They equate using indirect techniques with loss of control in the classroom. While admittedly there is some risk involved in using these techniques, careful planning and preparation can minimize the dangers and enhance the experience for teacher and learner alike. For the indirect-learning activity to be effective, the teacher must maintain even more control over the situation than in the direct approach. Although the learners are given the freedom to interact with each other and the material, the teacher sets the stage, determines the rules, monitors, facilitates, and generally keeps things moving in the appropriate direction. Learners must be kept on task and it is the teacher's job to make sure that is happening. The teacher must also set up the activity so that everyone gets a chance to participate. Finally, the teacher must summarize, synthesize, and put closure on the activity (Eble, 1988; Elliott et al. 1996). See Chapter 6 for more about active learning and ILI.

No matter how much thought we put into the design of the activity in advance, the nature of indirect learning is that it is to some extent unpredictable. Each time we use the activity may be a bit different from the last. That unpredictability can actually add to the technique's appeal. When faced with the prospect of repeating our sessions many times in a week or even in a single day, it is hard not to become stale and lose interest in our task. In a less-structured indirect learning setting, the material remains fresh. Each group brings its unique insights to the activity, and each class session has its own individual character.

One final advantage of the indirect, active-learning method is that it puts more of the responsibility for learning in the hands of the learners. Students are not viewed as passive receptacles into which our collective wisdom is poured. Learning under these circumstances is a shared responsibility and the students are as culpable as we are for the outcome. Viewing them as partners in the process communicates our respect for them and our belief in their ability to learn. When students are given ownership in the process, they are more likely to buy into the ideas being presented (Chickering and Gamson, 1987; Cook, Kunkel, and Weaver, 1995; Frederick, 1981). Indirect learning allows people to put the material into a meaningful context and to make the information part of their personal world-view. Motivation increases and more attention is paid to the material. Retention improves as students grasp the importance of the material and see how they can apply it to their lives.

Whatever format you decide to use in your sessions, remember that one of our goals is to send our students away feeling better about the material and their abilities to interact with it. In psychological terms, we wish to improve their self-efficacy (Bandura, 1977a). Self-efficacy refers to the judgments that people make about themselves, not about the actual skills people may have. It is about a person's belief in his/her abilities to use the skills appropriately (Mager, 1997b, 1997c). Giving people the chance to not only interact with but also to succeed with new material can greatly enhance their feelings of self-efficacy. Your enthusiasm for the subject coupled with the learners improved attitudes toward it should increase their willingness to approach the material in the future and an eagerness to learn more about it.

Many of the characteristics of the Humanist approach to teaching enhance this learner-teacher relationship and create an environment that promotes this self-efficacy. Humanist teachers are accessible and real as they allow their passion about the material to show. Student input is valued and rewarded. These teachers believe in the capability of their learners to succeed and indicate that belief in words, gestures, and deeds. They are empathic and understanding of their learners' fears and anxieties about learning the material (Rogers and Freiberg, 1994). Humanistic learning experiences tend to be student-centered, in many cases student-directed, and seem to be preferred by the learners themselves (Lowman, 1995). For more information about the Humanistic approach to teaching see Chapter 3.

CLASSROOM MANAGEMENT

If you have done your homework, prepared an engaging and relevant session, and have honed your performance/presentation skills, you should have little trouble keeping the class motivated and on track. If you are fortunate enough to be in a situation where people are attending your sessions because they want to, half the battle is won already. Sometimes, however, learners, especially in the school and academic environments, are required to attend the "library session." The relationship between the session and their regular course work is unclear to them and they may view themselves as unwilling "victims." It will be up to you to win them over. In most cases you will succeed. But what do you do about learners who not only remain unconvinced about the worth of session, but also actually expend some energy to disrupt it?

This is an example of where we run into the special problem of being a guest in someone else's class. It is hard for us to assert ourselves when we know we have no real power over the group. We cannot flunk them for interfering with our session; we may even find it difficult to ask them to leave the room. As hard as we might have tried to establish a relationship with these learners, it still may be a very tentative one. So what are we to do? If we are fortunate to have good rapport with the person who has sent them to us, we can ask him or her for assistance at this point. An even better approach is to ask in advance how he or she would like you to handle disruptions. Try including management questions into your pre-instruction information gathering discussions.

If you end up on your own, here are a few things you might try. First of all, remember that most of the group is probably interested or at least sympathetic to you. The loud mouth is generally the exception, not the rule. Do not judge your effectiveness by one or two unruly people. If someone is being really loud, stop talking. You probably cannot compete anyway, so do not even try. Suddenly the disrupter is the only voice in the room. This could be sufficiently embarrassing to cause the disrupter to shut up. Walking toward the disrupter can also be effective. If you feel comfortable about confronting the person, ask him or her if there is a problem that you could address. Finally, you can tell the person that if he or she is not interested in what is going on, then perhaps he or she should leave and let the rest of the class proceed with the instruction.

This may not be the most comfortable of situations. But if you have set the right tone from the beginning of the session, most of the group will be on your side and will support your action. They are probably just as annoyed at the disrupter as you are and will admire you for taking a stand. This is just another example of how you take what your are doing seriously and care about getting the information across to your learners. Do not worry too much about this sort of thing. It rarely happens, especially if you have created a positive learning environment from the start. The most effective classroom management techniques are those that prevent problems from happening in the first place (Elliott et al., 1996; Laslett and Smith, 1984). Create a positive learning environment. Mix formats so that everyone remains involved. Stress the relevance of the material to the students. Display your interest and enthusiasm and you will head off problems before they begin.

PASSION—THEIRS AND OURS

Motivating our students begins with motivating ourselves. We should be role models of enthusiasm for our material. We must exhibit care and concern for our students—and we must help them make the connection between what we are doing in our session to what they will need to be doing throughout their lives.

How can we make sure we care? First of all, a good match between who you are, what you teach, and how you are teaching is crucial. Your comfort with the task at hand communicates itself to the group. If you are well prepared, care about what you are teaching, believe in the methods you have selected, and have developed a personal performance style that really suits you, you cannot help but create a classroom environment conducive to learning.

Continuing to challenge yourself by incorporating new ideas and techniques into your sessions is also a way to keep your passion high. You must continue to expand your horizons by reading literature not only in ILI, but in that of education and psychology as well. Attend workshops and classes on teaching and performing. Develop a critical eye whenever you view any presentation. What did you like about the presentation that you might be able to use? What did not work for you? Why did not you like it? How would you do it differently?

Can you motivate your students merely by modeling your personal passion? To a certain extent, the answer is "Yes." Passion is contagious and your students will pick up on the excitement you are communicating.

Passion, however, may not be enough. You already know the relevance of the material. It is so obvious to you that you may forget that it is not quite so obvious to your students. It is up to you to show your students how what you are teaching relates to them both in the short run and over the long haul. Furthermore, you want to encourage them to continue to explore this material on their own and without the need for external rewards to spur them on. In other words, you would like to move them from being extrinsically rewarded (working for tangible rewards) to intrinsically rewarded (the learning being its own reward) (Eble, 1988; Elliott et al., 1996). Once you have done that, your students will become more self-sufficient and they will have taken a step closer to being people who have learned how to learn.

Since we generally will have little in the way of external rewards to offer, we must pay special attention to demonstrating the relevance of our information. Use examples during your class that the students can relate to. This is another place where background work pays off: The more you know about your learners and their information needs, the better you can incorporate meaningful examples into the session. Giving people some freedom in choosing topics for the activities can also help them relate the experience to their own needs. Including some activities that gives learners a chance to interact with the material in a meaningful way will also help them to discover how the information fits into their lives.

PLAYING TO OUR STRENGTHS

People who are drawn to public service in our libraries seem to be naturals for the task of teaching. They genuinely want to help people and in general have strong interpersonal skills, are excellent communicators, and show interest in and respect for a diverse clientele. All these traits serve as a sound foundation for teaching. However, many institutions require that all librarians participate in live, in-person, group instruction whether they are motivated to do so or not. Unfortunately, reluctant teachers may not be the most effective ones. It is hard for such a person to motivate the students or engage their interest. It is vitally important that those who are recruited into a teaching role be given training and support in order to develop the skills necessary for in-person group instruction.

Today's instructional technology provides a variety of opportunities for people to teach in a more virtual setting. Although everyone may be part of the teaching community, not everyone must be the person who is center-stage. There are many places where such librarians can contribute to the instructional mandate of an institution without ever having to be the person in the spotlight. They may be able to develop and teach fully online classes, develop interactive Web-based tutorials, or other virtual instructional material. The in-person presenter will also appreciate assistance in the development of handouts, slides, and other visual presentations, as well as any course-related Web pages. All these activities contribute to the ILI effort and in many ways make life easier for the live presenter who can then concentrate on getting the content together for the session. The presenter may also need volunteers to try out proposed activities, to attend rehearsals, and to give honest and constructive feedback. Having rovers during hands-on exercises is also useful. Working in teams and playing to the strengths of each member of the team can in the end improve the over-all instructional program.

Playing to your strengths is also relevant when assigning people to the various types of instruction that we do. In the name of equity we frequently try to develop instructional sessions as a group. The goal is to come to consensus about the session so that it is acceptable to all those who will teach it. The end product, however, may not be a session that fits all, but rather one that fits none. While it is important to agree on the goals and objectives for a given session that will be taught by a variety of people, the methods used to present that material should be left to each individual instructor.

Another consideration is preferred teaching style. Since people vary in their comfort levels regarding direct versus indirect methods, perhaps we should make our teaching assignments accordingly. While some enjoy the free and open atmosphere of the question-and-answer, active-learning, indirect format, others prefer a more structured, direct approach. The solution may be to allow more choice in the type of teaching we do, match teaching style to type of session, or to use a team teaching approach in which different types of teaching styles can be used for different segments of the session. In any case, no one should be forced into someone else's presentation mold. An extra advantage of team teaching is that it exposes us to other styles. Trying new techniques can be scary. But they can also be energizing and breath new life into our work. Watching someone else take the risk may very well be the first step toward our taking the risk ourselves.

Whatever you decide to do in relation to teaching, you must find your own voice and be true to your inner teacher (Palmer, 1998). Not everyone is equally comfortable being center stage, but everyone can contribute to the process—each according to his or her particular strengths, interests, and abilities.

FINAL REMARKS

Teaching can be fun. It is exhilarating to be in front of a group and see them gain new insight and understanding. Seeing our learners acquire not only new information and skills but also a more positive attitude toward it, and an eagerness to learn more, rewards us. Our contact with students is often limited. We have very little time to really get to know them during our sessions. By modeling our enthusiasm for the subject, by allowing students to interact with the material and experience success with it, and by showing respect for students' thoughts, opinions, and capabilities, we can create a positive learning environment. In the end we will win them over with our sincere and heartfelt passion for what we are doing. Our students leave us feeling better about both the material we have presented and their own abilities to apply what we have taught to their own lives.

EXERCISES

Exercise One

1. Think about some good teachers that you have had. What made them good (effective) teachers? Make a list of the characteristics that made them good teachers.
2. Now think about some bad teachers you have had. What made them bad (not effective) teachers? Make a list of the characteristics that made them bad teachers.
3. Group the characteristics from your lists into categories. Use these categories to identify your particular strengths and weaknesses. Be honest with yourself. Identify your strengths and weaknesses to help you design more effective instructional sessions. Try working on correcting any weaknesses that seem to be interfering with your effectiveness as a teacher.

Exercise Two

1. Identify your favorite methods for teaching. Identify those you do not like.
2. Develop an instructional piece that is not in your preferred style. Plan this piece for only a limited portion of a bigger session. Try to adjust the piece for your own comfort level.
3. You do not have to use this small instructional piece right away. Look for an opportunity where you are willing to try it out. Just thinking about using a non-preferred style may help you get used to the idea.
4. Once you do try the piece, analyze the results. How did it work? How did it make you feel? Can you adjust it to not only make the piece more effective, but to increase your comfort level with it?

5. Keep working at it until it becomes your own. This is a good method for expanding your instructional bag of tricks.

READ MORE ABOUT IT

Eble, Kenneth Eugene. 1988. *The Craft of Teaching: A Guide to Mastering the Professor's Art*. 2nd ed. *The Jossey-Bass Higher and Adult Education Series*. San Francisco: Jossey-Bass.

Elliott, Stephen N., Thomas R. Kratochwill, Joan Littlefield, and John F. Travers. 1996. *Educational Psychology: Effective Teaching, Effective Learning*. 2nd ed. Madison, WI: Brown and Benchmark.

McKeachie, Wilbert J. 1986. *Teaching Tips: A Guidebook for the Beginning Teacher*. 8th ed. Lexington, MA: D.C. Heath.

Mager, Robert F. 1997. *Making Instruction Work, or, Skillbloomers: A Step-by-Step Guide to Designing and Developing Instruction that Works*. 2nd ed., completely rev. ed. Atlanta: Center for Effective Performance.

Palmer, Parker. 1998. *The Courage to Teach: Exploring the Inner Landscape of a Teacher's Life*. San Francisco: Jossey-Bass.

Roland, David. 1997. *The Confident Performer*. Sydney; London: Currency Press; Nick Hern Books.

Smith, Terry. 1991. *Making Successful Presentations: A Self-Teaching Guide*. 2nd ed. New York: Wiley.

14

Designing ILI Programs for Diverse Populations

Many do not know that we are here in this world to live in harmony.
—Buddha

REACHING AND TEACHING DIVERSE POPULATIONS

The United States is a nation built on immigration and our communities and schools reflect this rich ethnic mix. Furthermore, increased numbers of international students are being encouraged by our colleges and universities to leave their home countries to do some or all of their higher education here. The Americans with Disabilities Act (ADA) of 1990 has raised awareness of the needs of people with disabilities in our schools and libraries (Norlin, 1992) and has put in place requirements that we accommodate those disabilities. Gender and social class issues and the needs of the older adult and other special populations can all influence the educational experience. Although the principles of good instruction should apply to every group we teach, the more we know about group characteristics and are conscious of how people can and do differ, the better we can design relevant, effective instruction.

Know Your Learners

Underlying all this is the need to know the make-up and backgrounds of the people involved in your ILI. If properly done, a Needs Assessment (see Chapter 7) will identify the various groups and special populations that comprise your intended audience. This assessment process can sensitize you to the needs of those who are different from you (in language, cultural, gender, age, ethnic or geographical background, physical or mental disabilities, and so on). Finding out more about the characteristics of these groups can help you identify ways to make the instructional experience a welcoming one for all concerned. Contacting appropriate offices or agencies in your institution or community who deal with diverse groups is key to this process.

Once you have identified the various groups, spend some time learning more about them. Pay special attention to differences that may have been identified in the way people view libraries and librarians in their cultures, child-rearing practices that can influence interpersonal interactions, and attitudes toward education. The more you know about a group, the more barriers to cultural compatibility you can eliminate when designing your instruction (Gilton, 1994; Moeckel and Presnell, 1995). Finally, engage in a little bit of self-reflection. Ask yourself how you feel about the groups with which you will be interacting. Do you have any prejudices toward the various groups or associate any stereotypes with them? Are you unfamiliar with some of the groups? Do you need to find out more about their cultures? Examine their beliefs and values for possible conflicts with your own (Elliott et al., 1996). In general, identify points of potential conflict in advance and work to correct them.

Group versus Individual Characteristics

Knowing the composition of your population is always the first step in instruction. Developing an understanding about the special needs of the groups that comprise your population is also a key element in good instructional design. However, making rash decisions about how any individual group member may respond to you or your instruction is detrimental to the process. To do so would only promote stereotypes and lead to false expectations and interpersonal misunderstanding

Each person who walks through your classroom door, visits your Website, or approaches you at the reference desk is a unique individual. At the same time, everyone belongs to and identifies with a variety of different groups. Groups tend to have their own set of affective, behavioral, and cognitive attributes. These characteristic beliefs, values, habits, and ways of thinking can affect how each group member approaches the educational process in general and ILI in particular. A person's gender, race/ethnicity, social class, religion, age, exceptionality (disabled or gifted), and geographical region can each be a contributing factor. How closely a person identifies with a group and is committed to that group's belief or value structure also affects his or her behavior.

Researchers in gender and ethnic studies, cross-cultural psychology, and sociology have contributed to our overall understanding of this issue. Although results of these studies may be mixed as to which characteristics are typical for which group, one point continues to be reinforced. These studies are discussing characteristics associated with an entire group. They are not meant to describe the characteristics of any particular member of that group. Keep in mind that these studies are talking about what is referred to as the modal personality for the group. "Modal" in this context is a statistical term referring to anything that occurs most frequently in a given group. Therefore, the term "modal personality" merely refers to traits that occur most often in a sample of the population. It does not imply that everyone in that group exhibits those traits (Shade, Kelly, and Oberg, 1997). Furthermore, people tend to belong to several groups and have varying levels of commitment to these groups. That makes using the findings of these studies to predict how a specific individual might think, feel, or behave in any particular situation difficult, if not impossible (Banks, 1993; Banks and Banks, 1993; Elliott et al., 1996; Grant and Sleeter, 1993).

Varying your presentation modes and methods in order to reach the maximum number of people in your audience is just good instructional practice. However, since we rarely know the complete background of each individual student, it is important to refrain from forming expectations about how individuals from specific groups might react to your instructional methodology. The more you know about the learners in your environment, the better you can develop a mix of instructional methods that will address the variety of cognitive, affective, and behavioral styles represented by members of your population.

Socialization, Acculturation, and Culture Clash

Group or cultural characteristics can be thought of as filters through which people view their world. They provide rules and guidelines for dealing with and interpreting events, people, and ideas encountered in daily life (Kabagarama, 1997; Shade and New, 1993). In general, these rules or filters are learned as children grow up within a given culture. Since these aspects are culturally defined, the style associated with a particular group is learned through this socialization or acculturation process. Socialization to group norms depends on children's interactions with those around them. Adult behavior acts as a model for their children to emphasize those things that a culture or group values (Vygotsky and Cole, 1978). Gender role expectations and views about race and ethnicity, as well as what constitutes exceptionality, are all transmitted from parent to child in this manner (Banks, 1993).

People who share a common culture, therefore, share a set of common rules through which they view and respond to the world around them (Shade, Kelly, and Oberg, 1997). Culture shock occurs when a person finds that the unwritten rules that have always worked before no longer apply in a new situation. Gestures, vocal quality, conversational distance, and so on vary in meaning from group to group. Furthermore, when different groups of people interact, these rules of behavior may actually conflict. Culture clash can occur when these cultural expectations differ from the demands of the environment. Each person you encounter has acquired a set of rules for verbal and nonverbal communication; orientation modes (use of time and space); social patterns, which include written and unwritten rules of behavior; and intellectual modes, including the learning styles valued by his or her group. In a very real sense, every interaction with another individual, either virtual or in-person, has the potential for culture shock.

These culturally defined behaviors can affect how people use the library, how they approach a reference desk, and how they react in an instructional setting (Gilton, 1994; Longstreet, 1978). Certain behaviors may appear strange to someone from another culture or group; however, these behaviors may appear unconventional only because they are unfamiliar. The more we know about the customs and mores of our users, the less unusual their behavior becomes and the more we can accommodate their needs with our instruction. *Culturgrams* (Brigham Young University and eMSTAR Inc., 1999) provide information about customs and mores in a variety of countries, and are a good starting point for increasing your background in these areas.

Macro versus Microcultures

When two people from different cultures meet, their different filters or worldviews can conflict, leading to uncertainty, confusion, and anxiety. Neither completely understands the rules by which the other is behaving and so can misunderstand the meaning behind that behavior. This can potentially lead to further misunderstanding and the possibility that each will wish to avoid such interactions in the future (Brigham Young University and eMSTAR Inc., 1999; Kabagarama, 1997). School culture is usually carefully defined to reflect the socialization process of the cultural majority. Any deviation from this defined norm may be viewed as either a disciplinary problem or evidence of lack of ability (Shade and New, 1993). However, the classroom is really made up of members of this cultural majority or macroculture and those who belong to a variety of microcultures (Banks, 1993). Clashes between micro and macrocultural rules and norms can result in a disproportionate number of microculture learners being labeled as behavior problems or as learning deficient (Hilliard, 1993; Shade, Kelly, and Oberg, 1997). Cultural compatibility between the school environment and the learner's home culture can therefore have a great deal of influence on individual achievement. Children from microcultures that emphasize different ways of thinking, interacting, and behaving from that of the macro or dominant culture, often find it difficult to work in a classroom climate that is counter to their accustomed ways of behaving (Shade, Kelly, and Oberg, 1997). However, changing our perspective from one where learners who are not compatible are viewed as deficient to one where these differences are appreciated and incorporated into teaching can enrich the experience for all concerned (Elliott et al., 1996; Natowitz, 1995).

CHARACTERISTICS AND VARIATIONS

Groups can vary in many ways. Rather than discuss these variations group by group, let's look at the characteristics themselves. In order to avoid the perpetuation of any cultural or group stereotypes, no group will be labeled as being more or less identified with specific characteristics. Furthermore, since every individual belongs to an assortment of groups, and thus represents a conglomerate of specific characteristics, it is better to acquire an understanding of the characteristics themselves rather than looking at those that might be associated with specific groups. Characteristics reviewed below include context factors, social interaction, separate versus connected learning, rewards and punishment, and communication styles.

Context Factors

Let's begin by looking at context factors. Generally, cultures are considered high or low context. The majority or dominant culture in the United States tends to represent the low context approach. Low context groups are very open to outsiders. Members of these groups view time in a linear fashion in which things happen sequentially rather than simultaneously. Low context cultures value competition over cooperation and promote self-sufficiency and independence rather than interdependency. In the low context approach the emphasis is on questioning and challenging authority (Banks, 1993; Elliott et al., 1996; Hall, 1976; Moeckel and Presnell, 1995; Roberts and Blandy, 1989). There is also a strong tendency toward individualism and independent work. In low context approaches, asking questions or seeking help can be frowned on as a sign of weakness (Keefer, 1993; Shade, Kelly, and Oberg, 1997).

High context groups, on the other hand, are characterized by greater interdependency among group members. High context cultures tend to be less accepting of outsiders than low context ones. Language involves subtlety in discussion in which vocal inflection, gestures, and the association of words in a sentence can influence meaning. Members of high context groups also have the ability to deal with poly-chronic time (many things happening at the same time). Cooperation is a highly valued trait in these cultures. Learning is a process of imitation and rote memory in high context cultures. The teacher is viewed as an authority figure whose statements are absorbed without question. For groups in which authority is unquestioned and cooperation is valued, neither copying from an expert or from a fellow student is considered wrong. The high context individual is rewarded for exact replication of authoritative material. The teacher, through his or her vast store of experience, is expected to be able to identify the source without further information. Citing the authority is unnecessary. In addition, since working together is encouraged, copying from a fellow student is considered a cooperative act without the negative connotations attached to it in a low context environment, so even the ideas of plagiarism and cheating are not universal concepts (Liu, 1993; Natowitz, 1995).

Many minority or non-dominant cultures in the United States represent high context groups. Problems can therefore arise when high context learners encounter an instructional experience that stresses low context characteristics. For example, learners with high context backgrounds refrain from asking questions during instruction for a number of reasons. First, since learning is dependent on absorbing authoritative material, asking questions might display their "shameful" ignorance. Furthermore, they do not wish to appear to be questioning the authority of the instructor. When asked if they understand presented material, high context individuals may politely nod and say yes rather than ask for clarification. Learners with English as a second language may also be self-conscious about speaking up in class and displaying their linguistic errors. An instructional situation that emphasizes student participation, discussion, and debate can be very uncomfortable to the high context learner. Engaging such learners in active learning experiences and group discussions can be quite challenging (Elliott et al., 1996; Gilton, 1994; Grossman, 1990; Moeckel and Presnell, 1995; Natowitz, 1995).

Growing up in a high or low context environment also influences how people perceive and process information. The high context individual tends toward a holistic worldview, while the low context individual is more a serial thinker. In other words, the high context person wishes to understand the big picture before trying to absorb specific details, while the low context person wants to start with specific examples and build up to the more global view. If you try to teach holistic learners individual skills without first presenting the context, they may become confused. Conversely, starting with the big picture may bore the low context learner who wants to acquire the skills to use specific tools and finds discussion of the overall system irrelevant (Lin, 1994). High context individuals may also be more field dependent in their learning style. The field dependent individual tends to pay attention to the whole pattern instead of the individual objects that make up the pattern and concentrates on relationships between concepts rather than individual bits of information. They learn best when material is directly relevant to their own experience (Dembo, 1988). Advance organizers can be very helpful to the high context individual. They provide a framework for the high context, field dependent learner to follow and highlight the important aspects that will be covered. Low context people, on the other hand, tend toward field independence in their learning style. Field independent learners prefer to focus on individual objects. They process information sequentially and try to impose their own structure on the material (Dembo, 1988). Low context learners appreciate the chance to try things out for themselves. Hands-on practice is very appealing to this type of learner. See Chapter 4 for more information on these learning styles concepts.

Social Interaction

The degree to which social interaction influences behavior also varies from group to group. People from high context cultures that emphasize interdependency tend to be viewed as people specialists. They are taught to be empathic with people and social dimensions and to pay less attention to impersonal or inanimate cues. These people specialists attend to facial expressions and social situation nuances and frequently use the interpersonal dimensions of a situation to determine decisions rather than depending solely on the content being presented. Classroom environment and teacher-student interactions are critical to successful instruction with these learners. Cooperative or group experiences, peer coaching, and curriculum material with social applications and meaning are particularly successful techniques for them (Shade and New, 1993). Real-world examples are crucial to this type of learner. Showing how the Web can be searched to find information about global warming and its implication for society should capture their attention. People specialists need to see that what they are learning matters to themselves, the people in their lives, and society in general. Low context cultures that favor independence and individuality pay less attention to these interpersonal and social components of learning. They are more inclined to search for topics of personal relevance rather than something with more broad-based societal implications. Learners from these cultures might be engaged by asking them to search the Web for information about a particular drug that they themselves are considering taking.

Separate versus Connected Learning

Related to social influence is the concept of separate versus connected learning (Clinchy, 1994). The heart of separate learning is detachment. Separate learners hold themselves aloof from the object being analyzed. They are impersonal and objective in their analysis and follow explicit rules and procedures to insure unbiased judgments. Personal feelings are discounted. The primary mode of discourse is the argument. Separate learners look for what is wrong in whatever they are examining. They tend to take a position that is contrary to that which they are examining regardless of whether or not they agree with that position. On the other hand, connected learners look at ideas and try to make sense out of them. Connected learners try to figure out how each position might be correct. They are not dispassionate, unbiased thinkers. Rather they bias themselves in favor of getting inside all the opinions and views. Connected learners put aside their own views and try to see the logic behind every approach. They may not in the end agree with the position, but while they are examining it they empathize with it and try to think and feel like the person who created it. Although emotion is not outlawed as it is in separate learning, reason is also present. Personal experience is drawn upon as a means of understanding what produced the idea under examination. It is a non-judgmental, non-critical approach that accepts all points of view as equally valid. While the separate thinker takes nothing at face value, the connected learner takes everything at face value. These connected learners do not try to evaluate the perspective under review. They try to understand it. Connected learners are not asking whether a viewpoint is right or wrong. They are trying to determine what it means. Separate learners favor the directive, argumentative approach while connected learners are looking for consensus. Connected learners enjoy group discussions in which all views are valued. The separate learner prefers debate and other competitive situations in which the goal is to determine which viewpoint is the most correct. Teachers who fail to appreciate and encourage both modes of learning can disenfranchise what might be large segments of their student population. Obviously no one mode of learning will appeal to both types, but allowing for some collaborative learning experiences as well as more competitive ones can widen the appeal of any instruction session and give both types the opportunity to learn in a way most suited to their individual styles.

Rewards and Punishments

The nature of reward (and punishment) can also vary from group to group. For example, some children are raised in an environment with lots of attention and frequent rewards. Progress toward a final product is encouraged through this attention and reward system. Others are encouraged to work more independently and unsupervised until the job is done. They are more comfortable working in private and do not expect rewards until they are finished. The more interdependent, socially oriented groups tend to view isolation and loss of attention as punishment. Loss of privilege or autonomy may be experienced as punishment in more individually oriented groups where independence and self-sufficiency is valued. Teachers who engage in active questioning with the goal of getting the student to the correct answer can therefore be viewed as either very helpful or quite intrusive depending upon the student's upbringing and background (Elliott et al., 1996; Grossman, 1990). Singling people out in class and asking for responses to individual questions appeals to those learners who enjoy this type of competitive challenge and the opportunity for frequent rewards. But for those who prefer a more reflective approach in which they are allowed time to think through a problem on their own, this targeted attention is disconcerting, often anxiety provoking, and can even be counter-productive to learning.

Communication Styles

The most obvious differences between groups lie in the area of communication style. Message transmission is accomplished through the verbal and nonverbal codes used in a particular group as well as a set of rules or guidelines about the appropriate application of those codes (Shade and New, 1993). These codes and rules are acquired during the socialization process. Children learn not only the vocabulary and grammar necessary to communicate. They are also oriented toward what types of information are important to transmit and receive, how to listen, methods for getting attention, appropriate vocal quality and level, and how to interpret nonverbal cues.

Communication style differences can create serious problems in and out of the classroom. Those who share the same style are better able to interpret each other's spoken and unspoken messages. They can make fairly accurate predictions about behavior based on that message. When people who do not share the same communication style attempt to interact, they are unable to correctly interpret the cues. Since they cannot count on their interpretations, they frequently fail to understand the meaning behind the message. This uncertainty is uncomfortable and leads to anxiety. In an attempt to reduce anxiety, people may fall back on stereotypes to make their predictions, or try to use their own stylistic rules to interpret the conversational cues. The net result can be communication misunderstanding, misinterpretations, and false predictions (Gross, 1997; Kabagarama, 1997).

There are many contributing factors to a communication style. First, there is the concept of personal space or comfortable conversational distance. Imagine someone whose acceptable space is one foot from the speaker trying to communicate with someone who is only comfortable with a three-foot separation and you can see how this factor can be problematic. Eye contact is another consideration. Many groups favor direct eye contact. However, others view this direct eye contact as rude, overly assertive, and intrusive. Then there is rhythm of speech and length of speaking turns. This variation is usually reflected in number and length of pauses. One person, thinking the other has completed a response, may interrupt what to the other was only a pause for thought. In addition, some people need to verbalize their thoughts. What appears to be intentional, disruptive outbursts during the communication process (or in the classroom setting) may only be the student verbalizing that he or she has gotten the concept or perceived a relationship. Physical gestures and facial expressions are also not universal. What may be acceptable to one group may turn out to be offensive to another. Whether and how people touch each other during communication is yet another parameter. Furthermore, words may acquire shades of meanings dependent upon these possible variations in intonation, facial expression, and body language (Elliott et al., 1996; Jenkins et al., 1989; Johnson, 1997; Kabagarama, 1997; Longstreet, 1978; Moeckel and Presnell, 1995; Shade and New, 1993).

Expressiveness of verbal delivery can also vary. Theatricality of presentation, amount of emotion exhibited, response rate, and energy levels all contribute to this dimension. On the one hand is the informal, animated, percussive, and active style. On the other hand is the more formal, detached, literal, and legalistic mode with a range of possibilities in-between (Seton and Ellis, 1996; Shade and New, 1993).

Immediacy Factors

Studies on what many researchers refer to as immediacy factors in in-person instruction indicate a relationship between these factors and teacher effectiveness. Immediacy cues include the use of vocal expressiveness, eye contact, gestures, relaxed body position, directing body position toward the student, smiling, movement, and proximity, as well as soliciting student views and using personal examples during instruction. The results of these studies can be extrapolated to distance education situations as well. The effectiveness of a presenter in a video or teleconference presentation can also be affected by these immediacy factors. Certainly the difficulty of maintaining some of these factors such as eye contact or proximity must be taken into account when the teacher and the learner are not sharing the same physical space. A further factor to consider is that research also indicates that members of different groups react differently to these immediacy cues. Certain immediacy cues may be positively viewed by members of one group and negatively by members of another. Groups with more formal interpersonal and communication styles might find particular expressions of immediacy uncomfortable or distasteful. Since groups vary in their reaction to immediacy cues, it stands to reason that the effectiveness of these cues will also vary (Sanders and Wiseman, 1994).

SPECIFIC GROUP ISSUES

A general understanding about how groups can vary is only part of the equation. Since most of our institutions and schools are organized in keeping with macroculture rules and norms, helping members of specific microcultures benefit from our ILI also depends on knowing something about their special needs. So let us take a look at some of these groups. Keep in mind that the general variations discussed above can be applied to the following situations. But each of the groups discussed below also has some identifiable group-related characteristics.

Adult Learners

This group is made up of people returning to school after having been in the workforce or raising a family. On the whole, they have a very strong need to succeed and may feel at a disadvantage when comparing themselves to their younger classmates. This combination can lead to very high levels of anxiety (Grabowski, 1980).

Studies on the characteristics of the adult learner indicate a different approach to learning from that of the child or adolescent. As a result a different teaching paradigm has been proposed, called andragogy, to differentiate it from the standard pedagogy used with younger learners (Knowles, 1980, 1996). A major consideration when dealing with the adult learner is that for these learners participation in the educational process is voluntary. Adult learners also bring vast amounts of life experience and highly developed life skills to the instructional setting and expect these to be acknowledged. Adult learners benefit from an atmosphere of mutual respect. In an effective adult learning environment all participants are viewed as both learners and potential teachers. No one member is regarded as having a monopoly on insight. Adopting the interactive, self-directed, and collaborative style of teaching that appeals to the adult learner requires the instructor to abandon the more authoritative "keeper of the keys" model of teaching. Knowledge is no longer dispensed in carefully measured doses. Reaching the adult learner requires an atmosphere of mutuality and shared responsibility. The adult learner will ask questions, demand clarification, and will not settle for imperfect understanding. Dissension and criticism are regarded as inevitable and desirable elements of the learning process (Brookfield, 1995; Roberts and Blandy, 1989; Sheridan, 1986).

Adult learners can be expected to take a more active role in deciding what is relevant or useful to them. The extent of their participation will therefore be shaped more by their own circumstances and perceptions than by passive acceptance of what is being presented to them. They tend to have relevant life experiences that can be drawn upon and are more motivated than younger learners. Adult learners tend to be pragmatic, practical, and extremely goal oriented. They expect to be taught skills that have direct application in their lives. These learners prefer being taken through progressive steps starting with the essentials and ending with the "nice to know" but not essential material. The adult learner has more clearly defined ideas about what is useful in an educational setting than younger learners, who may not as yet have settled on their ultimate goals. Because their time is limited adults want to learn very practical, efficient methods of gathering information and creating specific end products. Their wider life experiences and the fact that they may be juggling multiple roles lead to selection of more personally relevant research topics. These topics are frequently interdisciplinary, and thus more difficult and complex to research (Howard, 1983; Roberts and Blandy, 1989). Finally, adults often travel long distances to get to campus and may wish to use facilities closer to their home or workplace to do their research. Therefore, ILI needs to be a bit more generic for this group to prepare them for work in a variety of library environments, public as well as all levels of academic, and may focus more on what can be accomplished remotely through the use of electronic resources.

Ethnicity and Learning Styles

A good deal of research has been undertaken in an attempt to identify specific learning styles associated with particular ethnic groups. Excellent reviews of this material appear in Daisy Kabagarama's *Breaking the Ice* (1997) and Barbara Shade, Cynthia Kelly, and Mary Oberg's *Creating Culturally Responsive Classrooms* (1997). Stylistic variations that have been studied include modality preferences, field dependence versus independence, mobility needs, and cooperation versus competition. While these studies may indicate a modal personality for a given ethnic group, such as African Americans, Asian Americans, Mexican Americans, or Native Americans, they are not meant to indicate that every member of a given group will exhibit those characteristics. For a further discussion of learning styles and ethnicity, see Chapter 4.

Gender Issues

Although males and females can be members of a variety of different groups and thus exhibit characteristics associated with those groups, research has identified some specific gender-related traits or tendencies. On the whole, studies seem to indicate that females are more connected learners and males more separate learners (see above). However, although these results indicate the characteristic is gender-related, it is not gender exclusive. Again, this is an example of being able to predict group characteristics but not individual behavior. While it is more likely that females in general prefer the connected approach, some may in fact be separate learners. The same holds true for males. The United States educational system at all grade levels seems to favor separate learning, so connected learners are often forced to adapt their style to that of the school's in order to succeed.

Another gender-related variation seems to be in the way males and females approach research. One study (Burdick, 1996) examined gender differences in Carol Kuhlthau's Information Search Process (1993). Burdick was particularly interested in determining if there were differences in the emotional components that Kuhlthau had identified as accompanying the process. According to Kuhlthau, the researcher experiences uncertainty, anxiety, and lack of confidence at the beginning of the research process. These feelings diminish as the process continues. Kuhlthau marks topic formulation as the turning point in the process. At this point anxiety begins to decline and confidence starts to grow.

Burdick's study identified several gender-related differences among college students. Males emphasized information collection and detached themselves from the topic. Females were less detached and more involved emotionally with the topic. This seems to support the separate/connected research discussed above. Females were more likely to work together, while males worked more independently and were less likely to ask for help. In general, males emphasized activity while females emphasized reflection. Interestingly enough, this study showed little evidence of a gender gap in the use of computers and electronic information; however, males were more likely to describe computers as fun. Females tended to concentrate on the computer's utility. Anxiety and confidence levels did not appear to be strictly gender-related either. Females were neither more nor less likely to be confident or anxious about the research process than males. See Chapter 5 for more about various aspects of library anxiety.

There is some evidence to suggest that teacher gender can affect student-teacher interaction (Statham, Richardson, and Cook, 1994). Male teachers tend to run teacher-centric classrooms while female teachers are more student-centric in their approach. In a female led classroom, student involvement is encouraged and student input is valued. Women teachers see students as valuable resources and student participation as a source of stimulation and learning for both teacher and student. The relationship that develops between teacher and learner is also valued in the female led classroom.

Male teachers do not refer to the value of learners as contributors, collaborators, or as sources of knowledge, nor do they mention the importance of relationships that they form with their learners. Rather, they see themselves as the center of the classroom, as the sources of knowledge. Males discuss methods they might devise to convey material more effectively. Those males who prefer student involvement talk about the necessity of "permitting" it for comprehension checking and motivation. They do not regard learners as having a genuinely active part in the learning process. Male teachers tend to see themselves as the locus of learning. Females see the focus of learning in the learners. This difference can greatly influence what each gender views as good or bad learning experiences. While this study focused on teacher behavior, it is possible to extrapolate to the learners as well. Female learners may prefer the more student-centric approach and males prefer the more teacher-centric one. In any case, a mismatch between approaches favored by student and teacher can certainly lead to problems if not addressed.

International Students

Students from countries outside the United States, especially those for whom English is a second language, face many difficulties when attempting to study in this country. Library jargon such as "stacks," "checked out," and "on reserve" can present particular difficulties and should always be defined when used in instructional situations. Even those students coming to the United States from other English-speaking countries could experience problems. They may not understand the cultural nuances provided by both verbal and nonverbal cues that affect the meaning of words as spoken in this country. Furthermore, the informality of interpersonal interactions both in and out of the instructional setting may be very different from their experiences at home. The tendency toward active participation, interactive discussion, and the emphasis on independent research, all of which are so much a part of the "Western" educational process, may be quite disconcerting to someone with a very different background and upbringing. Depending upon their cultural background, international students may also have difficulty with many characteristics of Western-type libraries. These can include left to right arrangements, alphabetical arrangements used in call numbering systems, asking a woman for help, returning materials on time, doing things for themselves, questioning authority in the form of either the instructor or the written text, and learning outside the classroom. Furthermore, these students are frequently those who have excelled in their home countries and may even hold advanced degrees there. As they struggle to make sense not only of the content material but also of the language in which it is being taught and the social and cultural context that surrounds it, they may feel insecure and anxious. Finally, they may find it difficult adjusting to what seems like a loss of status. After all, they have moved from being a respected professional at home to a somewhat lowly student in an environment quite unlike their own (Ball and Mahony, 1987; MacDonald and Sarkodie-Mensah, 1988; Onwuegbuzie, 1998; Roberts and Blandy, 1989; Seton and Ellis, 1996).

Studies indicate that students for whom English is not their native language experience high levels of library anxiety (Jiao, Onwuegbuzie, and Lichtenstein, 1996; Onwuegbuzie, 1998). This may be due not only to language difficulties, but to cultural differences as well. The way libraries are organized, as well as how information is accessed, also has cultural variations. In many countries, library resources are scarce and books are considered precious commodities whose use is strictly regulated. The concepts of open stacks, traditional research tools, centralized catalogs, classification systems, and Western style reference service may all be unfamiliar to varying degrees. Self-service often does not exist in many developing countries. As a result, even doing their own photocopying may be a totally new experience to some international students. In some cultures, wealthy students are used to buying whatever sort of information they need rather than sharing material placed in reference or reserve collections for all students to use.

Many international students are reluctant to approach the reference desk with their questions. This may be due to insecurities about their communication skills or because of the lack of attention paid to reference service in their home countries. In many cultures the library is primarily a place to study. Students who are accustomed to learning by passively listening to lectures and reading and absorbing textbook material may find the idea of using the library for independent, creative research a strange one indeed. Furthermore, depending upon whether they are from a high or low context environment (see above) the concepts of copying another's work may have very different meanings. What constitutes cheating and plagiarism is culturally defined and so can vary from country to country (Ball and Mahony, 1987; Gilton, 1994; Liu, 1993; Moeckel and Presnell, 1995; Natowitz, 1995; Seton and Ellis, 1996).

People with Disabilities

Disabilities can be either physical or mental. With the passage of the ADA in 1990, many libraries have been mandated to improve library services for patrons with disabilities. The physically disabled can often be helped by the removal of physical barriers. Special devices for the visually or hearing impaired can be employed to help them make use of library materials. Workstations can be set at levels that accommodate those in wheelchairs. Computers can be equipped with software that reads Web pages to the visually impaired user for example. People with learning disabilities, however, present a special challenge since their disability may not be obvious (Norlin, 1992). However, a combination of common sense, sensitivity, courtesy, and good teaching practices goes a long way to make people with disabilities feel welcome in our libraries and our classrooms. For example, facing the class when you speak, speaking clearly and at a moderate rate of speed, and checking for comprehension are examples of good teaching techniques that will be helpful to all of your learners. But these techniques are crucial if you have hearing-impaired people in the group. If given enough notice, you might also request that a signer be assigned to the classroom for the hearing impaired. Reading aloud the material written on the board will help the visually impaired learners in your group, as will repeating important points (Roberts and Blandy, 1989). Do your best to teach in a mix of mediums. Use verbal as well as written explanations followed by hands-on practice. This approach will ensure you reach everyone, regardless of learning styles or disabilities (Applin, 1999). The key is sensitivity. Be aware of where your learners might need help, identify the barriers that make it difficult for your physically or mentally challenged learners to acquire the IL skills they need, and modify your instruction accordingly.

Socioeconomic Factors

In many ways, socially or economically disadvantaged learners are very similar to international students. They too have had experiences and backgrounds very different from that of the environment in which they now find themselves. It might help to return for a moment to the idea of macro and microcultures. The socially or economically disadvantaged student may have grown up in a microculture with its own rules of behavior and communication styles (Elliott et al., 1996). Their accustomed styles may seem at odds with that of the macroculture to which they must now adapt. As a result, these learners often experience high levels of anxiety and feel unwelcome and uncomfortable in what to them is a strange, new world. They may also be unfamiliar with the culture of both the school in general and the library in particular, and need to be introduced to rules under which they must now operate (Roberts and Blandy, 1989). Be particularly careful about jargon and making assumptions about previous library experience. Care and consideration, as well as good teaching practices, should help these learners adapt to and make the most of ILI.

SOLUTIONS

Our schools, communities, and libraries are made up of a rich mix of diverse individuals. How can we accommodate them all in our ILI? One solution is to develop specialized instruction directed at a particular group. Teaching to a homogeneous population offers the advantage of addressing the group's specific needs. However, targeting special groups (international students, older adults, or people with disabilities for example) must be done carefully and diplomatically. The members of a particular group may not wish to be identified as needing special attention. They may feel they are being labeled as less competent than the general population. Part of your Needs Assessment should be to contact agencies and offices that deal with the special groups. In doing so, try to determine how the group members themselves wish to receive instruction. Would they be interested in targeted instruction or would they prefer to be incorporated into the general group?

Opportunities to actually teach to a targeted, homogenous group may be rare. But the likelihood that the learners you encounter in any ILI situation will be representatives of a variety of groups is high indeed. So how do you cope? First, know the composition of your overall population and educate yourself on the various characteristics of as many members of this population as possible. Then be sensible and alert to the needs of all your learners. And finally, vary your teaching techniques and delivery modes in order to maximize the possibility of reaching everyone you are trying to teach. No matter how we categorize group differences, varying your methods and mixing approaches increases the likelihood that you will reach everyone regardless of their background, culture, gender, language, age, communication mode, or learning styles. Add large doses of sensitivity, courtesy and mutual respect, and clear and jargon-free language and you have the formula for teaching in a diverse environment.

The rules, as always, are:

- Know your audience
- Relate in a positive manner to your audience
- Help your audience put the information into a context that makes sense to them

One stylistic change teachers often find helpful when operating in a diverse environment is to move from the teacher-centric to the student-centric mode of behaving. Involve the learners in the process and invite their participation. Demonstrate or model what you are trying to teach. Observational learning is reinforced in many communities and cultures. By showing rather than telling, the teacher can overcome both behavioral and communication barriers that make it difficult for learners from a variety of backgrounds to process the information. Keep in mind that your learners do not all share the same frame of reference for the material you are teaching—they have the added problem of trying to fit the information into a context that makes sense to them. You can help them by starting with some kind of conceptual framework or mental model (see Chapters 3 and 5). This method also appeals to global thinkers who prefer to see the big picture before being presented with the individual pieces.

Although many learners come to our instruction with very little experience with active or collaborative learning methods, these very techniques can be applied to great advantage in a multicultural, diverse setting. By encouraging learners to interact with each other, many cultural and language barriers can be overcome. Concepts can be discussed in the context of each student's traditional values of heritage, history, custom, and language (Johnson, 1997). Working in group settings provides the opportunity for many different ideas to be expressed. Learners, who may be reluctant to speak up in the larger forum, may be willing to do so in the smaller, more intimate situation that small group work provides. Collaborative methods also provide opportunities for learners to take a more responsible role for their own education. It improves interpersonal skills, helps develop critical thinking, and encourages the recognition, acceptance, and value of diverse opinions (Hanson, 1995). See discussions of active and collaborative learning in Chapter 6.

However, since the idea of active participation is unfamiliar to many, instructors must make opportunities for everyone to contribute and respect those who wish to participate on a minimal level or not at all. Learners may opt out of discussions due to past unpleasant experiences in the academic setting because they lack confidence in their language skills or because they are reflective types who need to think about a topic for longer than is allowed in a quick-paced, interactive discussion. Set up a variety of situations that encourage different types of participation. In other words, invite them all to the dance by giving everyone a chance to perform each in his or her own way. See Chapters 6 and 13 for suggestions about indirect and active learning techniques.

Giving learners the opportunity to practice what is being taught is also valuable when dealing with a diverse population. It allows learners to test out what they think they understand from your demonstration, lecture, Web-based material, or other forms of instruction. What receives nods of understanding when described may prove more perplexing and difficult when put into practice (Hanson, 1995; MacDonald and Sarkodie-Mensah, 1988). Hands-on practice, therefore, can serve as a comprehension check for both in-person and remote synchronous instructional situations. It also allows the instructor to offer immediate feedback, answer specific questions, and address individual concerns that learners may not have been willing to bring up to the full group for fear of appearing stupid. Web-based tutorials can also provide opportunities for practice. Be sure to build in mechanisms for feedback such as e-mailing quizzes to the instructor for review or self-correcting exercises that provide the learner with information about the appropriateness of his or her responses.

Appealing to a variety of sensory modes is also good practice, especially in a diverse environment. Handouts, guided exercises, and print and Web-based teaching aids are especially important. Many learners may find it difficult to follow the spoken lesson due to language, learning styles, or communication differences. However, they may be able to follow along in print, on a Web page, or through the use of PowerPoint or other presentation software programs. Remember to use the chalk or whiteboard, or even a flip chart, to emphasize important points. Combine verbal instructions with visual cues and hands-on experiences to accommodate auditory, visual, and kinesthetic learners (Jiao, Onwuegbuzie, and Lichtenstein, 1996). Finally, prepare glossaries of library terminology. Remember that learners vary in their experience with and exposure to the types of services and procedures you will be discussing. If you have a large international student population, consider developing glossaries in both English and several native languages. See ACRL's Instruction Section's Instruction for Diverse Populations "Multilingual Glossary Language Table" (www.libraries.rutgers.edu/is/publications/glossary) for assistance. Try to avoid the use of jargon, little-known words, ambiguous statements, abbreviations, and acronyms. If you must use them, make sure you define the terms and refer learners to glossaries. Repeat important points to emphasize their significance. Learners may be too shy or embarrassed to ask for clarification. Above all, avoid using ethnic or culturally tinged words or phrases that might be offensive to some or all of your learners (Downing and Diaz, 1993; Liu, 1993; MacDonald and Sarkodie-Mensah, 1988).

Provide a friendly and welcoming environment. Indicate by words and deeds that you recognize and value the diversity represented in your population. Developing a climate that acknowledges, accepts, understands, and accommodates various interpersonal and communication styles is crucial, especially for those learners who have felt disenfranchised in the past. Rather than forcing the learner to choose between his or her own cultural style and that of the majority or macroculture represented by the educational system, the culturally responsive teacher allows learners to build bridges between both worlds (Shade, Kelly, and Oberg, 1997; Shade and New, 1993). Remember that learners work best and are more highly motivated when the curriculum reflects their own culture, experiences, and perspective. Reflect on how you felt in situations where you were viewed as an "outsider." Empathize with learners who do not find themselves reflected in textbooks, instructional material, or even the library's collections. Work at making your material relevant to everyone. Be inclusive, not exclusive, in your illustrative choices and examples (Downing and Diaz, 1993). Whenever you have a choice, use examples that reflect diversity rather than homogeneity.

Teaching to different cultures and different learning styles requires a shift in how instruction is organized. It depends upon the use of more interactive, student-centered, problem-solving, self-directed forms of teaching. Research indicates that cooperative or collaborative learning experiences are especially successful in reaching a variety of learners. Problem- or case-based instruction in which learners can bring their own perspectives and experiences into play as they deal with some real-life issue has also been shown to be successful (Shade, Kelly, and Oberg, 1997).

FINAL REMARKS

While you need to be familiar with the demographics of your institution, it is important to avoid making assumptions based on easy group stereotypes. Effective teaching in a diverse environment requires viewing each student as an individual and not merely a representative of a specific group (Downing and Diaz, 1993). Avoid making judgments based on age, physical appearance, speech, or behavior. Both teacher and student bring certain expectations about diverse groups to the classroom. The resulting interactions affect classroom atmosphere. As a teacher, you must be aware of your own expectations and attitudes. Become sensitive to the reasons why you react to certain people in particular ways. If the interaction is a negative one, try to identify the cause and determine what you can do to change the interaction. Such self-analysis will help you develop more respectful interactions that will result in a better learning environment for everyone (Elliott et al., 1996).

Remember that your attitude toward your learners has enormous influence on the effectiveness of your instruction. If you have formed expectations about your learners based on physical, cultural, gender, age, or socioeconomic factors, you will consciously or unconsciously communicate them to your learners. Learners will quickly grasp the message and react to it accordingly. The impact of these reciprocal interactions is clear and easy to observe (Elliott et al., 1996). You expect certain behavior from the student. The student interprets your spoken and unspoken message and responds accordingly. You have set up a self-fulfilling feedback loop where learners perform only as well as you think they will. But you can make this situation work for you. Develop a teaching style that communicates a positive attitude about everyone's abilities. Expect the best from everyone, let them know that is what you expect and that is what you will receive. It is up to the teacher to create a climate in which everyone feels welcome, all learners are viewed as competent, and all ways of thinking are accepted (Shade, Kelly, and Oberg, 1997). Many principles associated with the Humanist theories of learning are applicable here. See Chapter 3 for more on the Humanist approach to teaching.

Our classrooms can serve as laboratories where people from different backgrounds, cultures, and experiences can interact and broaden their perspectives. Raising your own consciousness about all types of diversity will help you create instructional sessions that are more meaningful and effective for all of your learners. Encourage your institution to offer staff development opportunities so that you and your colleagues can enhance your understanding about all members of your population. The more we know about people the easier it is for us to respond appropriately (Liu, 1993; Moeckel and Presnell, 1995; Natowitz, 1995; Norton, 1992). Becoming knowledgeable about your population will alert you to the needs of all your learners. It will help you create an atmosphere of mutual respect where diversity is not only recognized but also celebrated and valued.

EXERCISES

Working with Homogeneous Groups

1. Make a list of all the groups that are represented in your populations.
2. Write down all that you know about each group.
3. Now write down information that you need to find out.
4. Research the groups to check the accuracy of what you know and to fill in the gaps in your knowledge.
5. Pretend that you were preparing instruction for each of the groups listed. Assume that the group would be homogeneous (made up of members of only one group). What three things would you include in your instructional plan to make it especially appropriate for each of the groups you have identified? Make a separate list for each group.

Working with Heterogeneous Groups

1. Now assume that you are preparing instruction for a group made up of representatives of all the groups listed in the first exercise.
2. Review your responses to the fifth step. Can you combine the methods identified for each group into an instructional design that accommodates the needs of all these different groups?
3. List three methods, techniques, or strategies that you would employ to ensure the effectiveness for instruction for this type of heterogeneous group.

READ MORE ABOUT IT

Banks, James A., and Cherry A. McGee Banks. 1993. *Multicultural Education: Issues and Perspectives.* 2nd ed. Boston: Allyn and Bacon.
Kabagarama, Daisy. 1997. *Breaking the Ice: A Guide to Understanding People from Other Cultures.* 2nd ed. Boston: Allyn and Bacon.
LOEX. National LOEX Library Instruction Conference. 1989. *Reaching and Teach-*

ing Diverse Library User Groups. 16th Annual LOEX Library Instruction Conference, edited by Teresa Mensching. Ann Arbor, MI: Pierian Press.

Metoyer-Duran, Cheryl. 1993. *Gatekeepers in Ethnolinguistic Communities*. Norwood, NJ: Ablex.

Shade, Barbara J., Cynthia Kelly, and Mary Oberg. 1997. *Creating Culturally Responsive Classroom*. 1st ed. Washington, DC: American Psychological Association.

15

Delivering ILI in
Various Environments

No man is an island, entire of himself; every man is a piece of the continent.
—John Donne

IL AS NATIONAL MANDATE

One of the most fundamental aspects of Information Literacy is the desire to promote lifelong learning (ALA-Presidential Committee on Information Literacy, 1989). To accomplish this requires libraries at all levels and in all environments to participate in ILI. Although instruction in some form has long been incorporated into the mission of most academic and school libraries in the past, it has played a much smaller part in public and special libraries. However, advances in information technology and the proliferation of information in both print and electronic formats have created an even more pressing need to develop an information literate society. Both the Secretary's Commission on Achieving Necessary Skills (U.S. Department of Labor-Secretary's Commission on Achieving Necessary Skills, 1991) and America 2000 (U.S. Department of Education, 1991) can be viewed as national policy statements. Both called for the restructuring of the American educational system with the goals of producing a population equipped for the Information Age (Doyle and ERIC Clearinghouse on Information & Technology, 1994; Spitzer et al., 1998). These reports emphasize the necessity of lifelong learning, critical thinking and problem solving skills, and the importance of being able to use a variety of information technologies. Implicit in all of this is the idea that it is more valuable to know how to find and utilize useful information than to merely memorize and store specific facts that will probably quickly become out of date.

In 1994 the United States Congress passed legislation creating Goals 2000 thus granting legal status to the aims of America 2000. A national mandate, thus, existed to not only promote higher levels of individual student achievement, but to also build a globally competitive American work force (Doyle and ERIC Clearinghouse on Information & Technology, 1994; Spitzer et al., 1998). Six goals were proposed covering issues to be addressed ranging from education of preschool-aged children to adult literacy. Goals 2000 committed the resources of the government and the country to strengthening the public education system nationwide ("Goals 2000 and America 2000," 1994).

Three of the six goals are of particular interest to the library and information science profession and to the concept of IL. These three goals highlight the importance of information in our society, and thus have implications for the various types of libraries that provide access to and instruction in the use of that information. Goal One stresses the preschool years and the formative, affective aspects of developing a value for information. Goal Three is concerned with K–12 schooling and points to the attainment of skills necessary for lifelong learning. Goal Five addresses the widespread application of skills to employment and citizenship. IL skills are at the heart of successful attainment of each of these three goals (Doyle and ERIC Clearinghouse on Information & Technology, 1994; Doyle, 1992). A closer examination of each of these goals indicates how they can be tied to specific types of libraries (public, school, academic, and special).

LIBRARIES AND NATIONAL GOALS

Goal One and the Public Library

This goal calls for all children to start school ready to learn. Preschool children should be encouraged to value information through positive interactions with parents and other role models. Strong public libraries promote this goal not only by providing a place for the preschool child to learn about and gain access to information, but also by creating an environment where the adults in a community can interact in a positive way with information and learn to value it. These adults then encourage their children to do likewise.

Goal Three and the School Library

This goal stresses learning how to process information and apply information to problem solving and critical thinking skills required in an active learning format. The inquiry approach is basic to this active learning and requires an information-rich environment. The emphasis here is on resource-based learning and the library is viewed as an extension of the classroom. A strong, proactive school library that works in close collaboration with the classroom teacher is essential to the success of this approach.

Goal Five and the Academic and Special Libraries

This goal focuses on adult literacy and skills for employment and citizenship. It recognizes the need for addressing IL at the college level, but it also discusses the necessity of having an information literate workforce. Goal Five encourages both communities and businesses to support the concepts of IL and lifelong learning. It also promotes the idea of resource sharing among public and business institutions. So Goal Five has implications for special, academic, and even public libraries.

UNIFYING THEMES

The ALA 1989 report, the SCANS report, and Goals 2000 have much in common. The unifying thread running through all these initiatives is the need for an IL populace. The goal of creating an IL populace impacts libraries in all types of environments and serves as the impetus for various types of libraries to work more closely together to provide a framework in which IL permeates all aspects of life. These initiatives identify a continuum and a connection between all libraries. IL is no longer seen as the sole property of the K–College environment. The contributions of industry and the community are also highlighted, thus creating a place for the public and special library in the mix. From the community to schools to colleges and on to the workplace, people are expected to be able to access, use, understand, and apply information. The shared aim is to develop people who are ready to enter the workforce as competent, ethical, and productive users of information and technology (Ark, 2000). All four environments must work together in a coordinated and synergistic manner if the ultimate goal of an IL populace is to be reached. Thus the teaching role that has so long been associated with the school and academic libraries has now been expanded to the public and special libraries as well.

Advances in information technology and the delivery of information are also contributing to this synergy. In a world where a growing number of libraries truly have no walls, and libraries emphasize access over ownership, the concept of library as a place loses its meaning. Resources that were previously available only in the library are now accessible in the user's home, office, and even in Internet cafes attached to coffee shops and restaurants. Users not only can find information remotely, that material can be delivered (albeit sometimes for a fee) directly to their doorsteps. Document delivery either in print or via electronic transfer of information is rapidly becoming more and more standard.

A further consideration for remote users is licensing agreements that limit use of certain resources to specific user groups. For example, a remote user may be able to visit a particular library's Web page but will be blocked from using certain resources due to license agreements that restrict use to people with authorized IP addresses only. Remote users are understandably confused and frustrated when they can freely use a library's online catalog and certain publicly accessible databases such as the National Library of Medicine's PubMed® system, but are asked for a password when trying to search other proprietary databases.

The impact of these remote users needs to be examined in all types of libraries. Although libraries will continue to be defined by the ways in which they relate to their parent organizations, their clientele will develop more and more mixed loyalties. People may go to the most conveniently located library rather than one to which they have some sort of institutional association. They may visit many different libraries via those libraries' Web pages. If a specific library is no longer identified as an individual's special place to go for information, then all libraries must work together to provide the ILI that is necessary to make use of the information however and wherever it is found.

THE ENVIRONMENTS

What Are They?

Although this brave new technological world has somewhat blurred the distinctions between types of library, environments are still typically categorized into four distinct groups—public, school, academic, and special. Each has a unique relationship to the organization or institution in which it exists. While people of all ages may indeed use the public library, and community members may consult the resources found in academic libraries, each type of library considers certain users its primary clientele. The public library's main function is to serve its community's recreational and self-educational needs as well as the needs of school-age children in the area. The school and academic library share the educational goals of their parent institutions and contribute to the instructional and research needs of its students, faculty, and staff. The special library's job is to support the organization's employees in the production of their jobs and to contribute to the overall success of the organization.

The relationship between the library and its parent organization affects the way in which instruction is undertaken in that library. Public libraries, with their varied and diverse user groups, have traditionally tended toward individualized instruction and teach-yourself or self-help type instruction. Instruction is frequently one on one, and often occurs via the reference desk interaction. Workshops targeted toward particular user groups such as older adults are also a feature of the public library environment. Since the local public library may be many people's only means of computer access, these libraries have taken on a major responsibility for providing instruction in computer use to their constituents. Public libraries also rely heavily on signs, handouts, point-of-use instruction, and CAI and other electronic tutorials that people can use whenever the need arises.

School and academic libraries tend to work in conjunction with classroom teachers and faculty. ILI is intended to support the curriculum and works best when integrated with it. In both environments the aim of instruction is to provide the student with skills that will eventually result in his or her ability to be independent information users. Teaching tends to be to groups and is meant to promote self-reliance and the acquisition of transferable skills. The differences between school and academic library settings center around age level, and also on the magnitude of the enterprise. The K–12 school librarian must be concerned with issues of developmental readiness and appropriate levels of both materials and instruction. The academic librarian deals with a wide range of adult learners including those fresh out of high school and up to those older adults who are returning to school after along absences. In general, the school librarian is dealing with a narrower range of subject material, a smaller body of research resources, and fewer users than the academic librarian. However, ILI for students in both settings works best when integrated into the curriculum. Strong partnerships between the teachers and the librarian are crucial for this type of ILI to succeed. Faculty and staff are also part of the school and academic librarians user group. An awareness of new technological initiatives and educational reform movements provides the school and academic librarian with opportunities to be proactive in offering ILI support related to these changes.

Librarians in a special library setting tend to emphasize service over teaching. Instruction is tied to public relations and efficiency. Demonstrations and promotional outreach are aimed at alerting the library's potential clientele to new services and products available through the library. Efficiency is the watchword here. Instruction is for the purpose of helping employees become more aware of the library and its resources. It may not always be intended to teach them how to use those resources themselves. Much like the public library, individual information needs frequently are unique. So instruction tends toward the individual rather than the group setting. Furthermore, due to the growth of intranets and other electronic communication technologies, the special librarian often communicates with an invisible clientele that rarely if ever enters the library in-person. Online tutorials in the use of many of the library's resources can also be mounted on the company's intranet, providing ILI wherever and whenever the employee needs it.

What Do They Have in Common?

Although the environment in which each type of library operates has a strong influence on how, when, and where instruction takes place, many of the principles discussed in other chapters certainly still apply. Information professionals need to be familiar with their environmental climate and culture in order to design appropriate and effective instruction. Needs Assessments are still crucial before you begin the planning process. Clear, appropriate goals and objectives must be written. Mode and methods have to be selected and instructional efforts should be evaluated for effectiveness. But the success of your programs also depends upon making the right connections in your environment, finding the appropriate partners in your institution, and promoting the value of your programs to your community at large.

Find out who needs to be convinced, get them involved, continue to keep them informed about your successes and any need for new programs that might have been identified as you go along. You may have to start small and build on your successes. Use your assessments and evaluations to gain more support. Show how the library is a key element in the environment's goals and mission. Who the key players are will differ in each environment and thus methods of contact, promotion, and communication will also vary. But the principles remain the same. Know your population (both your users and the movers and shakers in your environment), target your programs accordingly, and promote the reasons for your decisions with the people who can help you make it happen. The next sections will look at each type of library and highlight unique characteristics and the resultant special aspects of ILI in that environment. Since the overriding goal is to promote IL and life-long learning to all our users, the type of libraries will be discussed in the order in which they relate to Goal 2000, discussed above.

SPECIAL CHARACTERISTICS AND CONSIDERATIONS: NEEDS, POPULATION, AND RELATION TO PARENT ORGANIZATION

The Public Library

Goal One is directed at preparing preschool children for school. Its overall aim is to promote the value of information in general and the use of information in reaching decisions in daily life. Children are invited into the process directly through library programs, and indirectly by observing the behavior of adults in the community. The ultimate goal is to prepare both children and adults to utilize information productively, in any context and from any source. Underlying this goal is the idea that every American should be able to access information and that communities should provide facilities for them to do so (Doyle and ERIC Clearinghouse on Information & Technology, 1994). The public library through its relationship to its community can provide the focus for this goal. To do so, it must promote itself, through its instructional efforts, as the place to go for information (Doyle and ERIC Clearinghouse on Information & Technology, 1994; Jackson, 1995) and to learn about how to access that information both in the library and remotely.

The public library is a reflection of the community it serves. The users in a public library can represent a diverse mix of ages, cultures, ethnic groups, educational and socioeconomic levels, lifestyles, and languages. Information needs tend to be specific and are often unique to the particular individual requesting help. In addition, use of the library can be intermittent and random. The diversity of user needs coupled with a lack of consistent contact has resulted in public libraries tending to adopt a more informal and ad hoc approach to instruction (Woods et al., 1990).

The public library's mission and its role in the community depend upon determining the needs of those who live in that community. As communities differ, so do the roles, missions, and activities of the library it serves. In order for a library to best meet its public's current and future needs, a thorough Needs Assessment must be undertaken. For the public library, a crucial part of the Needs Assessment stage of the planning process is a Community Needs Analysis (Woods et al., 1990).

All Needs Assessments start with an examination of the library's target population. See Chapter 7 for details on how to design a Needs

Assessment. Since the public library tends to serve a more diverse population than other types of libraries, information should be collected about how the library's population vary as to age, sex, family life cycle (singles, young marrieds, retirees), income, occupation, educational levels, race/ethnicity, cultures, languages spoken, etc. This data can be found in census reports, the city planner's office, the zoning office, and other government agencies. In addition find out who uses and who does not use the library. For what purposes do people use the library? What barriers keep others from using the library? Are there geographical or physical barriers to use? Do some members of the community feel that they are not welcome in the library? Interviews with users, community leaders and representatives from community organizations, focus groups, and surveys of both users and non-users can provide this information.

The community analysis also needs to look at transportation. Do people use public transportation or own their own cars? How difficult is it to get to the library? Look at travel time, parking, traffic patterns, and public transportation routes and schedules. The community's transportation office as well as its city planning office should have this data. Scheduling in-person instruction may depend on these travel considerations. If a large proportion of your population has transportation difficulties, issues of distance or remote education may need to be considered.

The businesses, stores, and organizations (cultural, educational, and recreational) that are located in the community also help to define it. Check on what types of businesses or industrial organizations are located in your community. Where do people shop? Are there daily, weekly, or seasonal patterns to their shopping behavior? What types of organizations are located in your community? Can you identify times of the year when these organizations are most active? Newspapers, community directories, telephone books, and the Chamber of Commerce should be able to provide this information.

Once the community scan is completed, you will be able to determine the needs of the various groups that make up your population. You will probably identify more groups and more programs than can be handled by your library. Remember that part of your Needs Assessment is to determine what your library is currently doing and a rational examination of facilities, staff, and budget constraints that might impact future programs. List all the possibilities and then prioritize them. You may be faced with some hard decisions as you select which groups and programs to concentrate on. If you have more than one primary user group with a variety of needs, where will you focus your efforts first? Community politics and your library's long- and short-term goals will affect your selection of which programs to implement. Your goal is to make the most positive, productive impact as possible on the community based on the library's available resources (Woods et al., 1990).

Use your Needs Assessment to identify potential inter-institutional partners. Local agencies, businesses, and even academic institutions may be willing to form alliances to provide resources and services to members of the community. Local businesses may be willing to provide financial support for equipment or supplies in exchange for a display in the library acknowledging their contributions (and thus creating positive public relations for the business itself). Schools with limited resources and local companies with no library of their own may wish to use the public library as their instructional setting. Academic libraries might provide information about when it is appropriate to refer public library users to a nearby academic institution and some information about the type of services and resources that would be available to these community users. Make sure you determine how the responsibility for delivering these joint efforts will be shared. Where will instruction actually take place? Who will pay for materials? Does the proposed joint effort fit into the overall goals of the library's IL plan? Finally, how does working with the outside agency impact the programs and services for those who are more regular users of the library (Woods et al., 1990)?

Inter-institutional cooperation and collaborative efforts with government agencies, community groups, and the private sector can pay off in many ways. Libraries that actively form alliances with other organizations learn even more about the information needs of their community. Teachers and schools are the natural allies of the public library in promoting the concept of information as a useful commodity. Business and industry are taking a steadily increasing role in workforce development. Employers are beginning to perceive the importance of having IL employees, thus opening a wedge for the enterprising public librarian. Connecting with social service agencies also opens the door for libraries to respond more directly to societal needs. Overall, partnerships and alliances such as these are a way to work effectively in the community, overcome institutional isolation, and promote the value of information and the library's role in making that information available to all (Jackson, 1995). These alliances also create positive public relations for the library and may even pay off financially. The more friends the library has in the community the more likely it will be seen as a valuable asset that deserves fiscal support.

The public library is used for both recreational and educational purposes. The users' ultimate goal determines which library resources they use and how they use these resources, as well as the types of interactions they have with the library staff. How and why a person is using the library will also determine what type of instructional effort will be most appropriate and effective in that particular situation (Webb, 1986; Woods et al., 1990). Although all users at some point will probably need to know how to use the library's catalog to locate relevant material, the way they learn how to use that catalog varies. The casual users or browsers tend to use the library in a rather hit-or-miss fashion. Since they are only intermittent users, they have little need for intensive instruction in the use of the library or its resources. What they learn during one visit may or may not be relevant to subsequent visits, so they tend to have little or no interaction with the staff and try to be as self-reliant as possible. These browsers appreciate a good sign system that directs them to appropriate areas of the facility, and handouts and self-help guides (both print and electronic) they can refer to as they make their way through the library. Browsers also like orientation programs that can help familiarize the user with the library's layout, its floor plan, and the general services offered by the library.

People researching the answer to a specific question also use public libraries. These researchers become involved with library staff and resources when they need help finding information on a specific question. They are very focused and project-oriented. Instruction for the researcher generally occurs during the course of a reference interaction and is specific to the question at hand. Researchers also like point-of-use guides and online tutorials so that they can teach themselves how to use specific resources at the moment they need them. Systems that are designed with easy-to-understand interfaces and readily available help screens access the researcher to move quickly from information need to appropriate resource. Context-sensitive help screens in online catalogs and databases are of particular use to both the browser and the researcher.

Finally, there is the independent learner whose aim is more extensive than other users. These learners tend to invest longer time commitments to their projects and are more likely to approach library staff for assistance. They also tend to make more use of services and resources (both print and electronic) provided by the library. These independent learners are interested in more in-depth instruction in the overall research process and in the use of specific resources. Since they have made a long-term time commitment to this project, they are often willing to attend more formal types of library instruction programs or meet with librarians for individual consultations. Pathfinders and other print handouts that help guide the learner through the research process are also useful, as are Web-based or online instructional materials.

Formal instruction programs are developed in the academic and school library settings because of the way the library relates to the educational process. Group needs are identified and instruction can be implemented within the framework of the academic or school enterprise. The parallel for this sort of sustained instructional contact does not generally exist in the public library where populations are diverse and it is difficult to identify a commonality of backgrounds among users. Instructional needs in such an environment are amorphous and constantly shifting. The focus in the public library is on the independent, individual library user and his or her unique needs (Jackson, 1995). It makes sense, therefore, that instruction in public libraries has tended to center around informal, one-on-one instruction, either through the reference desk or via individual consultation appointments. The typical public library user says "Teach me what I need to know and do it now! Don't make me wait and don't embarrass me by forcing me to exhibit my ignorance in a group setting." Public libraries' instruction often relies on methods that allow for the most flexibility of presentation. The emphasis is on materials that support self-directed learning. Signs, video or audio tapes, CAI, print materials, tutorials, and point-of-use instruction are all heavily used in the public library setting (Woods et al., 1990).

Many forces currently in play are causing this to change somewhat. Although there will always be a need for informal, ad hoc, individualized instruction, the national emphasis on IL, lifelong learning, and the development of an informed citizenry has created a place for more formal instruction in the public library environment. These concepts fit closely with the historic values of the public library as the "People's Universities" (Jackson, 1995). Furthermore, the constant and rapid changes in information technology have created global instructional needs that cut across the diversity of groups that use the public library. Though users may have varying levels of sophistication regarding technology, they all share a need to be brought up to date on these technological advances as they happen.

The public library is the natural place for people in a community to come together and explore this new technology. Public libraries such as the Deerfield Public Library in Illinois and the New York Public Library's Science, Industry, and Business Library offer open classes that promote the use of both print and electronic resources. Classes on how to search the Web are particularly popular (Bentley, 1997; Spitzer et al., 1998). Librarians, in these settings, provide instruction not only on the latest technological advances but also use the opportunity to advance the cause of IL by showing how the technology fits into the bigger picture of information access and research. Web sites such as the "Virtual Reference Desk" (Information Institute of Syracuse, 2000) and the "Internet Public Library" (University of Michigan School of Information, 2000) allow people to access typical public library reference and instructional services without ever going to the library at all.

The vision embraced by IL challenges libraries to make a difference in people's lives and calls upon libraries to contribute to the betterment of society by creating a population of independent seekers of truth (ALA-Presidential Committee on Information Literacy, 1989). Public libraries have historically seen themselves as committed to the needs of both their particular community and society at large. It is only natural and right that the public library has become the primary setting for its constituents to come together and develop the skills necessary to become IL individuals.

The School (K–12) Environment

Goal Three is directed toward information literacy in the school-age child. It targets a well-stocked school library, offering access to both print and non-print resources, as critical to the integration of information literacy into the K–12 curriculum. Goal Three encourages the close collaboration between the K–12 librarian and the classroom teacher in support of classroom and IL goals. Educational reform movements that emphasize resource-based learning rather than the lecture and textbook method of instruction place the school library at the focal point of the educational process. School librarians are seen as playing a vital role in this educational process as teachers move away from the traditional teacher-centered model to one that emphasizes real-world or authentic student-centered problem solving (Doyle and ERIC Clearinghouse on Information & Technology, 1994; Pappas, 1998). The library becomes the school's information hub, and is viewed as crucial to preparing today's children for an information-based society in which information skills are survival skills (Kuhlthau, 1995).

The evolution of the school library's role from the 1950s to the present can be characterized in four stages. In the early and mid–1950s the concentration was on collections. The 1960s saw the library program used to promote the usefulness of the collections. A major emphasis on instruction developed in the 1970s and 1980s. Today's focus is on integrating instruction into the curriculum and a move toward teaching process rather than the use of individual tools (Stripling, 1996).

Several process-oriented methods for presenting ILI in the school environment have been developed over the past several years. These include the Big Six Skills Approach (Eisenberg and Berkowitz, 2000), the Information Search Process (Kuhlthau, 1989), Pathways to Knowledge (Pappas and Tepe, 1997), Virginia Rankin's meta-cognition approach (Rankin, 1988), and the Research Process Model (Stripling and Pitts, 1988). All of these methods are based on current learning theory that emphasizes personal knowledge construction and a more holistic approach that integrates content and process skills. This movement toward a more integrated, process approach to ILI closely mirrors current school reform initiatives that emphasize thinking and inquiry skills and the fostering of communities of learners. Both educational reform movements and the process-oriented ILI approach challenge students to assume responsibility for their own learning in today's global society where information and knowledge are the key elements for success (Harada and Tepe, 1998; Stripling, 1996).

These more constructivist models of learning promote active participation in the learning process, and direct interaction with materials used to support that learning. Resource-based teaching techniques are a good fit with this model. In this approach, learners spend time prior to engaging in library research determining what understandings, experiences, and knowledge they already possess. It is only after they have identified what they know, and even more importantly what additional information they need to find out, that they proceed to the library to engage in research. Both teacher and librarian work together to provide learners with opportunities to expand and extend their baseline understanding and then to construct new knowledge for themselves (Hainer, 1998; Paige, 1996; Rankin, 1988). For examples of how teachers and school librarians at all grade levels are applying this constructivist approach to Web-based instruction, see WebQuest (Dodge, 2000). A WebQuest makes use of Web resources to promote an inquiry-oriented learning experience. WebQuests focus on using information rather than just locating it. They are intended to promote the analysis, synthesis, and evaluation of information, and as such support the goals of IL in the school environment.

Position papers and standards published by state and national organizations, both here and in Canada, are emphasizing this new image for the school librarian. The librarian's role is described as having shifted from passive "keeper of information" to key participant in the learning process (ALA-American Association of School Librarians and Association for Educational Communications and Technology, 1988, 1998; Association for Teacher-Librarianship in Canada and Canadian Library Association, 1998; CMLEA, 1994; Kentucky Department of Education, 1995; Utah State Office of Education, 1996). Today's school librarians are perceived as agents for change in the restructuring of the educational process. Their role is to provide a variety of resources as the basis for experiential or authentic learning, share with teachers the process by which students acquire needed information skills, and encourage students' pursuit of individual interests (Doyle and ERIC Clearinghouse on Information & Technology, 1994; Farmer, 1999; Spitzer et al., 1998).

With the school library as their classrooms, school librarians are uniquely qualified and situated to develop programs to teach students information skills. The most successful information skills programs are taught as integral parts of the school's basic curriculum. This focus assumes an academic need and a classroom connection. Programs thrive in schools where the administration views school librarians as teachers and information gathering skills as a necessary part of every student's education. Subject area curricula include the appropriate information gathering and usage skills as part of their learning objectives. The superintendent and the principal encourage team planning by the classroom teacher and the school librarian. Evaluation of the program is an annual event in order to keep the information skills curriculum fresh and current with curriculum changes. The program is recognized as a partnership of the principal, teacher, and librarian and is supported by the school district and the community. Both teachers and principals acknowledge that the processing and use of information is a schoolwide concern. In such an environment, the librarian should take the initiative for developing collaborative programs and encourage the team approach to instructional planning (Association for Teacher-Librarianship in Canada and Canadian Library Association, 1998; Corcoran and Langlois, 1990).

Today's students need a variety of skills in order to access information. The most effective way for them to acquire these skills is for the teacher and school librarian to be active partners in the learning process. Instruction works best when it is in context and should include tasks of relevance to the student. Library assignments are not busy work. They directly relate to and are integrated into the classroom endeavor. Librarians must be proactive in showing teachers the vital link between IL and learning. The traditional perspective of librarian as resource provider must be expanded to that of co-teacher and curriculum collaborator. Librarians must be seen as partners in curriculum planning as well as delivery (Harada and Tepe, 1998). By being aware of any reform initiatives that are proposed for their school, school librarians can develop collaborative relationships with the teaching faculty that will position the library at the center of these changes (Farmer, 1999; Hainer, 1998).

To successfully meet the information demands placed on them by their schoolwork, students need to acquire three different types of IL skills. They need to develop skills in exploiting specific resources such as how to use library catalogs to locate books. They need to develop search strategies that employ these resources as part of a systematic search directed at solving specific problems. Finally, they need application skills—what to do with the information once it is gathered (Corcoran and Langlois, 1990). Furthermore, these three skills need to be tied into the bigger picture of IL and lifelong learning. The classroom teacher assigning projects that will require information skills should confer with the librarian prior to assigning the task. This will ensure that the librarian will be forewarned about any upcoming impact on the library and can help structure the most appropriate ILI support for the project. The most common pitfalls of library assignments can be avoided when the school librarian and the classroom teacher collaborate on the development, delivery, and evaluation of these assignments (Gross and Kientz, 1999). This collaboration ensures not only that the library's resources can support the assignment, but also that the assignment incorporates IL learning outcomes along with its curriculum objectives and outcomes.

Unfortunately this type of collaboration does not always occur, regardless of the environment. Librarians frequently find out about an assignment only when large groups of students descend on the library all working on the same task. Instruction at this point becomes reactive as the librarian attempts to deal with the information needs of these students on the spot. Developing a close working relationship with classroom teachers is key to avoiding this reactive situation. Librarians who promote the services of the library and make themselves visible in the academic life of the school have a better chance of developing a cooperative relationship with the school's teaching community. Librarians should create opportunities for classroom teachers to use the library, the library's online materials, or its Website for their own needs. Provide special services and courtesies for the teachers, and make sure the library is a part of all schoolwide endeavors. The library can serve as a meeting place and sanctuary for teachers. Advertise the fact that the library subscribes to the morning newspaper. Create a welcoming environment in which teachers can relax and exchange ideas with each other and you. Keep teachers up to date on research and new teaching techniques in their subject areas. Provide interlibrary loan and document delivery services if possible or arrange for the local public library to do so. Create teacher-directed publications that publicize new resources, materials, and services. Join schoolwide committees. Make sure the library is featured during Open School nights (Corcoran and Langlois, 1990). Admittedly all this takes time, effort, and even money. But the payoff can be well worth it. As teachers become familiar with the library and its resources, they will begin to appreciate where the library and the school librarian fit into their overall instructional program. The more the library is seen as an integral part of the educational process, the more likely it will be that teachers will turn to the librarian when developing their classroom assignments. This is particularly true at the high school level where students are preparing to transition to higher education institutions.

The school librarian can also be the intermediary for teachers when it comes to new technology. The school library is frequently the first place where technology is successfully installed and used. It may also serve as the primary access point for this technology. If the school district has adopted a computer literacy requirement, the K–12 school librarian can perform a tremendous service by demonstrating how computers can be used to support curricula objectives. Combining computer literacy instruction with ILI increases student involvement and motivation. Incorporating computer skills into ILI provides a meaningful framework for the student that teaches these computer skills not for their own sake, but as an integral part of the entire educational process. It also enhances the role of K–12 school librarian by placing them center-stage as vital and indispensable instructors who can help assure that all students master the skills they will need to thrive in a technologically-based and information-rich world (Johnson and Eisenberg, 1996).

An excellent example of the use of technology in the school environment is the KidsConnect project (ALA-American Association of School Librarians, 2001; Spitzer et al., 1998). This AASL-sponsored initiative is an Internet question-answering, help, and referral service for K–12 students. The service is made possible through the efforts of 250 volunteer K–12 school librarians from the United States, Australia, Canada, England, Israel, Japan, and New Zealand. When a student sends an e-mail question to AskKC@ala.org, the question is routed to a school librarian who helps the student work through the IL process. Specialists may answer the question, but more often they provide students with an example of the metaprocesses involved in solving their information need (Spitzer et al., 1998). As of late 1998, more than 12,600 questions from 51 different countries had been answered.

The librarian working in the K–12 environment can be an advocate for this integrated approach by making sure teachers are kept aware of new technology-based resources and services. The library can host special workshops and in-service training opportunities so teachers can enhance their skills and become familiar with how to use these new resources. Take advantage of these opportunities to demonstrate how new resources can be effectively incorporated into the classroom experience. Show how technology can enhance the classroom experience.

Convincing the faculty of the value of information skills in general and informing them about new information resources (both print and electronic) should be a high priority for the school librarian. If classroom teachers do not see the need for using the library and its resources, they will not only leave the library out of the process, they may communicate this lack of enthusiasm to their students (Corcoran and Langlois, 1990). Providing a safe place for teachers to experiment with and learn about new technologies will go a long way toward developing the collaborative and cooperative environment in which teacher and librarian are viewed as partners in the educational process.

As in all environments, the more the librarian knows about the students who make up the school's population the better. Performing regular Needs Assessments (see Chapter 7) should be part of the school library's routine. A special aspect of Needs Assessments in the school environment, however, is the curriculum analysis. An examination of curriculum guides and classroom textbooks can help pinpoint where information skills might help students attain instructional objectives. A careful study of course descriptions indicates the type of information skills that students need to successfully complete their academic program. The information skills demanded by the academic curriculum represent the actual information needs of the students. Take a look at standard tests, review some representative written assignments and, of course, talk to the teachers (Corcoran and Langlois, 1990). Take any and all opportunities to learn about the material being taught and the methods in which it is being presented. See if you can develop a file of assignments and a calendar of units being covered by the different grades in your school. Encourage teachers to send you copies of all assignments in advance. Use this information to create coordinated displays and exhibits in the library, to develop appropriate library experiences for the students, and as a starting point for discussions with teachers that will result in a closer integration of the library into the classroom teaching process.

Creating a dynamic, integrated ILI in the school environment can be a major undertaking. Faced with limited space, staff, and funding, K–12 school librarians must be creative and flexible in their approaches. Since resource-based instruction is more student-centered, the library may need to expand its hours and provide for more open access to the facility. However, budgetary constraints as well as union issues must be taken into consideration. Self-help material such as pathfinders, self-guided tours, videotapes, and computerized tutorials will allow for more individualized instruction at a point of need. Remember the importance of a good sign system as well. These indirect teaching methods can go a long way toward easing the day-to-day workload on you and your staff (Corcoran and Langlois, 1990). Although supplementing your staff by the use of parent or community volunteers may be an appealing idea, consider the time and effort necessary to train and supervise these aides.

Adding services, extending hours, and enhancing instructional methods and materials can all have financial implications and may impinge on union contracts. Here is where outreach and communication with your community is extremely important. Contact community libraries to discuss how your students can make use of these facilities during hours your library is not available. Appeal to your principal, district supervisor or coordinator, the PTA, local businesses, the school board, the city council, and other interested community groups for assistance. Show how ILI can enhance the educational experience. Make sure that you have thoroughly assessed and evaluated the effectiveness of any programs you currently have in place (Corcoran and Langlois, 1990). Use positive outcomes to promote the value of ILI and as a means of gaining support. Assessment and evaluation can also be used to highlight what equipment and resources might be needed to enhance the program. See Chapter 12 for help with this assessment process.

Librarians working in the K–12 environment occupy a unique position in their schools. With a more holistic view of the entire curriculum, these librarians can promote interdisciplinary collaboration and a spirit of cooperation among both teachers and students. They can connect process with content, teacher with resources, and students with information, both within the library and in the world at large (Stripling, 1996), especially through the Internet. The successful attainment of Goal Three and the continued development of IL in the school-age child depend upon school librarians at all grade levels taking a proactive and dynamic place in their individual schools, their communities, and in the educational process as a whole.

The Academic Library

Goal Five is directed at IL in adults. It is meant to promote the development of IL in both the workplace and in society at large. Its ultimate aim is the development of IL citizens who can apply IL skills wisely and well in their daily lives. As such, this goal has implications for ILI in academic, public, and special library environments.

The academic library shares much in common with the school library. Both serve as supports for the educational mission of their parent institutions. Both need to work within the framework of the classroom curriculum and the institution as a whole. Librarians in both environments must form strong partnerships with classroom instructors and their administrators. In a way, the school library environment can be viewed as a microcosm of the larger and more complex academic library environment where the targeted user population includes faculty and staff as well as students. Granted, there is the obvious difference in the age of the user and the scope and diversity of programs being supported. But just as in the school library, many forms of ILI in the academic setting work best when they are integrated into the overall curriculum.

Although there is some variation in the type of academic environment (two-year and community colleges, four-year colleges, and universities offering both undergraduate and graduate/professional programs) all share the same goal, which is to educate their users for the information age. ILI should equip students, faculty, and staff to function as independently as possible to meet their information needs for work and leisure and provide them with lifelong learning skills. The emphasis of ILI in an academic library is on teaching the process of research. Just as in the school library, the goal is for students to learn how to apply what they have been taught and to replicate the process in a variety of different circumstances with little or no further assistance from the librarian (Ready et al., 1990).

ILI in its many forms and under a variety of names has had a long history in the academic library setting. The current emphasis on lifelong learning only serves to strengthen this instructional function. Colleges and universities concerned with the quality of learning on their campuses and how effectively they are preparing students for lifelong learning are being encouraged to foster new approaches to teaching. More and more emphasis is being placed on independent research and self-directed learning. Faculty are being encouraged to reexamine their teaching role and move from the teacher as lecturer to the teacher as facilitator model (Breivik and Gee, 1989). This student-centered learning movement invites students to go beyond their textbook and reserved readings in their search for information. It is intended to mimic the real world and to prepare students for the future by teaching them how to gather, evaluate, and utilize resources on their own (Moran, 1990). A similar trend has been identified in the K–12 school setting with its movement toward resource-based learning. With students at all levels being encouraged to pursue their own independent research, the implication for both school and academic libraries is obvious.

Needs Assessments in the academic library should focus on student, faculty, and staff characteristics. The institution's definition of user is key. This definition is expanded or limited by the institution's mission statement, sources of funding, and community mandates. Is the institution directed by state mandate to serve community citizens as well as the campus community? How restrictive are licensing agreements for electronic resources? In a private institution, are students of faculty from surrounding local public institutions welcomed or barred? In either case, what is the status of K–12 students who wish to use the college or university library? Are visiting scholars and outside researchers welcome or must they have a letter of introduction from administration on their home campus? What is the status of extension students, distance-education enrollees, private-sector partners, and friends and patrons courted by the development office? Are members of the public allowed to use the facility (Wilson, 1992) and licensed material? The answer to these types of questions will help you define who your users actually are. Contact appropriate campus offices to acquire the documentation that can help you develop a true picture of the mix of users your library is mandated to serve.

The academic community can also be quite diverse in its make-up. Be sure your Needs Assessment addresses issues of culture, ethnicity, gender, age, disabilities, languages, etc. This is of particular importance in the community-college environment where students can represent a wide gamut of academic skills and a variety of educational goals. Students may have aspirations of transferring to a four-year school or may only be taking a few courses to upgrade their job skills. Community-college students may be pursuing a technical certificate or just attending classes for intellectual stimulation. Designing instruction for this very diverse group can be extremely challenging (Miller, Patty, 1999; Ready et al., 1990). See Chapter 14 for a discussion of ILI for diverse populations and Chapter 7 for more suggestions about Needs Assessments.

Determining the make-up of your population is only the first step. You also need to do an environmental scan that looks at the curriculum, types of special research, professional or interdisciplinary programs, levels of enrollment in different departments, and so on. Course catalogs and campus Web pages can be very useful in performing this scan. Students, faculty, and administrators should be approached either in person, in focus groups, or by surveys to gather information about their perceived needs, attitudes toward using the library and information, as well as recommendations for where they feel ILI might best fit into the curriculum (Ready et al., 1990). Integrating ILI instruction into course requirements increases its relevance and its effectiveness.

Developing good relationships with the teaching faculty in your institution improves the likelihood that this connection can be made. Administrators can also provide information about campus initiatives that might affect ILI. Their knowledge of available financial resources could also prove useful as well as their willingness to provide other types of resources for your program. Administrators can put you in contact with appropriate departments, agencies, and offices on your campus that might be interested in partnering with the library. Having the backing of the campus administration can go a long way to promoting the library as a key player on campus.

The success of any instruction program depends on support from campus and library administrators, colleagues, and especially the teaching faculty (Ready et al., 1990; Spitzer et al., 1998). Identify faculty who consistently assign library work to their students and who themselves are regular users of the library. These faculty members are more likely to cooperate in developing an instructional program. By selecting an audience where there is academic support and by promoting library instruction as enrichment for an existing curriculum, the library can gain strong allies on campus.

The development of a successful ILI program requires that teaching faculty and instruction librarians engage in frequent contact and view each other as partners in the educational enterprise. It requires collaboration about course content, requirements, and assignments. Collaborative relationships are encouraged when librarians invite faculty to take part in collection development. The relationships benefit from frequent updating of the faculty about resources available, and frank discussions about those resources the faculty feel are lacking (Stoffle et al., 1984). If funding is an issue, these discussions can help the library prioritize purchases or may even result in departments offering to help fund a resource they feel is of particular interest. If good relations are consistently cultivated, collaboration has a better chance of occurring. Good friends tend to work together better than do total strangers (Kotter, 1999). Successful teacher-librarian collaboration results in more appropriate ILI that truly supports the educational objectives of the institution. The final result is improved student products and an enhanced learning experience for everyone: student, teacher, and librarian.

Establishing credibility for you and the library instruction program takes visibility and rapport with the teaching faculty. Advanced degrees in subject disciplines promote collegiality with the teaching faculty. Make any membership and involvement in professional associations known. Find out about individual faculty's research interests and contact them when relevant material or resources are added to the library. Help them keep up to date by alerting them to the online current awareness resources such as the Current Contents® database. Inform them about the library's interlibrary loan and document delivery services. Participate in campus committees and governance, universitywide clubs and organizations, and any other groups where you can keep in contact with both faculty and administrators. Promote the library at every opportunity and be alert for ways to connect the library to existing or new campus initiatives. Key players are the faculty senate and the faculty senate committees. Examine committee charges and campus initiatives to see if IL outcomes are being incorporated. Are IL outcomes being assessed, and, if so, how and where (Iannuzzi, 1998)? As always, make sure that any new ILI initiative has the support of your library colleagues and can be supported by current staffing, space, and budgetary constraints.

Advances in information technology have also changed the face of instruction in the academic library setting. By removing the physical barriers separating the classroom and the library, the library can become an integral part of the classroom experience. Students no longer have to go to the library, the library can become part of every classroom, dormitory room, and faculty office. However, if the student is not coming to the library, new ways of delivering ILI to these remote users must also be developed (Breivik and Gee, 1989; Moran, 1990). New information technologies can deliver information directly to the user, but this information remains inaccessible if the user cannot utilize the technology or systems so readily available. It is up to librarians to participate in the creation of simple, easy-to-understand interfaces that remove these technological and intellectual barriers to locating and accessing information.

Remote access complicates the ILI mission. Accustomed to face-to-face interactions, librarians must now anticipate needs and respond to and help those they cannot see. Librarians have responded to this challenge by developing systems and implementing services tailored to the needs of these remote users. They are taking a proactive role in the creation of intuitive, user-friendly interfaces (Rader, 1999). Many such examples of these librarian-developed interfaces exist. Ohio State's Gateway to Information (Tiefel, 1995) was an early example of this approach. Many professional organizations monitor and review these types of interfaces. Check ACRL's Instruction Section's list of Innovation in Instruction Recipients (ALA-ACRL-Instruction Section, 2000b), ALA's Library Instruction Round Table's Library Instruction Tutorials (ALA-Library Instruction Round Table, 2000), and the LOEX Clearinghouse for Library Instruction's Instruction "Links" page (LOEX, 2000b) for more examples of this sort of Web-based ILI.

At the same time these technological changes complicate ILI they also offer opportunities for the academic librarian to develop collaborative partnerships with teaching faculty. As the teaching faculty needs to become more technologically adept, they turn to the information professional for assistance. Collaborative curriculum development projects are becoming more and more common. Both EduCom (www.educom.com) and the User Education Roundtable of the International Federation of Library Associations (www.ifla.org/VII/rt12/rtued.htm) Web pages offer examples of these types of collaborations. The Coalition for Networked Information (www.cni.org/home.html) highlights collaborative efforts between librarians, faculty, and computer experts. Joint efforts between the Association of College and Research Libraries and the American Association for Higher Education also showcase the faculty-librarian partnerships. The Middle States Association of Colleges and Schools accrediting agency has been influential in elevating the importance of IL in higher education. Faculty and librarians in college and university systems in New York, Washington, and California are preparing IL competency standards, as are those in individual institutions such as the University of Arizona and Florida International University (Iannuzzi, 1998; Rader, 1999; Spitzer et al., 1998).

The Special Library

Special libraries as a group represent the most eclectic type of libraries. Special libraries can be part of an academic or public system. They can be found in corporate, museum, medical, legal, government, religious, cultural, nonprofit, and private research facilities settings. What they tend to have in common is a service rather than a teaching orientation. However, Goal Five encourages the promotion of IL in the workplace and so has an impact on the special library. The mission of the special library is to support the function of its parent organization. Services are directed at improving employee efficiency and productivity. ILI in this setting is developed not necessarily to teach employees how to use library resources, but to promote the library and its services.

Interactions in special libraries are generally one on one and question specific. Group presentations to demonstrate new services or systems are viewed as marketing opportunities. They are used to promote the goals of the library, to build a loyal customer base, and to solidify the library's place as a valued part of the organizational structure (Strife, 1995). Justifying an ILI program in a special library, where users expect the librarian to provide answers, is much more difficult than in other settings where ILI is seen in terms of an extension of the educational process. However, as employees learn to access library resources previously unknown to them, their job performance will improve. They will be able to use their time more efficiently and find better information to support their work. As employees learn more about the library and its services, they will be able to make more efficient and appropriate use of library staff. Special libraries can educate the organization's employees to make more and better use of the library's resources. As a result, these employees will be able to formulate more effective information searches. They will be more aware of what information is available and will know how to access it most thoroughly, systematically, and easily. Their interactions with the library staff will be enhanced as employees will be able to determine when to do research themselves and when it is more efficient to turn it over to an information professional (Birch, Bergman, and Arrington, 1990).

Because the existence of the library is so closely related to its perceived value to the overall organization, it is imperative that the special librarian develops an in-depth knowledge of the organizational structure and politics, especially where the library fits into the overall hierarchy. Make sure you are identifying the information needs of your organization and are determining if you are meeting those needs. Special librarians must make sure they have positioned themselves and their library so that those making budget decisions recognize the library's contributions to effectiveness of the organization (Adams, 1995; Strife, 1995).

When completing a Needs Assessment in this environment, the librarian should pay attention to the importance of each group within the organization. A group that does not show much interest on the Needs Assessment may actually take priority based on its place in the organization. Consider the political aspects as well, such as which groups provide financial or influential support for the library. Finally, primary or heavy users may already be very knowledgeable, but at the same time services and instruction for them may take priority because of their relation to the library (Birch, Bergman, Arrington, 1990). Make sure your Needs Assessment is used to identify potential allies in the company or organization. Marketing departments can help with the design of materials. Computer centers may assist in the delivery of instructional material via e-mail, the company's intranet systems, or other computer-based technology. Human resource departments and training and development units may have suggestions for the best approaches to instruction in your environment.

Take part in new-employee orientations to make sure newcomers feel welcome in the library, will be familiar with its resources and services, and will view the library staff as allies who can assist them in the performance of their jobs. Publicize the library via company newsletter, flyers, e-mail distributions, etc. Target supervisors for special attention—you need their support to encourage employees to use the library. Take the time and energy to set up special early morning coffee hours or other types of informal meetings in the library specifically for supervisors. You can use the time to promote new services and resources and to address concerns or answer questions about your facility. Your efforts will be appreciated and you and your staff will be seen as friendly and professional contributors to the organizational enterprise (Strife, 1995).

Since productivity is so important in this environment, employees may be reluctant to take time away from their primary job responsibilities to attend special presentations in the library. Take advantage of technology to send the instruction to them. Even in a small company, your users may only access the library and its resources remotely. They may even prefer to do their research during hours the library is not open. The development of electronically accessible user aides, especially Web-based ones, and the design of remote instruction methods will not only be valuable for the user, it will also keep the library and its services visible and at the heart of the organization. It will also enhance the image of the library as a cutting-edge facility that provides support and access to information in the most appropriate format and at the exact moment when people need it. For example, the Bank of Boston offers over 100 self-paced courses to its employees, thus providing training where and when it is most useful (Kanter, 1996). Helping to promote the value of information in the workplace, acting as an intermediary for accessing that information, and as a facilitator who helps employees maintain their IL skills will support the national mandate toward creating an IL population.

FINAL REMARKS

Goals 2000 established a national mandate for providing every person in this country with the necessary skills for lifelong learning. As such, it called on all types of libraries to account as participants in the process. If people of all ages and in every walk of life are to develop and maintain IL skills in the support of these goals, then every library bears the responsibility for providing ILI. Teaching becomes the obligation not only of the school and academic libraries that have traditionally seen it as part of their role, but also of the public and special library as well. Whenever a lifelong learner turns to his or her library—at work, at school or in the community—the means of further developing his or her IL skills should be available. Every librarian in every library plays a part in seeing that the aims of Goals 2000 become a reality.

Partnerships and collaborations between a library and appropriate members of its population are crucial to the success of ILI in every environment. But partnerships can also cut across library lines. School and academic libraries should work together to ensure that IL skills are both appropriate at each grade level and form a continuum that builds as children move through the educational process. Public and school libraries form a natural alliance in providing ILI to the children of their communities and can link to academic libraries through their high schools. Special libraries can work closely with academic and public libraries to make sure potential employees are developing IL skills appropriate to the workplace.

Developing effective ILI in any library requires effort, knowledge, and a firm understanding of where the library fits within its environment. However, changes in the delivery of information, the national mandates for lifelong learning and the development of an informed citizenry, and educational reform movement that emphasize independent, self-directed learning have created a situation where no single type of library can afford to operate in isolation. Skyrocketing costs of both print and electronic materials are encouraging libraries of all types to develop consortiums for the provision of information to all their constituents. Public, school, academic, and special libraries are beginning to see the benefit of acting together. The University of California's California Digital Library (California Digital Library, 2000), for example, negotiates systemwide subscriptions to electronic journals, monographs, and services on behalf of all the nine UC campuses. The Library of California project (California State Library, 2000) will link all types of libraries into an even broader network of sharing.

Where people go for their information is also changing. Once people went to a particular physical place when they had an information need. They looked for and visited the nearest, appropriate library facility. But with information being packaged in a variety of ways and being accessible from almost anywhere, which library actually "owns" the information becomes moot. The lines are blurring, and users can no longer tell which library is theirs or where the information is coming from. The successful development of an IL population depends on creating alliances between libraries, developing collaborations between libraries and appropriate interest groups in their respective environments, and a proactive approach that champions the cause of IL at every opportunity. Librarians must act as IL advocates in their communities and schools, on their campuses, and in their organizations. If we value the goals of the IL movement, it is up to us to promote those goals and make IL a reality for all.

EXERCISES

1. Identify three organizations, agencies, or community groups within your environment that you feel would be useful partners for your ILI program. How would this alliance benefit your ILI program? Develop an action plan developing an alliance with each of those groups.
2. Identify three administrators, managers, or community leaders whose support you need to implement an ILI in your environment. Develop an action plan for contacting these people.
3. Create an ILI advocacy packet that can be used to promote the value of ILI in your environment. Include references to national and local mandates for IL, as well as concrete evidence about the success of current IL endeavors in your library.
4. Develop a sequential plan that would link public, school, academic, and special libraries in your community in a joint IL ef-

fort. Identify the IL aspects that would be the responsibility of each type of library. Show how each type of library contributes to the overall aims of IL and how each aspect relates to and builds on other aspects.

READ MORE ABOUT IT

For information on developing ILI programs in each type of library environment see

The LIRT Instruction Handbook, edited by Mary Brottman and Mary Loe (1990, Englewood, CO: Libraries Unlimited).

To keep current on trends in a particular environment, scan the following journal publications:

Public Libraries

Library Journal
The Reference Librarian
Research Strategies
RQ

School Libraries

Emergency Librarian
The Reference Librarian
School Library Media Quarterly
Teacher Librarian

Academic Libraries

College and Research Libraries
Journal of Academic Librarianship
Research Strategies
The Reference Librarian
RQ

Special Libraries

The Reference Librarian
Special Libraries

16

Teaching Technology

How do you catch a cloud and pin it down?

—Maria, *The Sound of Music*

THE NATURE OF TECHNOLOGY

Fleeting, flimsy, and amorphous—today's technology very much resembles clouds, sometimes cumulus-like, with a well-defined outline—sometimes cirrus-like, "narrow bands or patches of thin, generally white, fleecy parts," (*American Heritage Dictionary*, 1991). Though difficult to pin down, clouds are usually not frightening, while technology is. What do we mean when we use the word "technology"? What makes it so frightening, and how can people learn how to understand and take control of it?

Today we talk about technology taking over our lives and the pace of technological change. Yet teaching technology in relation to libraries has special meaning, particularly as it relates to computers and computerized information. To librarians on the razor's edge of new technology, it may mean teaching the use of Web browsers, chat, discussion boards and more, by means of interactive Web tutorials, presentation software shows mounted on Websites, fully online courses, and so on. Other librarians may think of technology as the online catalog (OPAC), online article index databases, and CD-ROM reference tools, taught by means of in-person group sessions using varying levels of technology, including overhead transparencies, whiteboards, flip charts, videos, presentation software, and computers for learners.

Yet many, librarians and users alike, fear and abhor the steadily increasing use of technology and see it as a rising tide about to drown them. Why is this so? What can we do about it? What kinds of technology should librarians teach? What sorts of technology are available in or accessible through libraries, and how can we teach "mutating" technology?

TECHNOPHOBIA AND EMPOWERING USERS

Fear of technology, especially "the computer," cuts across gender, age, ethnicity, and cultural groups. Weil and Rosen's 16-year-long research study of computerphobia, published in 1997, reveals that in any group of the 20,000 subjects studied, 25 to 50 percent were computerphobic. In addition, contrary to popular opinion, age and gender made no difference as computerphobic people were " . . . just as likely to be young as old, and were equally divided between men and women" (Weil and Rosen, 1997: 12). The same researchers identified three broad categories of technology users, called "Techno Types": "Eager Adopters" (10–15% of the population), "Hesitant 'Prove-Its'" (50–60% of the population), and "Resisters" (30–40% of the population). "Eager Adopters" generally expect to have problems with computers and enjoy solving them. "Hesitant 'Prove Its'" also expect problems with technology, but they do not enjoy solving these problems and think they themselves have caused these problems to occur. "Resisters" generally try to avoid technology altogether because it makes them feel intimidated, embarrassed, or stupid, and they are sure they will break anything they touch. "User-hostile" error messages and the fear of one's privacy being invaded also contribute to technostress and computer avoidance (McGrath, 1999).

It is bad enough when you are a "Hesitant 'Prove-It'" and have to wend your way through an enormous number and variety of information tools and resources just to identify and locate a book or an article—and how much more so if you happen to be a "Resister." Add to these initial fears the lack of interface standardization in library systems and differing search command terminology and syntax, even with Web-based systems. To make matters even worse, the struggle to learn one system may very well need to be repeated for most other systems. So, even if an anxious library user learns how to use some library resources, especially if their mental models for using these systems are sketchy or minimal, when systems are upgraded or replaced by others with different interfaces or command structure, the poor user is back to square one. "Resisters" may very well just give up as learning obstacles may seem insurmountable, and even "Hesitants" may be loathe to venture into the physical or virtual library world.

It is important to understand why this computerphobia exists and to take a kind, gentle, and encouraging approach to helping people feel more comfortable about using computers. You might begin by helping users acknowledge and learn about their own TechnoType, so that they will see they are not alone. Weil and Rosen offer a "TechnoType Quiz" to help people self-identify, and they recommend a ten-step approach to learning new technology, including "Press the keys yourself," "Learn to expect problems with technology," and "You don't have to learn it all." At one time, the Thousand Oaks Library in California (a public library) offered computer classes to senior citizens that began by familiarizing attendees with the parts of the keyboard. Keyboards were removed from workstations and brought into a separate room where learners could manipulate them and learn the functions of the various keys before they were hooked up to workstations. This is an excellent way to help Weil and Rosen's "Resisters" overcome their computerphobia.

Another important way to make technology understandable is to provide pressure-free practice times and locations where people will begin to understand the basic rules of the system so that, ideally, they will be able to look for similar rules in other systems. Research indicates that there is hope, even for the most technologically inexperienced or computerphobic. The more people actually use computers, the more they get used to them and the less anxious many tend to feel. An international study of teachers who taught in two languages indicated that the more general computer use they had, the less anxious they were, as long as the training they received encouraged them to make use of computers rather than fear them (Yaghi and Abu-Saba, 1998). By extension, ILI librarians hope that the same will be true even for the most library- and information-research inexperienced.

WHAT KINDS OF TECHNOLOGY SHOULD WE TEACH?

Tension: Teach What Is Available Through the Library or Teach What They Want to Know?

As libraries and librarians have become more and more entranced with the computerized or electronic world, some librarians have taken on the role of technology trainers, teaching users the mechanics of how to use e-mail software, how to design Web pages, and other sorts of training in mechanics of use. For example, the University of Texas at Austin's General Libraries and their Computation Center separately offered standalone basic, intermediate, and advanced HTML classes from 1994 to 1999. Library staff also taught e-mail and listservs as requested in course-integrated sessions during that period (Dupuis, 1999a, 1999b).

The two units are now combined and the library staff no longer teaches HTML classes (Dupuis, 1999b). Others have focused on teaching more traditional library-related tools, such as online catalogs, online article indexes, and computerized reference tools.

Libraries like the Los Angeles Public Library (LAPL) are making licensed databases available remotely to users with LAPL library cards. Are these users able to figure out how to use multiple interfaces on their own? What sorts of help do these libraries provide for asynchronous remote users? Can users easily find and utilize the help we provide remotely? It is important to keep in mind that for the most part just mounting a system or database on the Web does not automatically make it easy to use or understand. Whether they are in the library or getting to library materials remotely, users may need clear and simple help in navigating systems and databases. It is sad to say, but many vendors rely on librarians to provide this sort of help to their users. So our users need help in selecting and using a variety of information research tools, and may want help in learning how to use other tools like e-mail, FTP, telnet, and various pieces of software. How much and what sorts of technology should librarians be teaching and how does the librarian's approach differ from that of the computer trainer? Is there a point at which we become interchangeable with computer trainers? Should we be doing something different, and if so, what should it be? How can we resolve the tension between what the librarians may be willing or able to teach, and what users want to learn?

Assess the Technological Landscape and User Needs

In considering what sort of approach to take, it would be useful to begin by surveying the landscape, reviewing both what is already available and has been prepared by other librarians in your own institution or organization and elsewhere and what your own users need and want to know. The first step in this process is to familiarize yourself with technology-related programs and products available locally. Ask other library staff to fill you in on your library's and institution's ILI history, and to give you sample materials. Next, review some ILI literature, surf ILI Websites at other libraries, and check out instructional development sites at colleges and universities as well. In the meantime, try to find out exactly what your users know and do not know about the use of various technologies like Web browser software. A fairly quick and non-threatening way to do this is by means of self-assessments or checklists. A self-assessment, of course, reflects only the user's own opinion of her/ his skill levels. A pre-test that asks users to demonstrate skills will reveal the actual mastery level of those skills. Whichever it is to be, it will be much easier to customize instruction to user needs if the assessment instrument is distributed in advance of instruction, and the results used as input in deciding where to begin and what sorts of instructional goals and objectives to set.

Competencies

Before ALA's Association for College and Research Libraries posted "Information Literacy Competency Standards for Higher Education" on its Website in January 2000, many libraries had developed or were in the process of developing information literacy competencies, the achievement of which served as goals and objectives for their instructional programs (Grassian and Clark, 1999). Some were simply lists of basic skills and detailed plans and proposals for teaching them, while others provided historical information, instructional materials which progressed from basic to advanced, and provided links to other similar instruction information and materials (California State University, 2000; Wisconsin Association of Academic Librarians, 2000). Most recently developed ILI material is now Web-based and includes reference to competencies related to technology use and evaluation. The IL *Standards* posted on ACRL's Website, along with the ALA-ACRL Instruction Section's revised model objectives based on those *Standards* provide an important structure on which to hang important technology-related competencies. These technology-related competencies, subsumed under IL, form important elements of many ILI goals and objectives.

There is no question that users need to know the mechanics of using various types of software and hardware in a variety of different interfaces or they will be unable to use the many electronic information resources we have so generously made available to them. Web instructional designers, with all good intent, often make some basic assumptions about users, including easy access to the latest Web browser software, up-to-date hardware, and facility with using a mouse. As we acknowledged in Chapter 5, discomfort with or fear of using hardware and software can stop a person in her/his tracks and block out any additional information you may wish her/him to learn, including database content, structure, and critical thinking about electronic resources. However, in today's world, technology competency, especially computer literacy, is a prerequisite to gaining information literacy competency, and this is where the computer trainer can be of great help. Partnership with a good computer trainer can mean that users get a solid foundation in basic mechanics of computer use, and will then be prepared to move on to information literacy competency taught by a librarian. Computer trainers too will gain respect for librarians as people who are aware of information resources in all sorts of formats, have been trained to evaluate information resources objectively, and can advise users on important features, as well as potentially useful resources.

A BASELINE LEARNING APPROACH

After Needs Assessment results are in and librarians have surveyed existing instructional materials regarding teaching technology, they may want to consider a baseline teaching/learning approach for their primary learner group(s). This approach focuses mainly on teaching the basics of the most highly used information-research-related tools available in the library and to remote library users, in order to help them achieve particular competencies. For example, in order to help users learn how to identify, locate, and evaluate books, librarians will need to teach the mechanics of getting to and using the OPAC, as well as critical thinking about what the OPAC contains and how to evaluate its search results. If the OPAC is Web-based, librarians may need to teach Internet and Web basics, and use of a Web browser in addition.

ON BEYOND THE BASELINE . . .

Once you have met baseline learning goals for primary users, you may want to meet requests for instruction in other sorts of technology, such as HTML programming, e-mail software, or bibliography formatting software (for example, ProCite). As time and staff permit, you might consider partnering with computer trainers or technical support staff to develop instructional materials and also offer computer literacy instruction jointly. This would be a wonderful opportunity to begin building an organization-wide or institution-wide ILI coalition. Just wishing for this ideal situation will not make it happen, though. We need to be proactive and take the first step toward open and generous sharing of our materials and our expertise. Librarians *and* technical support/computing center staff in all sorts of environments (school libraries, special libraries and information centers, organizations, businesses, government libraries, academic libraries, public libraries, etc.) deserve respect for and acknowledgment of their expertise. We have a lot to learn from each other, and as the world of information resources continues to expand geometrically, partnerships of all kinds will become increasingly important.

SYSTEMATIC APPROACHES TO DESIGNING INSTRUCTION IN TECHNOLOGY USE

The idea of "teaching technology" can seem enormous and overwhelming. How can one teach technology without knowing what "technology" encompasses? Even if you know what you are teaching, how can you best approach such a huge task? It may help to focus first on the value of a particular piece of technology (why would you want to use it?), and then on the basic mechanics of using it, weaving critical thinking and other concepts throughout. Kobelski's and Reichel's concept types and others mentioned in Chapter 5 offer useful categories, which may be applied in different ways, and which may need to be stretched to accommodate newer formats of materials and newer forms of instruction such as interactive Websites, as well as new means of scholarly communication. Teaching the mechanics of using information resources is a necessity, however, and we must do our best to incorporate evaluation and critical thinking into this process from the get-go.

The Barclay Approach

Barclay primarily takes a "mechanics" approach to IL technology instruction. He recommends teaching users that there are standard features of many databases; for example, means of searching and means of getting online help. This is an extremely useful introduction to any sort of technology-related instruction. It can help users make sense of an amorphous collection of technology tools and understand that there are similar concepts underlying many of them. It can also help the instruction librarian make sense of electronic resources and tools by categorizing them as "full-featured," that is, having all or most of a series of features, including "luxury" items as opposed to the "stripped down" variety with just the basics.

For example, the University of California's California Digital Library's (CDL) "PsycINFO" interface is full-featured. There are twenty-one different ways to search (keyword, exact title, explode exact subject, etc.) in any or all of eleven different time periods, and there are ten other limit categories, each with its own menu. For example, you can limit to any of ten different general topics such as "Attitude Measures" and "Learning Disorders." On the other hand, the CDL system's "Current Contents" interface is fairly simple and basic. There are only seven means of searching the database (author, title, exact title, etc.), and just five categories of limits (language, date, etc.), though again, each limit category has a menu of choices. Yet both of these databases have certain common features. They both allow searching, they both allow the user to display and e-mail results, and the search interface, displays, and search history all look very much the same. In a brief instruction session or in a reference interaction, it is fairly simple to explain the common features of databases such as these, and focus attention on their differences instead—content coverage, date coverage, limits available, and so on.

Each of these concepts or features has to do with how a database functions and what it is designed to do. It is tempting to take the "functional" road and offer simple, brief explanations of basic features and mechanics, which may in fact be all the learner can or needs to absorb in a short period of time. Brief as learning time may be, however, the librarian can and should insert critical thinking elements throughout, focusing on what is important to the learners. For example, you might appeal to undergraduates by emphasizing that they will save time and end up with better research papers if they learn and apply critical thinking criteria as they proceed through the research process. You might want to pose provocative questions such as: "Who created a particular online index and how did they decide which journals to index?" or "How did they decide which terms to use as subjects?" The idea is that information tools do not simply appear out of thin air. People make decisions about structure, contents, means of access and use, how information will be displayed or laid out in a print publication, how it will be indexed, etc. Whether intended or not, these are political decisions that impact how information seekers search for information and what sort of information they can find readily.

A New Ten-Step Model

When there is more time to design instruction, and more learning time available, a different approach may make the librarian's task seem less daunting and can offer more in-depth evaluation of resources. First, you will need to take the preliminary steps necessary in designing all kinds of instructional programs: identify the audience and conduct one or more Needs Assessments to determine where they are and what they need to know. Once you have identified the audience, and conducted Needs Assessments, there are ten steps to designing instruction for technology.

STEP 1: LIST THE TECHNOLOGY(IES) YOU PLAN TO TEACH

Will you be teaching the OPAC, CD-ROM indexes, full-text CD-ROM items, online indexes, the Internet in general, Websites, some combination of these, or other sorts of technology? The instructional approaches

---

Figure 16–1
Teaching Technology: a Ten-Step Model

Step 1:   List the technology(ies) you plan to teach

Step 2:   Place these items into "classes" and "subclasses," if necessary

Step 3:   Examine these classes to identify general overall concepts

Step 4:   Establish evaluative, critical thinking criteria for each class or type of technology

Step 5:   Examine items within classes for intended use vs. creative use

Step 6:   Study the mechanics of use of different items within a class

Step 7:   Establish further evaluative, critical thinking criteria for each class and for items within a class, focusing on "filters" and the filtering process

Step 8:   Develop content-based, measurable goals and objectives or learning outcomes, based on Needs Assessments

Step 9:   Select teaching/learning methodologies, flesh out curriculum, and provide instruction

Step 10: Evaluate instruction, assess learning outcomes, and revise and update all aspects of the instructional program continuously

---

you take may depend partly on what sort of technology you are planning to teach, as well as the audience. For example, if you are teaching undergraduates and want them to learn how to use and think critically about online indexes in a synchronous (at the same time) in-person group session, you might want to begin, for example, with small group exercises. These exercises can be designed to help users learn the differences between magazines and journals, and then the differences between indexes that list journal articles as opposed to magazine articles. (See Figure 16-2 for an exercise example.) An OPAC instructional session might include some Web basics and hands-on practice, as well as means of getting online help for remote users.

STEP 2: PLACE THESE ITEMS INTO "CLASSES" AND "SUBCLASSES," IF NECESSARY

These classes may include OPACs, article indexes, and full-text databases, whatever the technological format or means of access. Subclasses might include subject-specific article indexes as opposed to general indexes. The Internet presents a special problem, however, because this format encompasses a large and growing number of different classes and sub-classes, all of which users tend to lump together as "the Internet."

Figure 16–2
Small Group Exercise

Ask learners to pair up. Give each pair a set of two Websites, either in paper or on a Web page. Tell them they will have ten minutes to complete the exercise, and then will participate in reporting back to the class.

1. They must go to "Evaluating Web Resources" (Alexander and Tate, 1999), categorize their Websites based on the categories at the Alexander and Tate site, and come up with one or two reasons for selecting a particular category for each site.
2. After categorizing their Websites, each pair must go to the "Thinking Critically About World Wide Web Resources" Web page (Grassian, 1998) and evaluate each Website, using one evaluative criteria from each of the three categories on the page.
3. When the ten minutes are up, call the large group back together and ask pairs to report on their Websites. As they report, show the Websites on a large screen for the entire group to see. Ask the group to vote on whether or not they agree with the pair's opinions. If the audience agrees, give the pair a treat—candy.

Classifying Internet technology into two basic categories can be quite helpful as a precursor to developing a variety of ILI for technology.

There are two basic types of Internet technology, which may be represented by answers to the following questions:

a. **Is it software and does it make the Internet function?**
Primary examples of software by which the Internet itself functions are telnet, ftp, Web browsers, and "attached" Web search engines. Attached search engines are placed within a specific Website and are used to search only that site, for example, "Labyrinth" (Georgetown University, 2000).
b. **Is it software and does it simply make use of the Internet as a vehicle?**
"Standalone Web search tools," such as Google, AltaVista, and Yahoo! have their own databases of information and are independent of other Websites. They search these databases in response to queries entered by visitors. Standalone Web search tools, Web-based OPACs, and Web-based article index databases are examples of software or resources which use the Internet as a means to provide access to information or data.

"Internet Function," or "IF," software is quite distinct from "Internet Use," or "IU," software. Generally, libraries tend to teach IU software more than IF software, so once the distinction has been made between IF and IU software, it may be easier to focus on important differences among the types of software or resources within the IU category. Many items within the IU category can have a similar look and feel simply by virtue of the fact that they are viewed or utilized via a Web browser, and yet can be further categorized in a number of different ways.

The most obvious categories relate to scholarly research as opposed to personal interest or "vanity" sites, though it is particularly important to draw distinctions among the various types of databases available through the Web. Web search tools, for example, gather or simply receive information in a variety of ways and either dump it into a database (for example, Google), or select and categorize it and then dump it into a database (for example, Yahoo!). Queries to these search tools do not search the entire Web. They search their own collections of information, that is, their own databases, and mostly for free. Some, like Northern Light, require a fee to display some full-text materials gleaned or retrieved from their database. (Northern Light labels this material "Special Collection.") Most, however, are maintaining a list of Web-based items in their databases. These databases contrast sharply with commercial-vendor-produced article index databases, many of which are indexes to refereed or edited material, or the material itself, and are usually available only to institutions or groups who have paid a licensing fee for their use.

Interestingly, developers of Web search tools such as Google are now selling their software for use as attached search engines for specific Websites. For example, Google software now "powers" Yahoo! searches. In this example, Google appears to be serving multiple functions, as Web users may see it stand on its own and also may see it on the Yahoo! site. Yet, it is still software designed to search a database of information and display results in ranked order.

The challenge here is to provide simple, easy-to-follow guidelines that will help users understand the differences among these categories and types of items. Alexander and Tate have risen to this challenge and developed an excellent Website that helps people learn how to identify Website categories in a highly engaging manner. For example, they categorize Web pages as "Advocacy," "Business/Marketing," "News," "Informational," and "Personal" (1999). "Hoax? Scholarly Research? Personal Opinion? You Decide!" is a useful active learning exercise based on Alexander and Tate's site (Grassian and Zwemer, 2000).

Figure 16–3
Small Group Exercise

1. Divide the audience or class into small groups. Provide each group with cards, each of which has an information tool written on it with a few words of description, for example:

   - PsycINFO database
     Lists articles with abstracts.
   - ORION2: UCLA Libraries & Collections
     Lists library books and subscriptions to periodicals.
   - Magazine & Journal Article Index database
     Lists articles with abstracts and some full articles.
   - Ethnic Newswatch
     Gives full articles from over 200 ethnic publications.
   - "Mr. Shakespeare" (Website)
     Gives full text of works.
   - "Yahoo"
     Lists web pages by category.
   - California Digital Library: MELVYL™ Catalog
     Lists library books.
   - "Google"
     Allows searching for web pages

2. Give the groups three minutes to sort their cards into categories and label each category. Categories can include:

   - Article indexes
   - Web pages or sites
   - Web search tools
   - Full-text works online
   - OPACs

3. Ask groups to take three minutes to identify general overall identifying characteristics for two of the categories they've defined.
4. Give the groups five minutes to come up with three critical thinking criteria for each of these two categories; that is, list the most important features to look for when evaluating the value of items fitting into these categories. For example, dates of coverage are important in assessing the value of article indexes.

STEP 3: EXAMINE THESE CLASSES TO IDENTIFY GENERAL OVERALL CONCEPTS

Through careful study and preparation, librarians can help users see similarities and differences between items within a class, and between classes. An obvious similarity among various types of technology we might be teaching is that they all require use of a computer at some point, though it may or may not be hooked up to a network or to the Internet. Some technology may involve use of a graphic user interface, or GUI, while others may not. Some classes, like article indexes, differ from others, like OPACs, by virtue of their function. Generally, article indexes are designed to provide access to individual articles by topic, author, title, keyword, subject, and so on. OPACs, on the other hand, are designed to help users identify and locate materials that physical libraries own, or to which they subscribe, such as online journals. (See Figure 16-3 for an example of an exercise that you can use to help people learn Steps 2 and 3.)

STEP 4: ESTABLISH EVALUATIVE, CRITICAL THINKING CRITERIA FOR EACH CLASS OR TYPE OF TECHNOLOGY

Computer trainers can draw users' attention to some of the more obvious similarities and differences among these types of technology. However, the librarian's instructional role is quite distinct from that of the computer trainer when it comes to teaching users how to evaluate and think critically about them, and how to "triangulate" data, particularly in order to verify the accuracy of Web-based information. This can be accomplished by helping users learn to ask a series of questions.

FOR WHAT PURPOSE WAS THIS ITEM DESIGNED?

It may be fairly easy for the general user to understand that an OPAC is a computerized version of a card catalog, that is, a listing of library materials. It will be more difficult to draw clear distinctions between Web search tools such as Yahoo! or Google, and licensed article index databases such as Contemporary Women's Issues. Web-based databases such as the National Library of Medicine's PubMed site (U.S. National Library of Medicine, 2000b) and AskERIC (Syracuse University, 1999), on the other hand, fulfill purposes similar to licensed article index databases, yet are freely available to all.

Why is it important for people to be able to distinguish among licensed databases, unlicensed or free databases, and Web search tools? The answer revolves around the political issue of filtered information. All of us filter information through our own experiences and knowledge. Many of us have forgotten Paddy Chayefsky's warnings in the

1976 movie, *Network,* and are rather uncritical of typical information sources such as newspapers or television network news. What would Chayefsky have thought about the Web? Research has shown that those of us who are the least skilled and knowledgeable tend to have the highest opinions of our intellectual abilities (Kruger and Dunning, 1999). Yet these are the very people who most need to get in the habit of asking critical thinking questions. How many and what sorts of "filters," if any, have been applied to these items, and by whom? Do certain databases index only peer-reviewed material published in specific publications? If so, who decides which publications will be indexed? OPACs are often designed by commercial vendors. Who are these vendors, what sorts of design decisions have they made, and how do these decisions affect the user's access? Can everyone have access to everything contained in the OPAC? If a freely accessible OPAC lists URLs for licensed electronic journals, will the general public have access to these journals online?

WHO IS THE AUDIENCE? IS IT GEARED TO SPECIFIC GROUPS OR INDIVIDUALS?

The Yahooligans! Website is designed for children, while Fodor's site has an adult audience in mind, yet users of all ages may visit these sites and might find useful information there. The majority of licensed databases provide access to peer-reviewed or edited materials geared to particular audiences. There are many freely available quality Websites geared to a variety of audiences, as well, and often they are not reviewed or edited, or do not provide access to peer-reviewed or edited materials. This free and open environment is exhilarating, but also requires caution on the part of the users. For example, The Smoking Section Website presents a heavily slanted view on this topic, in contrast to The American Cancer Society site. Even within a large Website, the audience may differ from one database to another. For example, PubMed (U.S. National Library of Medicine, 2000b) is geared to those interested in scholarly research articles, while MEDLINEplus (2000a) is geared to general health consumers.

HAS SOMEONE OR SOME GROUP PAID A LICENSING OR SUBSCRIPTION FEE IN ORDER TO MAKE THIS RESOURCE AVAILABLE? ARE CERTAIN PORTIONS OF A SITE FREE WHILE OTHERS ARE NOT?

The distinction between Web search tool databases, licensed databases, and unlicensed databases is particularly confusing for learners, as many databases (free or fee), now use the Web as a vehicle, thereby creating the illusion that they simply represent more freely available Websites or pages. The Los Angeles Public Library wisely labels its licensed databases "subscription databases," and indicates which are available remotely (2000). Academic library users, though, often do not see the distinction between free and fee sites because academic libraries do not clearly differentiate these databases or systems from other Websites that are freely available to all users. The word "database" often does not even appear in the names of databases, for example, America: History and Life, ABI Inform, and Sociological Abstracts.

PsycINFO is a licensed database; Cambridge Scientific Abstracts is a licensed system consisting of a number of databases. Institutions or organizations pay fees for their use by specific user groups. PubMed, on the other hand, is freely available to everyone, as is MEDLINEplus, both paid for by U.S. tax dollars. Hoover's Online, a Web-based database and Northern Light, a Web search tool, offer certain portions of their sites for free, while others require a fee.

WHO CREATED AND MAINTAINS THIS RESOURCE?

It is important to help users learn to step back and think about who created the various types of technology they use. How do the producers of article index databases decide which items to index—magazines, journals, books, dissertations? Which words do they use to describe these items? Who writes the abstracts in article index databases, if there are any, and what guidelines do they use in writing them? Are they free or is a fee required for use? Does advertising have any influence on the contents or approach of Websites?

Some Websites, like the Internet Movie Database, provide a wealth of information in specific areas or disciplines. Does it all come for free or is there some kind of sponsorship or advertising involved? Who designed the various article indexes to which many academic libraries subscribe and for what purpose?

Amazon.com and many other dot com Websites have advertising banners right at the top of their home page. Does Travelocity.com list airfares for all airlines or just particular ones? Which listings come to the top of their results pages? Who pays to provide this service free of charge to users, and why? Skepticism.net's Global Warming site offers a list of many links that question global warming claims. How objective is this site and what sort of expertise do the authors have? Brian Carnell claims to be a freelance writer "currently writing a book on the animal rights movement" (2000). Elizabeth Carnell claims to be a grad student in the Medieval Institute at Western Michigan University, "particularly interested in early modern witchcraft in continental Europe" (2000). What does this have to do with global warming? Authorship and sponsorship are not always obvious or easy to determine, and yet we need to know who authors and sponsors are, as well as their expertise and bias, so we can make our own judgments about the reliability and quality of a par-

---

Figure 16–4
Small Group Exercise

1. Show the entire group a bogus Website and a scholarly Website and model an evaluation process by pointing out which features to look for when examining Web pages critically.
2. Tell the group that they will be divided into pairs, and will have five minutes for the following hands-on exercise (or use paper printouts of Web pages).
3. Assign two pages to each group and ask them to analyze:

   ✓ audience
   ✓ purpose
   ✓ viewpoint
   ✓ author(s)
   ✓ criteria for inclusion of information

   Include an OPAC or an article index, a personal Website and a Web search tool.
4. At the end of the five-minute period, call the group back together and ask for reports from the pairs.
5. Show Websites as pairs report back, and focus on how sites may serve as personal and political tools by filtering information using stated or unstated criteria.
6. Ask learners how they would determine who created the pages, what their criteria are for inclusion, and whether or not they have a means of influencing these criteria.

---

ticular Website or other information tool. (See Figure 16-4 for a sample exercise to help people learn Step 4.)

STEP 5: EXAMINE ITEMS WITHIN CLASSES FOR INTENDED USE VERSUS CREATIVE USE

Generally, OPACs are used to identify and locate library materials. In the past, the phrase "library materials" has referred to physical objects, primarily paper, but also microform. As Web-based OPACs become more prevalent, though, library materials listed in them may come in a larger variety of formats. Some journals, for example, are now available only in electronic form. In addition to providing cataloging records for these journals, libraries may provide a link to the journal's home page where users can search, view, print, save, or download the full text of articles published in these journals.

Examples of creative uses of OPACs include searches for publishers to see what kinds of materials they publish, searches by date to see what was published in a particular year, and searches for answers or clues to help answer reference questions that can be found in book titles or subject headings.

Article indexes in a variety of formats, of necessity, have always had some distinctive features. Wilson print indexes, for example, index different periodicals and cover different subject fields even though they are very similar in look, feel, indexing arrangement, frequency of publication, and dates of coverage. Web interfaces like the California Digital Library's locally mounted databases have provided a comfortingly similar look and feel to numerous article index databases. Search buttons, search history, means of display, printing, and e-mailing, for example, look the same and operate the same way for databases ranging from ABI/Inform to PsycINFO. Whatever the format, the primary purpose of all of these indexes is to enable users to identify, locate, and if available, read abstracts or the full text of articles and other materials.

Creative or unintended uses of article indexes are often similar to unintended uses of OPACs. You can search by journal title, for example, to get an idea of the kinds of articles published in a particular journal over a period of years. Students may also search for items published recently in order to find "hot topics" for papers, or in order to get an idea of how much attention a book has received via book reviews.

Alexander and Tate, among others, have classified Web resources in a similar fashion (1999). A general user can learn to get in the habit of quickly classifying and evaluating Websites by using Web-based or paper exercises based on sites like Alexander and Tate's.

As we see more and more research tools enter the online arena, users are more and more confused about which to use for a particular information need. It is important to help learners get in the habit of stepping back and taking a hard look at information tools. Focusing attention on the main purpose of an item will help learners select more appropriate tools as they search for information. Creative uses of information tools add a serendipitous twist, as well, which can be especially useful in multidisciplinary information research.

STEP 6: STUDY THE MECHANICS OF USE OF DIFFERENT ITEMS WITHIN A CLASS

For most electronic tools, there are generic "mechanics" concepts, though how these concepts are carried out by the user may depend on the interface design, as well as the software and hardware used. Though Barclay's standard database features (searching, viewing results, saving results, and getting help online) may apply to many different information-research tools, specific search options actually may vary greatly from one database or system to another. You may use full Boolean searching in some, while others may only allow use of "and." Truncation is available in some, but not in others. Of course, the more standardization and the more generic are the concepts we can define, the easier it will be for people to learn, as they will be able to transfer what they know about using one tool to another.

For example, OPACs all allow you to search for materials, display results, and get some sort of help online. Some go further and allow you to limit searches, sort results, to establish personal profiles, to save lists beyond the current session, e-mail individual items or lists, and connect or link to other OPACs, other databases or other Websites, including online periodicals.

In teaching the mechanics of use of an online periodical index, you could focus on how to get to the main menu, what buttons to press in order to select an appropriate database for searching, what to enter for a title search, or how to e-mail results, and how to return to the main menu. These are all features that a good computer trainer could teach just as well as a librarian, if not better. The librarian's unique contribution lies in teaching which databases to select and why, as well as how to evaluate both the results of a search and the tool used to search.

STEP 7: ESTABLISH FURTHER EVALUATIVE, CRITICAL THINKING CRITERIA FOR EACH CLASS AND FOR ITEMS WITHIN A CLASS, FOCUSING ON "FILTERS" AND THE FILTERING PROCESS

Web search tools are a mystery to most Internet users. Many people think that all Web search tools search the entire Web, if not the entire world of knowledge, and bring it all back free of charge. They are unaware of the fact that Web search tools collect information and store it in their own databases. Some search tools, like Yahoo! select Websites to include in their database, and then list these sites in category menus. The Librarians' Index to the Internet is a highly selective site that includes librarians' signed reviews of Websites, also categorized in menus. Both of these sites act as filters by selecting Websites and then categorizing them. Google began as a Web search tool with a simple search box. Type in your search words and press enter, and Google will provide a ranked list of results. It now has a link to its own directory too, a list of the items in its database, arranged in categories. Dogpile is a metasearch engine that hunts through a number of different Web search tools and provides results from each. How do these sites differ, and when might you want to use one as opposed to the other?

The librarian can teach people how to think critically about infor-

---

Figure 16–5
Individual Exercise
(Optional: Report Back to Entire Group)

---

1. Ask individuals to look up a topic of their choice in Yahoo!, AltaVista, and Google and note the first item listed in the results.
2. Then ask them to look up the same topic in The Librarian's Index to the Internet to see if the items they found in Yahoo!, AltaVista, and Google appear here.
3. Ask what, if anything, this tells them about these Web-based resources and the items they list.

---

mation tools and their producers/creators, as well as the items they retrieve by asking questions such as: How do Yahoo! and Google decide what to include in their databases? Why does Yahoo! list "Humanities" as a category under "Social Science"? Why do Looksmart and GoTo.com search tool results display first in most Dogpile searches? What operation is Google performing behind the scenes before displaying the results of a search? For how long will Google keep cached copies of Web pages? What are Yahoo!'s plans regarding archiving? Is there a limit to the number of items Yahoo! will include in its database? Is there a limit to the number of search tools Dogpile will use for its meta-searches? How does Yahoo! decide which categories to use, which labels to use for these categories, and how to apply them? Does Yahoo! list multidisciplinary sites under more than one category? Is there a limit to the number of different categories they may use for a particular site? What time period do all of these tools cover?

We can help people learn how to ask similar evaluative questions of licensed databases and systems. For example, how did Information Access Corporation decide which fifteen hundred magazines and journals to index for its "Magazine and Journal Articles" index available to the University of California community through the California Digital Library? Who made this decision and what factors were taken into account in making it?

In the pre-Web world, information was largely filtered before it ever got to users. Librarians selected books by reading book reviews written by reviewers hired by publishers or editors of magazines, newspapers, and journals. Many books were not reviewed, and, with limited budgets, librarians had to pick and choose for their collections even among those that were reviewed, trying, of course, to develop and maintain collections balanced by differing viewpoints. Articles published in most kinds of media, including newspapers, were reviewed by an editorial board or by peers. Self-published materials were often suspect and thought to be of poor quality. Compare that situation to the current open Web environment. Today, anyone or any group can self-publish on the Web. In addition, publishers and publications with solid reputations also publish on, or through the Web, using it as a delivery mechanism. Instead of filtering materials before they ever get to the user, librarians now need to help users learn to filter on their own, or at least learn to identify trustworthy sites which will filter for them. It is the librarian who should be helping users learn to ask these questions and then where and how to look for answers. (See Figure 16-5 for a sample exercise that will help people learn Step 7.)

STEP 8: DEVELOP CONTENT-BASED, MEASURABLE GOALS AND OBJECTIVES OR LEARNING OUTCOMES, BASED ON NEEDS ASSESSMENTS

It is important to write learning outcomes for instruction, or use existing ILI standards appropriate to your learner group, once general and specific concepts and mechanics have been identified. These goals and objectives should incorporate critical thinking throughout, and should include expected learner outcomes, learning outcomes assessment, program evaluation, and a plan for ongoing revision based on assessment and evaluation results. (See Chapter 7 for details.)

STEP 9: SELECT TEACHING/LEARNING METHODOLOGIES, FLESH OUT CURRICULUM, AND PROVIDE INSTRUCTION

Instruction in technology can and probably should take many forms, both synchronous (real time) and asynchronous (any time, any place), group instruction, one-on-one instruction, tutorials (electronic), point-of-use guides (paper), and exercises or workbooks to accommodate a variety of learning styles and situations. Depending on the library's fiscal and physical environment, as well as staffing and time constraints, these exercises and workbooks can be Web-based or in paper. They can be hands-on exercises to be completed during a group instruction session, or self-paced to be completed at one's leisure. Web-based exercises may be one of the most important means of helping remote users learn to use and think critically about technology.

STEP 10: EVALUATE INSTRUCTION, ASSESS LEARNING OUTCOMES, REVISE AND UPDATE ALL ASPECTS OF THE INSTRUCTIONAL PROGRAM, CONTINUOUSLY

You can conduct evaluation in-person, as well as remotely and synchronously as well as asynchronously. For example, you can use technology to evaluate learning about technology through the use of online quizzes and interactive exercises that actually test learning in addition to measuring user satisfaction. (See Chapter 12 for a detailed discussion of evaluation, and Chapter 17.)

IL LIBRARIANS AND COMPUTER TRAINERS

As we have noted, computer trainers can help users learn about the basic major features of various types of technology. However, they do not have a grasp of the range of resources available on specific topics in a range of formats, nor their relative value. Library school students learn how to evaluate information resources objectively, no matter the format. They learn to be non-judgmental about information resources, to present information of all kinds and in all formats to users in response to requests for help. Librarians have done this at reference desks and in classroom situations for many years, and this effort was little noticed for much of that time. Now that the general public is drowning in an incredible tidal wave of information, the librarian alone can supply a lifejacket in the form of critical thinking skills. It is the librarian who will be able to guide users to the most likely sources to meet their information needs, and will be able to help them learn how to evaluate both the information retrieved and the tool used to retrieve it. The librarian can teach users how to think critically about information tools and their producers or creators, as well as the items they retrieve. Systematically categorizing and analyzing the different types of technology you plan to teach will make the task of designing suitable instruction seem much less overwhelming.

FINAL REMARKS

Information tools are migrating to the Web in such numbers that it almost takes a purposeful effort to consider print, CD-ROM, and other formats in ILI instruction. Yet these are the ILI librarian's strengths; knowledge of the range of information resources in a variety of disciplines and the ability to help people learn to evaluate tools and items, select those most appropriate, and use them effectively. Like many other large tasks, teaching technology can seem overwhelming until it is broken down into manageable units. We began this chapter by facing and discussing the fear of technology. We discussed how to grapple with teaching technology by looking at our history, at the types of technology we have in (or available through) our libraries, by examining user needs, and then by taking a systematic approach to categorizing and teaching various types of technology. Remember, we are not alone in this effort. Computer trainers may be working on parallel tracks, teaching the mechanics of using the same or similar tools. We can and should work together to help our users achieve ILI learning outcomes so they will utilize technology appropriately as it fits their needs, rather than feeling overwhelmed and terrified of it.

EXERCISES

1. Come up with an exercise that will teach users how to distinguish an Internet Function (IF) resource from an Internet Use (IU) resource.
2. Interview a computer trainer and an instruction librarian about their method(s) of teaching the use of software. Compare and contrast their approaches.
3. Critique the following exercise for users:

INDIVIDUAL USER/LARGE GROUP EXERCISE

People use the Internet in a variety of ways, some of which are questionable, if not controversial. For example, the September 20, 1999 issue of *Newsweek* reported that Zack Exley bought the domain name "gwbush.com" for $70 and then offered to sell it to George W. Bush staffers for $350,000. When he was turned down, Exley created a site that parodies Bush and his official election site (Brant, 1999). Bring to class an example of Internet use that illustrates a controversial or questionable use of the Internet. Be prepared to share your example and discuss it with the class.

READ MORE ABOUT IT

Alexander, Jan, and Marsha Tate. 1999. "Evaluating Web Resources" [online]. Available: www2.widener.edu/Wolfgram-Memorial-Library/webeval.htm [December 28].

Barclay, Donald A. 1995. "Teaching the Standard Features of Electronic Databases." In *Teaching Electronic Information Literacy: A How-To-Do-It Manual*, edited by Donald A. Barclay. New York: Neal-Schuman.

Kruger, Justin, and David Dunning. 1999. "Unskilled and Unaware of It: How Difficulties in Recognizing One's Own Incompetence Lead to Inflated Self-Assessments." *Journal of Personality and Social Psychology.* 77 no. 6:1,121–34.

Weil, Michelle M., and Larry D. Rosen. 1997. *Technostress: Coping With Technology @Work @Home @Play*. New York: Wiley & Sons.

17

Using Technology to Teach

We need to remember that the measure of a civilization is not the tools it owns but the use it makes of them.
                                    —Editors, *The New York Times*, 3 Jan 1999, 4: 8

GIVE US THIS DAY OUR DAILY TECHNOLOGY?

Passwords are out; fingerprints are in! Ethentica has developed a swappable PCMIA card for your computer with a sensor that "tests for the electrical properties of human skin" (Corcoran, 2000:238). The MIT Media Lab is developing affective wearable computers that can sense your stress levels and other affective patterns through measurements of your temperature, blood pressure, heart rate, and other factors, and beam that information to others (Picard and Healey, 2000). Neil Gershenfeld confidently predicts that our refrigerators will soon be telling our shoes that the milk is spoiled (1999). The June 11, 2000 *New York Times Magazine* reported on new developments in technology like grass that may be genetically engineered to grow no more than one and a half inches tall, so you may never need to mow your lawn again (Farnham, 2000).

Are you thrilled? Do you welcome these advances? Or do you worry that technology is advancing too quickly, perhaps altering and taking over our lives? Technology is such an integral and yet subliminal part of lives today that we hardly seem to notice it unless it is brand new or beeps, blinks, buzzes, rings, rotates images at us, or even speaks to us. At one extreme, some of us are preoccupied with computers to the point of addiction, while others are terrified of them or go to great lengths to avoid them, or worse yet, have little or no access at all. Those on the "dark side" of the digital divide (see Chapter 2) are particularly concerned about the pace and scope of technology. Yet most of us drive cars, use microwave ovens, toasters, clock radios, and watches, often not realizing that many of these items contain computer chips that keep time, regulate temperature, set off a variety of alarms, and generally keep them running smoothly. We have become comfortable with many forms of impersonal technology, both obvious and subtle, but we are in a semi-permanent transitional state when it comes to using technology for instruction, partly because we are continuously surprised and even taken aback by wonderful, or grotesquely mutating, forms of "technology," which in turn make us question its unexamined use in teaching and learning. So, let us examine the use of technology in instruction.

QUESTIONS ABOUT TECHNOLOGY USE IN INSTRUCTION

It is important to note that your definition of and comfort with various forms of technology often depend upon your level of exposure to and experience with each. What constitutes technology use in an instructional setting, though? What sorts of technology can and should we use, and for what purpose? Does it hinder or help learning? Which kinds of technology should you use in teaching, if any, and for which purpose? How much technology is too much? What can be done to help ILI librarians and other library staff feel comfortable using the technology of their choice? How do we handle the issue of lack of human contact so often associated with technology use?

What Is It?

Most people would call computers, data projectors, Websites, Web browsers, and presentation software, "technology," but what about blackboards, whiteboards, flip charts, overhead transparencies and projectors, slide/tapes, and videotapes? The *Oxford English Dictionary* defines "technology" broadly, as "the scientific study of the practical or industrial arts." Today, most people think of technology as what the same venerable dictionary calls "high-technology," referring to "a firm, industry, etc., that produces or utilizes highly advanced and specialized technology, or to the products of such a firm" (1989).

Yet, in the nineteenth century, chalk, slate, books, and pictures were innovative instructional technologies. Film, a major technological innovation, was first used in a classroom in 1910. Radio and television use in the classroom came next, beginning respectively in 1923 and 1939. When each of these technological innovations was introduced, it promised

" . . . individualized instruction, relief of the tedium of repetitive activities, and presentation of content beyond what was available to a classroom teacher" (Cuban, 1986:4).

In the twentieth century, instructional innovators have eagerly used radio, television, film, whiteboards, presentation software, and more. Yet, according to at least one researcher, all of these technologies (with the exception of chalk, slate, books, and pictures) have failed as widely used teaching tools (Cuban, 1986). The reasons given for this failure sound remarkably familiar to reasons given today for lack of widespread implementation of current technology in educational settings of all kinds, including libraries:

- Teachers' lack of skills in using equipment . . .
- Cost of . . . equipment, and upkeep . . .
- Inaccessibility of equipment when it is needed . . .
- Finding and fitting the right . . . [tool] to the class (Cuban, 1986:18)

Another researcher supports this claim by stating that numerous studies have concluded that there is no significant difference in learning, no matter what sort of technology you use in instruction, radio, television, video, Web, or if you use no technology at all (Russell, 1999a, 1999b, 1999c).

What Good Is It?

So, what good is technology? As we pointed out in Chapter 5, computers have aggravated stress levels among library users. Library staff too suffer from technostress. In addition to other stressors, Kupersmith states that they may suffer from the "Zeigarnik effect," where "interrupted tasks tend to be remembered better than completed tasks, especially when the individual is highly involved in the task and when the interruption is unplanned" (1993:25). As people juggle an ever larger variety of tasks and responsibilities, many of which involve technology use, they feel more and more anxious and stressed. They feel continuous pressure to learn new technology and new versions of technology the minute they are released, both in order to teach it and in order to use it to support other forms of instruction such as Web page creation.

Likewise, new technology for teaching or new technological approaches to teaching seem to pop up almost daily. Yet we are at different skill levels on the technology continuum, and we have differing ideas about which technology to use in teaching, as well as their effectiveness. Learning how to write on a board or flip chart while maintaining the learners' attention is a learned skill, for example, as is creating a Web page, setting up and using a discussion board or a chat room, and using other forms of technology. It is natural for us to be fearful and stressed about what we do not understand; or at the other extreme, to be carried away with glitzy new technology and use it simply because it looks attractive. These good looking "shows," however, may be ineffective or little used by learners if they do not support or enhance pedagogical goals. In this chapter we shall see that many kinds of technology can be useful in helping people achieve learning outcomes, as long as we take the time to define goals, objectives, and expected learning outcomes, and if we spend some time planning and developing before implementing, as well as evaluating and revising afterwards. For those on the hesitant end of the spectrum, we shall try to dispel your fears by demystifying a representative sample of technology and technological approaches that may be useful in instruction. Our focus throughout will be on the judicious use of technology to support IL instructional goals.

Advantages and Disadvantages of Technology Use in Instruction

Technology use in instruction is a controversial issue in some arenas, but not in others. The U.S. armed forces see technology use in instruction as a boon, an important and easily accessible means of training and educating personnel scattered all over the world, both for job-related and for personal development (Masie, 2000). Syllabus Press reports that the U.S. Army " . . . will spend $600 million over the next six years to allow interested soldiers the opportunity to take distance education courses on the Internet at little or no cost" (2000). The U.S. Navy is planning to offer " . . . 24-hour access to 400 courses for 1.2 million Navy personnel and Marines, including reservists and civilians" (Bill Communications, Inc., 2000). The private sector too is quite interested in e-learning and e-training, for three main reasons:

1.   to gain a profit-making share in what they see as the lucrative, wide-open field of education, from Kindergarten through higher education and beyond (IBM, 2000; Learn2.com, 2000)
2.   for employee training (Franklin, 1999; Learn2.com, 2000)
3.   as a device to lure customers to a Website and to establish and maintain their loyalty to that Website as a portal, as their entry point to the Web in general (Barnes & Noble.com, 2000).

Some look at the rapidly expanding e-learning world, and believe that technology promoters inevitably will take over education at all levels . On the other hand, technology critics like David Noble insist that technology use in instruction is not inevitable if we object publicly to its use. He believes quite strongly that it endangers the highly personal, interactive, and dynamic nature of teaching and learning in higher education, and has fought desperately to beat off what he sees as Big-Brotheresque use of technologies such as e-mail and online course builders like WebCT and Blackboard.com (Noble, 1998, 2000a, 2000b). These online software suites and others like them allow instructors to track students' use of a Website to such an extent that some consider it to be a serious invasion of privacy. Noble further sees technology use in education as a tool for financial gain and administrative control over personal intellectual property created by faculty. He worries too that, in higher education at least, institutions may try to gain ownership of course syllabi mounted on Websites, may videotape or otherwise record courses, and then dispense with expensive faculty and instead just use these materials for courses. Other faculty reject most of these views as unsupported claims, and see technology as simply a tool (White, 1999).

However, some do fear that institutions may contract to offer common undergraduate courses like introductory chemistry delivered to their students online, rather than continuing to pay faculty to teach basically the same course in institution after institution, term after term, year after year. In what may turn out to foreshadow this development, though at a lower level, in October 1999 *The Chronicle of Higher Education* reported that the state of Kentucky contracted with the University of Nebraska's for-profit company, Class.com, to provide courses for a completely online high school in Kentucky (Carr, 1999b). Two other universities (Indiana University and University of Missouri at Columbia) have provided distance education for high school students for many years. They have now have been granted accreditation by the North Central Association of Colleges and Schools for online courses to meet the needs of students not enrolled in traditional high schools, for example, home-schooled children (Carr, 1999a). The University of Nebraska's Class.com and Stanford University's Education program for Gifted Youth are also planning to advertise their courses in a number of other countries, including Argentina, Brazil, and Australia, as well as several Asian countries (Carr, 2000).

Is this a trend that will impact education globally at all levels? It may be that necessity will lead many of us down this path as the "Echo" generation—the children of the Baby Boomers—flood higher education establishments that do not have the physical space to handle the demand.

It is true, as Nardi and O'Day put it, that "Every technology change needs critical friends to watch what happens, think about it, and provide useful feedback" (1999: 42). But why should ILI librarians care about all of this? These trends in the educational realm have major implications for libraries, for librarians, and for ILI. The number and variety of both fee and free online information tools and resources continues to expand dramatically. Will educational administrators, businesspeople, and the general community continue to see a need for libraries and librarians if they are under the impression that all information is freely available on the Internet? The British Open University (OU) states that it offers a research course that 18,000 people have taken (2000). What does this course teach and who teaches it? What sort of research materials do participants use? Is there any other sort of help available to OU students who need to do research? Or do they operate similarly to the Los Angeles Public Library, whose Website offers wonderful access to scores of licensed databases with a large variety of interfaces, but no help guides to using them?

In the school environment, one has to wonder what sort of personal interactions students in an online high school can have with their teachers, with librarians (if they have any), and with other students. Who owns online course materials created by teaching faculty and IL instructors? Are there benefits to using technology for instruction of all kinds, including ILI, that outweigh the negatives? How can we best use technology to support IL teaching and learning?

Of course, like faculty and others who develop instructional curriculum and materials, ILI librarians need to be aware of concerns about quality and intellectual property issues related to the use of technology in instruction. As Bransford, Brophy, and Williams put it, we need to consider " . . . *what* students need to learn, *how* they learn, and *what counts as evidence* for their learning" (2000: 67). Have we identified learning outcomes, selected a variety of learning modes, and developed a means of measuring learning? Have learners used technology at appropriate points to get an overview, test ideas, to review, and to self assess (Castellan, 1993)? Have we, in fact, considered whether or not technological tools can help us improve the effectiveness of our instructional handouts, syllabi, Websites, and other materials and programs?

As we have seen, some researchers see no added value to teaching with technology (Cuban, 1986; Ruth, 1997; Russell, 1999a, 1999b, 1999c). Their admonitions are valuable antidotes to those who make technology use the center of their instructional efforts, rather than being guided by pedagogical goals. However, only briefly do they acknowledge that computers and the Internet have opened many doors to learning (Pallis, 1997).

In spite of its drawbacks, technology use in instruction, including computers, can serve varied teaching and learning styles, both in-person and remotely. Some forms of technology offer learners new and more flexible ways to learn and interact that do not have easily accessible (any time/any place) or reasonably priced, quality in-person equivalents. The British Open University, for example, offers numerous distance education courses in many parts of the world to those who live in remote areas or cannot afford the time or money to attend traditional educational institutions. School library media centers, public libraries, and "Street Libraries" may in fact provide the only access to computers and the Internet for low-income people in extremely rundown U.S. neighborhoods (Tardieu, 1999).

Whether you are using technology for ILI in a wealthy urban area or in an isolated disadvantaged area, you need to remember that technology is no more than a tool (Ruth, 1997). In-depth teaching and learning, of necessity, involves interchange between learner and teacher in order to meet pedagogical goals. The use of technology can and should support these pedagogical goals and the teaching-learning interchange. As a complete substitute, currently it may fall short of face-to-face interaction, but the nature of support it can offer is truly astounding, and new technological developments are minimizing many of the differences.

LEARNING AND TRYING OUT TECHNOLOGY FOR INSTRUCTION

In Chapter 9 we described a number of different instructional modes, including some technology-based modes that you might want to try out. Presentation software like Microsoft's PowerPoint is a good example of new technology that seems dauntingly complex. Those who use it seem to create and alter slide shows with ease, making slides fade in and out and making bulleted points fly onto slides. Colors, clip art, and captured images on slides appear as if by magic. Yet presentation software can help get users' attention, quickly reinforce important points, and even help you organize a synchronous group instruction session. You know it can be useful, but how can you learn the basics of new technology like this quickly?

You may be surprised to find that you know more than you think you do about technology, that you can apply what you already know in order to learn the basics of new technologies more easily. You might begin by trying to identify familiar elements from other technologies you have already used. If you have used a word-processing program like Microsoft's Word, then you already have many skills that you can apply to a number of other applications (software programs). For example, both PC and Macintosh programs come with menus that have standard labels, like "File" and "Help." The choices listed under these

---

Figure 17–1
Ten Quick Steps to Creating a PowerPoint Slide Show

1. Open PowerPoint and use the AutoContent Wizard to create a new presentation.
2. Select a presentation type, like "Presentation Guidelines."
3. Indicate whether you want to use the slide show for a presentation or online.
4. Choose a presentation style, like "on-screen presentation," and decide whether or not you want to be able to print out handouts.
5. Enter information that will appear on the title screen.
6. Select "Outline" from the "View" menu, and alter text by highlighting and typing over words, or by backspacing over them.
7. To add hidden notes to slides that only you will be able to see and print out, switch to the "Notes Pages" in the "View" menu.
8. Click in the text box area just under the slide, and type your notes.
9. Switch to "Slide Sorter" in the "View" menu, highlight a slide, click in the box at the top of the screen labeled "No Transition," and select the way you would like that slide to pop on the screen, for example, "Fade Through Black."
10. Click on the icon of a movie screen at the bottom left to see your slide show, pressing enter or clicking with the mouse button to advance through the screens.

---

menu labels vary, but often there are some commonalities like "Save" and "Print."

Many applications come with "wizards," quick, step-by-step guides to help you get started using the program. For example, you can learn how to use PowerPoint in ten steps by beginning with the "AutoContent Wizard." (See Figure 17-1.) If you follow the instructions in Figure 17-1, you can create a basic PowerPoint slide show. The PowerPoint slide show on the CD-ROM that accompanies this book is a somewhat more complex example. If you want to try using a presentation slide show in synchronous instruction, at first you might want to start with just two slides, an outline for the introduction, and a review slide for the conclusion. You can still put points to remember and examples on any number of notes pages and just use those for yourself. You will need to learn how to open the slide show, how to interact with the learners as you use the software, and how to move forward and backward between slides while you are conducting an instruction session (Bit Better, 2000). The next step is to practice incorporating the new technology you learn into a class session, especially if you can get a colleague or a naïve user to provide some constructive criticism. At this point you may feel ready to try using the new technology with learners in an electronic classroom, or remotely through distance learning.

This is one way to get started trying out a technology that is new to you. Some people prefer to learn new technology by following basic instructions on their own or by reading a guide, or even by trying out all the options and printing out all the help screens. Others may only want to learn bits and pieces of technology as the need arises. Still others prefer to take a class or find it easier to learn the software from someone who is familiar with the technology and is willing to serve as a mentor. Which approach is best? The answer is whichever is best for you. If you are overwhelmed by new technology and need to take it one step at a time, then try using a brief guide and focus on mastering just one element of it at a time. If you learn best by watching a demonstration and listening to a linear presentation, and possibly trying out technology at intervals, then take a class or get some one-on-one help from someone who remembers what it is like to be a novice user of this technology.

Keep in mind, though, that it takes time to learn anything new, and that learning to make effective use of technology can take quite a lot of time. In deciding whether or not to use a particular type of technology in teaching/learning situations, you will need to weigh two factors. First, you will need to consider whether or not using the technology will actually improve the learning experience and learning outcomes. Second, you will need to figure out in advance approximately how much of your own time you are able to expend on learning how to make effective use of this particular technology.

Just as we need to set goals and objectives or learning outcomes for our audience, we also need to set goals and objectives or learning outcomes for our own learning. In teaching synchronously, in-person or remotely, we must work within specified time frames. We must decide what are the most important points we want people to learn, and similarly, what the expected technology learning outcomes should be for ourselves. Which technologies should we learn? A good rule of thumb is to invest your time in the simplest form of technology that would help improve learning outcomes for your audience. If you are in an environment with more than one staff member, you may be able to share the burden of keeping up with new technology by divvying up responsibility for becoming the "expert" in different technologies. If possible, you might consider team teaching with your colleagues, with each of you using the technology with which you feel most expert or most comfortable. Electronic classrooms can be good settings for this sort of team teaching, since they often have a variety of technologies in one physical location.

ELECTRONIC CLASSROOMS

When online library catalogs (OPACs) were new and other electronic resources were few, librarians often did in-house and end-user training by lecturing and by drawing or writing on blackboards and whiteboards. Demonstrations in classrooms or meeting rooms came next. At first some libraries used screen prints turned into overhead transparencies, then progressed to using data monitors, and then data projectors.

As computer prices declined and data projector technology improved, and also declined in price, many libraries began to establish electronic classrooms or labs where learners could try out electronic resources during a class session.

ILI librarians were then faced with the dilemma of figuring out how best to utilize the riches of learner workstations and at the same time help people achieve increasingly complex learning outcomes for a mushrooming number of electronic resources. Faced with the 50-minute (one-shot) dilemma, ILI librarians like Barclay have attempted to distill the essence of electronic resources for teaching purposes. (See Chapter 6.) Many have also begun to lean more heavily on print point-of-use guides for the myriad databases and systems that cannot be covered in detail in one brief session. In addition, it takes longer to teach a hands-on session, as learners tend to wander off on their own if the session proceeds too slowly for them, or may not be able to keep up if it proceeds too quickly. In other words, it can be quite a bit more difficult to find and teach to the middle level of any given group when you are teaching a hands-on, in-person group session, especially to learners whom you will encounter as a group only once. One way to help determine the mid-level is to do a quick oral pre-test. Ask how many have used the Web or ask them to rate themselves on a scale of 1 to 5, from someone that has never used a computer or mouse or the Internet to a skilled computer user on one or more platforms with excellent mouse and Web skills. (See Figure 8–1 for detailed definitions of range of computer and information literacy skills.) Then ask experienced learners to sit next to and partner up with those less experienced.

You may want to control the learning environment, since learners do tend to wander off and explore on their own, even during what you may consider to be the most relevant portions of a session. If you decide to go this route, you might want to use classroom control software. This type of software allows you to control all of the learners' screens. You can display the instructor's screen and disable the keyboards, or you may "grab" a learner's screen and display it for the group to see. Classroom control software can come to the rescue if the projection system fails, or if you are teaching in a very large room with forty or more work-

---

Figure 17–2
Sample Class Outline

❑   Welcome learners, go over the outline of the session, and ask for questions (2 minutes)
❑   Define "database," "online database," and "online system" (collection of online databases) (2 minutes)
❑   Introduce the local OPAC and draw a pyramid to describe the search strategy process from local OPAC to regional OPAC to national/international OPAC (2 minutes)
❑   Demonstrate and invite learners to follow along hands-on or watch as you search one of these OPACs (15 minutes):
  √   Have users logon, if necessary
  √   Do one keyword or title word search
  √   Identify subject headings
  √   Do a subject search using one of those headings
❑   Weave critical thinking throughout, for example (15 minutes):
  √   Get learners in groups of two or three
  √   Give them two minutes to look through the list of results and pick out the one they think would be most useful for a research paper
  √   Ask students to explain why they picked particular items and fill in any of the following that they miss: publication date, publisher, author, length, language
❑   Ask for questions (2 minutes)
❑   Review the main points (2 minutes)

---

stations, where you may not be able to walk around to see what is on all the learners' screens. This type of software can be useful, too, if you want to get the learners' attention from time to time by displaying a particular screen. There are pitfalls to this approach, however. Learners may become quite frustrated because they have workstations in front of them, but are not allowed to use them. You may also unintentionally embarrass a learner by using her/his screen as an example for all to see. So, difficult as it may seem, depending on the learners' age and educational level, you should try to balance your desire for control of the learning environment with a more learner-centered approach where learners have the option of following along during a session, just watching, or working with a partner, or simply wandering on their own.

Try breaking your session into ten- to fifteen-minute chunks, and include some partnering or small group exercises, for example, one or two of the exercises from *Designs for Active Learning* (Gradowski, Snavely, and Dempsey, 1998). Alternate between using or showing electronic resources and interacting personally with the learners by asking questions, drawing on a board, and walking around.

It is important, of course, to map out your session in advance, based on the learning outcomes you selected, since it is very easy to get sidetracked by a myriad of points regarding mechanics of using one or another databases or systems. A good rule of thumb is to balance concepts and mechanics equally, if possible, seamlessly weaving them together. For example, if your goal is to help people learn how to identify and locate useful books, you might outline your group session with approximate times indicated for each segment, as in Figure 17-2, "Sample Class Outline."

When learners can follow along or watch, as they choose, the learning environment changes and the electronic classroom can become a less threatening place. In sum, we can help people improve learning outcomes by using a hands-on electronic classroom if we are organized, keep on track, and maintain a positive, friendly, and helping environment, just as we should in non-electronic teaching/learning environments.

Putting It All Together

If you are new to ILI, all of this may seem daunting, if not overwhelming. After all, in addition to determining instructional needs and setting goals, objectives, or expected learning outcomes, coming up with content (including illustrative examples), writing an outline or script that incorporates active learning, preparing supplementary materials like handouts and/or a presentation slide show, and rehearsing and timing your session, you need to figure out how to handle both the instructor's and learners' workstations and other equipment, when and how to meld it all together smoothly, all the while keeping learners interested, motivated, and on task. That is not only a mouthful to say, it requires an incredibly complex set of skills, all of which need to be blended together for a smooth, effective, and efficient session. Take heart! You can learn to do this by working with the ILI technology manager to find out how to use the equipment, and then by observing other ILI librarians teaching live sessions, by taking notes on the techniques and wording you liked, by practicing with them in rehearsals, by keyboarding for a class, and even by team-teaching (LaGuardia et al., 1996). Ask for or make up your own simple checklist for using technology to teach and for how to set up an electronic classroom before a session, based on whatever sort of equipment training or other instructions you receive regarding the electronic classroom (LaGuardia et al., 1996; see also Figures 17-3 and

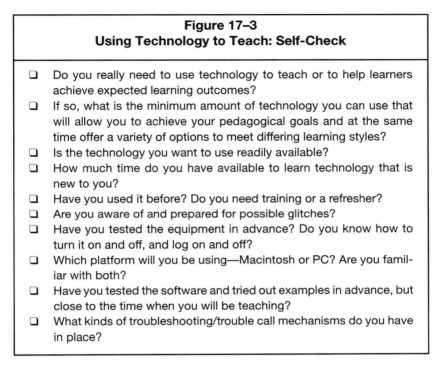

Figure 17–3
Using Technology to Teach: Self-Check

❑   Do you really need to use technology to teach or to help learners achieve expected learning outcomes?

❑   If so, what is the minimum amount of technology you can use that will allow you to achieve your pedagogical goals and at the same time offer a variety of options to meet differing learning styles?

❑   Is the technology you want to use readily available?

❑   How much time do you have available to learn technology that is new to you?

❑   Have you used it before? Do you need training or a refresher?

❑   Are you aware of and prepared for possible glitches?

❑   Have you tested the equipment in advance? Do you know how to turn it on and off, and log on and off?

❑   Which platform will you be using—Macintosh or PC? Are you familiar with both?

❑   Have you tested the software and tried out examples in advance, but close to the time when you will be teaching?

❑   What kinds of troubleshooting/trouble call mechanisms do you have in place?

17-4). Be sure to allow plenty of time to set up the equipment, check your handouts, and review your session script, outline, and/or presentation software slide show before the session begins—set aside, generally, about an hour.

The electronic classroom, of course, represents an effective means of helping users in a synchronous, face-to-face group instruction environment. Remote instruction offers many other benefits and challenges.

DISTANCE LEARNING

Poverty, isolation, disabilities and physical distance from educational institutions—thankfully, these too commonplace barriers to achieving one's potential are melting quickly as technology access broadens, and as distance education begins to take hold at many levels. Synchronous (simultaneous, real time) and asynchronous (any time/any place) learning over the Internet suits learners who are unable to attend traditional in-person classes at a particular physical location, scheduled at regular intervals during a term. They may need to work full time when a particular class is offered, or may not be able to get to the physical location

---

Figure 17–4
Sample Electronic Classroom Preparation Checklist

❑   Turn on the main power in the media cabinet by pressing top POWER button.

❑   Turn on the data projector by pressing the green ON button.

❑   Switch the display to VHS or some other medium by pressing button 2, 3 or 4 to the right of the data projector ON button. (This will blank the screen so it does not display what appears on the instructor's monitor.)

❑   Lower the electronic screen.

❑   Turn on the monitor on the instructor's workstation, log on to the network and open the Web browser you are going to use for the session.

❑   Turn on the monitors on each of the 14 student workstations, log on to the network and open the Web browser you are going to use for the session.

❑   Go back to the instructor's workstation
 √   go over your script or outline
 √   test out each site and example you plan to use and make any necessary changes
 √   test out your presentation slide show if you plan to use one
 √   decide and test out how you will point to items on the electronic screen (mouse, pointer pen, laser pointer, your hand)

❑   If you want to distribute handouts at the beginning of the session, have them in packets and place them on chairs in the room.

❑   If you want to distribute handouts at intervals during the session, make sure you have enough of them, stacked in the order in which you want to distribute them, and in handy reach.

❑   Test out the lighting.

❑   Write your name and e-mail address or phone number on the board, or have this information on the first slide in your slide show.

❑   Switch the display back to the instructor's monitor by pressing button 1 to the right of the data projector ON button.

❑   When the session is over, if the room will not be used for the rest of the day, go back through each step, picking up leftover handouts, turning off lights, logging off workstations, etc.

at all or on a regular basis. They may even be in a different part of the country or the world, with scant opportunities for education.

What does "distance learning" mean today when learners can be at a "distance" a mere building away, or anywhere in the world? Geographical boundaries have eroded. Day and night are losing meaning as companies, organizations, and educational institutions, including libraries, furiously scramble to offer 24/7 (24 hours a day/7 days a week) services of all kinds, including self-service asynchronous Web pages.

The Encyclopedia of Educational Technology lists four types of distance education interactions: learner-to-learner; learner-to-instructor; learner-to-interface; learner-to-content (Schutt, 2000). Distance learning can include remote instruction in the form of static and interactive Web pages, discussion boards, chat, and online courses that incorporate all of these modes and more.

Library Involvement in Distance Learning

For ILI, distance learning refers to remote learning, synchronous or asynchronous, in formal distance education environments away from a physical "campus," or in any setting, including the physical campus, that involves no face-to-face interaction. However, some distance education courses do involve minimal in-person interaction, for example, one or two face-to-face meetings of all students enrolled in an online course. For the purposes of this book, we shall consider these forms of instruction "remote," since the learners do not spend the majority of their instructional time face-to-face with each other or with an instructor.

ILI librarians have been using Web-based exercises, tutorials, online courses, and even "cybermobiles" to help their users and staff achieve both narrow and broad information literacy learning outcomes remotely, and news about their efforts is spreading. Morgan reports that the St. Louis (Missouri) County Library turned one of its bookmobiles into a "cybermobile." They completely replaced the interior of the bookmobile, and installed a local area network (LAN) hooked up to the Internet for seven workstations, and an LCD panel and projector. They traveled around to their nineteen branches in this cybermobile, training 700 staff (Morgan, 1999). In its February 23, 2000 issue, *The Chronicle of Higher Education* lauded Ellen Chamberlain's online tutorial, titling its article, "Lost in Cyberspace? A Librarian Offers an Online Course on Search Engines" (McCollum, 2000). Libraries also offer help for distance learners taking academic courses. For example, the University of South Florida offers an information-packed Web page called "USF Distance Learners Library Services" (2000). A consortium of academic libraries in Virginia offers a Website called "VIVA: The Virtual Library of Virginia" (2000).

This site quite simply links to "Electronic Collections," "Access to Libraries," and "Internet Search Tools." The University of Tennessee, Knoxville offers a Web page entitled "Off-Campus Library Services: Providing Library Services to UT Students Involved in Off-Campus/Distance Education Programs" (2000).

Principles for Success

What underlies successful distance education efforts? How are they distinct from programs that merely utilize technology? The ALA-ACRL Distance Learning Section published revised and helpful "Guidelines for Distance Learning Library Services" in 2000, which define distance education from an academic library perspective. The guidelines cover topics such as management, finances, personnel, resources, services and documentation, and finances (2000c). They focus on library resources and services for distance education or extended campus programs, though they include "courses attended in-person" as well as electronically. The ACRL guidelines strongly emphasize the importance of lifelong learning, to be instilled through "general bibliographic and information literacy instruction" (2000:1,025). At a minimum, they state that the librarian administrator of library support services for distance education conduct needs assessments, assess IL learning outcomes, and participate in curriculum development and course planning "to ensure that appropriate library resources and services are available" (2000:1,027). They also state that originating institutions should have on hand a minimum of types of documentation to prove that they are meeting these guidelines. Interestingly, "printed user guides" is first on their list of eighteen different kinds of documentation recommended for this purpose.

The Canadian Library Association's (CLA) Services for Distance Learners Interest Group has also developed useful draft "Guidelines for Library Support of Distance and Distributed Learning in Canada" (2000). The two documents cover similar topics, and both are meant to delineate clearly what distance education is and what are the responsibilities of libraries and institutions regarding their own distance learners as well as those affiliated with other institutions.

Penn State, Lincoln, and Cheyney Universities developed a set of five guidelines for designing and developing distance education for higher education in general (Ragan, 1999). It may be useful to examine these guidelines as well to see how and where ILI fits in. Their Category II, "Interactions," for example, emphasizes that it is through interaction with an instructor and others that people learn. This is true both for in-person and for distance learning. In a distance learning environment, the ILI librarian could offer to monitor the class discussion board for information research issues, and could be available via e-mail for individual consultation. The ILI librarian could work with the instructor to devise a series of interactive Web-based exercises or a workbook which the distance ed learners could complete asynchronously. But who is our audience and what is their level of expertise and experience with technology? What are their age and skill levels? What do they already know about the topics you want to cover and about related areas?

AUDIENCE AND PURPOSE

As we have mentioned in previous chapters, audience is one of the most critical factors we need to consider in developing and providing ILI in any format. This is particularly true for distance or remote learning, as our potential learner base has grown to include anyone who has an Internet connection anywhere in the world. For distance learning in particular, we must define and actively target our primary learner groups, gearing ILI to their needs first. In public libraries, for example, primary learner groups include all levels of society, all age groups, and all educational levels within particular geographical regions. Academic, school, and special libraries each have smaller bites of the user pie, often defined in their mission statements.

IS DISTANCE ED BEST?

Almost as soon as there was a quick way to use the Internet, by means of Gopher software, ILI librarians began building IL Internet instruction, though remote ILI really took off with the advent of the Web in 1994. Both passive and interactive IL instructional Websites have evolved and matured since 1994 as the Web has become the focus of distance learning efforts at many levels. As Kirk and Bartelstein point out, distance education is not just another fad (1999). An increasing number of colleges and universities have distance education programs. In January 2000, *The Chronicle of Higher Education* reported that "1,680 [U.S.] institutions offered a total of about 54,000 online-education courses in 1998, with 1.6 million students enrolled," a 72 percent increase over 1995 offerings (Carnevale, 2000). As we have seen, e-learning businesses are popping up all the time as well.

Physical distance of any kind becomes almost irrelevant once you have defined targeted user groups. For example, academic libraries will want to provide ILI to undergraduates in dorm rooms at 2 a.m., as well as to their own faculty doing research while on sabbatical in other parts of the world. It is easy to keep campus or local community populations in mind when planning ILI, even if they are in dorm rooms or at home, since they have a physical connection to the institution when they attend classes or come to a library building for materials.

It is more difficult to think about distance learners' information research needs when they are essentially invisible unless they make themselves visible through technology like e-mail. How are these people getting their research materials? Are they using Web search tools like Yahoo! and Google to identify and locate materials? Are they using sites like Northern Light or going directly to magazine and journal Websites, and paying for articles and other items they could get for free through licensed databases? Who is helping them sort through the information muddle? As Kirk and Bartelstein emphasize, librarians must be proactive. We must reach out to distance ed instructors and learners who are part of our larger community (Kirk and Bartelstein, 1999). If we do not, we may be left behind as dot com sites like refdesk.com take over one of our most important roles as objective information evaluators and advisors. How can we address distance learning IL needs? Many of the sample technologies we have already discussed could be utilized for this purpose, but what sorts of distance ed techniques should you use?

Techniques

In addition to its "Guidelines for Distance Learning Library Services," the ALA-ACRL Distance Learning Section (2000c) has links to many distance learning tools, including "Courseware and Groupware Products" such as Web-based conferencing software and "Courseware Development and Collaboration Tools." These links focus on academic libraries, though many of the tools and examples could be adapted for other environments. Similarly, approaches used in school or private sector environments could be adapted for use in academic or public libraries. For example, academic libraries have developed Web-based online courses and tutorials, as well as Web pages targeted specifically at distance learners (SUNY, Buffalo, 1999); the business community and the U.S. government have focused on Web-based training (WBT), including simulations; schools have developed WebQuests for K–12 students, and public libraries have led in developing digital collaboration for reference. WebQuests, for example, provide a structured approach to using the Web to support instruction (Dodge, 2000). Teachers select topics and Websites, develop research focus, and assign members of student teams to investigate various aspects of a topic like the art and environment of the Navajo (Dodge, 2000). WebQuests make learning fun, interesting, and relevant, and as a result students may be more motivated to complete instruction and to retain learning.

Instructional games also attract interest and can hold learners' attention (DeLorenzo, 1999; Blum and Yocom, 1996; Childers, 1996; Doolittle, 1995). Elaborate, graphically rich computer games require much development time, expertise, and expensive software. People do enjoy learning through games, though, so why not investigate some simple approaches like the "Save the Village" game, created completely remotely by high school students from three countries for their award-winning ThinkQuest Website, "Volcanoes Online" (1998). Challenge learners to test their "Information Literacy IQ," solve an IL puzzle, or find answers to interesting questions.

Tutorials, WebQuests, and games can be highly useful in ILI, and address preferences for both learner-to-learner and learner-to-interface instructional modes, though remember that some people prefer learner-to-instructor modes. Each of these approaches should be selected and designed to support your pedagogical goals of course, and you will need to consider all of the mode selection factors mentioned in Chapter 8, as well as copyright, intellectual property, and privacy issues. Access is a critical issue. You will also need to consider whether or not there will be free and easily accessible technology sophisticated enough to handle whatever ILI you devise.

How effective is distance education? Are learners achieving expected learning outcomes? Are they meeting the standards or goals you have set? Evaluation and assessment of learning will help answer these questions. Schrock has created excellent Website evaluation tools for grade levels ranging from primary through high school. These forms could be assigned as homework and used to assess learning following a group instruction session (Schrock, 2000a). You may also want to adapt these or other forms for adult learners, with the authors' permission, of course.

Every day it seems there are more Web-based ILI tutorials, many of which are listed on the LOEX Website. These tutorials may address different audiences and have different purposes, but the primary question is whether or not their primary audience is achieving the learning outcomes expected of them after they have completed the tutorial. Online quizzes and tests may help, if you can get the learners to your site, and if they complete the instruction. At this point, there are more questions than answers regarding the effectiveness of ILI distance education. Admittedly, this is an uncertain state, but it offers great opportunity for small-scale experimentation. You may be pleasantly surprised at the results of such experiments or you may be disappointed, but in any case you will surely learn a lot and will be better prepared for the next experiment.

USING TECHNOLOGY TO PREPARE FOR BOTH LOW-TECH AND HIGH-TECH ENVIRONMENTS

How do you prepare when you are unsure of whether or not you will be using technology at the higher end of the instructional technology continuum? If you are prepared, organized, and have a variety of backup plans and materials, people will learn whether or not the network is up, the workstation is running, and there is a continuous flow of electricity. Be prepared to pose questions to the learners, go through interactive exercises that help people learn concepts, and provide paper handouts for mechanics. For example, if all equipment fails, you may still have a speaker's outline and point-of-use guides for the OPAC, as well as one or more licensed databases. You can still do small and large group exercises on topic selection, on the flow of information, on Boolean operators, and on the differences between magazines and journals, including critical thinking about what you can expect to get from each. You can even begin by asking learners to write questions on blank cards, and then use their questions to frame and conduct the session.

If the network connection fails, but you still have electricity, and you have prepared in advance, you may still be able to demo Web pages. Inexpensive offline Web browsers like WebWhacker allow you to save to a disk one or a series of Web pages, along with their images. Generally, you specify which page you want to save and how many levels of links you want to save from that page. Once the pages have been saved, you can use a Web browser like Netscape or Internet Explorer to view them without being connected to the Internet. For all intents and purposes, these saved pages make it seem as though you have a live connection, though links will only work as far down as you have saved the pages. However, if a learner wants to see something you have not saved, or wants you to do a search you have not prepared, you will be unable to accommodate her/him. In addition, most offline Web browsers do not allow you to specify which links you would like to save off the page you save first. So you may end up with a number of files that you do not want or need. Also, if files are very large, you may only be able to save them in networked storage, on a hard drive, or on a Zip disk. This may make them unusable for synchronous in-person use in remote locations if you do not have equipment that can handle so many files, some of which may be quite large. With some advance planning, though, you can make good use of an offline Web browser to create backups. Decide which pages are most important, and how many levels of links you need. In most cases just one or two levels of links should be sufficient. Any more than that and you may very well run out of room to save all the files, especially since graphic images can take up a lot of computer memory. Then save two copies of the files on floppy or Zip disks, just in case one of the disks is unreadable.

You can also use word-processing software to prepare a session outline, and you can use presentation software to prepare overhead transparencies. You can send follow-up information or answer questions later though a class bulletin board or by e-mail. Many kinds of technology can be useful in instruction in a range of environments and circumstances, indirectly as well as directly, but it is possible to lose learners with too much technology.

HOW MUCH TECHNOLOGY IS TOO MUCH?

Are in-person groups of learners falling asleep? Are their eyes glazed over? Do they seem dazed and overwhelmed or turned off? Are they having trouble following along in a hands-on environment or grasping basic concepts in a demonstration or other synchronous learning environment? Stop. Ask questions to check for comprehension. Above all, listen carefully and respectfully to the learners' answers (or lack of them). Always blame the machines and the software for difficulties rather than the learners (Agre, 2000). Turn off the display, slow down, simplify, and offer friendly words of encouragement and support. Proceed with machines and other electronic/electric equipment in-person only when learners indicate they are ready to do so. Drop back to simpler electronic/electric modes if synchronous online participation drops off.

Is your wonderful new interactive Web-based tutorial unused or underused? Are learners starting it, but not finishing? Are faculty ignoring your Web-based exercises, hints, tips, and forms? Usage statistics can provide some indication of the success of your Website, though testing for learning outcomes is the real indicator of success. If usage is low and learning outcomes are not satisfactory, usability testing with naïve users and subsequent revisions may help (see Chapter 11). Most of all, we should not be discouraged by underuse of our electronic products and services. It takes time for new forms of instruction to take hold, and we may have to do some marketing to bring them to the attention of those who need them.

SYNCHRONICITY AND ASYNCHRONICITY, REDUX

There is still much demand for synchronous ILI, in-person and remote, paper and electronic/electric. However, the development of asynchronous electronic/electric instruction presents a singular opportunity for

ILI to meld with academic curricula at all levels, from Kindergarten through higher education, and to provide support and lifelong learning opportunities for learners in all sorts of environments. This is a very exciting opportunity for ILI librarians, as it opens the door to many creative approaches to ILI that will be able to reach many more people at many different levels. Scarcity of staff time has long been a mitigating factor in offering in-person, synchronous ILI, and has in effect forced us to focus on our primary users largely to the exclusion of others. Synchronous remote learning and particularly Web-based asynchronous learning allow us to reach out to a larger variety of user groups by offering various forms of ILI in learner-centered approaches. For example, academic libraries could create ILI self-tests designed for high school students who would like to prepare in advance for their freshman year in college. These self-tests could help students identify weak areas, and also link to instruction designed to strengthen skills or knowledge, such as critical thinking about Web pages.

THE CRUX OF LEARNING AND TEACHING

With or without technology, however, most people would probably agree that "Effective teaching is that which leads to engaged and intelligent learning" (Koppi, Lublin, and Chaloupka, 1997: 245), or "deep learning" (Koppi, Lublin, and Chaloupka, 1997). In other words, the core of effective teaching and learning is interaction between learner and teacher. Interaction between learners can support and enhance interaction between learner and teacher. Both types of interaction can take place synchronously, in face-to-face group instruction, or remotely in group sessions, but can also take place asynchronously, any time, any place, one person at a time (Chickering and Ehrmann, 2000).

It seems fairly obvious that teacher and learners can interact synchronously in face-to-face group instruction. The instructor can ask questions, answer questions, query learners about puzzled looks, set up active learning exercises for large and small groups, get learners to lead discussions, organize debates, use Think-Pair-Share and other creative problem-solving techniques, and even use active learning assessment techniques to review and stimulate learning (ALA-ACRL-IS, 1998; Angelo and Cross, 1993). Instructors can use many of these same techniques in synchronous remote instruction, such as chat, but the instructor has to work harder to engage learners and there are more caveats. There is no body language, so verbal cues are very important, as is lack of participation. It can help to ask questions and to chunk learning into manageable bites, interspersed with activities or exercises.

But how, you may ask, can teacher and learners interact asynchronously?

They can interact remotely through discussion boards or listservs where an entire group or a subset can respond to issues and questions. They can also interact privately via e-mail. Instructors can post messages that take controversial stands on issues of interest to the group, encourage debate and discussion, and draw attention to key points, as well as strengths and weaknesses of arguments.

Learners can interact asynchronously as well with interactive Web-based materials and with printed materials. They can do Web-based exercises and receive feedback on their answers. They can send e-mail reference questions and receive e-mail answers which help them learn how to learn. In print, they can complete worksheets, turn them in, and receive corrections and comments.

It is difficult, if not impossible, however, to predict which form of interaction between learner and teacher would work best for a particular individual with a given information or learning need, at any given time or place. From the learner's standpoint, the best approach for one situation may not be best for another, and the same is true for the teacher. Ideally, the teacher should provide several different alternative means of interacting with learners, and respond flexibly to whichever method the learners use. Of course, little of this will simply happen on its own. You must plan for interaction in teaching, especially for successful distance learning, and you will need help because any sort of teaching with technology hinges on well organized, timely, capable, and supportive technology management (Schutt, 2000).

FINAL REMARKS

Does technology hinder or help? Is there a significant difference in learning when we utilize technology in teaching? Do people learn more, better, or differently when we use technology in instruction? What levels and percentages of use, as well as types of technology are best, for which situations? What sort of technology can and should we use in-person and remotely in order to support our ILI goals? We have attempted to help you along in your search for answers to these important questions, answers that will vary according to your institution's or organization's current needs and circumstances. Most importantly, we need to keep asking questions and keep developing and adjusting our questions and answers as often as necessary in our exciting, frightening, and ever-changing world.

EXERCISES

1. In which of these situations would you want to use technology to teach? Why or why not?
   - Face-to-face group instruction
   - Individual instruction
   - Distance/remote instruction
2. Which sorts of technology would you use for a class of 15? Which sorts of technology would you use for a group of 50? What would work best for distance learning? What about individual remote users?
3. Sample situation:
   You have 50 minutes to teach the use of a new Web-based OPAC to a class of 25 freshmen.
   a. How could your use of technology help or hinder their learning?
   b. Which types of technology would you want to use for this class, if you knew how to use them?
   c. Given your current state of knowledge and experience with technology, which types of technology do you think you would use right now?

READ MORE ABOUT IT

Agre, Philip. 2000. "How To Help Someone Use A Computer" [Online]. Available: dlis.gseis.ucla.edu/people/pagre/how-to-help.html [November 4].

ALA. Association of College and Research Libraries. Distance Learning Section. 2000. [Online]. Available: http://caspian.switchinc.org/~distlearn/ [August 6].

Cuban, Larry. 1986. *Teachers and Machines: The Classroom Use of Technology Since 1920*. New York: Teachers College Press, Columbia University.

Russell, Thomas L. 1999. *The No Significant Difference Phenomenon: As Reported in 355 Research Reports, Summaries and Papers*. Raleigh, NC: North Carolina State University.

Ruth, Stephen. 1997. "Getting Real About Technology-Based Learning: The Medium is NOT the Message." *Educom Review* (September/October):32–37.

Tardieu, Bruno. 1999. "Computer as Community Memory: How People in Very Poor Neighborhoods Made a Computer Their Own." In *High Technology and Low-Income Communities: Prospects for the Positive Use of Advanced Information Technology*, edited by Donald A. Schoen, Bish Sanyal, and William J. Mitchell. Cambridge, MA: MIT Press.

Part V

The Future of ILI

18

Visions of the Future:
Two Perspectives

Wise men come, ever promising, the riddle of life to know.
                                        —"Sands of Time," *Kismet*

ESTHER S. GRASSIAN'S PERSPECTIVE

Have we solved the riddle of effective ILI for you? I think not. Riddles are perplexing. Some are insolvable while others simply require concentrated thought. We have tried to give you the tools to help you think about and solve the riddle for yourself within your environment. As you use these tools, I hope three principles will guide you: patience and respect for the past, judicious use of technology as a tool, and joy in empowering all learners.

Patience and Respect for the Past

In this impatient world it may seem incongruous to suggest slowing down, waiting, building relationships, and letting people chew on ideas. After all, opportunities may pass us by. Technology does not stand still while we think about positives, negatives, and costs, and experiences of the past cannot possibly mean anything now in the technological realm. Or can they? Do your colleagues have experience with pre- and post-testing? Have they tried interactivity in the paper-based world with exercises or workbooks? Have you observed their instructional techniques,

413

examined their instructional materials, talked to them, and listened carefully to what they have to say about the benefits and drawbacks of their approaches to teaching and learning? You may know a lot about present capabilities, but your patient and respectful queries directed at colleagues can uncover invaluable treasures that may be reused or reformulated to fit new uses.

Judicious Use of Technology as a Tool

Many of us are caught up in the endless cycle of new and upgraded technology, and worry about being replaced by e-reference and e-learning commercial enterprises if we do not jump on each new form of technology as it comes along. Some are hooked on change, constantly seeking the next new technological high. This new world is enticing and so bedazzling that it is difficult to look away and think about our purpose. Why are we using technology to teach? What pedagogical goals does it support? Which form of technology would best meet our needs? Would it be better in some cases simply to interact on a personal basis, face to face?

On the other hand, new technology may be able to help us improve all of our instructional efforts. For example, does it seem as though learners only remember there is an ILI Web page for their class and nothing else from your one-shot group sessions? You can use technology to see if your impression is correct. Ask faculty/teachers to put a link to a pre- and post-test on the class Web page. Before the session, ask learners to take the pre-test. A month after your instructional session, ask learners to take the post-test. Compare the results to the pre-test and you will have your answer. If indeed learners only remember the Web page, you may want to replace time-intensive, one-shot group instruction with other instructional modes that will do a more effective job of helping them achieve expected learning outcomes and retain what they learn.

Just remember that you are in control of technology and can make it work for you and for your learners. As long as you focus on your destination, the learning outcomes you expect to see and their retention, you maintain power over your technological tools.

Joy in Empowering All Learners

ILI is also supposed to empower learners so that they have control over information tools and know how to learn. It is easier to do this on a college campus with computer labs and widespread access to the Internet, and where more and more information tools appear daily. But how do we help the Internet have-nots? We need to make Internet access a part of everyone's life.

Can you make this happen? Yes! ILI librarians like you, from all sorts of environments, have worked to develop standards and objectives that define information literacy in measurable terms. As we mentioned in Chapter 2, accrediting agencies in the U.S. are revamping accreditation standards for schools and colleges, and are considering adding IL standards to them.

If IL standards are incorporated into accreditation standards, there may be a day when the SAT and the GRE measure IL competencies. In order to get into college, and in order to continue on to graduate school, students will need to demonstrate increasingly complex levels of IL skills. Administrators may exhort faculty/teachers to incorporate ILI into their curricula. Businesses will expect high school and college graduates to be computer and information literate, just as they now expect them to be able to read. Students will acquire these skills beginning in elementary school, just as they acquire reading and math literacy skills, and will be tested for them at various educational levels, and in the workforce, based on expected learning outcomes.

It is our role and our privilege to work toward these goals, to bring information power to everyone through information literacy, especially underrepresented minority groups and the impoverished, those whom the Consumer Federation of America has labeled the "Disconnected, Disadvantaged, and Disenfranchised" (Cooper, 2000).

The Solution?

I hope you see now that there is no one solution and there may not be one instructional program that will meet all of your learners' needs. You, your colleagues, faculty/teachers, and your administrators alone can answer questions such as: "How can we adapt these lessons to our environment?", "What can we learn from past experiences?", "What are the newest questions?", "How can we continue to create new opportunities for learning and teaching in our swiftly evolving technological world?", or "How can we best support and assess what we do?"

In the end, ILI is what you make of it. You will need to decide for yourself when continuous change becomes change for its own sake, how you will judge the effectiveness of instruction, which instructional modes will best suit your environment and circumstances, whether or not to create a single program or a multi-pronged one that can flex with shifting needs and circumstances, and when to let go of a mode that is no longer effective. You can create collegial coalitions by building on the past, by working in the present, and by looking to the future. You have the power to transform and empower your learners through information literacy instruction, and I am confident that you will.

JOAN R. KAPLOWITZ'S PERSPECTIVE

Whenever anyone asks me to look into my crystal ball and predict what I see for the future of ILI, I tend to reply, "The more things change, the more they remain the same." While I fully expect new and different types of technology to transform not only the ways in which we access information, but also how we deliver it, I believe that the issues we have always faced as ILI librarians will remain the same. We will continue to struggle with how to provide the type of quick instructional support our users require at any given moment. Furthermore, we will still be faced with the problem of convincing our users that they need additional instruction if they are to gain the deeper and more transferable skills that will move them toward being information literate individuals.

Two issues complicate the delivery of both the quick answer type of instructional support, and the more in-depth ILI. First, there is the issue of remote users. With access to more and more resources being made electronic, large percentages of our "regular" clientele will be accessing our material remotely. It will become difficult to even know who these users are, and extremely challenging to determine what their information and instructional needs might be. While we may be able to provide easy access and even seamless, invisible gateways to information, we may find it difficult to get the "evaluating for quality" idea across. How will we be able to convince users to be selective in their information choices? Even now we see users opt for articles that appear in electronic format and reject those available only in print with no regard to the relative merit of the articles themselves. Convincing users that they should actually make a trip to the library for material when they can access a wide range of information without leaving their bedrooms will become even more of an issue in the future. Somehow ILI professionals will have to find a way to get the message across that "easy to get" does not always equal "best information available." Libraries can help alleviate this problem by enhancing document delivery services and speeding up the process, perhaps by scanning material and faxing items to users. Still, being available for immediate printing from a desktop will continue to be faster and more convenient than ordering items, perhaps at a cost, and then waiting for the delivery of that information. Obviously the more material we can get into electronic format the better. But it will be many years down the road (if ever) before everything is available that way.

Second is the related issue of library loyalties or the question of "Which library is mine?" Although users may have primary affiliation with only a particular library or consortia of libraries, they can and will be using a variety of others. Their rights and privileges will be determined by their status in relation to the library they are accessing remotely. While some services and resources will be provided freely, others may cost or may not be available at all to someone who is not counted as a primary user of that library. How do we provide instructional support for this mix of users, some of whom can access the whole range of resources and others who have varying levels of access? How do we teach those who do not have the whole range of resources what their options are and, furthermore, explain to them why the restrictions exist? Who will be the advocate for the remote user when we are unsure who they are and what their status might be?

One solution to these issues of remote access and mixed library loyalties is to increase cooperation and collaboration between libraries of all kinds. Resource sharing among all libraries in a given geographic area, for example, would mean that people could access all material regardless of which library they were using (in-person or virtually). Collaborative instructional projects between libraries at all levels would help to promote the idea of ILI throughout a person's life span, wherever and whenever he or she interacts with a library and its resources.

With the proliferation of e-commerce, the use of the Internet by the news media, the promotion of Websites as a means of providing health information, and even the mounting of Websites as a major part of political campaigning, becoming IL is rapidly turning into a life survival skill. Providing the means of acquiring this essential skill is the shared responsibility of ILI librarians in every library—public, school, academic, and special. A coordinated effort by all ILI librarians will ensure that appropriate ILI will be available to all and that instruction provided in each environment will complement that given in the others. Building a sequential approach is not only sensible, it is imperative if we are to reach our goal of having an IL populace. The instructional sequence should begin at the public library level for the very young child, move through all stages of education (K–12 and on into the higher education environment), out into the workplace via the special library, and back to the public library for our seniors. The public library should also take ILI responsibility for those adults who use the public library as their primary source of both print and electronic resources. Working together, IL professionals can make sure that IL initiatives are prominently considered (and funded) by governing bodies, administrators, and voters alike. Schools and academic institutions should be encouraged to include IL competencies in their educational objectives and provide a means for testing the acquisition of these competencies. Being IL should be as much a graduation requirement as being able to read and write. Furthermore, employers should be shown the value of having IL workers, and be encouraged to make IL part of the screening process when hiring.

Clearly, the needs of the primary users at each different type of library will vary. But this very variety can be used to advantage if IL professionals in those libraries are working together in a coordinated fashion. We need better communication between those IL professionals working in each of the various environments and a better understanding of exactly what piece of the IL skills puzzle is most appropriate to present under differing circumstances. We can no longer afford to isolate ourselves from our colleagues based on our type of library. Each of us needs to know what is going on in library environments other than our own in order to make sure this sequencing is happening in the most efficient and appropriate way possible. We need to be building upon, not replicating each other's work, and coordinating our efforts throughout our profession. The economic impetus toward resource sharing among libraries can work to our advantage as it promotes more interactions between libraries of all kinds. IL professionals should use these opportunities to promote the sequential, cooperative, collaborative approach to ILI that is so necessary to make IL a reality for everyone.

Advances in information technology are not only a factor in the access and delivery of information. These advances also provide a way for IL to improve the delivery of instruction as well. One approach is to develop user-friendly front ends. The goal of these front ends or gateways is to provide seamless access to information. Users do not choose the online catalog when they want a book. They merely fill in a search request asking for the book they want and the system takes them where they need to go. Some systems may even search a number of OPACs at the same time to locate the desired item. Similar query boxes are provided for journal articles. Again, users do not have to specify (or even know) the appropriate database to search. They merely pick a broad category such as "Psychology" or "Education" and the system searches the appropriate database or databases for them.

While this approach provides a high level of service to the user, there are several caveats to be aware of. First, gateways such as these are only as good as the person who designed them. The interface may look easy to the user, but a great deal of work is required to program these systems to search efficiently and correctly. Furthermore, since users are not aware of how or where the system is looking for information, it is often difficult to determine why they are getting the particular results, and to adjust the search appropriately to get more focused information. For example, a user may think that his or her topic might be found in medical literature but in fact it would be better to search sociology material. These interfaces must have some kind of feedback loop built in that instructs the user how to modify their searches when results are not what they want.

Finally, in order for these interfaces to work across a range of resources, a uniform search strategy must be developed that will work in all the resources. This often means that some of the elegant and sophisticated features that are specific to certain resources will not be used. There is a definite trade-off between ease of use and relevance of retrieval. The easier search paradigm may allow the user to find information quickly, and without real knowledge of the databases. However, a great deal of relevant information may be missed because the database is not being used to its full capabilities. On the other hand, the more sophisticated the search interface becomes, the more instruction becomes necessary. At the very least, on-screen (preferably context specific) help is essential. Links to additional instructional support that aid the user in designing search strategies to take advantage of these sophisticated options are also useful.

Another aspect to consider when thinking about user-friendly interfaces or gateways is transferability. If users remain unaware of how they obtained their information, how will they be able to reconstruct the process in another context? In a way, the development of a seamless gateway creates a dependency situation. The user can operate quite successfully within that particular gateway. But what happens when they must access information some other way? While one of our goals is certainly to assist users in obtaining what they need quickly and easily, another very important goal is for them to learn how they did it so that they can do it anywhere, anytime, and for any information need. One of our real dilemmas is and will continue to be how to balance the "providing information quickly and easily" aspect with the need to instruct our users on some of the more complex concepts of accessing, using, and evaluating information resources.

Ironically, technology both hinders and helps us in this task. It provides us with the means of delivering excellent, interactive, and engaging instructional material to people where and when they need it. But getting people to take that extra step of learning how to find quality information can be a very daunting task. It is hard to expect people to spend time on our tutorials when they already have found enough (in their view) material to suit their needs. Getting people to take advantage of the many wonderful tutorials that are being developed and will certainly continue to be developed in the future will be one of our biggest challenges. This becomes an even bigger issue if we are trying to promote these tutorials to our virtual users. How do we suggest the use of a tutorial to someone with whom we are not personally interacting? Methods of live, real-time, Web-based reference or even e-mail reference services may help to address this question. But with our material being accessible to a wider and wider audience, we must be directing some of our attention to the promotion and publicity of our instructional material. Whenever possible we need to form partnerships with employers, supervisors, faculty, and community leaders so that they, too, will promote our endeavors.

ILI and its predecessors—bibliographic instruction, user education, and the like—can be seen as the means of helping people get around or over the hurdles or barriers placed between them and the information they need by the very people who are providing this information. One aspect of ILI is to help people cope with difficult, unintuitive, and just plain confusing databases, OPACs, and a variety of print and electronic resources. If the resources were designed with user needs in mind, there would be less of a need for our Web tutorials, handouts, classes, and the like. Furthermore, if some standardization for these resources were in effect, instructional efforts would have more widespread effect. If all OPACs or journal article databases had more uniform interfaces, our job would be much easier. But they are not uniform nor will they be unless we as a profession are strong advocates for such a change. We must take a larger role in the production of information resources in order to make this happen. We can do this directly by working with the vendors who are providing material and by being an advocate for user-friendly, intuitive interfaces. But even if we are not working for or with the vendors, we should make our opinions known to them. We, after all, are the consumers for much of their material. We must take careful measure of any new resource that becomes available. We should take advantage of any opportunities that may come our way in order to field-test resources before they are in general release. And we should let vendors and developers know what we find useful and, perhaps more importantly, what we find unacceptable and demand that those things be changed before we purchase them for the library or recommend their use to our users. We have a power-base and we should use it to be advocates for our users.

Since new resources are being developed at an exponential rate, instruction of some kind will continue to be needed. If we use our collective power to influence resource providers during developmental, prototype stages, we can perform a great service for our users. Users often do not know which button to click, when to scroll down the page to get other options, or how to move forward or backward through a list of results. Once we explain how to do that to them, we are often faced with the plaintive question "But how would I know that?" And how would they if there are no on-screen directions or help options to tell them so? If we become actively involved in the development of new resources, we can help ensure that these resources are intuitive enough to use so that we can reduce or even eliminate the "How would I know that?" type of questions. If our users can easily teach themselves the mechanics of using a new resource, we can concentrate our ILI efforts on helping them use these resources wisely and well. We can concentrate on teaching transferable IL skills and abilities during our in-person sessions and via our remote Web-based and other-technology-based instruction.

How do I see the role of IL professionals in the future? I see us as being advocates and intermediaries for our users. This is not a new role for us. IL professionals have always tried to bring people together with the information they need. In the past we concentrated on in-person sessions, pathfinders, handouts, point-of-use pieces, workbooks, and so on to help people learn how to select appropriate resources and use those resources efficiently and effectively. All of these modes are still widely used and very valid. Face-to-face instruction remains a very popular and widespread mode. But technology has expanded how, where, and when we play out our advocacy and intermediary roles. We can now take our show on the road and be available to our users when and where they need us via e-mail, Web reference, teleconferencing, and interactive tutorials. We can use technology to provide a range of instructional experiences that address a variety of learning styles and preferences. We can use this technology during face-to-face encounters and / or for the distribution of instructional material to complement our instruction or as aids for users who are accessing the library remotely. And we can use the technology as a hook to get our voices heard. Our expertise and knowledge of information technology provides us unprecedented access to the movers and shakers, the decision makers in our environment, and in the information technology industry at large. We are the ones to whom people in our environments should turn in order to learn about new technological advances. We should be the ones alerting people to new resources and helping them learn how to use those resources effectively. We should be making sure that those resources are user-friendly and intuitive. In short, we should continue to do what we have always done—be teachers in every sense of the word—to ensure that our users have the IL skills and abilities to survive in an ever-changing and complex information-rich world.

References

Absher, Linda. 2000. "The Lipstick Librarian" [Online]. Available: www.teleport.com/ ~petlin/liplib/ [November 4].

Ackerman, Edith. 1996. "Perspective Taking and Object Construction: Two Keys to Learning." In *Constructionism in Practice: Designing, Thinking and Learning in a Digital World,* edited by Yasmin B. Kafai and Mitchell Resnick. Mahwah, NJ: Erlbaum.

Adams, Mignon. 1993. "Evaluation." In *Sourcebook for Bibliographic Instruction,* edited by Katherine Branch. Chicago: American Library Association.

_____1995. "Library Instruction in Special Libraries: Present and Future. In *Information for a New Age: Redefining the Librarian,* edited by LIRT Fifteenth Anniversary Task Force. Englewood, CO: Libraries Unlimited.

Adobe Photoshop n.d. www.adobe.com/products/photoshop/main.html Last update: n.d. Visited: 25 Jan 2001.

Agre, Philip. 2000. "How to Help Someone Use a Computer" [Online]. Available: dlis.gseis.ucla.edu/people/pagre/how-to-help.html [November 4].

Alexander, Jan, and Marsha Tate. 1999. "Evaluating Web Resources" [Online]. Available: www2.widener.edu/Wolfgram-Memorial-Library/webeval.htm [December 28].

Allen, Eileen E. 1995. "Active Learning and Teaching: Improving Postsecondary Library Instruction." *Reference Librarian* 51/52:89–103.

Allen, Susan M. 1993. "Designing Library Handouts: Principles and Procedures." *Research Strategies* 11 no.1:14–23.

Aluri, Rao, and Mary Reichel. 1984. "Learning Theories and Bibliographic Instruction." In *Bibliographic Instruction and the Learning Process,* edited by Carolyn A. Kirkendall. Ann Arbor, MI: Pierian Press.

Alverno College Faculty. 1994. *Student Assessment as Learning at Alverno College.* Milwaukee, WI: Alverno College Institute.

American Association for Higher Education. 1992. *Principles of Good Practice for Assessing Student Learning.* Washington, DC: American Association for Higher Education.

American Cancer Society. 2000. www.cancer.org/ Last update: 14 Jul 2000 Visited: 16 Jul 2000.

American Heritage Dictionary. 2d ed. s.v. "Cirrus" 1991. Boston: Houghton-Mifflin.

ALA. 2000a. "Information Literacy Community Partnerships Initiative" [Online]. Available: www.ala.org/kranich/literacy.html [June 24].

_____. 2000b. "21st Century Literacy" [Online]. Available: www.ala.org/work/ literacybrochure.html [June 15].

ALA. American Association of School Librarians. 1998. *Information Literacy Standards for Student Learning.* Chicago and London: American Library Association.

_____. 2001. "KidsConnect" [Online]. Available: www.ala.org/ICONN/kidsconn.html [February 2].

ALA. American Association of School Librarians and Association for Educational Communications and Technology. 1988. *Information Power: Guidelines for School Library Media Programs.* Chicago: American Library Association.

ALA. Association of College and Research Libraries. 2000. *Information Literacy Competency Standards for Higher Education*. Chicago: American Library Association. Available online: www.ala.org/acrl/ilcomstan.html [November 11].

ALA. Association of College and Research Libraries. Bibliographic Instruction Section. 1983. *Evaluating Bibliographic Instruction: A Handbook*. Chicago: Bibliographic Instruction Section, Association of College and Research Libraries, American Library Association.

_____. 1991. *Read This First: An Owner's Guide to the New Model Statement of Objectives of Academic Bibliographic Instruction*, edited by Carolyn Dusenbury, et al. Chicago: ACRL Bibliographic Instruction Section, American Library Association.

_____. 1993a. *Learning to Teach*. Chicago: American Library Association.

_____. 1993b. *Sourcebook for Bibliographic Instruction*. Chicago: American Library Association.

ALA. Association of College and Research Libraries. CARL. 2000. [Online]. Available: www.carl-acrl.org/Reports/rectoWASC.html [January 4].

ALA. Association of College and Research Libraries. Distance Learning Section. 2000a. [Online]. Available: caspian.switchinc.org/~distlearn/ [August 6].

_____. 2000b. "ACRL Guidelines for Distance Learning Library Services" [Online]. Available: caspian.switchinc.org/~distlearn/guidelines/ [September 1].

_____. 2000c. "Guidelines for Distance Learning Library Services." *College & Research Libraries News* 61 no.11:1,023–30.

ALA. Association of College and Research Libraries. Institute for Information Literacy. 2000a. [Online]. Available: www.ala.org/acrl/nili/nilihp.html [September 2].

_____. 2000b. "Best Practices and Assessment of Information Literacy Programs" [Online]. Available: www.earlham.edu/~libr/Plan.htm [June 15].

_____. 2000c. "Best Practices Project" [Online]. Available: www.ala.org/acrl/nili/bestprac.html [June 24].

ALA. Association of College and Research Libraries. Instruction Section. 1999. [Online]. Available: www.libraries.rutgers.edu/is/ [November 29].

_____. 1998. *Designs for Active Learning*. Chicago: American Library Association.

_____. 2000a. "Instruction for Diverse Populations—Multilingual Glossary Language Table" [Online]. Available: www.libraries.rutgers.edu/is/publications/glossary [December 27].

_____. 2000b. "Miriam Dudley Instruction Librarian Award Winners" [Online]. Available: www.libraries.rutgers.edu/is/awards/dudley-winners.html [October 23].

_____. 2000c. "Model Statement of Objectives for Academic Bibliographic Instruction: Draft Revision" *College & Research Libraries News* 48(5):256–261. Available online: www.libraries.rutgers.edu/is/publications/mso.html [June 15].

_____. 2001a. "Objectives for Information Literacy Instruction: A Model Statement for Academic Librarians" [Online]. Available: www.libraries.rutgers.edu/is/publications/objs.html [March 23].

_____. 2001b. "Innovation in Instruction Award Recipients" [Online]. Available: www.libraries.rutgers.edu/is/awards/dudley-winners.html [April 3].

ALA. Association of College and Research Libraries. New England Chapter. New England Bibliographic Instruction Committee (NEBIC). 2000. [Online]. Available: www.holycross.edu/departments/library/website/NEBIC/Nebic.htm [April 28].

ALA. Library Instruction Round Table. 1999. [Online]. Available: diogenes.baylor.edu/Library/LIRT [September 9].

_____. 2000. "Library Instruction Tutorials" [Online]. Available: Diogenes.Baylor.edu/Library/LIRT/lirtproj.html [April 2].

ALA. LITA. Human/Machine Interface Interest Group. 2000. "Usability Testing Resources" [Online]. Available: www.vancouver.wsu.edu/fac/campbell/hmiig/usabres1.htm [September 11].

ALA. Office for Information Technology Policy. 2000. "[TUTORIAL:1] WELCOME TO THE ONLINE COPYRIGHT TUTORIAL." Personal e-mail to author. 14 February 2000.

ALA. Presidential Committee on Information Literacy. 1989. *Final Report*. Chicago: American Library Association.

ALA. Presidential Committee on Information Literacy. 1998. "A Progress Report on Information Literacy: An Update on the American Library Association Presidential Committee on Information Literacy: Final Report." www.ala.org/acrl/nili/nili.html. Last update: March 1998 Visited: 24 Jun 2000.

American Psychological Association. 2000. "Mental Models." *Encyclopedia of Psychology* 5. Oxford, UK; New York: Oxford University Press.

Amsel, Abram. 1989. *Behaviorism, Neobehaviorism and Cognitivism in Learning Theory: Historical and Contemporary Perspectives*. Hillsdale, NJ: Erlbaum.

Anderson, James A., and Maurianne Adams. 1992. "Acknowledging the Learning Styles of Diverse Student Populations: Implications for Instructional Design." *New Directions for Teaching and Learning* 49:19–33.

Anderson, L. W. 1988. "Likert Scales." In *Education Research, Methodology and Measurement: An International Handbook,*" edited by J. P. Keeves. New York: Pergamon Press.

Angelo, Thomas A., and K. Patricia Cross. 1993. *Classroom Assessment Techniques: A Handbook for College Teachers*. 2nd ed. *The Jossey-Bass Higher and Adult Education Series*. San Francisco: Jossey-Bass Publishers.

Anthony, Robert. 2000. "The Digital Divide Network." *Black Enterprise* 30 no. 11:80–84.

AOL Instant Messenger. 2000. www.aol.com/aim/home.html. Last update: 20 Oct 2000 Visited: 21 Oct 2000.

Apple. 2000. [Online]. Available: www.apple.com [October 8].

Applin, Mary Beth. 1999. "Instruction Services for Students with Disabilities." *Journal of Academic Librarianship* 25:139–41.

Areglado, Ronald J., R. C. Bradley, and Pamela S. Lane. 1996. *Learning for Life: Creating Classrooms for Self-directed Learning*." Thousand Oaks, CA: Corwin Press.

Armstrong, David G., and Tom V. Savage. 1983. *Secondary Education: An Introduction*. New York: Macmillan.

Ark, Connie E. 2000. "A Comparison of Information Literacy Goals, Skills and Standards for Student Learning." *Ohio Media Spectrum* 51 no. 4:11–15.

Arp, Lori. 1990. "Information Literacy or Bibliographic Instruction: Semantics or Philosophy?" *RQ* 30 no. 1:46–49.

———. 1993. "An Introduction to Learning Theory." In *Sourcebook for Bibliographic Instruction*, edited by Katherine Branch. Chicago: American Library Association.

Association for Teacher-Librarianship in Canada and Canadian Library Association. 1998. "Competencies for Teacher-Librarians in the 21st Century." *Teacher Librarian* 26:22–25.

Ausubel, David P. 1960. "The Use of Advance Organizers in the Learning and Retention of Meaningful Verbal Material." *Journal of Educational Psychology* 51:267–272.

———. 1977. "The Facilitation of Meaningful Verbal Meaning in the Classroom." *Educational Psychologist* 12:162–178.

Ausubel, David P., Joseph D. Novak, and Helen Hanesion. 1978. *Educational Psychology: A Cognitive View*. 2nd ed. New York: Holt, Rinehart and Winston.

Ausubel, David P., and Floyd G. Robinson. 1969. *School Learning: An Introduction to Educational Psychology*. New York: Holt, Rinehart and Winston.

Ball, Mary Alice, and Molly Mahony. 1987. "Foreign Students, Libraries and Culture." *College and Research Libraries* 48 no. 2:160–66.

Bandura, Albert. 1977a. "Self-efficacy Toward a Unifying Theory of Behavioral Change." *Psychological Review* 84 no. 2:191–215.

———. 1977b. *Social Learning Theory*. Englewood Cliffs, NJ: Prentice-Hall.

———. 1986. *Social Foundations of Thought and Action: A Social Cognitive Theory*. Englewood Cliffs, NJ: Prentice-Hall.

Banks, James A. 1993. "Multicultural Education: Characteristics and Goals." In *Multicultural Education: Issues and Perspectives*," edited by James A. Banks and Cherry A. McGee Banks. Boston: Allyn and Bacon.

Banks, James A., and Cherry A. McGee Banks. 1993. *Multicultural Education: Issues and Perspectives*. 2nd ed. Boston: Allyn and Bacon.

Banta, Trudy W., Jon P. Lund, Karen E. Black, and Frances W. Oblander. 1996. *Assessment in Practice: Putting Principles to Work in College Campuses*. San Francisco: Jossey-Bass.

Barbe, Walter Burke, and Raymond H. Swassing. 1988. *Teaching Through Modality Strengths: Concepts and Practices*. Columbus, OH: Zaner-Bloser.

Barclay, Donald A. 1995. "Teaching the Standard Features of Electronic Databases." In *Teaching Electronic Information Literacy: A How-to-Do-It Manual*, edited by Donald A. Barclay. New York: Neal-Schuman.

Barlow, John Perry. 1999a. "A Declaration of the Independence of Cyberspace" [Online]. Available: www.eff.org/~barlow/Declaration-Final.html [December 29].

_____. 1999b. "The Economy of Idea: Selling Wine Without Bottles on the Global Net." [Online]. Available: www.eff.org/~barlow/EconomyOfIdeas.html [December 29].

Barnes & Noble.com. 2000. "Barnes & Noble University" [Online]. Available: www.barnesandnoble.com/ [July 24].

Barron, Tom. 1999. "Harnessing Online Learning." *Training & Development* 53(9):28–34.

Bartlett, John. 1992. *Familiar Quotations*. 16th ed., s.v. "Murphy's Law." Boston: Little, Brown & Co.

Bates, Marcia J. 1979. "Information Search Tactics." *Journal of the American Society for Information Science* 30:205–14.

_____. 1989. "The Design of Browsing and Berrypicking Techniques for the Online Search Interface." *Online Review* 13 no.5:407–24.

Baysinger, Geoff. 2000. "Consistent Color on ALL Browsers—10 easy steps" [Online]. Available: www.netscapeworld.com/common/nw.color.html [March 14].

Beaubien, Anne K., Sharon A. Hogan, and Mary W. George. 1982. *Learning the Library: Concepts and Methods for Effective Bibliographic Instruction*. New York: Bowker.

Bechtel, Joan. 1986. "Conversation, a New Paradigm for Librarianship." *College & Research Libraries* 47 no.3:219–24.

Behrens, Shirley J. 1990. "Literacy and the Evolution Toward Information Literacy: An Exploratory Study." *South African Journal of Library and Information Science* 58 no. 4:353–58.

_____. 1994. "A Conceptual Analysis and Historical Overview of Information Literacy." *College and Research Libraries* 55, no. 4:309–22.

Belenky, Mary Field, Blythe McVicker Clinchy, Nancy Rule Goldberger, and Jill Mattlock Tarule. 1986. *Women's Ways of Knowing*. New York: Basic Books.

Bell, Colleen. 1999. "re: template for web design" [electronic bulletin board]. 27 Sep 1999 [cited 27 Sep 1999]. Available from: BI-L.

Bentley, Mark. 1997. "User Education at NYPL's New SIBL." *College and Research Libraries* 58 no. 9:633–36.

Beyer, Barry K. 1985a. "Critical Thinking: What Is It?" *Social Education* 49 no.4:270–76.

_____. 1985b. "Teaching Critical Thinking: A Direct Approach." *Social Education* 49 no.4:297–303.

Bigge, Morris L., and S. Samuel Shermis. 1992. *Learning Theories for Teachers*. 5th ed. New York: HarperCollins.

BI-L BI-L@listserv.byu.edu. n.d.

Bill Communications, Inc. 2000. "You and e-stories: OLL News." *Online Learning News*. 22 Aug 2000. listserv message. 11 September 2000.

Birch, Tobeylynn, Emily Bergman, and Susan J. Arrington. 1990. "Planning for Library Instruction in Special Libraries." In *The LIRT Library Instruction Handbook*, edited by May Brottman and Mary Loe. Englewood, CO: Libraries Unlimited.

Bit Better. 2000. "PowerPoint Tips & Tricks" [Online]. Available: www.bitbetter.com/powertips.htm [September 17].

Bjorner, Susanne. 1991. "The Information Literacy Curriculum: A Working Model." *IATUL Quarterly* 5 no. 2:150–160.

Black, Leah, and Denise Forro. 1999. "Humor in the Academic Library: You Must Be Joking! or, How Many Academic Librarians Does It Take to Change a Lightbulb?" *College & Research Libraries* 60 no.2:165–72.

Blakey, Elaine, and Sheila Spence. 1990. "Thinking for the Future." *Emergency Librarian* 17 no.5:11,13–14.

Bloom, Benjamin Samuel. 1981. *All Our Children Learning: A Primer for Parents, Teachers, and Other Educators.* New York: McGraw-Hill.

———. 1956. *Taxonomy of Educational Objectives: The Classification of Educational Goals. Handbook 1: Cognitive Domain. Handbook 2: Affective Domain.* 2 vols. New York: McKay.

Bloom, Benjamin Samuel, George F. Madaus, and J. Thomas Hastings. 1981. *Evaluation to Improve Learning.* New York: McGraw-Hill.

Blum, H. Timothy, and Dorothy Jean Yocom. 1996. "A Fun Alternative: Using Instructional Games To Foster Student Learning." *Teaching Exceptional Children* 29 no.2:60–63.

Bober, Christopher, Sonia Poulin, and Luigina Vileno. 1995. "Evaluating Library Instruction in Academic Libraries: A Critical Review of the Literature 1980–1993." *Reference Librarian* 51/52:53–71.

Bodi, Sonia, 1988. "Critical Thinking and Bibliographic Instruction: The Relationship." *Journal of Academic Librarianship* 14 no.3:150–53.

———. 1990. "Teaching Effectiveness and Bibliographic Instruction: The Relevance of Learning Styles." *College and Research Libraries* 51 no.2:113–119.

Bonn, George. 1960. *Training Laymen in the Use of the Library.* Volume 2, pt. 1 of *The State of the Library Art,* edited by Ralph R. Shaw. New Brunswick, NJ: Rutgers University Press.

Bonwell, Charles C. 1996. "Enhancing the Lecture: Revitalizing a Traditional Format." In *Using Active Learning In College Classes: A Range of Options for Faculty,* edited by Tracey E. Sutherland and Charles C. Bonwell. San Francisco: Jossey Bass.

Bonwell, Charles C., and Tracey E. Sutherland. 1996. "The Active Learning Continuum: Choosing Activities To Engage Students in the Classroom." In *Using Active Learning In College Classes: A Range of Options for Faculty,* edited by Tracey E. Sutherland and Charles C. Bonwell. San Francisco: Jossey Bass.

Bower, Gordon H. and Hilgard, Ernest R. 1981. *Theories of Learning.* 5th ed. Englewood Cliffs, N. J.: Prentice-Hall.

Bowling Green State University. 2000. "Falcon: an Interactive Web Tutorial." http://www.bgsu.edu/colleges/library/infosrv/tutorial/tutor1.html. Last update: 22 Jul 2000 Visited: 4 Nov 2000.

Boyd, Robert. 2000a. "Anthropology 7 Class Web Site" [Online]. Available: www.sscnet.ucla.edu/classes/fall97/anthro7/ [February 28].

———. 2000b. "Fossil Flash Cards" [Online]. Available: www.sscnet.ucla.edu/classes/fall97/anthro7/new/flashcard.pl?quiz=fossils [February 28].

Bradley, Lynne E. 2000. "Washington Hotline." *College & Research Libraries News* 61 no.11:1035.

———. 2001. "E-Rate Under Fire." *College & Research Libraries News* 62 no.3:324.

Brandon, David. P., and Andrea B. Hollingshead. 1999. "Collaborative Learning and Computer-Supported Groups." *Communication Education* 48 no.2:109–26.

Bransford, John, Sean Brophy, and Susan Williams. 2000. "When Computer Technologies Meet the Learning Sciences: Issues and Opportunities." *Journal of Developmental Psychology* 21 no.1:59–84.

Brant, Martha. 1999. "The Mouse That Roars: A Cyberguerrilla Takes Shots At the Bush Camp." *Newsweek,* Sept. 20, 1999, p. 53.

Breivik, Patricia S. 1985. "Putting Libraries Back in the Information Society." *American Libraries* 16 no. 1:723.

————. 1991. "Literacy in an Information Society." *Information Reports and Bibliographies* 20 no. 3:10–14.

Breivik, Patricia S., and E. Gordon Gee. 1989. *Information Literacy: Revolution in the Library.* New York: Macmillan.

Brigham Young University and eMSTAR Inc. 1999. *Culturgrams: The Nations Around Us.* Provo, UT: Brigham Young University and eMSTAR Inc.

Brookfield, Stephen. 1995. *Becoming a Critically Reflective Teacher.* 1st ed. *The Jossey-Bass Higher and Adult Education Series.* San Francisco: Jossey-Bass.

Brophy, Jere. 1987. "Teacher Influences on Student Achievement." *American Psychologist* 41:1,069–77.

Brosnan, Mark. 1998. "Avis Sets Sights on Technophobes." *Travel Trade Gazette UK & Ireland* (September 2):45.

Brottman, May, and Mary Loe, eds. 1990. *The LIRT Library Instruction Handbook.* Englewood, CO: Libraries Unlimited.

Brown, Cathy, Debe Costa, Esther Grassian, Lise Snyder, and Diane Zwemer. 2000. "Who Dunnit: What Kind of Web Page Is This?" UCLA College Library [Online]. Available: www.library.ucla.edu/libraries/college/instruct/environ/envindex.htm [June 29].

Bruce, Christine. 1994. "Portrait of an Information Literate Student." *Herdsa News* (December):9–11.

————. 1997. *The Seven Faces of Information Literacy.* Adelaide, Australia: Auslib Press.

"Bruin OnLine." 1995. Videotape, 10 min. Produced and directed by the UCLA Academic Technology Center. Los Angeles, CA: UCLA Office of Academic Computing.

Bruner, Jerome S. 1963. *The Process of Education.* 2nd ed. New York: Random House.

————. 1966. *Toward a Theory of Instruction.* Cambridge, MA: Harvard University Press.

BUBL LINK. 2000. [Online]. Available: bubl.ac.uk/link/index.html [October 8].

Burdick, Tracey A. 1996. "Success and Diversity in Information Seeking." *School Library Media Quarterly* 25:19–26.

Burton, Susan. 1977. "Objective Tests as an Evaluation Tool: Problems in Construction and Use." In *Library Instruction in the Seventies: State of the Art,* edited by Hannelore B. Rader. Ann Arbor, MI: Pierian Press.

Bushong, Sara. 1998. "Utilization of PowerPoint Presentation Software in Library Instruction of Subject Specific Reference Sources." Master's thesis, Kent State University.

California Clearinghouse on Library Instruction, North. 1999. [Online]. Available: www.scu.edu/SCU/Library/Orrardre/ccli/ccli.htm [September 9].

California Clearinghouse on Library Instruction, South. gort.ucsd.edu/dtweedy/ccli.html Last update: 10 Apr 2000 Visited: 24 Jun 2000.

California Clearinghouse on Library Instruction, South. 2000. "Guidelines for Effective Assignments" [Online]. Available: gort.ucsd.edu/dtweedy/EffectiveAssignments. html [October 24].

California Community Colleges. Board of Governors. 2000. "An Information Competency Plan for the California Community Colleges (1998)" [Online]. Available: www.santarosa.edu/~kathy/ICC/bog98–9.html [June 29].

California Digital Library. 2000. "Overview of the California Digital Library" [Online]. Available: www.cdlib.org/about/overview/ [November 13].

California State Library. 2000. "Library of California" [Online]. Available: www.library. ca.gov/loc/index.html [November 13].

California State University. 2000. "CSU Information Competence Project" [Online]. Available: www.lib.calpoly.edu/infocomp/ [October 24].

California State University, San Marcos, Library. 2000. "CSUSM General Education Program" [Online]. Available: www.csusm.edu/library/ILP/ge.html [June 24].

Canadian Library Association. 2000. "Guidelines for Library Support of Distance and Distributed Learning in Canada" [Online]. Available: www.cla.ca/about/intgroup. htm#16 [October 5].

Candy, Phil 1996. "Major Themes and Future Directions: Conference Summary and Implications." In *Learning for Life*, edited by D. Booker. Adelaide, Australia: University of South Australia Library.

Canfield, Marie P. 1972. "Library Pathfinders." *Drexel Library Quarterly* 8 no.3:287–300.

Carnell, Brian. 2000. "Brian's Bazaar" [Online]. Available: www.carnell.com/brian/index.html [April 2].

Carnell, Elizabeth. 2000. "Elizabeth's Study" [Online]. Available: www.skepticism.net/index.html [April 2].

Carnevale, Dan. 2000. "Survey Finds 72% Rise in Number of Distance Education Programs." *Chronicle of Higher Education* (January 7):A57.

Carr, Sarah. 1999a. "2 More Universities Start Diploma-Granting Virtual High Schools." *Chronicle of Higher Education*, December 10, 1999, p. A49.

———. 1999b. "U. of Nebraska's Class.com Hooks Up With a Kentucky School" *Chronicle of Higher Education*, October 22:A56.

———. 2000. "Online High-School Programs Plan to Market Courses Internationally." *Chronicle of Higher Education*, May 5:A49.

Carroll, John M., and Hans van der Meij. 1996. "Ten Misconceptions about Minimalism." *IEEE Transactions on Professional Communication* 39 no.2:72–86.

Carspecken, Phil, and Michael Apple. 1992. "Critical Qualitative Research: Theory, Methodology, and Practice." In *The Handbook of Qualitative Research*, edited by Margaret D. Le Compte, Wendy L. Millroy, and Judith Preissle. New York: Academic Press Inc.

Casey, Carol. 1999. "Accessibility and the Educational Web Site." *Syllabus* 13 no.2:26–30.

Caspers, Jean S. 1998. "Hands-on Instruction Across the Miles: Using a Web Tutorial to Teach the Literature Review Research Process." *Research Strategies* 16 no.3:187–97.

CAST. 2000. "Welcome to Bobby 3.2" [Online]. Available: www.cast.org/bobby/ [September 17].

Castellan, N. John, Jr. 1993. "Evaluating Information Technology in Teaching and Learning." *Behavior Research Methods, Instruments, & Computers* 25 no.2:233–37.

Chayefsky, Paddy. 1976. "Network". Produced by Howard Gottfried and directed by Sidney Lumet. Motion Picture. 120 min. Metro-Goldwyn Mayer/United Artists.

Chickering, Arthur W., and Stephen C. Ehrmann. 2000. "Implementing the Seven Principles: Technology as Lever" [Online]. Available: www.aahe.org/technology/ehrmann.htm [October 9].

Chickering, Arthur W., and Zelda F. Gamson. 1987. "Seven Principles of Good Practice in Undergraduate Education." *AAHE Bulletin* 39 no.7:3–7.

Childers, Cheryl D. 1996. "Using Crossword Puzzles as an Aid to Studying Sociological Concepts." *Teaching Sociology* 24 no.2:231–35.

The Chronicle of Higher Education.2000. "Information Technology: Jargon Monitor" [Online]. Available: chronicle.com/free/it/jargon.htm [September 12].

Clement, John. 1983. "A Conceptual Model Discussed by Galileo and Used Intuitively by Physics Students." In *Mental Models*, edited by Dedre Gentner and Albert L. Stevens. Hillsdale, NJ: Lawrence Erlbaum Associates.

Clinchy, Blythe McVicker. 1994. "Issues of Gender in Teaching and Learning." In *Teaching and Learning in the College Classroom*, edited by Kenneth A. Feldman and Michael B. Paulsen. Needham Hts, MA: Ginn Press.

CMLEA. 1994. *From Library Skills to Information Literacy: A Handbook for the 21st Century*. Castle Rock, CO: Hi Willow Research and Pub.

Coalition for Networked Information. www.cni.org/. Last update: n.d. Visited: 2 February, 2001

Coffman, Steve. 1998. "What If You Ran Your Library Like a Bookstore?" *American Libraries* 29 no.3:40–44.

Coffman, Steve, and Susan McGlamery. 2000. "The Librarian and Mr. Jeeves." *American Libraries* 31 no.5:66–69.

Colborn, Nancy Wooton, and Rosanne M. Cordell. 1998. "Moving from Subjective to Objective Assessments of Your Instruction Program." *Reference Services Review* 26 no. 3/4:125–37.

Commings, Karen. 1996. "Two 'All in One' Workstation Projects." *Computers in Libraries* 16 no.5:26–27.

Cook, Kim N., Lilith R. Kunkel, and Susan M. Weaver. 1995. "Cooperative Learning in Bibliographic Instruction." *Research Strategies* 13 no.1:17–25.

Coombs, Norman. 2000. "Untangling Your Web." *Syllabus* 14 no.5:28–30.

Cooper, James, and Pamela Robinson. 1998. "Small Group Instruction in Science, Mathematics, Engineering, and Technology: A Discipline Status Report and a Teaching Agenda for the Future." *Journal of College Science Teaching* 27 no.6:383–88.

Cooper, Mark N. 2000. "Disconnected, Disadvantaged, and Disenfranchised: Explorations in the Digital Divide." Washington, D.C.: Consumer Federation of America.

The Copyright Web Site. 2000. [Online]. Available: www.benedict.com/ [February 19].

Corcoran, Cate T. 2000 "Just Outta Beta: Under My Thumb." *Wired* 8(8):238.

Corcoran, Fran, and Dianne Langlois. 1990. "Instruction in the Use of Library Media Centers in Schools. " In *The LIRT Instruction Handbook*, edited by May Brottman and Mary Loe. Englewood, CO: Libraries Unlimited.

Corno, Lyn, and Ellen B. Mandinach. 1983. "The Role of Cognitive Engagement in Classroom Learning and Motivation." *Educational Psychologist* 18 no. 2:88–108.

Cote, Joseph A., James McCullough, and Michael Reilly. 1985. "Effects of Unexpected Situations on Behavior-Intention Differences: A Garbology Analysis." *Journal of Consumer Research* 12 no.2:188–94.

Courts, Patrick L., and Kathleen H. McInerney. 1993. *Assessment in Higher Education: Politics, Pedagogy, and Portfolios.* Westport, CT: Praeger.

Craver, Kathleen W. 1986. "The Changing Instructional Role of the High School Library Media Specialist: 1950–1984." *School Library Media Quarterly* 14, no.4:183–191.

Cross, K. Patricia. 1998. "Classroom Research: Implementing the Scholarship of Teaching." *New Directions for Teaching and Learning* 75:5–12.

Cross, K. Patricia, and Mimi H. Steadman. 1996. *Classroom Research: Implementing the Scholarship of Teaching.* San Francisco: Jossey-Bass.

Crozier, W. Ray. 1997. *Individual Learners: Personality Differences in Education.* London: Routledge.

Crumlish, Christian, and Malcolm Humes. 1996. *Web Publishing with Netscape for Busy People.* Berkeley, CA: Osborne/McGraw.

Cuban, Larry. 1986. *Teachers and Machines: The Classroom Use of Technology Since 1920.* New York: Teachers College Press, Columbia University.

Cunningham, Jim. 1999. "Ten Ways to Improve Your Web Site. *College & Research Libraries News* 60 no.8:614–15, 628.

Curtis, Donnelyn. 1995. "Writing for Information Literacy Training." In *Teaching Electronic Information Literacy: A How-To-Do-It Manual,* edited by Donald A. Barclay. New York: Neal-Schuman.

Curtis, Ruth V., and Charles M. Reigeluth. 1984. "The Use of Analogies in Written Text." *Instructional Science* 13:99–117.

"CU-SeeMe" 2000. [Online]. Available: www.cuseeme.com/ [November 14].

"CU-SeeMe Networks: Singapore National Institute of Education Selects CUSEEME Networks Technology to Facilitate Learning Programs." 2000. www.cuseeme.com/news/20000615.htm

Dagher, Zoubeida R. 1995. "Review of Studies on the Effectiveness of Instructional Analogies in Science Education." *Science Education* 79 no.3:295–312.

Darwin, Charles. 1859. *On the Origin of the Species by Means of Natural Selection.* London: J. Murray.

Davis, Barbara Gross. 1993. *Tools for Teaching.* 1st ed. *The Jossey-Bass Higher and Adult Education Series.* San Francisco: Jossey-Bass.

DeArmond, Celita V. 1999. "Web as database" [electronic bulletin board]. 2 Feb 1999—[cited 3 Feb 1999]. Available from bi-l@listserv.byu.edu.

DeCandido, GraceAnne A. 1999. "Bibliographic Good vs. Evil in Buffy the Vampire Slayer." *American Libraries* 30 no.8:44.

DeLorenzo, Ron. 1999. "When Hell Freezes Over: An Approach To Develop Student Interest and Communication Skills." *Journal of Chemical Education* 76 no.4:503.

Dembo, Myron H. 1981. *Teaching for Learning: Applying Educational Psychology in the Classroom.* Santa Monica, CA: Goodyear Publishing Company.

_____. 1988. *Teaching for Learning: Applying Educational Psychology in the Classroom.* 2nd ed. Santa Monica, CA: Goodyear.

Dempsey, Paula R., and Beth Mark. 1998. "Human Boolean Exercise." In *Designs for Active Learning*, pp. 117–118. ALA. Association of College and Research Libraries. Instruction Section. Chicago, IL: ALA.

DeMulder, Elizabeth K., and Kimberly K. Eby. 1999. "Bridging Troubled Waters: Learning Communities for the 21st Century." *American Behavioral Scientist* 42 no.5:892–901.

Dervin, Brenda, and Patricia Dewdney. 1986. "Neutral Questioning: A New Approach to the Reference Interview." *RQ* 25 no.4:506–13.

DesForges, Charles, ed. 1995. *An Introduction to Teaching: Psychological Perspectives.* Oxford, UK: Blackwell.

Deutsch, Suzanne. 1999. *Encyclopedia of Educational Technology*, s.v. "COLOR." San Diego State University [Online]. Available: coe.sdsu.edu/eet/Articles/usingcolor/start.htm [December 29].

Dewald, Nancy. 1999. "Transporting Good Library Instruction Practices Into the Web Environment: An Analysis of Online Tutorials." *The Journal of Academic Librarianship* 25 no.1:26–32.

Dewald, Nancy, Ann Scholz-Crane, Austin Booth, and Cynthia Levine. 2000. "Information Literacy at a Distance: Instructional Design Issues." *Journal of Academic Librarianship* 26 no. 1:33–44.

Dewey, Melvil. 1876. "The Profession." *American Library Journal* 1:6.

Digital Divide Network. 2000. [Online]. Available: www.digitaldividenetwork.org/ [September 17].

"Dr. Strangelove, or: How I Learned to Stop Worrying and Love the Bomb." 1964. Produced and directed by Stanley Kubrick. Motion Picture. 93 min. Columbia Pictures Corporation.

Dodge, Bernie. 2000. "A WebQuest About WebQuests" [Online]. Available: edweb.sdsu.edu/webquest/webquestwebquest-es.html [March 16].

Dods, Richard. 1997. "An Action Research Study of the Effectiveness of Problem-Based Learning in Promoting the Acquisition and Retention of Knowledge." *Journal for the Education of the Gifted* 20 no.4:423–37.

Dolphin, Philippa. 1990. "Evaluation of User Education Programmes." In *User Education in Academic Libraries*, edited by Hugh Fleming. London: Library Association.

Doolittle, John H. 1995. "Using Riddles and Interactive Computer Games to Teach Problem-Solving Skills." *Teaching of Psychology* 22 no.1:33–36.

Downing, Karen, and Joseph Diaz. 1993. "Instruction in a Multicultural/Multiracial Environment." In *Learning to Teach: Workshops on Instruction*, edited by Learning to Teach Task Force. Chicago: American Library Association.

Doyle, Christina S. 1992. *Final Report on the National Forum on Information Literacy.* Syracuse, NY: ERIC Clearinghouse on Information, Resources.

_____. 1996. "Information Literacy: Status Report from the United States." In *Learning for Life*, edited by Di Booker. Adelaide, Australia: University of South Australia Library.

Doyle, Christina S., and ERIC Clearinghouse on Information & Technology. 1994. *Information Literacy in an Information Society: A Concept for the Information Age.* Syracuse, NY: ERIC Clearinghouse on Information & Technology, Syracuse University.

Driscoll, Marcy Perkins. 1994. *Psychology of Learning for Instruction*. Boston: Allyn and Bacon.

Dudley, Miriam. 1978. *Library Instruction Workbook*. Los Angeles: University of California Library.

_____. 1983. "A Philosophy of Library Instruction." *Research Strategies* 1 no.2:58–63.

_____. 2000. "History of BIS." Interview by the author. March 26.

Dunn, Rita S., and Shirley Griggs. 1995. *Multiculturalism and Learning Styles: Teaching and Counseling Adolescents*. Westport, CT: Praeger.

Dupuis, Elizabeth A. 1999a. "The Creative Evolution of Library Instruction." *RSR: Reference Services Review* 27 no.3:287–90.

_____. 1999b. "RE: Classes" Personal e-mail to author 27 September 1999.

_____. 1999c. "RE: What Is an Interactive Tutorial?" [electronic bulletin board]. 28 Jan 1999—[cited 17 Jul 1999]. Available from: martin_raish@byu.edu.

Dwyer, F. M. 1978. *Strategies for Improving Visual Learning*. State College, PA: Learning Services.

Eadie, Tom. 1990. "Immodest Proposals: User Instruction for Students Does Not Work." *Library Journal* 115 no. 17:42–45.

"Earlham College" 1999. [Online]. Available: www.earlham.edu/ [November 10].

Eble, Kenneth Eugene. 1988. *The Craft of Teaching: A Guide to Mastering the Professor's Art*. 2nd ed. *The Jossey-Bass Higher and Adult Education Series*. San Francisco, CA: Jossey-Bass.

Eco, Umberto. 1983. *The Name of the Rose*. San Diego, CA: Harcourt, Brace, Jovanovich.

Eisenberg, Michael and Robert E. Berkowitz. 1990. Information Problem-Solving: The Big Six Skills Approach to Library and Information Skills Instruction, Information Management, Policy, and Services. Norwood, N.J.: Ablex Pub. Corp.

_____. "The Big 6 Skills Information Problem-Solving Approach" [Online]. Available: www.big6.com/ [June 29].

Eisenberg, Michael, and Michael Brown. 1992. "Current Themes Regarding Library and Information Skills Instruction: Research Supporting and Research Lacking." *School Library Media Quarterly* 20 no. 2:103–109.

Electronic Frontier Foundation. 2000. [Online]. Available: www.eff.org/ [February 19].

Elliott, Stephen N., Thomas R. Kratochwill, Joan Littlefield, and John F. Travers. 1996. *Educational Psychology: Effective Teaching, Effective Learning*. 2nd ed. Madison, WI: Brown and Benchmark.

Encyclopedia of Library and Information Science. 1978. S.v., "Ranganathan". New York: Marcel Dekker, Inc. v. 25, p. 66.

Encyclopedia of Library and Information Science. 1978. S.v., "Rochester, University of, Library." New York: Marcel Dekker, Inc., v. 25, p. 449.

Ensor, Pat. 1998. "Virtual Library Instruction: Training Tomorrow's User Today." In *Recreating the Academic Library: Breaking Virtual Ground*, edited by Cheryl LaGuardia. New York: Neal-Schuman.

Farber, Evan Ira. 1974. "Library Instruction Throughout the Curriculum: Earlham College Program." In *Educating the Library User*, edited by John Lubans, Jr. New York: Bowker.

_____. 1993. "Bibliographic Instruction at Earlham College." In *Bibliographic Instruction in Practice: A Tribute to the Legacy of Evan Ira Farber*, edited by Larry Hardesty, J. Hasteiter, and D. Henderson. Ann Arbor, MI: Pierian Press.

_____. 1995a. "Bibliographic Instruction, Briefly." In *Information For a New Age: Redefining the Librarian*, edited by ALA Library Instruction Round Table. Englewood, CO: Libraries Unlimited.

_____. 1995b. "Plus ca Change?" *Library Trends* 44 (2):430–38.

Fargo, Lucile F. 1939. *The Library in the School*. Chicago: ALA.

Farmer, Lesley S. J. 1999. "Making Information Literacy a Schoolwide Reform Effort." *Book Report* 18 no.3:6–8.

Farnham, Brian. 2000. "The Lawn That Never Needs Mowing." *New York Times Magazine*, June 11: 55.

Fidler, Donald. 2001. "Producing Educational Video" [Online]. Available: www.hsc.wvu.edu/admin/facultydev/video/video_production.htm [March 29].

"The 50 Best." 1995. *Advertising Age*. 66:36–40.

Fink, Deborah. 1989. *Process and Politics in Library Research*. Chicago: American Library Association.

Ford, Nigel. 1990. "Learning Styles, Strategies and Stages." In *User Education in Academic Libraries*, edited by Hugh Fleming. London: Library Association.

Foster, Mike. 22 Aug 2000. "Multimedia Design Controversies." *The Encyclopedia of Educational Technology*. San Diego State University. coe.sdsu.edu/eet/Articles/MessMulti/ Last update: 22 Aug 2000 Visited: 4 Nov 2000.

Foster, Stephan. 1993." 'Information Literacy': Some Misgivings." *American Libraries* 24 no. 4:344–46.

Fox, Richard. 1995. "Development and Learning." In *An Introduction to Teaching: Psychological Perspectives*," edited by Charles Desforges. Oxford, UK: Blackwell.

Franklin, Harriet, 1999. "Five Steps to Effective Training." *Franchising World* 31 no.5:24-26.

Fraser-Fazakas, Lindsay 1996. "Re: Internet and analogies" [electronic bulletin board]. 1 Mar 1996—[cited 2 Mar 1996]. Available from nettrain.bit.list.

Frederick, Peter J. 1981. "The Dreaded Discussion: Ten Ways to Start." *Improving College and University Teaching* 29 no. 3:109–14.

Freedman, Janet L., and Harold A. Bantly. 1982. *Information Searching: A Handbook for Designing & Creating Instructional Programs*. Rev. ed. Metuchen, NJ: Scarecrow Press.

French, Nancy, and H. Julene Butler. 1988. "Quiet On the Set! Library Instruction Goes Video." *Wilson Library Bulletin* 63 no.4:42–45.

Frick, Elizabeth. 1975. "Information Structure and Bibliographic Instruction." *Journal of Academic Librarianship* 1 no. 4:12–14.

_____. 1990. "Qualitative Evaluation of User Education Programs: The Best Choice?" *Research Strategies* 8 no. 1:4–13.

Fry, Thomas K., and Joan Kaplowitz. 1988. "The English 3 Library Instruction Program at UCLA: A Follow-up Study." *Research Strategies* 6 no.3:100–08.

Frye, Colleen. 1999. "Learning Online: Style Matters." *Inside Technology Training* 3:40–42; 47.

Fryer, Wesley A. 2000. "Writing Webpages with Wesley: Web Authoring Concepts/Basic Terms" [Online]. Available: www.wtvi.com/html/www2.html [October 24].

"The Future of Learning: An Interview with Alfred Bork." 1999. *Educom Review* 34 no.4 [Online]. Available: www.educause.edu/ir/library/html/erm9946.html [November 4].

Gagne, Robert M. 1985. *The Conditions of Learning*. 4th ed. (New York: Holt, Rinehart & Winston.

Gaines, Lawrence S., and Robert D. Coursey. 1974. "Novelty Experiencing, Internal Scanning, and Cognitive Control." *Perceptual and Motor Skills* 38:891–98.

Garfield, Bob. 1992. "Freberg." *Advertising Age* 63 no.3:52.

Gaynor, Kathy. 1999. "Summary: Hands-on exercises" [electronic bulletin board]. 10 Jun 1999—[cited 19 Jul 1999]. Available from bi-l@listserv.byu.edu.

Georgetown University. 2000. "Labyrinth." [Online]. Available: georgetown.edu/labyrinth/labyrinth-home.html [November 4].

Germain, Carol Anne, Trudi E. Jacobson, and Sue A. Kaczor. 2000. "A Comparison of the Effectiveness of Presenting Formats for Instruction: Teaching First-Year Students." *College and Research Libraries* 61 no. 1:65–72.

Gershenfeld, Neil A. 1999. *When Things Start to Think*. New York: Henry Holt.

Ghaphery, Jimmy, and Dan Ream. 2000. "VCU's My Library: Librarians Love It...Users? Well, Maybe." *Information Technology and Libraries* 19 no. 4:186–90.

Gibson, Craig. 1992. "Accountability for BI Programs in Academic Libraries: Key Issues for the 1990s." *Reference Librarian* 138:99–108.

Gilchrist, Debra. 1997. "To Enable Information Competency: The Abilities Model in Library Instruction." In *Programs that Work: Papers and Sessions Material Presented at the*

24th National LOEX Library Instruction Conference, edited by Linda Shirato. Ann Arbor, MI: Pierian Press.

Gilton, Donna L. 1994. "A World of Difference: Preparing for Information Literacy Instruction for Diverse Groups." *Multicultural Review* 3 no. 3:54–62.

"Goals 2000 and America 2000." 1994. *Congressional Digest* 73 no.1:8.

Gordin, Douglas N., Louis M. Gonzalez, Roy D. Pea, and Barry J. Fishman. 1996. "Using the World Wide Web to Build Learning Communities in K–12." *Journal of Computer Mediated Communication* 2 no.3. Available online: www.ascusc.org/jcmc/vol2/issue3/gordin.html [1999, November 29].

Gorman, Michael. 1991. "Send for a Child of Four! or Creating the BI-Less Academic Library." *Library Trends* 39 no. 3:354–62.

Gould, Ted. 1977. "6 Ways to Ask a Reference Question." Videotape, 6 min. Produced and directed by Ted Gould. Davis, CA: University of California, Davis.

Grabowski, Stanley M. 1980. "What Instructors Need to Know about Adult Learners." *National Society for Performance and Instruction Journal* 19:15–16.

Gradowski, Gail, Loanne Snavely, and Paula Dempsey, eds. 1998. *Designs for Active Learning.* Chicago: American Library Association.

Grant, Carl, and Christina Sleeter. 1993. "Race, Class, Gender and Disability in the Classroom." In *Multicultural Education Issues and Perspectives,* edited by James A. Banks and Cherry A. McGee Banks. Boston: Allyn and Bacon.

Grassian, Esther. 1993a. "The One-Shot Lecture." In *Learning to Teach,* edited by ALA, Association of College and Research Libraries, Bibliographic Instruction Section. Chicago: American Library Association.

_____. 1993b. "Setting up and Managing a BI Program." In *Sourcebook for Bibliographic Instruction,* edited by Katherine Branch and Carolyn Dusenbury. Chicago: American Library Association.

_____. 1998. "Modeling Topic Selection." In *Designs for Active Learning,* ALA. Association of College and Research Libraries. Instruction Section. Chicago: American Library Association.

_____. 1999a. "Using Netscape Navigator 3.0 (Windows NT)" Los Angeles, CA: UCLA College Library. Available: www.library.ucla.edu/libraries/college/instruct/n3/n3nt/n3nt.htm

_____.1999b. "Using Netscape Navigator 3.0 (Macintosh)" Los Angeles, CA: UCLA College Library. Available: www.library.ucla.edu/libraries/college/instruct/n3/n3mac/n3mac.htm

_____. 2000a. "Information Literacy Assignment Ideas" [Online]. Available: www.library.ucla.edu/libraries/college/instructors/ilassignment.htm [October 24].

_____. 2000b. "Thinking Critically About World Wide Web Resources" [Online]. Available: www.library.ucla.edu/libraries/college/help/critical/index.htm [October 14].

_____. 2000c. "Topic Selection Exercise," UCLA College Library. Available: www.library.ucla.edu/libraries/college/instruct/research/tfocus.htm

Grassian, Esther, ed. 1986. *Directory of Library Instruction Programs in California Academic Libraries.* 3d ed. Los Angeles, CA: California Clearinghouse on Library Instruction.

Grassian, Esther, and Susan E. Clark 1999. "Internet Resources: Information Literacy Sites: Background and Ideas for Program Planning and Development." *College & Research Libraries News* 60 no.2:78–81, 92 (Available online at: www.ala.org/acrl/resfeb99.html [September 13].

Grassian, Esther, and Diane Zwemer. 2000. "Hoax? Scholarly Research? Personal Opinion? You Decide!" [Online]. Available: www.library.ucla.edu/libraries/college/instruct/hoax/evlinfo.htm [June 30].

Graves, Rebecca S. 1997. "Ref: Internet/paper/TV" [electronic bulletin board]. 20 Mar 1997—[cited 21 March 1997]. Available from bi-l@listserv.byu.edu.

Greenbaum, Thomas L. 1998. *The Handbook for Focus Group Research.* 2d ed. Thousand Oaks, CA: Sage Publications.

Greenfield, Louise W. 1987. "Publication Sequence: The Use of a Conceptual Framework for Library Instruction to Students in Wildlife and Fishery Management." In *Conceptual Frameworks for Bibliographic Education*, edited by Mary Reichel and Mary Ann Ramey. Littleton, CO: Libraries Unlimited, Inc.

Gribas, Cyndy, Lynn Sykes, and Nick Dorochoff. 1996. "Creating Great Overheads with Computers." *College Teaching* 44 no.2:66–68.

Griggs, Shirley, and Rita S. Dunn. 1996. "Learning Styles of Asian-American Adolescents." *Emergency Librarian* 24 no. 1:8–13.

Grigorenka, Elena L., and Robert J. Sternberg. 1995. "Thinking Styles." In *International Handbook of Personality and Intelligence*, edited by Donald H. Saklofske and Moshe Zeidner. New York: Plenum.

Gross, Bertran W. 1997. "Intercultural Communication Competencies: A Strategy for a Multicultural Campus." In *Strategies for Promoting Pluralism in Education and the Workplace*, pp. 21–29. Edited by Lynne B. Welch, Betty J. Cleckley and Marilyn McClure. Westport, Conn: Praeger.

Gross, June, and Susan Kientz. 1999. "Collaborating for Authentic Learning." *Teacher Librarian* 27:21–25.

Grossman, Herbert. 1990. *Trouble-Free Teaching: Solutions to Behavior Problems in the Classroom*. Mountain View, CA: Mayfield Pub. Co.

Guyonneau, Christine H. 1996. "Re: Analogies" [electronic bulletin board]. 9 Feb 1996— [cited 10 Feb 1996]. Available from bi-l@listserv.byu.edu.

Hacker, Donald J., John Dunlovsky, and Arthur C. Graesser , eds. 1998. *Metacognition in Educational Theory and Practice*. Mahwah, NJ: Lawrence Erlbaum Associates, Publishers.

Hackman, J. Richard. 1998. "Why Teams Don't Work." In *Theory and Research on Small Groups*, edited by R. Scott Tindale, et al. New York: Plenum Press.

Hagle, Claudette. 1990. "Presentation Skills and Classroom Management." In *Learning to Teach: Workshops on Instruction*," edited by Learning to Teach Task Force. Chicago: American Library Association.

Hainer, Eugene. 1998. "Information Literacy in Colorado Schools." *Colorado Libraries* 24 no.4:5–9.

Hall, Edward Twitchell, 1976. *Beyond Culture*. 1st ed. Garden City, NY: Anchor Press.

Hanson, Michele G. 1995. "Joining the Conversation: Collaborative Learning and Bibliographic Instruction." *Reference Librarian* 51/52:147–59.

Hara, Noriko and Rob Kling. 1999. "Students' Frustrations with a Web-Based Distance Education Course." *firstmonday: Peer-Reviewed Journal on the Internet* 4 no.12 [Online]. Available: www.firstmonday.dk/issues/issue4_12/hara/index.html [September 16].

Harada, Violet, and Ann Tepe. 1998. "Pathways to Knowledge." *Teacher Librarian* 26 no. 2:9–15.

Hardesty, Larry, and John Mark Tucker. 1989. "An Uncertain Crusade: The History of Library Use Instruction in a Changing Educational Environment." In *Academic Librarianship Past Present, and Future; a Festschrift in Honor of David Kaser*, edited by John Richardson, Jr., and Jinnie Y. Davis. Englewood Cliffs, NJ: Libraries Unlimited.

Hartnett, John. 2000. "Tag, You're It! How to Decipher the HTML Tags in a Typical Web-Based Training Page." *Inside Technology Training* (February): 58–60.

Harvey, Douglas. 2000. "Web-Based Instruction Resource Site: MAIN" [Online]. Available: www.stockton.edu/~harveyd/WBI/main.htm [April 2].

Haycock, Ken. 1999. "Public Library Standards" [Online]. Available: ALA Council List Listserv [1999, October 31].

Haynie, Nancy Ann. 1994. "Wundt, Wilhelm." In *Encyclopedia of Psychology*, edited by Raymond J. Corsini. New York: John Wiley and Sons.

Hensley, Randy Burke. 1993. "Teaching Methods." In *Sourcebook for Bibliographic Instruction*, edited by Katherine Branch. Chicago: American Library Association, Association of College and Research Libraries, Bibliographic Instruction Section.

_____. 2000. "Learning Communities and Information Literacy." *ALA. ACRL. IS Newsletter* 17 no.1:5.

Hergenhahn, Baldwin R. 1988. *An Introduction to Theories of Learning.* Englewood Cliffs, N. J.: Prentice-Hall.

Herman, Douglas. 1994. "But Does It Work? Evaluating the Brandeis Reference Model." *RSR: Reference Services Review* 22 no.4:17–28.

Hewitt, Robert L. 1995. "The Nature of Adult Learning and Effective Training Guidelines." In *The Importance of Learning Styles: Understanding the Implications for Learning, Course Design and Education,"* edited by Ronald R. Sims and Serbrenia J. Sims. Westport, CT: Greenwood Press.

Hickson, Joyce, and Michael Baltimore. 1996. "Gender Related Learning Styles: Patterns of Middle School Pupils." *School Psychology International* 17, no. 1:59–70.

Hilliard, Asa G. 1992. "Behavioral Style, Culture and Teaching and Learning." *Journal of Negro Education* 61 no. 3:370–77.

Hinchliffe, Lisa Janicke. 1999. "Summary Bibliography on Research/Search Logs" [electronic bulletin board]. 11 Jun 1999—[cited 12 Jun 1999]. Available from bi-l@listserv.byu.edu.

Hodges, Mark. 1996. "Videoconferencing for the Rest of Us." *Technology Review* 99 no.2:17-18.

Hofstadter, Douglas R. 2000. "Analogy as the Core of Cognition." In *The Best American Science Writing 2000,* edited by James Gleick. New York: HarperCollins Publishers.

Hogan, Sharon. 1980. "Training and Education of Library Instruction Librarians." *Library Trends* 29 no.1:105-26.

Hogle, John. 2000. "Storyboarding a Web Site" [Online]. Available: www.blueroom.com/internet/HD-storyboarding.htm [April 2].

Howard, Sheila. 1983. "Library Use Education for Adult University Students." *CLJ* 40:149–55.

HTML Manual of Style. 1994. Emeryville, CA: Ziff-Davis Press.

Iannuzzi, Patricia. 1998. "Faculty Development and Information Literacy: Establishing Campus Partnerships." *Reference Services Review* 26 no.3/4:97–102, 116.

_____. 1999. "We Are Teaching, but Are They Learning: Accountability, Productivity, and Assessment." *Journal of Academic Librarianship* 28 no. 4:304–05.

IBM. 2000. "IBM Launches e-learning Business Unit —IBM Mindspan Solutions" [Online]. Available: www.can.ibm.com/news/latest_news/051600_mindspan. htm [July 24].

ICQ. n.d. web.icq.com/index Last update: n.d. Visited: 13 Nov 2000.

Iding, Marie K. 1997. "How Analogies Foster Learning From Science Texts." *Instructional Science* 25 no.4:233–53.

Information Institute of Syracuse. 2000. "The Virtual Reference Desk" [Online]. Available: www.vrd.org/index.html [December 18].

Information Literacy: Advancing Opportunities for Learning in the Digital Age. A Report of the Aspen Institute Forum on Communications and Society. 1999. Washington, D.C.: The Aspen Institute.

Inhelder, Bärbel, and Jean Piaget. 1958. *The Growth of Logical Thinking from Childhood to Adolescence: An Essay on the Construction of Formal Operational Structures.* London: Routledge & Kegan Paul.

IFLA. User Education Roundtable. www.ifla.org/VII/rt12/rtued.htm. Last update: 3 November 2000 Visited: 2 February, 2001

"Internet Movie Database." 1999. www.imdb.com/ Last update: 28 Dec 1999 Visited: 28 Dec 1999.

"Internet Navigator" 1999. [Online]. Available: www.navigator.utah.edu/ [November 10].

Jackson, Rebecca Jackson. 1999. "Learning Communities Summary" [electronic bulletin board]. 8 Jul 1999—[cited 9 Jul 1999]. Available from bi-l@listserv.byu.edu.

Jackson, Susan. 1995. "Information Literacy and Public Libraries: A Community Based Approach." In *Information for a New Age: Redefining the Librarian,* edited by LIRT Fifteenth Anniversary Task Force. Englewood, CO: Libraries Unlimited.

Jacobson, Trudi E. 1996. "The Effect of CD-ROM Instruction on Search Operator Use." *College and Research Libraries* 57:68–76.

Jacobson, Trudi E., and Beth L. Mark. 1995. "Teaching in the Information Age: Active Learning Techniques to Empower Students." *Reference Librarian* 51/52:105–20.

James Madison University. 2000. "Go for the Gold" [Online]. Available: library.jmu.edu/library/gold/modules.htm [October 24].

Jeng, Ling Hwey. 2000. "Reference Questions" [electronic bulletin board]—[cited 13 June 2000]. Available from cala@csd.uwm.edu.

Jenkins, John M., Charles A. Letteri, Patricia Rosenlund, and James W. Keefe. 1989. *Learning Style Profile Handbook*. Reston, VA: National Association of Secondary School Principals.

Jiao, Qun G., Anthony J. Onwuegbuzie, and Art A. Lichtenstein. 1996. "Library Anxiety: Characteristics of 'At-Risk' College Students." *Library and Information Science Research* 18:151–63.

Johnson, Anna Marie, and Phil Sager. 1998. "Too Many Students, Too Little Time: Creating and Implementing a Self-Paced, Interactive Computer Tutorial for the Libraries' Online Catalog." *Research Strategies* 16 no.4:271–84.

Johnson, Dolores. 1997. "What's Love Got to Do with It: Strategies for Teaching in Multilingual and Multicultural Classrooms." In *Strategies for Promoting Pluralism in Education and the Workplace*, edited by Lynne B. Welch, Betty J. Cleckley, and Marilyn McClure. Westport, CT: Praeger.

Johnson, Doug, and Michael Eisenberg. 1996. "Computer Literacy and Information Literacy: A Natural Combination." *Emergency Librarian* 23 no.5:12–16.

Jonassen, D. H., and T.C. Reeves. 1996. "Learning with Technology: Using Computers as Cognitive Tools." In *Handbook of Research for Educational Communications and Technology*, edited by D. H. Jonassen. New York: Simon & Schuster Macmillan.

Kabagarama, Daisy. 1997. *Breaking the Ice: A Guide to Understanding People from Other Cultures*. 2nd ed. Boston: Allyn and Bacon.

Kafai, Yasmin B., and Mitchell Resnick, eds. 1996. *Constructionism in Practice: Designing, Thinking and Learning in a Digital World*. Mahwah, NJ: Erlbaum.

Kagan, Jerome. 1966. "Reflection-Impulsivity: The Generality and Dynamics of Conceptual Tempo." *Journal of Abnormal Psychology* 71:17–24

Kanter, Jerry. 1996. "Guidelines for Attaining Information Literacy Information Strategy." *The Executives' Journal* 12 no.3:6–11.

Kaplowitz, Joan. 1993. "Contributions from the Psychology of Learning: Practical Implications for Teaching." In *Learning to Teach*, edited by ALA, Association of College and Research Libraries, Instruction Section. Chicago: American Library Association.

_____. 1995. Evaluating Bibliographic Instruction: Issues and Influences. Unpublished manuscript, Santa Monica, CA.

_____. 1996. "A Pre and Post-test Evaluation of the English 3 Library Instruction Program at UCLA." *Research Strategies* 4 no. 1:11–17.

Kaplowitz, Joan, and Janice Contini. 1998. "Computer-Assisted Instruction: Is It an Option for Bibliographic Instruction in Large Undergraduate Survey Classes?" *College & Research Libraries* 59 no.1:19–27.

Kazdin, Alan E. 1994. *Behavior Modification in Applied Settings*. Pacific Grove, CA: Brooks/Cole.

Keefe, James W. 1987. *Learning Style : Theory and Practice*. Reston, VA: National Association of Secondary School Principals.

_____. 1988. *Profiling and Utilizing Learning Style, NASSP Learning Style Series*. Reston, VA: National Association of Secondary School Principals.

Keefe, James W., and John S. Monk. 1988. *Learning Style Profile: Technical Manual*. Reston, VA: National Association of Secondary School Principals.

Keefer, Jane. 1993. "The Hungry Rats Syndrome: Library Anxiety, Information Literacy, and the Academic Reference Process." *RQ* 32 no.3:333–39.

Keller, John M. 1987. "Strategies for Stimulating the Motivation to Learn." *Performance and Instruction Journal* 26 no. 8:1–7.

Kellough, Richard D., Noreen G. Kellough, and Eugene C. Kim. 1999. *Secondary School Teaching: A Guide to Methods and Resources: Planning for Competence*. Upper Saddle River, NJ: Merrill.

Kennedy, James R., Jr. 1974. *Library Research Guide to Religion and Theology: Illustrated Search Strategy and Sources*. Ann Arbor, MI: Pierian Press.

Kentucky Department of Education. 1995. *Online II: Essentials of a Model Library Media Program*. Louiseville KY: Kentucky Department of Education.

Kerns, Kathy. 2000. "Live Reference" [Online]. Available: www-sul.stanford.edu/staff/ infocenter/liveref.html [September 29].

Kirk, Elizabeth, and Andrea M. Bartelstein. 1999. "Libraries Close In On Distance Education." *Library Journal* 124 no.6:40–42.

Kirton, Michael J. 1976. "Adaptors and Innovators: A Description and Measure." *Journal of Applied Psychology* 61:622–29.

Klein, Michael. 1987. "What Is It We Do When We Write Articles Like This One—and How Can We Get the Students to Join Us?" *The Writing Instructor* 6:151–161.

Knapp, Patricia B. 1966. *The Monteith College Library Experiment*. Metuchen, NJ: Scarecrow.

Knowles, Malcolm Shepherd. 1978. *The Adult Learner: A Neglected Species*." 2d ed. Houston: Gulf Pub. Co. Book Division.

_____. 1980. *The Modern Practice of Adult Education: From Pedagogy to Andragogy*. Rev. and update ed. New York: Cambridge the Adult Education Company.

_____. 1984. "New Role for Teachers: Empowerers of Lifelong Learners. *Journal of Children in Contemporary Society* 16 no. 3/4:85–94.

_____.1996. "Andragogy: An Emerging Technology for Adult Learning." In *Boundaries of Adult Learning*," edited by Richard Edwards, Ann Hansen and Peter Raggatt. London: Routledge.

Ko, Susan, and Steve Rossen. 2001. *Teaching Online: A Practical Guide*. Boston: Houghton-Mifflin.

Kobelski, Pamela, and Mary Reichel. 1981. "Conceptual Frameworks For Bibliographic Instruction." *Journal of Academic Librarianship* 7, no.2:73–77.

Köhler, Wolfgang, and Ella Winter. 1925. *The Mentality of Apes*. New York, London: Harcourt Brace & Company Inc.; K. Paul Trench Trubner & Co. Ltd.

Kolb, David A. 1976. *Learning Styles Inventory: Technical Manual*. Boston: McBer.

_____. 1981. "Learning Styles and Disciplinary Differences." In *The Modern American College: Responding to the New Realities of Diverse Students and a Changing Society*, edited by Arthur W. Chickering. San Francisco: Jossey-Bass.

_____. 1984. *Experiential Learning: Experience as the Source of Learning and Development*. Englewood Cliffs, NJ: Prentice-Hall.

Koppi, A.J., J. R. Lublin, and M.J. Chaloupka. 1997. "Effective Teaching and Learning in a High-Tech Environment." *Innovations in Education and Training International* 34 no.4:245–51.

Kosower, Evie. 1995. "Is There a Generalist Learning Style?" *Academic Medicine* 70 no. 9:745–46.

Kotter, Wade R. 1999. "Bridging the Great Divide: Improving Relations Between Librarians and Classroom Faculty." *Journal of Academic Librarianship* 25 no.4:244–303.

Kounin, Jacob S. 1970. *Discipline and Group Management in Classrooms*. New York: Holt Rinehart and Winston.

Kozlowski, Ken. 1995. *Analysis of Reference Service at the Cleveland Law Library, April-September 1995*. Master's thesis, Kent State University.

Kranich, Nancy. 2000. "Building Partnerships for 21st-Century Literacy." *American Libraries* 31(September):7.

Kresh, Diane Nester. 2000. "Offering High Quality Reference Service on the Web: the Collaborative Digital Reference Service (CDRS)." *D-Lib Magazine* 6(6) [Online]. Available: www.dlib.org/dlib/june00/kresh/06kresh.html [September 13].

Kreunen, Ben. 2000. "Big Ben's Digital Imaging Tutorial: Web-safe Colour Palette [Online]. Available: www.bigbenpublishing.com.au/digital/websafe.html [October 6].

Kroenke, Kurt. 1984. "The Lecture: Where It Wavers." *American Journal of Medicine* 17 no. 3:393–96.

Kruger, Justin, and David Dunning. 1999. "Unskilled and Unaware of It: How Difficulties In Recognizing One's Own Incompetence Lead to Inflated Self-Assessments." *Journal of Personality and Social Psychology* 77 no.6:1,121–34.

Kuhlthau, Carol C. 1981. *School Librarian's Grade-by-Grade Activities Program: A Complete Sequential Skills Plan for Grades K–8.* West Nyack, NY: Center for Applied Research in Education.

_____. 1985. "A Process Approach to Library Skills Instruction: an Investigation into the Design of the Library Research Process." *School Library Media Quarterly* 13:35–40.

_____. 1989. "Information Search Process: A Summary of Research and Implications for School Library Media Programs." *School Library Media Quarterly* 17:19–25.

_____. 1990. "Information Skills for an Information Society: A Review of Research." *Information Reports and Bibliographies* 19 no. 3:14–26.

_____. 1993. *Seeking Meaning: A Process Approach to Library and Information Services, Information Management, Policy and Services.* Norwood, NJ: Ablex Pub. Corp.

_____. 1995. "The Instructional Role of the Library Media Specialists in the Information-Age School." In *Information for a New Age: Redefining the Librarian,* edited by LIRT Fifteenth Anniversary Task Force. Englewood, CO: Libraries Unlimited.

Kupersmith, John. 1984. "The Graphic Approach: Don't Do This! Don't Do That!" *Research Strategies* 2 no.4:185–87.

_____. 1987. "The Graphic Approach: 'Library Anxiety' and Library Graphics." *Research Strategies* 5 no.1: 36-38.

Kupersmith, John. 1993. "Technostress in the Bionic Library." In *Recreating the Academic Library: Breaking Virtual Ground,* pp. 23–47. Edited by Cheryl LaGuardia. New York: Neal-Schuman.

La Guardia, Cheryl, Michael Blake, Lawrence Dowler, Laura Farwell, Caroline M. Kent, and Ed Tallent. 1996. *Teaching the New Library: A How-To-Do-It Manual for Planning and Designing Instructional Programs.* New York: Neal-Schuman.

Landon, Bruce, Randy Bruce, and Amanda Harby. 2000. "Online Educational Delivery Applications: A Web Tool for Comparative Analysis" [Online]. Available: www.ctt.bc.ca/landonline/ [September 16].

Laslett, Robert, and Colin Smith. 1984. *Effective Classroom Management: A Teacher's Guide.* London; New York: Croom Helm; Nichols Pub. Co.

Lawson, Jerry. 1996. "Re: Internet and Analogies" [electronic bulletin board]. 2 Mar 1996— [cited 3 Mar 1996]. Available from nettrain.bit.list.

Learn2.com. 2000. [Online]. Available: www.learn2.com/index.asp [September 17].

Lessick, Susan, Kathryn Kjaer, and Steve Clancy. 2000. "Interactive Reference Service (IRS) at UC Irvine: Expanding Reference Service Beyond the Reference Desk" [Online]. Available: www.ala.org/acrl/paperhtm/a10.html [October 19].

Levine, Tamar, and Smadar Donitsa-Schmidt. 1998. "Computer Use, Confidence, Attitudes, and Knowledge: A Causal Analysis." *Computers in Human Behavior* 14 no. 1:125–46.

"Librarian's Index to the Internet." 2000. [Online]. Available: lii.org/ [July 16].

"Library Cartoons: An Annotated Bibliography." 2000. [Online]. Available: pw1.netcom.com/~dplourde/cartoons/index.html [October 24].

Liedtke, Michael. 2000. "Portals Return to Search for Niche." *Los Angeles Times,* 19 October 2000, section C.

Lin, Poping. 1994. "Library Instruction for Culturally Diverse Populations: A Comparative Approach." *Research Strategies* 12 no. 3:168–73.

Lindell, Ann, Mimi Pappas, Jana Ronan, and Colleen Seale. 2000. "Shall We Chat? Extending Traditional Reference Services with Internet Technology: A Survey of Online

Interactive Reference Services" [Online]. Available: web.uflib.ufl.edu/hss/ref/chat/cc3.html [October 8].

Linden, Julie. 2000. "The Library's Web Site *Is* the Library: Designing for Distance Learners." *College & Research Libraries News* 61, no.2:99–100.

Linn, Robert L., and Norman Gronlund. 1995. *Measurement and Assessment in Teaching*. 7th ed. New York: Macmillan.

Lippincott, Joan K. 1987. "End-User Instruction: Emphasis on Concepts." In *Conceptual Frameworks for Bibliographic Education*, pp. 183–191. Edited by Mary Reichel and Mary Ann Ramey. Littleton, CO: Libraries Unlimited, Inc.

Liu, Ziming. 1993. "Difficulties and Characteristics of Students from Developing Countries." *College and Research Libraries* 54 no. 1:25–31.

Loe, Mary, and Betsy Elkins. 1990. "Developing Programs in Library Use Instruction for Lifelong Learning: An Overview." In *The LIRT Library Instruction Handbook*, edited by May Brottman and Mary Loe. Englewood, CO: Libraries Unlimited.

LOEX. 2000a. [Online]. Available: www.emich.edu/~lshirato/loex.html [September 27].

_____. 2000b. [Online]. "Instruction links." Available: www.emich.edu/~lshirato/ISLINKS/TUTLINKS.HTM [October 30].

LOEX. National LOEX Library Instruction Conference. 1989. *Reaching and Teaching Diverse Library User Groups. 16th Annual LOEX Library Instruction Conference*, edited by Teresa Mensching. Ann Arbor, MI: Pierian Press.

LOEX. National LOEX Library Instruction Conference. 1997. *Programs That Work: Papers and Session Materials Presented at the 24th National LOEX Library Instruction Conference*, edited by Linda Shirato. Ann Arbor, MI: Pierian Press.

"LOEX of the West 2000." 1999. www.lib.montana.edu/loex/. Last update: 15 Sep 1999. Visited: 10 Nov 1999.

Longstreet, Wilma S. 1978. *Aspects of Ethnicity: Understanding Differences in Pluralistic Classroom[s]*. New York: Teachers College Press.

Los Angeles Public Library 2000. "Remote Access Databases" [Online]. Available: www.lapl.org/databases/db_home.shtml [July 16].

Lowman, Joseph. 1995. *Mastering the Techniques of Teaching*. 2nd ed. *The Jossey-Bass Higher and Adult Education Series*. San Francisco: Jossey-Bass.

Lubans, John, Jr., ed and comp. 1983. *Educating the Public Library User*. Chicago: American Library Association.

Lynch, Clifford A. 1998. "Recomputerizing the Library: New Roles for Information Technology in a Time of Networked Information." In *Recreating the Academic Library: Breaking Virtual Ground*, edited by Cheryl LaGuardia. New York: Neal-Schuman Publishers.

McCollum, Kelly. 2000. "Lost in Cyberspace? A Librarian Offers an Online Course on Search Engines." *The Chronicle of Higher Education: Information Technology* [Online]. Available: chronicle.com/free/2000/02/2000022301t.htm [February 23].

McCormick, Mona. 1983. "Critical Thinking and Library Instruction." *RQ* 22 no.4:339–42.

McCrank, Laurence J. 1991. "Information Literacy: A Bogus Bandwagon." *Library Journal* 116 no. 8:38–42.

McCrea, Fred, R. Keith Gay, and Rusty Bacon. 2000. "Riding the Big Waves: a White Paper on the B2B e*learning Industry." Thomas Weisel Partners: Merchant Banking.

MacDonald, Gina, and Elizabeth Sarkodie-Mensah. 1988. "ESL Students and American Libraries." *College and Research Libraries* 49:425–31.

McGrath, Peter. 1999. "Potholes on the Road Ahead." *Newsweek*, Sept. 20: 78.

McIntyre, Tom. 1996. "Does the Way We Teach Create Behavior Disorders in Culturally Different Students?" *Education and Treatment of Children* 19 no. 3:354–70.

McKeachie, Wilbert J. 1986. *Teaching Tips: A Guidebook for the Beginning Teacher*. 8th ed. Lexington, MA: D.C. Heath.

_____. 1999. *Teaching Tips: Strategies, Research and Theory for College and University Teachers*. 10th ed. Boston: Houghton-Mifflin.

McKiernan, Gerry. 2000. "LiveRef(sm):a Registry of *Real-Time* Digital Reference Services" [Online]. Available: www.public.iastate.edu/~CYBERSTACKS/LiveRef.htm [September 20].

Macromedia. 2001. "Dreamweaver" [Online]. Available: www.macromedia.com/software/dreamweaver/ [January 25].

Mager, Robert Frank. 1997a. *Goal Analysis: How to Clarify Your Goals So You Can Actually Achieve Them.* 3rd completely rev. ed. Atlanta: Center for Effective Performance.

_____. 1997b. *How to Turn Learners on Without Turning Them Off: Ways to Ignite Interest in Learning.* 3rd completely rev. ed. Atlanta: Center for Effective Performance.

_____. 1997c. *Making Instruction Work, or, Skillbloomers: A Step-by-Step Guide to Designing and Developing Instruction that Works.* 2nd completely rev. ed. Atlanta: Center for Effective Performance.

_____. 1997d. *Measuring Instructional Results, or, Got a Match?: How to Find Out if Your Instructional Objectives Have Been Achieved.* 3rd completely rev. ed. Atlanta: Center for Effective Performance.

_____. 1997e. *Preparing Instructional Objectives: A Critical Tool in the Development of Effective Instruction.* 3rd ed. Atlanta: Center for Effective Performance.

MOUSE, Inc. 2000. [Online]. Available: www.mouse.org/ [January 25].

Mallonee, Barbara C. 1981. "A Pitch for Collaborative Learning: Discovering a Paragraph Heuristic." ED218642 [unpublished ERIC document].

Mann, Thomas. 1993. *Library Research Models: A Guide to Classification, Cataloging, and Computers.* Oxford, UK; New York: Oxford University Press.

Maricopa County Community College. 2000. "Information Literacy" [Online]. Available: hakatai.mcli.dist.maricopa.edu/ocotillo/report94/rep7.html [June 24].

Mark, Beth L., and Trudi E. Jacobson. 1995. "Teaching Anxious Students Skills for the Electronic Library." *College Teaching* 43 no.1:28–31.

Markey, Karen, and Pauline A. Cochrane. 1981. *Online Training and Practice Manual for ERIC Data Base Searchers.* 2d ed. Syracuse, NY: ERIC Clearinghouse on Information Resources.

Masie, Elliott, ed. 2000. "TechLearn Trends—Technology & Learning Updates" [electronic bulletin board]. 15 May 2000[cited 15 May 2000]. Available from trends@masie.com.

Maslow, Abraham H. 1987. *Motivation and Personality.* 3rd ed. New York: Harper and Row.

Mason, Lucia. 1994. "Analogy, Metaconceptual Awareness and Conceptual Change: A Classroom Study." *Educational Studies.* 20 no.2:267–91.

MIT Media Lab. 2000. "MIT-Roxbury Projecct Aims to Close 'Digital Divide" [Online]. Available: http://web.mit.edu/newsoffice/nr/2000/roxbury.html [December 20].

Maul, Gary P., and David S. Spotts. 1993. "A Comparison of Computer-Based Training and Classroom Instruction." *Industrial Engineering* 25 no.2:25–27.

Mayer, Richard E. 1979. "Can Advance Organizers Influence Meaningful Learning?" *Review of Educational Research* 49 no.2:371–83.

Mellon, Constance A. 1986. "Library Anxiety: A Grounded Theory and Its Development." *College & Research Libraries* 47 no.2:160–65.

_____. 1987. *Bibliographic Instruction: The Second Generation.* Littleton, CO: Libraries Unlimited.

_____. 1995. "Library Instruction in the Information Age." In *Russian-American Seminar on Critical Thinking and the Library*, pp. 19–28. Edited by Cerise Oberman and Dennis Kimmage. Urbana-Champaign, IL: University of Illinois.

Mestre, Lori. 1998. "Structuring a Session with Questions." In *Designs for Active Learning*, edited by Gail Gradowski, Loanne Snavely, and Paula Dempsey. Chicago: ALA, ACRL.

Metoyer-Duran, Cheryl. 1993. *Gatekeepers in Ethnolinguistic Communities.* Norwood, NJ: Ablex.

Meyers, Chet, and Thomas B. Jones. 1993. *Promoting Active Learning: Strategies for the Col-lege Classroom*. 1st ed. *The Jossey-Bass Higher and Adult Education Series*. San Francisco: Jossey-Bass.

Microsoft. 2000. "Guidelines for Accessible Web Pages." www.microsoft.com/enable/dev/web/guidelines.htm. Last update: 12 Sep 2000 Visited: 17 Sep 2000.

Miller, Mari. 1999. Personal email "Re: Research Assistant." 13 Sep 1999.

Miller, Patty. 1999. The Hurried Student: NHCTC Library Finds Many Ways to Help Their Busy Users." *Community and Junior College Libraries* 8 no. 2:63–69.

Minneapolis Community & Technical College. 2000. "Information Literacy Tutorial" [Online]. Available: www.mctc.mnscu.edu/academicAffairs/library/tutorials/infolit/index.html [March 2].

Moeckel, Nancy, and Jenny Presnell. 1995. "Recognizing, Understanding and Respond-ing: A Program Model of Library Instruction Services for International Students." *Reference Librarian* 51/52:309–25.

Moran, Barbara B. 1990. "Library/Classroom Partnerships for the 1990s." *College and Re-search Libraries News* 51:511–14.

Moreland, Virginia. 1993. "Technostress and Personality Types." *Online* 17 no.4:59–62

Morgan, David.1997. *Focus Groups as Qualitative Research*. 2d ed. Thousand Oaks, CA: Sage Publications.

Morgan, Eric Lease. 1999. "A Different Type of Distance Education." *Computers in Librar-ies* 19 no.2:35.

Morse, Janice M., and Peggy-Anne Field. 1995. *Qualitative Research Methods for Health Pro-fessionals*. 2nd ed. Thousand Oaks, CA: Sage Publications.

Mountainside Press, Inc. 1980. "Reference Book Guides." Ann Arbor, MI: Mountainside Publishing, Inc.

Munro, George, and Allen Slater. 1985. "The Know-How of Teaching Critical Thinking." *Social Education* 49 no.4:284–92.

Murrell, Jeanette. 1996. "ANALOGIES" [electronic bulletin board]. 27 Feb 1996—[cited 16 June 2000]. Available from bi-l@listserv.byu.edu.

Nagumo, Takako. 1997. "Citation-> Article: Metaphors" [electronic bulletin board]. 7 Feb 1997—[cited 8 Feb 1997]. Available from bi-l@listserv.byu.edu.

Nahl, Diane. 1999. "Creating User-Centered Instructions for Novice End-Users." *RSR: Reference Services Review* 27 no.3:280–86.

Najjar, Lawrence J. 1998. "Principles of Educational Multimedia User Interface Design." *Human Factors* 40 no.2:311–24.

Nardi, Bonnie A., and Vicki L. O'Day. 1999. *Information Ecologies: Using Technology with Heart*. Cambridge, MA; London: MIT Press.

NCSA, University of Illinois. 2000. "A Beginner's Guide to HTML" [Online]. Available: www.ncsa.uiuc.edu/General/Internet/WWW/HTMLPrimerP1.html; www.ncsa.uiuc.edu/General/Internet/WWW/HTMLPrimerP2.html; www.ncsa.uiuc.edu/General/Internet/WWW/HTMLPrimerP3.html [April 2].

"National Forum on Information Literacy Overview 1999–2000 Report." 2000. [Online]. Available: www.ala.org/kranich/breivik_rep.html [November 6].

National Forum on Information Literacy. 2000. "The National Forum on Information Lit-eracy—An Overview." [Online]. Available: www.infolit.org/ [October 29].

Natowitz, Allen. 1995. "International Students in United States Academic Libraries: Re-cent Concerns and Trends." *Research Strategies* 13 no. 1:4–16.

Nelson, Craig E. 1994. "Critical Thinking and Collaborative Learning." *New Directions for Teaching and Learning* 59:45–58.

New Mexico Junior College. 2000. "A Visit to Copyright Bay" [Online]. Available: www.nmjc.cc.nm.us/copyrightbay/ [March 30].

Newby, Timothy J. 1995. "Instructional Analogies and the Learning of Concepts." *Educa-tional Technology Research and Development: ETR&D* 43 no.1:5–18.

Nielsen, Jakob. 1999a. "Differences Between Print Design and Web Design" [Online]. Available: www.useit.com/alertbox/990124.html [January 25].

_____. 1999b. "The Top Ten *New* Mistakes of Web Design" [Online]. Available: www.useit.com/alterbox/990530.html [June 2].

_____. 1999c. "Usability as Barrier to Entry" [Online]. Available: www.useit.com/alertbox/991128.html [November 30].

_____. 1999d. "When Bad Design Elements Become the Standard" [Online]. Available: www.useit.com/alertbox/991114.html [November 30].

_____. 2000a. *Designing Web Usability.* Indianapolis, IN: New Riders Publishing.

_____. 2000b. "Jakob Nielsen's Alertbox: End of Web Design" [Online]. Available: www.useit.com/alertbox/20000723.html [August 30].

_____. 2000c. "The Mud-Throwing Theory of Usability" [Online]. Available: www.useit.com/alertbox/20000402.html [April 3].

Nimmer, David. 2000. "A Riff on Fair Use in the Digital Millennium Copyright Act." *University of Pennsylvania Law Review* 148 no.3:673–742.

Nipp, Deanna. 1998. "Innovative Use of the Home Page for Library Instruction." *Research Strategies* 16 no.2:93–102.

Noble, David F. 1998. "Digital Diploma Mills: The Automation of Higher Education." *First Monday: Peer-Reviewed Journal on the Internet.* 3, no.1. Available online: www.firstmonday.dk/issues/issue3_1/noble/ [2000, July 24].

_____. 2000a. "Digital Diploma Mills, Part II: the Coming Battle Over Online Instruction: Confidential Agreements Between Universities and Private Companies Pose Serious Challenge To Faculty Intellectual Property Rights" [Online]. Available: communication.ucsd.edu/dl/ddm2.html [July 24].

_____. 2000b. "Digital Diploma Mills, Part III: the Bloom Is Off the Rose" [Online]. Available: communication.ucsd.edu/dl/ddm3.html [July 24].

Norlin, Dennis A. 1992. "We're Not Stupid You Know: Library Services for Adults with Mental Retardation." *Research Strategies* 10 no. 2:56–68.

Norman, Donald A. 1983. "Some Observations on Mental Models." In *Mental Models*, edited by Dedre Gentner and Albert L. Stevens. Hillsdale, NJ: Lawrence Erlbaum Associates.

"Northern Light." 1997–1999. www.nlsearch.com/. Last update: copyright 1997–1999 Visited: 28 Dec 1999.

Norton, Melanie J. 1992. "Effective Bibliographic Instruction for Deaf and Hearing-Impaired College Students." *Library Trends* 41 no. 1:118–30.

"Nuthin' But Links." 2000. nuthinbutlinks.com/graphics.htm. Last update: 2 Apr 2000 Visited: 24 Oct 2000

Oberman, Cerise. 1980. *Petals Around a Rose: Abstract Reasoning and Bibliographic Instruction: A Paper.* Chicago: ACRL.

Oberman, Cerise, and Rebecca A. Linton. 1982. "Guided Design: Teaching Library Research in Problem Solving." In *Theories of Bibliographic Education*, edited by Cerise Oberman and Katina Strauch. New York: Bowker.

Oberman, Cerise, and Katina Strauch. 1982. *Theories of Bibliographic Education; Designs for Teaching.* New York: Bowker.

Oberman, Cerise, and Betsy Wilson. 1998. "The Information Literacy IQ (Institutional Quotient) Test." *College & Research Libraries News* 59 (5):348–49.

Olsen, Erica. 2000. "Thwart Not the Librarian" [Online]. Available: www.msu.edu/~olseneri/library.html [April 2].

"Online Computer Training." 2000. [Online]. Available: computertraining.ucla.edu/ [February 19].

Onwuegbuzie, Anthony J. 1998. "The Relationship Between Library Anxiety and Learning Styles Among Graduate Students: Implications for Library Instruction." *Library and Information Science Research* 20 no. 3:235–49.

Open University. 2000. [Online]. Available: www.open.ac.uk/our-website/ [October 24].

Orme, Bill. 1999. "Re: information literacy—the role of librarians." Personal e-mail to author. 22 October 1999.

Oxford English Dictionary (OED), 2nd ed. 1989. Oxford: Clarendon Press.

Paige, Kathy. 1996. "Panel Session." In *Learning for Life: Information Literacy and the Autonomous Learner*, edited by Di Booker. Adelaide, Australia: University of South Australia Library.

Paivio, Allan. 1973. "Picture Superiority In Free Recall: Imagery Or Dual Coding?" *Cognitive Psychology* 5 no.2:176–206.

Pallis, J. M. 1997. "K–8 Aeronautics Internet Textbook." In *The World Wide Web As a Medium of Instruction: What Works and What Doesn't. Proceedings of the March Learning Technologies Conference.* NASA Dryden Flight Research Center, March 18–20, 1997. Edwards, CA: NASA. NASA Report CD–3358.

Palmer, Parker J. 1998. *The Courage to Teach:Exploring the Inner Landscape of a Teacher's Life.* San Francisco, CA: Jossey-Bass.

Pappas. Marjorie. 1998. "Designing Authentic Learning." *School Library Media Activities Monthly* 14:29–31, 42.

Pappas, Marjorie, and Ann Tepe. 1997. *Pathways to Knowledge (TM). Follett's Information Skills Model.* 3rd ed. McHenry, IL: Follett Software.

Parise, Pierina. 1998. "Information Power Goes Online: Teaching Information Literacy to Distance Learners. " *RSR: Reference Services Review* 26 no.3–4:51–59.

Parks, Eric 1999. "Online Learning News" [electronic bulletin board]. 20 Sep 1999—[cited 8 Oct 1999]. Available from listserv message (lakewood1@list.emailpbu.com).

Pask, Gordon, and B. C. Scott. 1972. "Learning Strategies and Individual Competencies." *International Journal of Man-Machine Studies* 4 no. 3:217–53.

Patton, Michael Quinn. 1980. *Qualitative Evaluation Methods.* Beverly Hills, CA: Sage Publications.

Pavlov, Ivan Petrovich. 1927. *Conditioned Reflexes.* New York: Dover.

———. 1928. *Lectures on Conditioned Reflexes.* New York: International Publishers.

Petruzelli , Barbara W. 1996. "Analogies" 13 Feb 1996. <bi-l@listserv.byu.edu> (14 Feb 1996).

Pero, Carlos. 2000. "Carlos' Forms Tutorial" [Online]. Available: robot0.ge.uiuc.edu/~carlosp/cs317/cft.html [September 16].

Perry, William Graves. 1981. "Cognitive and Ethical Growth: The Making of Meaning." In *The Modern American College*, edited by Arthur W. Chickering. San Francisco: Jossey-Bass.

Philbin, Marge, Elizabeth Meier, Sherri Huffman, and Patricia Boverie. 1995. "A Survey of Gender and Learning Styles." *Sex Roles* 32 no. 7/8:485–94.

Phipps, Shelley E. 1980. "Why Use Workbooks? or Why Does the Chicken Cross the Road? and Other Metaphors, Mixed." *Drexel Library Quarterly* 16 no.1:41–53.

Piaget, Jean. 1952. *The Origins of Intelligence in Children.* 2nd ed. New York: International Universities Press.

———. 1954. *The Construction of Reality in the Child.* New York: Basic Books.

Piaget, Jean, and Bärbel Inhelder. 1969. *The Psychology of the Child.* London: Routledge & K. Paul.

Picard, Rosalind, and Jennifer Healey. 2000. "Introduction: Why Affective Wearables?" [Online]. Available: vismod.www.media.mit.edu/tech-reports/TR–432/node2.html [August 1].

Pierian Press. 2000. "Library Orientation, Bibliographic Instruction, and Critical Reasoning Skills." www.pierianpress.com/3B03.HTM. Last update: 16 Jan 2000 Visited: 24 Oct 2000.

Plovnick, Mark S. 1975. "Primary Care Career Choice and Medical Student Learning Styles." *Journal of Medical Education* 50 no. 9:849–55.

Postman, Neil, and Charles Weingarten. 1971. *Teaching as a Subversive Activity.* New York: Delacorte Press.

Prior, Derek. 2000. "YOUR ENQUIRY/INFORMATION LITERACY" Personal e-mail to author. 6 January 2000.

Quible, Zane K. 1998. "A Focus on Focus Groups." *Business Communication Quarterly*. 61 no.2:28–37.

Rader, Hannelore B. 1990. "Bibliographic Instruction or Information Literacy?" *College and Research Libraries News* 51:18–20.

_____. 1991. "Information Literacy: A Revolution in the Library." *RQ* 31:25–29.

_____. 1999. "The Learning Environment—Then, Now and Later: 30 Years of Teaching Information Skills." *Reference Services Review* 27 no. 3:219–24.

Ragains, Patrick. 1997. "Evaluation of Academic Librarians' Instructional Performance: Report of a National Survey." *Research Strategies* 15 no. 2:159–75.

_____. 2000. "Assessment in Library and Information Literacy Instruction." [Online]. Available: www2.library.unr.edu/ragains/assess.html [December 20].

Ragan, Lawrence C. 1999. "Good Teaching Is Good Teaching: An Emerging Set of Guiding Principles and Practices for the Design and Development of Distance Education." *CAUSE/EFFECT* 22 no.1. Available online: www.educause.edu/ir/library/html/cem9915.html [April 29].

Rainey, Mary Ann., and David A. Kolb. 1995. "Using Experiential Learning Theory and Learning Styles in Diversity Education." In *The Importance of Learning Styles: Understanding the Implications for Learning, Course Design and Education*, edited by Ronald R. Sims and Serbrenia J. Sims. Westport, CT: Greenwood Press.

Rankin, Virginia. 1988. "One Route to Critical Thinking." *School Library Journal* 34 no.5:28–31.

Rayner, Stephen, and Richard Riding. 1997. "Toward a Categorisation of Cognitive Styles and Learning Styles." *Educational Psychology* 17 no. 1/2:5–27.

Ready, Sandy, Marvin E. Wiggins, Sharon Lee Stewart, Katherine Jordan, and Kathy Sabol. 1990. "Library Instruction in Academic Libraries including Graduate, Four-Year and Two-Year Institutions. In *The LIRT Library Instruction Handbook*, edited by May Brottman and Mary Loe. Englewood, CO: Libraries Unlimited.

RealNetworks. 2000. [Online]. Available: www.real.com/ [October 8].

Reichardt, Randy. 2000. "RE: Print/electronic pathfinders" [electronic bulletin board]. 17 Mar 2000—[cited 18 Mar 2000]. Available from bi-l@listserv.byu.edu.

Reichel, Mary, and Mary Ann Ramey, eds. 1987. *Conceptual Frameworks for Bibliographic Education: Theory into Practice*. Littleton, CO: Libraries Unlimited.

Reigeluth, Charles M. ed. 1987. *Instructional Theories in Action: Lessons Illustrating Selected Theories and Models*. Hillsdale, N. J.: L. Erlbaum.

Reusch, Christine. 1998. "Pathfinders—Business, Engineering, Computer Science" [electronic bulletin board]. 18 Sep 1998—[cited 19 Sept 1998]. Available from bi-l@listserv.byu.edu.

Revenaugh, Mickey. 2000. "Beyond the Digital Divide: Pathways to Equity." *Technology & Learning* 20 no. 10:38–48.

Richardson, Daniel. 1997. "Student Perceptions and Learning Outcomes of Computer-Assisted versus Traditional Instruction in Physiology." *American Journal of Physiology* 273 no.6:S55–59.

Riddle, John. 1996a. "BI Analogies" [electronic bulletin board]. 7 Feb 1996—[cited 8 Feb 1996]. Available from bi-l@listserv.byu.edu.

_____. 1996b. "More BI Analogies" [electronic bulletin board]. 9 Feb 1996—[cited 10 Feb 1996]. Available from bi-l@listserv.byu.edu.

Riding, Richard, and Indra Cheema. 1991. "Cognitive Styles —An Overview and Integration." *Educational Psychology* 11:193–215.

Roberts, Anne F., and Susan Griswold Blandy. 1989. *Library Instruction for Librarians*. 2nd rev. ed. Englewood, CO: Libraries Unlimited, Inc.

Robinson, Otis. 1880. "Rochester University Library—Administration and Use." U.S. Bureau of Education. *Circular of Information*, no. 1–880:15–27.

Rogers, Carl R. 1969. *Freedom to Learn: A View of What Education Might Become*. Columbus, OH: C. E. Merrill Pub. Co.

Rogers, Carl R., and H. Jerome Freiberg. 1994. *Freedom to Learn.* 3rd ed. New York, New York; Toronto: Merrill; Maxwell Macmillan International, Maxwell Macmillan Canada.

Roland, David. 1997. *The Confident Performer.* Sydney; London: Currency Press; Nick Hern Books.

Rollison, Carrie. 2000. "RE: Question." Personal e-mail to author 31 August 2000.

Rorschach, Hermann. 1942. *Psychodiagnostics: A Diagnostic Test Based on Perception, Including Rorschach's Paper—'The Application of the Form Interpretation Test'.* Translated by P. Lemkau and B. Kronenberg. 5th ed. Berne: Huber.

Roselle, Ann. 1997. "Using the ALA's Evaluating Library Instruction." *Journal of Academic Librarianship* 23 no. 9:390–97.

Rotter, Julian B. 1950. *The Rotter Incomplete Sentences Blank.* New York: Psychological Corp.

Russell, Thomas L. 1999a. "No Significant Difference" [Online]. Available: cuda.teleeducation.nb.ca/nosignificantdifference/ [November 24].

_____. 1999b. *The No Significant Difference Phenomenon: As Reported in 355 Research Reports, Summaries and Papers.* Raleigh, NC: North Carolina State University.

_____. 1999c. "Significant Difference" [Online]. Available: cuda.teleeducation.nb.ca/significantdiffference/ [November 24].

Ruth, Stephen. 1997. "Getting Real About Technology-Based Learning: The Medium is NOT the Message." *Educom Review* (September/October):32–37.

Sadler-Smith, Eugene. 1997. "Learning Style: Frameworks and Instruments." *Educational Psychology* 17 no. 1/2: 51–63.

St. Lifer, Evan. 2000. "2000 LJ Budget Report: Public Libraries Close Out Millennium on a Fiscal High Note." *Library Journal* 125 no. 1:45.

San Diego State University. 2000. *Encyclopedia of Educational Technology* [Online]. Available: coe.sdsu.edu/eet/ [November 26].

Sanders, Judith A., and Richard L. Wiseman. 1994. "The Effects of Verbal and Nonverbal Teacher Immediacy on Perceived Cognitive, Affective and Behavioral Learning in the Multicultural Classroom." In *The College Classroom,* edited by Kenneth A. Feldman and Michael B. Paulsen. Needham Hts., MA: Ginn Press.

Sarkodie-Mensah, Kwasi. 1998. "Using Humor for Effective Library Instruction Sessions." *Catholic Library World* 68 no.4:25–29.

"Save With Images." n.d. www.inquare.com/swi/index.phtml. Last update: n.d. Visited: 25 Aug 1999.

Schmeck, Ronald R., ed. 1998. *Learning Strategies and Learning.* New York: Plenum.

Schneider, Curtis R. 2000. "Netscape Communicator 4.05 Browser Tutorial on the Web" [Online]. Available: www.curtis1.com/netscape/ [June 30].

Schrock, Kathy. 2000a. "Critical Evaluation Survey: Middle School Level" [Online]. Available: school.discovery.com/schrockguide/evalmidd.html [June 30].

_____. 2000b. "Kathy Schrock's Guide for Educators" [Online]. Available: http://discoveryschool.com/schrockguide/eval.html [November 26].

Schutt, William. 2000. "Human Dimension in Distance Learning." *Encyclopedia of Educational Technology* [Online]. Available: coe.sdsu.edu/eet/Articles/humanizingde/start.htm [October 24].

Scriven, Michael. 1973. "The Methodology of Evaluation." In *Educational Evaluation: Theory and Practice,* edited by Blaine Worthen and James Sanders. Belmont, CA: Wadsworth.

Seifert, Kelvin L. 1991. *Educational Psychology.* 2nd ed. Boston: Houghton Mifflin Company.

Seton, Jo, and Ninette Ellis. 1996. "Information Literacy for International Postgraduate Students." In *Learning for Life,* edited by Di Booker. Adelaide, Australia: University of South Australia Library.

Severiens, Sabine, and Geert Ten Dam. 1997. "Gender and Gender Identity Differences in Learning Styles." *Educational Psychology* 17 no. 1/2:79–93.

Shade, Barbara J., Cynthia A. Kelly, and Mary Oberg. 1997. *Creating Culturally Responsive Classrooms*. 1st ed. Washington, DC: American Psychological Association.

Shade, Barbara J., and Clara A. New. 1993. "Cultural Influences on Learning: Teaching Implications." In *Multicultural Education: Issues and Perspectives*, edited by James. A. Banks and Cherry A. McGee Banks. Boston: Allyn and Bacon.

Shapiro, Jeremy J., and Shelley K. Hughes. 2000. "Information Literacy as a Liberal Art: Enlightenment Proposals for a New Curriculum." *Educom Review* 31 (March/April) [cited 2000, June 16]. Available: www.educause.edu/pub/er/review/reviewarticles/31231.html

Sheridan, Jean. 1986. "Andragogy: A New Concept for Academic Librarians." *Research Strategies* 4 no. 4:156–67.

_____. 1990. "The Reflective Librarian: Some Observations on Bibliographic Instruction in the Academic Library." *Journal of Academic Librarianship* 16 no.1: 22–26.

Shippensburg University of Pennsylvania.2000. "Ellis Skills Tutorial" [Online]. Available: www.ship.edu/~library/tutorial/intro.htm [October 24].

Shonrock, Diana, ed. 1996. *Evaluating Library Instruction: Sample Questions, Forms, and Strategies for Practical Use* . Chicago: American Library Association, Library Instruction Round Table.

Shores, Louis. 1970. *Library-College USA: Essays on a Prototype for an American Higher Education*. Tallahassee, FL: South Pass Press.

Silverplatter. 2000. "WebSPIRS Online Tutorial" [Online]. Available: www.silverplatter.com/tutor/mainintro.html [October 6].

Simkins, Scott P. 1999. "Promoting Active-Student Learning Using the World Wide Web in Economics Courses." *Journal of Economic Education* 30 no.3:278–87.

Sims, Ronald R., and Serbrenia J. Sims, eds. 1995. *The Importance of Learning Styles*. Westport, CT: Greenwood Press.

Skepticism.net. 1996–2000. "Global Warming" www.skepticism.net/global_warming/ Last update: 1996–2000 Visited: 2 Apr 2000.

Skinner, B.F. 1938. *The Behavior of Organisms*. New York: Macmillan.

_____. 1953. *Science and Human Behavior*. New York: Macmillan.

_____. 1968. *The Technology of Teaching*. New York: Appleton-Century-Crofts.

_____. 1974. *About Behaviorism*. New York: Knopf

_____. 1983. *A Matter of Consequences*. New York: Knopf.

_____. 1984. "The Shame of American Education." *American Psychologist* 39 no. 9:947–54.

Slavin, Robert E. 1997. *Educational Psychology: Theory and Practice*. Boston: Allyn and Boston.

Smith, Drew. 1999. "Re: template for web design" 24 Sep 1999 BI-L message 27 Sep 1999.

Smith, Jean. 1987. *Searchin' Safari*. Produced and directed by OLR Television. Videotape, 9 min. La Jolla, CA: School of Medicine, University of California, San Diego.

Smith, Terry C. 1991. *Making Successful Presentations: A Self-Teaching Guide*. 2nd ed. New York: Wiley.

SnagIt n.d. www.techsmith.com/products/snagit/default.asp. Last update: n.d. Visited: 31 Dec 2000.

SnapzPro n.d. www.ambrosiasw.com/Products/SnapzPro.html. Last update: n.d. Visited: 25 Jan 2001.

Snavely, Loanne, and Natasha Cooper. 1997. "The Information Literacy Debate." *Journal of Academic Librarianship* 23 no.1:9–14.

Snavely, Loanne. 1998. "Teaching Boolean Operators in a Flash Using a Deck of Cards" In *Designs for Active Learning*, pp. 114–116. Edited by Gail Gradowski, Loanne Snavely and Paula Dempsey. Chicago, IL:ALA, ACRL.

Soldat, Alexander S., Robert C. Sinclair, and Melvin C. Mark. 1997. "Color as an Environmental Processing Cue: External Affective Cures Can Directly Affect Processing Strategy Without Affecting Mood." *Social Cognition* 15 no.1:55–72.

SPARC (The Scholarly Publishing and Academic Resources Coalition). 1999. [Online]. Available: www.arl.org/sparc/factsheet.html [September 9].

Special Libraries Association. 2000. "New Cases." *Information Outlook* 4 no.7: 36–37.

Spitzer, Kathleen L., Michael Eisenberg, Carrie A. Lowe, and ERIC Clearinghouse on Information & Technology. 1998. *Information Literacy Essential Skills for the Information Age.* Syracuse, NY: ERIC Clearinghouse on Information & Technology, Syracuse University.

Spoon, Jerry G., and John W. Schell. 1998. "Aligning Student Learning Styles with Instructor Teaching Styles." *Journal of Industrial Teacher Education* 35 no. 2:41–56.

Stahl, Steven A. 1999. "Different Strokes for Different Folks: A Critique of Learning Styles." *American Educator* 23 no. 3:27–31

Stamatopolos, Anthony, and Robert Mackay. 1998. "Effects of Library Instruction on University Students' Satisfaction with the Library: A Longitudinal Study." *College and Research Libraries* 59:323–34.

SUNY. 2000. "Information Literacy Initiative Overview" [Online]. Available: www.sunyconnect.suny.edu/ili/iliover.htm [October 24].

SUNY Buffalo. 1999. "Help Guide for Distance Learners." [Online]. Available: ublib.buffalo.edu/libraries/help/distance.html [November 5].

_____. 2000a. "Library Skills Workbook" [Online]. Available: http://ublib.buffalo.edu/libraries/workbook/ [October 24].

_____. 2000b. "Library Skills Workbook: Psychology 101R Version—Spring 2000 (Dr. Thompson)" ublib.buffalo.edu/libraries/units/ugl/workbook/psy101.html Last update: 14 Jan 2000 Visited: 30 Jun 2000.

_____. 2000b. "Library Skills Workbook: Psychology 101R Version—Spring 2000 (Dr. Thompson)" [Online]. Available: ublib.buffalo.edu/libraries/units/ugl/workbook/psy101.html [June 30].

Statham, Anne, Laura Richardson, and Judith A. Cook. 1994. "Gender and University Teaching: A Negotiated Difference." In *Teaching and Learning in the College Classroom*, edited by Kenneth A. Feldman and Michael B. Paulsen. Needham Hts, MA: Ginn Press.

Steadman, Mimi Harris, and Marilla D. Svinicki. 1998. "CATs: A Student's Gateway to Better Learning." *New Directions for Teaching and Learning* 75:13–20.

Sternberg, Robert J. 1997. *Thinking Styles.* Cambridge, UK; New York: Cambridge University Press.

Sternberg, Robert J., and Elena L. Grigorenko. 1997. "Are Cognitive Styles Still in Style?" *American Psychologist* 52 no. 7:700–12.

Sternthal, B., and C.S. Craig. 1973. "Humor in Advertising." *Journal of Marketing* 37 no.4:12–18.

Stevens, Charles H., Marie P. Canfield, and Jeffrey J. Gardner. 1973. "Library Pathfinders: A New Possibility for Cooperative Reference Service." *College & Research Libraries* 34 no.1:40–46.

Stewart, Sharon Lee. 1998. "Assessment for Library Instruction: The Cross/Angelo Model." *Research Strategies* 16 no. 3:165–74.

Stocks, J. Timothy, and Paul P. Freddolino. 1998. "Evaluation of a World Wide Web-Based Graduate Social Work Research Methods Course." *Computers in Human Services* 15 no.2–3:51–69.

Stoffle, Carla J., Alan E. Guskin, and Joseph A. Boisse. 1984. "Teaching, Research, and Service: The Academic Library's Role." In *Increasing the Teaching Role of Academic Libraries*, edited by T. Kirk. San Francisco: Jossey-Bass.

Stover, Mark, and Steven D. Zink. 1996. "World Wide Web Home Page Design: Patterns and Anomalies of Higher Education Library Home Pages." *RSR: Reference Services Review* 24 no.3:7–20.

Strife, Mary L. 1995. "Special Libraries and Instruction: One on One Public Relations." *Reference Librarian* 51/52:415–19.

Stripling, Barbara K. 1996. "Quality in School Library Media Programs: Focus on Learning." *Library Trends* 44 no. 3:631–56.

Stripling, Barbara K., and Judy M. Pitts. 1988. *Brainstorms and Blueprints: Teaching Library Research as a Thinking Process*. Englewood, CO: Libraries Unlimited.

Stronck, David R. 1983. "The Comparative Effects of Different Museum Tours on Children's Attitudes and Learning." *Journal of Research in Science Teaching* 20 no.4:283–90.

Stroop, J. Ridley. 1935. "Studies of Interference in Serial Verbal Reactions." *Journal of Experimental Psychology* 18:643–62.

Sullivan, Eamonn. 1998. The Web Isn't Always the Best Teacher (Intersights) *PC Week* 15, no.6:43.

"Supermarket Psych-Out." 1999. *Tufts University Health & Nutrition Letter* 16 no.1:1.

Sutherland, Peter. 1995. "An Investigation into Entwistlean Adult Learning Styles in Mature Students." *Educational Psychology* 15 no. 3:257–70.

Svinicki, Marilla D. 1994. "Practical Implications of Cognitive Theories." In *Teaching and Learning in the College Classroom*, edited by Kenneth A. Feldman and Michael B. Paulsen. Needham Hts, MA: Ginn Press.

Svinicki, Marilla, and Barbara Schwartz. 1988. *Designing Instruction for Library Users: A Practical Guide*. New York: Marcel Dekker, Inc.

Svinicki, Marilla D., and Nancy M. Dixon. 1987. "The Kolb Model Modified for Classroom Activities." *College Teaching* 35 no. 4:141–46.

Syllabus Press. 2000. "News, Trends, and Resources: An Online Newsletter from Syllabus Press" listserv message. 15 August 2000.

Syracuse University. 1999. "AskERIC" [Online]. Available: ericir.syr.edu/ [December 28].

Tagliacozzo, R., and M. Kochen. 1970. "Information-Seeking Behavior of Catalog Users." *Information Storage and Retrieval*. 6 no.5:363–81.

Talbot, Janet Frey, Rachel Kaplan, Frances E. Kuo, and Stephen Kaplan. 1993. "Factors that Enhance Effectiveness of Visitor Maps." *Environment and Behavior* 25 no.6:7–25.

"Talking With Don Norman." 1999. *Educom Review* 34 no.3 [Online]. Available: www.educause.edu/ir/library/html/erm9936.html [November 4].

Tardieu, Bruno. 1999. "Computer as Community Memory: How People in Very Poor Neighborhoods Made a Computer Their Own." In *High Technology and Low-Income Communities: Prospects for the Positive Use of Advanced Information Technology*, edited by Donald A. Schoen, Bish Sanyal, and William J. Mitchell. Cambridge, MA: MIT Press.

Tennant, Roy. 1997. "Web Sites by Design: How to Avoid a 'Pile Of Pages'." *Syllabus* (August): 49–50.

Theory into Practice's *TIP database* 2000. [Online]. Available: www.hfni. gsehd.gwu.edu/ ~tip/ [December 27].

Thompson, Glenn J., and Barbara R. Stevens. 1985. "Library Science Students Develop Pathfinders." *College & Research Libraries News* 46 no.5:224–25.

Thorndike, Edward L. 1913. *Educational Psychology*. New York: Teachers College Columbia University.

Thousand Oaks Library. 1999. www.tol.lib.ca.us/. Last update: 15 Dec 1999 Visited: 28 Dec 1999.

3COM. 2000. "3COM Networking Solutions: E-Rate Central (1999)" [Online]. Available: education.3com.com/erate/erate_f.html [June 15].

Tiberius, Richard, and Ivan Silver. 2000. "Guidelines for Conducting Workshops and Seminars That Actively Engage Participants" [Online]. Available: www.hsc.wvu.edu/ aap/aap-car/faculty-development/teaching-skills/guidelines-workshops.htm [November 4].

Tiefel, Virginia. 1995. "Library User Education: Examining its Past, Projecting its Future." *Library Trends* 44:318–38.

Tighe, Thomas J. 1982. *Learning Theory: Foundations and Fundamental Issues*. New York: Oxford University Press.

Tolman, Edward Chace. 1932. *Purposive Behavior in Animals and Men.* New York: The Century Co.

Tucker, John Mark. 1980. "User Education in Academic Libraries: A Century in Retrospect." *Library Trends* 28:9–27.

Tufte, Edward R. 1983. *The Visual Display of Quantitative Information.* Cheshire, CT: Graphics Press.

Turner, Diane. 1993. "What's the Point of Bibliographic Instruction, Point-Of-Use Guides and In-House Bibliographies?" *Wilson Library Bulletin* 67 no.5:64–68.

Twigg, Carol A. 2000. "Who Owns Online Courses and Course Materials? Intellectual Property Policies for a New Learning Environment." The Pew Learning and Technology Program [Online]. Available: www.center.rpi.edu/PewSym/mono2.html [September 17].

Tyckoson, David. 1999. "What's Right with Reference?" *American Libraries* 30 no.2:57–63.

Tyler, Ralph Winfred. 1976. *Educational Evaluation: New Roles, New Meanings.* Chicago: University of Chicago Press.

Unger, Harlow G. 1996. *Encyclopedia of American Education,* s.v. "Active Learning." New York: Facts on File, Inc.

———. 1996. *Encyclopedia of American Education.* S.v., "Metacognition," New York: Facts on File, Inc.

U.S. Department of Commerce and National Telecommunications and Information Administration (NTIA). 1999. "Falling Through the Net: Defining the Digital Divide." Washington, D.C.: U.S. GPO.

U.S. Department of Education. 1991. *America 2000: An Education Strategy.* Rev. ed. Washington, DC: U.S. Dept. of Education.

———. 2000. "Virtual Reference Desk." [Online]. Available: www.vrd.org/ [October 8].

U.S. Department of Education. Office of Educational Technology. 2000. "Tool Kit for Bridging the Digital Divide in Your Community" [Online]. Available: www.ed.gov/Technology/tool_kit.html [December 20].

U.S. Department of Labor. Secretary's Commission on Achieving Necessary Skills. 1991. *What Work Requires of Schools: A SCANS Report for America 2000.* Washington, DC: Secretary's Commission on Achieving Necessary Skills.

U.S. Library of Congress. 2000. "Collaborative Digital Reference Service" [Online]. Available: lcweb.loc.gov/rr/digiref/ [October 8].

U.S. National Academy of the Sciences. 1999. "Being Fluent with Information Technology" [Online]. Available: www.nap.edu/readingroom/books/BeFIT [September 19].

———. 2001. "Being Fluent with Information Technology: Executive Summary" [Online]. Available: www.nap.edu/html/beingfluent/es.html [March 4].

U.S. National Library of Medicine. 2000a. "MEDLINEplus" [Online]. Available: www.nlm.nih.gov/medlineplus/ [October 24].

———. 2000b. "PubMed" [Online]. Available: www.ncbi.nlm.nih.gov/entrez/query.fcgi [April 2].

University of Arizona Library. 2000a. "RIO: Research Instruction Online" [Online]. Available: dizzy.library.arizona.edu/rio/ [September 8].

———. 2000b. "RIO: Research Instruction Online: Writing Research Papers" [Online]. Available: www.library.arizona.edu/rio/write1.html [October 21].

———. 2001. "RIO Research Instruction Online: Choosing the Right Index" [Online]. Available: www.library.arizona.edu/rio/journ4.html [March 22].

University of British Columbia Library. 2000. "Information Explorer" [Online]. Available: www.library.ubc.ca:8900/public/LibraryIntro/index.html [October 24].

University of California. California Digital Library. 1999. [Online]. Available: www.cdlib.org/ [November 29].

———. California Digital Library. 2000. "CDL Collections and Services." www.cdlib.org/collections/. Last update: 5 Jan 2000 Visited: 16 Jul 2000.

UCLA. College Library. 2000. "Selecting the Right Source" [Online]. Available: www.library.ucla.edu/libraries/college/insruct/selecting/select.htm [April 30].

UCLA. Young Research Library. 2000. "Reference Collection Online" [Online]. Available: www.library.ucla.edu/libraries/url/referenc/refonline.htm [October 6].

University of California, Santa Cruz. 2000. "UCSC' NetTrail" [Online]. Available: nettrail.ucsc.edu/nettrail/master/ [April 30].

University of Illinois. 2000. "NCSA: A Beginner's Guide to HTML" [Online]. Available: www.ncsa.uiuc.edu/General/Internet/WWW/HTMLPrimer.html [September 16].

University of Michigan School of Information. 2000 "The Internet Public Library" [Online]. Available: www.ipl.org/ [December 18].

University of Pittsburgh. 1997. "Navigating the Sea of Information." Produced by Center of Instructional Development and Distance Education. Videotape, 18 min. University of Pittsburgh. Media, PA: Media, Inc.

University of South Florida. 2000. "USF Distance Learners Library Services" [Online]. Available: www.lib.usf.edu/virtual/services/distancelearning.html [October 29].

University of Tennessee, Knoxville. 2000. "Off-Campus Library Services: Providing Library Services to UT Students Involved in Off-Campus/Distance Education Programs" [Online]. Available: aztec.lib.utk.edu/%7Epearls/ [October 29].

University of Texas. 2000. "Crash Course in Copyright" [Online]. Available: www.utsystem.edu/ogc/intellectualproperty/cprtindx.htm [March 30].

University of Texas System Digital Library. 2000. "TILT: Texas Information Literacy Tutorial" [Online]. Available: tilt.lib.utsystem.edu/ [September 8].

University of Washington. 2000. "UWired" [Online]. Available: www.washington.edu/uwired/ [April 2].

Utah State Office of Education. 1996. *Library Media Information Literacy Core Curriculum for Utah Secondary Schools*. Salt Lake City, UT: Utah State Office of Education.

Van der Meij, Hans, and Ard W. Lazonder. 1993. "Assessment of the Minimalist Approach to Computer User Documentation." *Interacting with Computers* 5 no.4:355–70.

Vander Meer, Patricia F., and Galen E. Rike. 1996. "Multimedia: Meeting the Demand for User Education with a Self-instructional Tutorial." *Research Strategies* 14 no. 3:145–58.

VIVA: The Virtual Library of Virginia. 2000. [Online]. Available: exlibris.uls.vcu.edu/ [October 29].

"Volcanoes Online." 2000. [Online]. Available: library.thinkquest.org/17457/ [May 29].

Vygotsky, Lev S., and Michael Cole. 1978. *Mind in Society: The Development of Higher Psychological Processes*. Cambridge, MA: Harvard University Press.

Walden University. 1998. "Templates for Editing Web Pages." www.waldenu.edu/templates/ Last update: 7 Dec 1998 Visited: 16 Sep 2000.

Walker, Donna E. 1998. *Strategies for Teaching Differently: On the Block or Not*. Thousand Oaks, CA: Corwin.

Wanzer, Melissa Bekelja, and Ann Bainbridge Frymier. 1999. "The Relationship Between Student Perceptions of Instructor Humor and Students' Reports of Learning." *Communication Education* 48 no.1:48–62.

Warmkessel, Marjorie Markoff, and Frances M. Crothers. 1993. "Collaborative Learning and Bibliographic Instruction." *Journal of Academic Librarianship* 19 no.1:4–7.

Watson, John B., and Rosalie Rayner. 1920. "Conditioned Emotional Reactions." *Journal of Experimental Psychology* 3:1–14.

Weaver, David. 1999. "Re: Annotated Pathfinders" [electronic bulletin board]. 5 Aug 1999— [cited 6 Aug 1999]. Available from bi-l@listserv.byu.edu.

Webb, J.D. 1986. "A Hierarchy of Pubic Library User Types. *Library Journal* 111:47–50.

Webb, Wendy. 2000. "Taking the Plunge: Authoring Tips for Novices." *Inside Technology Training* (February):44–49.

WebCT. 2000. [Online]. Available: www.webct.com/wyw [October 24].

"WebWhacker" 2000. www.bluesquirrel.com/products/whacker/whacker.html. Last update: 2000 Visited: 21 Oct 2000.

Wehmeyer, Lillian Biermann. 1996. "Teaching Online Search Techniques Your Students Can Use." *Syllabus* 10 no. 2:52–56.

Weil, Michelle M., and Larry D. Rosen. 1997. *Technostress: Coping With Technology @Work @Home @Play.* New York: Wiley & Sons.

Weiner, Bernard. 1995. *Judgments of Responsibility: A Foundation for a Theory of Social Conduct.* New York: Guilford Press.

Wergin, Jon F. 1988. "Basic Issues and Principles in Classroom Assessment." *New Directions for Teaching and Learning* 34:5–17.

Wertheimer, Max. 1912. "Experimental Studies of the Perception of Movement." *Zeitschrift fur Psychologie* 61:161–265

Westerbrook, Lynn. 1993. "Evaluation." In *Learning to Teach: Workshops on Instruction,* edited by Learning to Teach Task Force. Chicago: American Library Association.

West's Encyclopedia of American Law, 1998 ed., s.v. "copyright."

White, Frank. 1999. "Digital Diploma Mills: a Dissenting Voice." *First Monday: Peer-Reviewed Journal on the Internet* 4 no.7. Available online: firstmonday.org/issues/issue4_7/white/index.html [2000, October 29].

"Why Blue M&M's Make You Drowsy." 1997. *Forbes* 159 no.9:S82.

Wilcoxson, Lesley, and Michael Prosser. 1996. "Kolb's Learning Style Inventory (1985): Review and Further Study of Validity and Reliability." *British Journal of Educational Psychology* 66:247–57.

Williams, T. Craig, and Hyder Zahed. 1996. "Computer-Based Training Versus Traditional Lecture: Effect on Learning and Retention." *Journal of Business & Psychology* 11 no.2:297–310.

Wilson, Lizabeth A. 1992. "Changing Users: Bibliographic Instruction for Whom?" In *The Evolving Education Mission of the Library,* edited by Betsy Baker and Mary Ellen Litzinger. Chicago: American Library Association.

Winsor, Justin. 1880. "College Libraries as Aids to Instruction." U.S. Bureau of Education. *Circular of Information,* no. 1–880:7–15.

Wisconsin Association of Academic Librarians. 2000. "WAAL Ad Hoc Information Literacy Committee: Information Literacy and Academic Libraries" [Online]. Available: facstaff.uww.edu/WAAL/infolit/links.html [October 19].

Witkin, Herman A., Carol A. Moore, Donald R. Goodenough, and Patricia W. Cox. 1977. "Field-Dependent and Field-Independent Cognitive Styles and Their Educational Implications." *Review of Educational Research* 47 no. 1:1–64.

Wood, Leslie. 1995. "Prop Goes the Easel." *Office Systems* 12 no.2:32–37.

Woods, Kathleen G., Helen T. Burns, and Marilyn Barr. 1990. "Planning an Instructional Program in a Public Library. In *The LIRT Instruction Handbook,* edited by Mary Brottman and May Loe. Englewood, CO: Libraries Unlimited.

"World Lecture Hall" 2000. [Online]. Available: www.utexas.edu/world/lecture/ [June 30].

World Wide Web Consortium. 2000. "Web Accessibility Initiative (WAI)." www.w3.org/WAI/. Last update: 22 Sep 2000 Visited: 7 Oct 2000.

Yaghi, Hussein M., and Mary Bentley Abu-Saba. 1998. "Teachers' Computer Anxiety: An International Perspective." *Computers in Human Behavior* 14 no.2:321-36.

"Yahoo!" 2000. [Online]. Available: www.yahoo.com/ [February 22].

Zurowski, Paul G. 1974. *The Information Service Environment: Relationships and Priorities.* Washington DC: National Commission on Libraries and Information Science.

Zwemer, Diane. 2000. "Flow of Information." UCLA College Library [Online]. Available: www.library.ucla.edu/libraries/college/instruct/flow/flow.htm [June 29].

Index

About the Authors

ESTHER S. GRASSIAN

Esther S. Grassian received a Masters in Library Science from UCLA in 1969. Since that time, she has served in a variety of reference—and in-struction-related positions in the UCLA College Library. Her working title was first "Reference Librarian," then "Reference/Instruction Librar-ian," followed by "Electronic Services Coordinator" (1995–99) and cur-rently, "Instructional Services Coordinator" (1998-present). Her titles reflect both her involvement with reference, instruction and technology in an undergraduate library, and the development of the modern library instruction/bibliographic instruction/information literacy movement.

She has also held various elected and appointed positions in infor-mation-literacy-related organizations, including member of the ALA, ACRL Institute for Information Literacy Advisory Board, Chair of the ACRL Instruction Section, and Chair of the California Clearinghouse on Library Instruction, South. Her publications include "Thinking Criti-cally About World Wide Web Resources," as well as chapters in the ACRL publications, *Learning to Teach* and *The Sourcebook for Bibliographic Instruction*. She has led workshops and spoken at programs at the local, regional, state, and national level, on a variety of topics, including how to teach one-shot sessions, how to teach the Internet and critical think-ing, and the differences and similarities between information technol-ogy fluency and information literacy.

She taught UCLA's undergraduate "Library and Information Re-sources" course seven times in the mid–1980s, and in 1989 co-proposed (along with Joan Kaplowitz) a course for graduate students in the UCLA Department of Information Studies. The course title, "User Education/ Bibliographic Instruction: Theory and Technique," has been changed to "Information Literacy Instruction: Theory and Technique," again, re-flecting the changing nature of this field. Esther and Joan have alter-nated teaching this course since 1990. In 1995, she was named Librarian of the Year by the Librarian's Association of the University of California, Los Angeles, for her efforts at incorporating information literacy into the UCLA academic curriculum, and for her work in developing and implementing Internet training programs for UCLA Library staff and users.

JOAN R. KAPLOWITZ

Joan R. Kaplowitz has a doctorate in Psychology as well as a master's in library science. She has been at UCLA since graduating UCLA's Library and Information Science program in 1984. Dr. Kaplowitz began her UCLA career as reference/instruction librarian and later Educational Services Coordinator and Head of Public Services at the Education and Psychology Library. She is currently the Interim Head of Reference at the Louise M. Darling Biomedical Library and also serves as the Psychology Specialist as well as the liaison to both the School of Medicine and the Psychology Department for the library.

Dr. Kaplowitz has been heavily involved in library instruction at the local, state, and national levels for her entire career. During her early years at UCLA she taught several sections of UCLA's undergraduate "Library and Information Resources." In 1989 she collaborated with UCLA's Esther Grassian, to propose and develop the UCLA graduate library program's course "User Education/Bibliographic Instruction: Theory and Technique" (currently known as "Information Literacy Instruction: Theory and Technique"). She and Ms. Grassian have alternated presenting this course each year since 1990. Dr. Kaplowitz was also part of the faculty development team for ACRL's Institute for Information Literacy's Immersion Program and taught in both Immersion 1999 and 2000.

Dr. Kaplowitz has made numerous presentations on various topics such as the psychology of learning and cognitive styles, evaluating bibliographic instruction, the pros and cons of computer assisted instruction, and mentoring within the profession. She has been awarded several Librarian's Association of the University of California research grants to support her research endeavors. Dr. Kaplowitz has held several offices in ALA's New Members Roundtable and the California Clearinghouse on Library Instruction. Her most recent professional commitments involve working with ALA's Committee on Accreditation and various ALA scholarship and awards committees.